THE DIVISION OF LABOR IN SOCIETY

By ÉMILE DURKHEIM

Translated by GEORGE SIMPSON

The Division of Labor in Society
By Émile Durkheim
Translated by George Simpson

Print ISBN 13: 978-1-4209-6175-1
eBook ISBN 13: 978-1-4209-6176-8

This edition copyright © 2019. Digireads.com Publishing.

Cover Image: a detail of "Shell Making", Edinburgh, from British Artists at the Front, Continuation of The Western Front, c. 1918 (colour litho), by John Lavery (1856-1941) / Private Collection / The Stapleton Collection / Bridgeman Images.

Please visit *www.digireads.com*

CONTENTS

To

ROBERT MORRISON MacIVER

and

GEORGE EDWARD GORDON CATLIN

Boni praeceptores boni

Preface to the Translation

The need for an English translation of Emile Durkheim's *De la division du travail social* has long been felt. The first great work of a man who controlled French social thought for almost a quarter of a century and whose influence is now waxing rather than waning, it remains today, both from an historical and contextual standpoint, a book that must be read by all who profess some knowledge of social thought and some interest in social problems. First published in 1893 with the subtitle, *Étude sur l'Organisation des Sociétés Supérieures*, and a dedication "A Mon Cher Maître, M. Emile Boutroux, *Hommage respectueux et reconnaissant*" it has gone through five editions, the last having been brought out in 1926, nine years after Durkheim's death. The second edition appeared in 1902 with the now classic preface, *Quelques Remarques sur les Groupements professionnels.* The third edition appeared in 1907, the fourth in 1911.

In the second and subsequent editions Durkheim omitted many pages from the long introduction which he wrote for the first. I feel, however, that this introduction is fundamental to an understanding of Durkheim's position and valuable in itself, besides being indispensable to an appreciation of a study which Durkheim had again turned to in his last years and which he considered his crowning work, the science of ethics. Consequently, I have appended it at the end of this volume. Nowhere else, except in the first French edition (now out of print), can this, Durkheim's early development of the idea of a science of ethics, be found. Hence I consider it a great boon to sociological scholarship that I was enabled to have this first edition at my disposal, and present it to an English-speaking audience.

The translation has been made from the first and fifth editions only. The sole difficulty I encountered in thus having to restrict myself to these two is that Durkheim did not edit the last edition, and, from all appearances, neither did any of his students or colleagues. Besides the additional preface and the omission of much of the introduction, there was little omitted or added in any of the editions. The footnote to chapter one of book one in the first edition could not have appeared in later editions since it refers to material in the first edition which was omitted in all subsequent editions. I have placed it there with a note of my own. Near the end of chapter two of book two, three and a half lines were added which are important, since they answer the charge of jingoism made against Durkheim[1] and show his international leanings. They read thus: "Inversement, tout retour d'un nationalisme étroit a toujours pour conséquence un developpement de l'esprit protectionniste, c'est-à-dire une tendance des peuples à s'isoler, économiquement et moralement, les uns des autres." In its context it tacitly expresses a condemnation of nationalism and is the best refutation of Durkheim's *ad hoc* pamphlets published during the war, *Qui a voulu la guerre? Les origines de la guerre d'après les documents diplomatiques* (in collaboration with E. Denis); *"L'Allemagne au-dessus de tout" la mentalité allemande et la guerre*; and *Les lettres à tous les français*. In chapter one of book two in a sentence concerning suicide among lower peoples, certain words generalizing the main thought concerning the rarity of suicides among such people were omitted. I have noted this omission in a footnote. It is probable that Durkheim's work on suicide contained in that remarkable study in social causation, *Le Suicide*, led him to extenuate the broad generalization he was there making.

The title page of all the editions contained a quotation from Aristotle's *Politics* (B, I, 1261a, 24), reading as follows:

οὐ γὰρ γίνεται πόλις ἐξ ὁμοίων˙ ἕτερον γὰρ συμμαχία καὶ πόλις.

Mention should be made of my translation of terms peculiar to Durkheim's sociology. The French word "conscience" I have translated as *conscience*; the usual translation of Durkheim's term, *consciousness*, seems to me to be a gross misinterpretation of Durkheim's meaning. A conscience for Durkheim (although never expressly defined) is pre-eminently the organ of sentiments and representations; it is not the rational organ that the term "consciousness" would imply. The qualities possessed by a conscience whether collective or individual are not those generally imputed to consciousness in German, English, and American epistemology. Moreover, the moral character of the sentiments and representations in a conscience would seem to render my translation more in the spirit, as well as the letter, of the original. In fact, the term has resemblance to the term "unconscious" in psychoanalysis, rather than to consciousness in logical theory. The terms "collective" and "commune" Durkheim employed interchangeably in referring to a conscience of such a sort. Their

---

[1] See my estimate for the citation, p. 10.

interchangeable character is shown by an error made in calling the conscience "commune" in the subtitle of chapter three of book two of the main text, and printing it as "collective" in the heading of that chapter in the table of contents. In this instance, I have made both of them read *common.*

To translate Durkheim's term "anomie" I have called back to life an English word obsolete since 1755 and first used in 1591, *anomy.* The *Shorter Oxford English Dictionary* finds it used in its earlier period to mean "disregard of (divine) law," and in its later, "lawlessness." Its derivation is direct from the Greek *ἀνομία.* The adjective of this noun which Durkheim uses, "anomique," has no English counterpart, obsolete or current, and I have had to coin a word which I hope gains some currency because of its fullness of meaning. That word is *anomic.* The Greek for it is *ἄνομος.*

The words "sentiment" and "representation" I have translated as *sentiment* and *representation.* These words, too, Durkheim defined only by implication, but I think that the same English terms will convey the sense intended by the original. Sometimes I have translated "similitude" as *likeness* and sometimes as *similitude.* In the first chapter of book two, Durkheim refers to the plural "progrès" of the division of labor, implying not the ethical term, *progress,* but rather the vitalistic term, *advances.* Durkheim uses the word in the plural and I have sometimes translated it as *advances,* and sometimes by the singular, *progress.* This is mentioned here to warn the reader that it is not to be confused with Spencer's term, nor with the popular use of the word to mean *moral superiority.* I have often translated "la morale" as *ethics,* although sometimes as *morality.* I do not think Durkheim made any sharp distinction between them. At least the context never shows it.

The picture of Durkheim which appears as the frontispiece in this volume is not a late one; it dates from about 1903. I should have preferred to have used a later one, but the photographs to which I had access and which were of a later date are either very bad and very difficult of reproduction, or else show Durkheim when he was in the throes of the illness which was to be fatal to him and consequently do not catch the spirit and vigor of a great mind.

Where Durkheim has quoted Spencer directly from the French translations of Spencer's works, I have translated from the French and placed the matter in indirect statement; the page references I have left as referring to the French translations. Where Durkheim quotes Spencer in order to criticize him adversely, as in the majority of the cases, there would seem to be no reason for being interested in Spencer's ideas after Durkheim has finished with them. In truth, there is scarcely any mind, even though tutored in logic and philosophy, as Spencer's certainly was not, that can stand up under the attack of Durkheim's incisive thinking on topics to which he has given keen attention.

This volume I hope marks the beginning of interest in this country in Durkheim's work. He is certainly the greatest social thinker that has come out of France since Proud'hon, far greater than Comte on whom so much attention was lavished without commensurate results. My friend and former teacher, Mr. George E. G. Catlin, is now supervising a translation of *Les Règles de la méthode sociologique* which should do much to enhance Durkheim's reputation among the English-speaking peoples. Dr. Talcott Parsons, as I have noted in my Estimate, is writing an essay on Durkheim. The reputation of Durkheim in this country has suffered from the criticism of anthropologists, but that is because he was not an anthropologist; he made great contributions to anthropology, but it was not his *métier.*

A student of sociology, with only a general academic training in French, I early sought the aid of Mr. Herbert A. Brodsky, who rendered great service in the preliminary stages of the translation of the two prefaces, the introduction, and the appendix, as well as the greater part of the second book. Had other demands not forced themselves upon him, he might have been my collaborator in the whole task. As it is, I am extremely indebted to him, and realize how much better this book might have been if it had had the benefit of his knowledge of French. I thought it best, however, that the book see the light in English as soon as possible, since further delay would only serve to deprive English-speaking students of the work of a man they can ill afford to miss.

Whatever there is of worth in the English style of the book must be attributed to my friend, Mr. George H. Weltner, who has carefully gone over the entire translation and aided me in polishing it. There are parts, however, which even his skill could not polish, and I alone must be held accountable for them. I am sure that what is good in the style is his, and what is bad is mine.

My debt to Professors MacIver and Catlin I have been able to express, but only in a small way, in the dedication.

G. S.

New York City. November, 1933.

An Estimate of Durkheim's Work[2]

I. THE PRESENT STATUS OF DURKHEIM'S WORK

Rarely in the history of social thought has the best of a thinker's labor been as grossly misinterpreted as in the case of Emile Durkheim. And, in no other case is the misinterpretation to be laid at the door of the thinker himself. His reputation was established by the book here translated and *Le Suicide*, but his present place in social thought rests upon the views he expressed in other works,—views which, strange to say, were in contradiction to these two studies. *De la division du travail social* was the first of his *magna opera*, and undoubtedly the greatest. *Le Suicide* is directly in line with the conclusions of this book. But *Les Règles de la méthode sociologique* marks the beginning of a distortion of the results herein contained and misrepresents the logic of science, particularly of social science. Logic and rigorous analysis have never been, in any formal fashion, the great qualities of French thought. In this respect Durkheim is of his country. Of course, this does not mean that his work is illogical; it means that his methodology is incorrect. To the subject-matter of sociology he contributed a great deal, in this work and in *Le Suicide*; it is unfortunate that the same cannot be said for his methodology. If anything, his methodology disturbed the growth of sociology.

Nevertheless, his fame derives not from *De la division du travail social*, or from *Le Suicide*, but from *Les Règles*, from *Les formes élémentaires de la vie réligeuse*, and from his social psychology, a science in whose establishment he would never have believed had he not misunderstood the nature of social science. But formally to misinterpret the nature of social science does not necessarily imply the substantial misinterpretation of it. In this work and in *Le Suicide*, Durkheim contributed enough to social thought and sociology to gain

---

[2] Since writing my estimate, I have done considerable work and even more cogitating about Durkheim, and I now feel that there is more in his realism than I earlier saw. Moreover, the mass of unpublished manuscripts which Durkheim left will no doubt when published throw much light on the development and ramifications of his thought. (See Mauss' *In Memoriam, L'oeuvre inédite de Durkheim et de ses collaborateurs*, in *L'Année Sociologique*, New Series, Volume I (1923-24), Paris, 1925.) The reason for leaving this estimate as I wrote it is that it expresses a criticism of Durkheim from a certain point of view,—a point of view which I have held but whose retention will depend upon my own development and developments in the science of sociology. Also, there is the fact that I am not yet prepared to substitute any other critical expression and apparatus for the one I did employ, partly because I have latterly been impressed by the profundity of Durkheim's analysis, and partly because I cannot bring myself around to a position on either side which I consider sound.

everlasting fame; yet both works are comparatively little known and mentioned cursorily in "surveys" of social thought.

His fame today rests largely on what is termed his "social realism." This is an apt name for his work after the publication of the article entitled *Représentations individuelles et représentations collectives* which appeared in the *Révue metaphysique* for 1898. From that article we may justly date the development of his social realism, as well as Durkheim's misinterpretation of his own work. To be sure, in 1902 there came the highly significant preface to the second edition of *De la division du travail social* on occupational groups,[3] but this is an outgrowth of conclusions reached in that work, and not those contained in *Les Règles* or the article in which Durkheim's theory of collective representations appeared.

The analysis here will set forth the grounds which justify calling him a social realist, with a criticism of such realism; delineate the argument of *De la division du travail social*; and show Durkheim's relation to the socialist movement. Before doing so, it might be well to notice and add as another element in Durkheim's misinterpretation of his own best work a phase of his thought which has recently been brought to public attention; namely, his relation to the French nationalistic movement, and especially his activities during the late war as a fiery jingo.[4] His nationalism is a direct growth from his theory of the collective conscience. As we shall soon see, however, that theory carried over into the analysis of contemporary society a concept which Durkheim had found useful in anthropological work and the study of primitive peoples, but which, on his own assertion and splendid proof in *De la division du travail social*, was not only inadequate, but also outworn as an instrument for the interpretation of industrial societies where organic solidarity was in process of becoming.

This estimate of Durkheim is not to be wholly negative. We shall deal in some detail with his theory of the division of labor and show its surpassing importance in our present societies. It is over a quarter of a century since Durkheim proclaimed the need for a new moral code, and still we have not evolved it. His foresight and his ingenious proposal for such a moral code stand in striking contrast to some of the fatuous contemporary attempts to proclaim "disinterestedness," or a lame, weak, and blind "humanism" as the way out.

---

[3] See Barnes, H. E., "Durkheim's Contributions to the Reconstruction of Political Theory," *Political Science Quarterly*, Vol. XXXV.

[4] See Mitchell, M. M., "Emile Durkheim and the Philosophy of Nationalism," *Political Science Quarterly*, Vol. XLVI, March 1931.

II. DURKHEIM'S SOCIAL REALISM[5]

The term "realism" is generally used to denote a certain philosophical attitude towards the relation of the knowing subject to the object known. A realist is one who believes, and seeks to prove, that objects known have an existence outside of the knowing subject, and so exist even without their being known. There are, of course, all shades of realists, from the Platonic who conceive the Ideas or Forms as having an existence of their own to those who are realistic not about ideas, but about objects. Durkheim's realism is a theory not of the relation between the known and the knower, but of the individual to society; and realism, for Durkheim, means that society, its facts and products, exists outside of, and above individuals. The existence of society, in short, is not dependent upon individuals. During his lifetime, Durkheim was accused of being a Platonic realist by Tarde, his lifelong opponent. Tarde's charge Durkheim did not deny but regarded as a just attribution of likeness. He says that "face to face with this system of ideas, the individual mind is in the same position as the *nous* of Plato before the world of ideas. The individual mind is compelled to absorb them, for it needs them in order to be able to have communion with its fellows. But the absorption is always imperfect."[6] He later qualified this thorough-going realism, but the qualification was verbal and never carried out in practice.

The problem that Durkheim is here dealing with is the central, most crucial, and most vexing in all social thought,—the relation of the individual to society,—for upon an answer to this question will rest a whole theory of society and the methods to be employed in social research. The seemingly naïve and facile solution which Durkheim gives to it, in spite of the profound results on the same subject which he reached in *De la division du travail social* where the problem is the one which he poses for himself in the book, is the result of the, at that time, great and growing prestige of the science of psychology and its supposed worth in social analysis, and also of the conception of the nature of science which Durkheim inherited from a bad logician, Comte. To understand Durkheim's realism, we must understand these sources of his work.

---

[5] Dr. Talcott Parsons, who is making a study of Durkheim's work, finds much that is valuable in his realism. We have begun to see significant implications in the position, but still find difficulty in accepting coercion and externality as concepts applicable to contemporary society. Were we estimating Durkheim's work anew, we perhaps might assign greater importance to the doctrine. We hope that our criticism does not lead the reader to underestimate the possibilities latent in such a position. For the best that can be said for Durkheim's realism we await Dr. Parsons' exposition.

[6] *Les formes élémentaires de la vie réligeuse*, p. 622.

In *De la division du travail social*, written before he assumed the realistic position, Durkheim shows that the collective conscience has gradually become weakened through the course of social evolution and that with its effacement and the decline of mechanical solidarity, the individual has become autonomous and an entity in his own right. In this work, he is hesitant to answer the question whether the collective conscience, which results from likenesses, is a conscience as is the individual conscience. "By this term [collective conscience, also sometimes spoken of in the book as common conscience], we simply signify the totality of social likenesses without prejudging the category by which this system of phenomena ought to be defined."[7] But, five years later, in *représentations individuelles et représentations collectives*, he has already made this term not only a category of, but the very foundation-stone of what he calls socio-psychology and sociology. To accomplish this, he draws the analogy between individual représentations which are the object-matter of individual psychology and collective representations which are the object-matter of social psychology and sociology. And since individual representations are contained within the individual conscience, collective représentations must be contained within what he calls the collective or common conscience.

In the very beginning of this crucial essay, Durkheim admits that his argument is one from analogy. Unfortunately, he fails to realize that arguments from analogy evade the issue by assuming some available teleology without inquiring into the adaptability of the data at hand to such a teleology. Thus, Durkheim argues from psychology to sociology without seeing any inconsistency in that. The basic reason for this is that Durkheim, following in the positivist tradition, fails to realize the difference between the social and the natural sciences.[8] Otherwise, he could never have fallen into the pit-fall.[9]

The collective représentations are exterior to individual consciences because they are not derived from the individuals taken in isolation but from their convergence and union. The private sentiments do not become social except by combining under the action of the forces *sui generis* which association develops. As a result of these combinations, and of mutual

---

[7] *De la division du travail social*, p. 47, 5th ed.

[8] This is not the place for an analysis of the difference. The reader is referred to the work of Max Weber in Germany, as well as that of Rickert, Dilthey, and Spranger. In America, R. M. MacIver has become the leader of this school, which is attempting to steer social thought away from the easiest and most erroneous path which identifies the two.

[9] S. Jankelevitch in 1905 had already criticized the neo-positivists whose leader Durkheim was for asserting that they were strict scientists and consequently made no assumptions, and then making the most glaring assumption of all,—that "natural" and social science are of the same species. See his *Nature et Société*.

alterations which result therefrom, the private sentiments become something different. The resultant derived therefrom extends beyond the individual mind as the whole is greater than the part. It is this that thinks, that feels, that wills, although it may not be able to will, feel, or act except through the intermediation of individual consciences. This explains why the social phenomenon does not depend upon the personal nature of individuals.[10]

In *Les Règles* Durkheim expresses the same idea. He says that collective représentations manifest

the way in which the group conceives itself in its relations with the objects which affect it. The group has a different constitution from that of the individual, and the things that affect it are of a different nature. Representations expressing neither the same objects nor the same subjects cannot depend upon the same causes. To understand the way in which society represents itself, one must consider the nature of the society and not that of the individuals.[11]

These collective représentations form the content of what Durkheim calls the collective or common conscience. But there is here a mistaking of the like for the common and collective. In *De la division du travail social* he found that the common conscience which was concomitant with repressive law and mechanical solidarity had its roots in the great multitude of social likenesses (similitudes). But "to speak rigorously," as he is fond of saying, a conscience which has its roots in likenesses would be a conscience similar in individuals and not common to them. For a representation to be common, all individuals would have to partake of one and the same reaction to one and the same stimulus. Sensations are not common; they are communicable. On the basis of such communication, one may join with those who have like sensations, but one cannot penetrate into them. Durkheim might answer that the conscience is common because the same *sentiment* was forced upon each individual. But a sentiment, even in Durkheim's usage, is not a representation. Sentiments may be held in common, but they can only result from similar reactions. "Common" suggests an identity. But there are no identical sensations. If there are, mortal beings will never know of them.

One might be willing to admit a group mind as a physicist admits an atom into his system of categories, if it could be shown that the qualities of such a mind had some relation to objective phenomena. These objective phenomena, in the case of a group mind or a common

---

[10] *Rep. Ind. et Rep. Col*, p. 295.
[11] Pp. xvi-xvii.

conscience, would have to be common to that aspect of individual beings which was under consideration. In this instance, the aspect is the individual organism as psychology views it. But psychology, whatever brand one may choose, deals with memory, imagination, perception, thought, gestalts, neuro-muscular processes, and there is surely nothing in a group mind which remembers, thinks, perceives, or reacts as individual beings do. Tarde, to be sure, did speak of social memory, but it was a metaphor and science is not built on metaphors.

We must, therefore, conclude that Durkheim's theory of collective représentations is inadequate to solve the problem of the relation of the individual to society.

Durkheim's conception of the nature of science is decidedly in the positivist tradition. From it we can gain an understanding of his definition of a social fact, a concept fundamental in his later work and one which has gained wide vogue, and also of his reputation as a realist. Social facts, he tells us in *Les Règles*,

> consist in ways of acting, thinking, and feeling, exterior to the individual and endowed with a power of coercion, wherewith they impose themselves upon the individual. They must not, then, be confused with organic phenomena since they consist of representations and actions, nor with psychic phenomena which have existence only in the individual consciences and through it. Thus, they constitute a new type of phenomena, and to them must be given the name "social."

This definition of factuality in social science is traceable to two aspects of the positivist epistemology which Durkheim clings to. . The first is a distrust of metaphysics and theory; the second the desire to eliminate all personal biases, all values from social studies. Hence, he says that social facts must be treated as things. They must not be conceived of as part of individual consciences or inherent in the minds of individuals. It may be asked of Durkheim, Why must they be not so conceived? And Durkheim's answer would be because they are not then objective. Unfortunately, this objectivity Durkheim finds in what he is pleased to call the positive sciences, that is, the natural sciences. But, there are as many sciences as there are types of data, and if society exists only in the minds of individuals, or only in the interaction of individuals, as surely could be contended and upheld, it is still possible to be objective about these phenomena. Phenomena can be in the subject and yet be considered objectively. Just as there are as many types of science as there are types of data, so there are as many types of objectivity as there are types of objects to study. To make social facts exterior and coercive to the individual is a circumvention of the very problem which sociology must face. Durkheim's objectivity is a factitious one since it rests on a distortion of the data. Ultimately, it derives from a false conception of science and a failure to realize the difference between the natural and the social.[12]

To study social facts as things Durkheim contends that we must define the group of phenomena which constitute our science by some characteristic common to them all, but which is external to them. But no characteristic of any science is claimed to be external to the phenomena studied. It is inherent, or presumed to be so, or else it is factitious and artificial. The real difficulty in Durkheim is his desire, at any expense, to make sociology positive. But it is just because the object-matter of sociology is different from natural phenomena that sociology cannot be made positive. What MacIver has called the inner order which social phenomena present and what Znaniecki has termed the "humanistic coefficient" render social data of an order different from the natural order.[13]

Thus, Durkheim was enabled to make society external to and outside of individuals not through observation of social data, but through an attempt to impose a method upon the data which was not fitting to them. Social facts are exterior to the individual, not because they really are exterior, since there would be no social facts without individuals, but because Durkheim cannot conceive of a science which studies the inner order of phenomena. Just as he drew a false analogy from psychology to set up a theory of collective représentations and the common conscience, so he here draws a false parallel between the science which studies the social and those which study the natural. But, in reality, even the natural scientist does not proceed as Durkheim claims. He does not isolate some aspect for study by considering it outside of and determinate of his data. His data themselves determine his method, and he determines his data. Hence, Durkheim is doing a strange thing. Ultimately his argument reduces to something like this:—Social facts cannot be in individuals and cannot be a result of individual interaction and association alone because we could not then be able to set up a science of the social as are the positive sciences. Therefore, we must assert that that alone is social which is above and outside of individuals so that we can objectively determine it and study its content as facts. He is claiming that we must have a *positive* science

---

[12] For the type of objectivity that the social scientist can have while understanding the difference between the natural and the social, see Max Weber's article in his *Gesammelte Aufsätze zur Wissenschaftslehre*, Die Objectivität sozial-wissenschaftlicher und sozialpolitischer Erkenntnis.

[13] MacIver, R. M., *Is Sociology a Natural Science?* Publications of the American Sociological Society, May 1931; also the chapter on social causation in his *Society, Its Structure and Changes*. Znaniecki, F., "The Object-Matter of Sociology," *American Journal of Sociology*, Vol. 32, 1927.

of the social at any cost, even at the cost of the data themselves. The error is too obvious to labor over.

This criterion of objectivity and factuality led Durkheim to a statement on the question of values in sociology which is much too sweeping. Values are metaphysical and speculative; they deal with ethics, and Durkheim claims to be dealing with the science of ethics. We must study moral rules through some external symbol, and that external symbol is law and its sanctions. But law in modern society, as every realm of modern society, is in men, and not outside of them. It is considered to be outside of them in primitive societies, and Durkheim has well shown how it is outside of them there. Hence, morality does not force men to participate in it, but is something that men make. Morality still remains an individual matter despite its social bearing. Furthermore, Durkheim was not as free of values as he claimed. In *Les Règles* he sees as the duty of the statesman the keeping of society in equilibrium and a state of moral health. What that equilibrium is and what that moral health is Durkheim suggests. But, is it not true that other thinkers have suggested other conditions for the health of society? And is not Durkheim's solution of social ills a value of his own?

There is another phase of Durkheim's thought which explains his realism, although it, too, does little to validate its worth as an interpretation of the social. After *Le Suicide* he devoted himself, for the most part, to investigations of primitive societies. There he found that the collective conscience was strong and defined and that social facts were exterior and coercive to the individual. Thus, in *Les formes élémentaires de la vie réligeuse*, Durkheim was able to show that religion is originally social, and that it always partakes of a means for keeping society alive and healthy. We do not here wish to enter into a discussion of Durkheim's religious theories,[14] but we wish to point out that his study of primitive religion might well be made in terms of his own definition of social facts and the collective conscience and yet have no validity for the interpretation of modern society. This Durkheim himself showed in *De la division du travail social.* With the growth of free thought, religion has become an individual affair, and each man may choose his own, or refuse allegiance to any. The collective conscience has been weakened and each individual has become the carrier of his own society. Society becomes nothing more and nothing else than the individuals who compose it. That he did not so conceive society we can ascribe to a misinterpretation of his own work.

The evolutionary clue which Durkheim found in *De la division du travail social* he used to little advantage in his later work, and to this

---

[14] Criticism of these theories will be found in Clement C. J. Webb's *Group Theories of Religion.*

failure a great part of his social realism is due. Whereas he later was speaking of one type of society,—primitive where the collective conscience is strong and society is external and coercive to the individual—he mistook his doctrine for a theory of all types of society. Whereas in *De la division du travail social* he was speaking of societies, he later came to speak of society. And his monism was an appropriation of the means for interpreting one type for the interpretation of all types.

We have, then, shown wherein Durkheim's reputation as a social realist is justified, and also the shortcomings of the position. By a false analogy to psychology, through a bad theory of the nature of science and a failure to distinguish the natural from the social, and a mistaking of modern society for primitive, he was enabled to set society over and above the individual. To these three factors can be attributed, we believe, the criticism which has been levelled at Durkheim.

III. "THE DIVISION OF LABOR IN SOCIETY"

De la division du travail social had its origin, as Durkheim says, "in the question of the relation of the individual to social solidarity. Why does the individual, while becoming more autonomous, depend more upon society? How can he be at once more individual and more solidary? Certainly, these two movements, contradictory as they appear, develop in parallel fashion. ... It appeared to us that what resolves this apparent antinomy is a transformation of social solidarity due to the steadily growing development of the division of labor. That is how we have been led to make this the object of our study." But the division of labor is not a phenomenon that we observe universally in all societies; we find it only in higher societies. To understand it we must then investigate the type of solidarity which we find in societies where there is no, or very little, division of labor. These societies owe their integration to the large number of social similitudes. In them we find a homogeneity of sentiments and practices which is common to all their members. The proof of such homogeneity lies in the existence of only one type of law,—repressive. Since law is the symbol of the manner in which social relations are regulated, it is permissible to study it as an index of solidarity. This Durkheim does through a theory of crime and punishment. This theory has taken high rank in legal philosophy and the study of sanctions advocated by Durkheim has been a key to socializing the study of law. We are not here concerned with that theory except as it bears on the larger study of social evolution and the division of labor.[15] With a mass of detail and a breadth of knowledge

---

[15] Some penetrating criticism, as well as a keen appreciation of Durkheim as a legal philosopher, will be found in Pierre de Tourtoulon's *Philosophy in the Development of*

that is amazing, Durkheim proves his thesis of the preponderance of repressive law wherever the division of labor is in a rudimentary state.

Repressive law works mechanically; that is, there is no doubt in the minds of the members of the society in which a crime is committed as to what action should be taken. Moreover, the sanctions which attach penalties to crime are, as Durkheim says, engraven in every conscience. He says that the action is spontaneous, concerted, and unopposed. The individual is not a factor in executing the law; he is merely the instrument of society. In such a society, there is no recognition of those different from its members; such difference disrupts social solidarity and calls forth a passionate reaction from all members. This reaction is imposed; it is not planned; it is mechanical. Thus, Durkheim is led to call this type of solidarity mechanical.

The moral value of repressive law and mechanical solidarity is undoubted. The problem then is to show that the type of solidarity which the division of labor gives rise to, as evinced in some other type of law, has a function similar to that executed by mechanical solidarity. But the law which the division of labor makes for is not repressive law, but restitutive law, and there is no penalty attached to it. Moreover, the action, though it involves social sanctions and society is always keenly interested in the outcome of it, is between individuals who, in their own right, have contracted to exchange goods or services. Hence, the study of contract-law will show us the moral influence which the division of labor has. Whereupon Durkheim goes into a learned and valuable analysis of how contract-law works, how it supposes a division of labor, and how, throughout the course of history, it becomes ever more preponderant. But there is nothing mechanical about the relations which contract-law looks after. They are entered into by individuals of their free will, although watched over by society, and presuppose a liberty of movement in the individual which was never possible under repressive law and mechanical solidarity.

The type of solidarity to which the division of labor gives rise derives, then, from a co-operation of individuals within a system. This system is society, and each individual is an organ of society. But co-operation between organs demands an organism within which they co-operate. Thus, Durkheim is led to call the type of solidarity which the division of labor creates, organic solidarity. Mechanical solidarity acts in individuals just as physical forces act upon inanimate matter. The individuals are at the beck and call of society. Its summons must be obeyed. Organic solidarity demands an interaction of parts for the sake of the totality. The emphasis is thus shifted. Whereas in the former society is supreme and dictates the type of solidarity, in the latter the individual is the focus of interest and through his actions keeps the system healthy.

The causes for the development and steady advance of the division of labor lie in the growth of material and moral density which presupposes the effacement of the segmental social type and which is usually accompanied by a growth in volume.

The division of labor requires the specialization of each individual in some certain task to which he devotes himself and which constitutes his life-work. Dilettantism is abhorrent to the proper functioning of organic solidarity; it is merely a superficial development of all the faculties without the profound development of any one, or some few. Individuals become differentiated through the social functions they fulfill. They are no longer forced into certain functions that their ancestry formerly demanded they execute since the force of heredity has become weakened, and no one inherits anything more than very general dispositions. Not only is the individual not forced into any set occupation at birth, but society must see to it that he attains the position his ability merits notwithstanding his lineage. With the differentiation of functions within the social organism and the decline of the force of heredity, there has occurred the weakening of the power of the common conscience, and the growth of individualism. Moreover, the growth of cities has also weakened the common conscience, has pluralized it. This individualism, however, must not be understood as something over and against society, but as a quality which a certain type of society, that in which organic solidarity is dominant and the division of labor is advanced, forces upon individuals. Instead of being a cog in a machine, as it were, the individual becomes the prime factor in the proper working of organic life.

This felicitous working out of the division of labor does not always occur, and sometimes pathological cases arise. Industrial crises become more frequent as labor is divided more. This abnormality results from an insufficient regulation of the relations between capital and labor. Normally, the division of labor itself regulates functions so as to cause the harmonious working out of organic solidarity. But where the spontaneity of economic life is disrupted by over-production, strikes, boycotts, or some such strictly economic causes, then society, through the governmental organ, must step in to regulate the functions so as to make for harmony again. The second type of abnormal forms of the division of labor occurs in class-warfare. This can only come about through force being exercised upon the individual so as to keep him within a function which he finds unsuited to his abilities and possibly beneath them. Such constraint is a result of the inequalities in the external conditions of life which do not permit free competition to take its natural course. The solution for this lies in equalizing the external conditions of fife. There must no longer be rich and poor at birth, but all must start from the same point. There is to be no handicapping of individuals bereft of fortune. Inheritance of wealth is a phenomenon of segmental organization, and organized societies have evolved from, and gone beyond that stage. The third abnormal form occurs when the functional activity of each worker is insufficient. The further working of the division of labor, however, tends of itself to ameliorate this abnormality and to bring about the harmony of functions.

Thus, Durkheim concludes that the division of labor gives rise to organic solidarity and that organic solidarity is a moral phenomenon. It integrates individuals in society at the same time that it insists upon their individuality. Therefore, the question which was posed at the beginning of the investigation has now been answered. And on this note Durkheim ends.

In the preface to the second edition, however, Durkheim returns to a problem which he merely touched upon in the course of the work, that of occupational groups. Though the division of labor is a moral phenomenon, it does create anomalies. The most important of these is the isolation of the individual in some one task and the failure to integrate him in some larger social whole. This can be obviated by the setting up of occupational groups constituted as units on the basis of the type of labor done by the individuals in societies. In a learned argument, Durkheim shows that there is historical precedence for this besides the undoubted moral need for it. Not only will occupational groups integrate certain interests, but these groups should constitute the new basis for political representation. There should be groups of employers as well as groups of employees, and there should be meetings between duly appointed representatives of both types of groups. Though political representation hereafter should be based on occupations, still politics is inadequate to cope with the problems in economic fields which only those nearest them know. These occupations will not only have economic status, but they will undoubtedly develop into little societies of their own with recreational facilities, actuarial functions, and almost all others that men today require for existence. Durkheim finds these groups so completely the solution for our moral dilemma that in *Le Suicide* he contends that their institution will do much to lessen the number of voluntary deaths which are symptomatic of a society which has lost its hold on the individual and has left him to wander without spiritual pabulum.

The idea was not new, as Durkheim saw. It was as old as economic fife. Proud'hon had suggested it half a century earlier, and Durkheim, using new arguments and with true moral fervor, saw in it the hope for our future society.

IV. DURKHEIM AND SOCIALISM

The argument of Durkheim and his conclusion remain remarkably fresh to this day, and his doctrine of evolution is adequate to the material he presents. We are concerned to dispute his optimism concerning the felicitous working of the division of labor. Now, forty years after he wrote *De la division du travail social*, all the forms of the division of labor which are present in contemporary society seem to be abnormal forms. Surely on Durkheim's premises this should not be so. Abnormalities should be the rare exception. How does this come about?

In brief, Durkheim's misplaced optimism can be traced to his failure to understand the working of modern capitalism. Though he complains that the economists have failed to see a moral phenomenon in the division of labor, he nevertheless failed to see it in its full scope as an economic phenomenon. He views economic life, as most other aspects of society under the division of labor, as a spontaneous product of human interaction. Its only abnormality would seem to lie in constraining the individual in a function and the periodic appearance of crises. To alleviate this he suggests regulation of the external conditions of economic life. But this regulation would seem to imply a total capitalistic upheaval and the destruction of the profit-system. This Durkheim would never admit. As Mauss says of him, "All his life he found adherence to socialism properly so-called repugnant because of certain traits in it: its violent character; its more or less purely proletarian class-character, and also its political and politician-like character. Durkheim was deeply opposed to all class or nation warfare. He wished change for the benefit of all society and not one of its parts, even if that part was most numerous and had the force. He considered political revolutions and parliamentary evolutions superficial, costly, and more theatrical than serious. ... He "sympathized," as we say, with the socialists, with Jaurès, with socialism. He never gave himself to it."[16]

This can be traced to his failure to distinguish what he so justly called the division of labor in society from what Marx has called the division of labor in the workshop, or in manufacture, or the division of labor caused by capital, in another variant phrase of Marx. The division of labor in society Marx identifies as does Durkheim with that "known for centuries past, and which organized the laborers in the various handicrafts."[17] This, as Marx shows, in agreement with Durkheim, was

---

[16] Introduction, pp. viii-ix, to the posthumous work of Durkheim, *Le Socialisme*, 1928.

[17] *Das Kapital*, Vol. 1, Ch. 14.

an evolutionary process and a valuable one. "What," asks Marx, "characterizes the division of labor in manufactures?" And he answers,

> The fact that the detail laborer produces no commodities. It is only the common product of all the detail laborers that becomes a commodity. Division of labor in a society is brought about by the purchase and sale of the products of different branches of industry, while the connection between the detail operations in a workshop is due to the sale of the labor power of several workmen to one capitalist, who applies it as combined labor power. The division of labor within the workshop implies concentration of the means of production in the hands of one capitalist; the division of labor in society implies their dispersion among many independent producers of commodities. While, within the workshop, the iron law of proportionality subjects definite numbers of workmen to definite functions, in the society outside the workshop chance and caprice have full play in distributing the producers and their means of production among the various branches of industry. Division of labor within the workshop implies the undisputed authority of the capitalist over men, who are but parts of a mechanism that belongs to him. The division of labor within the society brings into contact independent commodity-producers who acknowledge no other authority but that of competition, of the coercion exerted by the pressure of their mutual interests.[18]

Why did Durkheim fail to distinguish between these two aspects of the division of labor? The answer is that he failed to realize the monopolistic nature of capitalism and the activities to which the profit-system lead. He saw economic life much as Adam Smith did, a spontaneous working out of harmony. In the case of industrial crises, it is not the functions which need further regulating, it is the system which warps these functions that must be replaced. And class-warfare does not come about from the individual's not being in harmony with his function within the system; it is caused by evils inherent in the system itself. Durkheim's solution would be a compromise between production for profit and production for use. Unfortunately, there can be no compromise since, as Marx says, production for profit (capitalism) is a monster that multiplies. It calls forth from individuals the basest desires in human nature, acquisitiveness at the expense of fellow-men and authority over the lives of others without respect for others. It is not the failure of functions to concur that produces depressions and crises; it is the over-production and financial manipulation which are inherent elements in capitalism. To plan

---

[18] *Ibid.*

production to meet consumption we must either surrender capitalism or surrender the attempt, and merely pay lip-service to socialism. The abolition of such abnormalities, as Durkheim calls them, requires that industries be owned by society at large for the service of its members, and that the banking system which fosters profit-making be made over into a national credit-institution that metes out credit as society demands.

Durkheim fails to see that the abnormalities he speaks of are inherent in a system, and that we cannot retain the system without also retaining the evils. The workers, even collectively, cannot bargain with those who hold the power, especially when the labor-supply is great enough for the employers to be able to dispense with workers making demands which eat into profits. Were they exchanging commodities, there might be some equality in the bargaining. But they are offering services. There is, then, really no exchange; there is exploitation. Unless the producing forces are themselves constituted for the best interests of the workers, these forces will not hold such interests to be of primary importance. The failure of labor unions the world over attests to this. The recent fiasco in the English labor movement has finally brought the Labor party to proclaim that its aim hereafter will be socialistic and uncompromising. For, ultimately, there can be no compromise between capitalism and socialism. They conflict on every important item. Only when manufactures and industry become social, can the division of labor in society really become paramount and the guiding force of civilization. For the division of labor in manufacture to become part of the division of labor in society, manufacture must become socialized.

Durkheim rightly saw that, eventually, the extension of the division of labor in society would make for internationalism, but here again he did not understand that under capitalism any hope for international co-operation and union is doomed. Tariff reprisals, imperialistic ventures, all make for war. To make nations conscious of other nations and their problems we must employ the same means as must be employed in making men conscious of other men and their problems, namely, involve them in a system where it is criminal and subversive of their own personalities to injure others. To make them conscious of one another is not enough; we must, as Durkheim implies, make it illegal for them to be otherwise. Unfortunately, our present legal system is built upon the inalienable right of national states and the sanctity of sovereignty. Living, as Durkheim might put it, in organized societies, we yet cling to codes which fit segmental types.

A new social world Durkheim certainly saw; the means to its attainment have yet to be developed.

THE DIVISION OF LABOR IN SOCIETY

Preface to the Second Edition

SOME NOTES ON OCCUPATIONAL GROUPS

In re-editing this book, we do not wish to change its original format. A book has an individuality of its own. It is best to keep intact the appearance by which it has become known.[19]

But there is an idea undeveloped in the first edition which it will be useful to bring to light, and further determine, for it will clarify certain parts of the present work, and even those we have since published.[20] It is the question of the role that occupational groups are destined to play in the contemporary social order. If, originally, we came into contact with the problem only by allusion,[21] that is because we expected to consider it again in a special study. As other activities have come up to turn us from the project, and as there does not seem to be any likelihood of our being able to follow it up later, we are going to take advantage of this second edition to show how this question is bound up with the subject treated in the course of this work, to indicate how the question appears, and especially to try to remove the prejudices which still prevent many from understanding the urgency and significance of the problem. Such will be the object of this new preface.

I

We repeatedly insist in the course of this book upon the state of juridical and moral anomy in which economic life actually is found.[22] Indeed, in the economic order, occupational ethics exist only in the most rudimentary state. There is a professional ethic of the lawyer and the judge, the soldier and the priest, etc. But if one attempted to fix in a little more precise language the current ideas on what ought to be the relations of employer and employee, of worker and manager, of tradesmen in competition, to themselves or to the public, what indecisive formulas would be obtained! Some generalizations, without point, about the faithfulness and devotion workers of all sorts owe to those who employ them, about the moderation with which employers must use their economic advantages, a certain reprobation of all

---

[19] We feel justified in suppressing about thirty pages of the old introduction, which appear useless to us today. Where the material formerly appeared, we have given an explanation of the omission.

[20] See *Le Suicide*, conclusion.

[21] See pp. 155-162 and 181-182.

[22] See pp. 181-182 and p. 277.

competition too openly dishonest, for all untempered exploitation of the consumer; that is about all the moral conscience of these trades contains. Moreover, most of these precepts are devoid of all juridical character, they are sanctioned only by opinion, not by law; and it is well known how indulgent opinion is concerning the manner in which these vague obligations are fulfilled. The most blameworthy acts are so often absolved by success that the boundary between what is permitted and what is prohibited, what is just and what is unjust, has nothing fixed about it, but seems susceptible to almost arbitrary change by individuals. An ethic so imprecise and inconsistent cannot constitute a discipline. The result is that all this sphere of collective life is, in large part, freed from the moderating action of regulation.

It is this anomie state that is the cause, as we shall show, of the incessantly recurrent conflicts, and the multifarious disorders of which the economic world exhibits so sad a spectacle. For, as nothing restrains the active forces and assigns them limits they are bound to respect, they tend to develop haphazardly, and come into collision with one another, battling and weakening themselves. To be sure, the strongest succeed in completely demolishing the weakest, or in subordinating them. But if the conquered, for a time, must suffer subordination under compulsion, they do not consent to it, and consequently this cannot constitute a stable equilibrium.[23] Truces, arrived at after violence, are never anything but provisional, and satisfy no one. Human passions stop only before a moral power they respect. If all authority of this kind is wanting, the law of the strongest prevails, and latent or active, the state of war is necessarily chronic.

That such anarchy is an unhealthy phenomenon is quite evident, since it runs counter to the aim of society, which is to suppress, or at least to moderate, war among men, subordinating the law of the strongest to a higher law. To justify this chaotic state, we vainly praise its encouragement of individual liberty. Nothing is falser than this antagonism too often presented between legal authority and individual liberty. Quite on the contrary, liberty (we mean genuine liberty, which it is society's duty to have respected) is itself the product of regulation. I can be free only to the extent that others are forbidden to profit from their physical, economic, or other superiority to the detriment of my liberty. But only social rules can prevent abuses of power. It is now known what complicated regulation is needed to assure individuals the economic independence without which their liberty is only nominal.

But what brings about the exceptional gravity of this state, nowadays particularly, is the heretofore unknown development that economic functions have experienced for about two centuries. Whereas formerly they played only a secondary role, they are now of the first

---

[23] See Book III, ch. i, 3.

importance. We are far from the time when they were disdainfully abandoned to the inferior classes. In the face of the economic, the administrative, military, and religious functions become steadily less important. Only the scientific functions seem to dispute their place, and even science has scarcely any prestige save to the extent that it can serve practical occupations, which are largely economic. That is why it can be said, with some justice, that society is, or tends to be, essentially industrial. A form of activity which has assumed such a place in social life evidently cannot remain in this unruly state without resulting in the most profound disasters. It is a notable source of general demoralization. For, precisely because the economic functions today concern the greatest number of citizens, there are a multitude of individuals whose lives are passed almost entirely in the industrial and commercial world. From this, it follows that as that world is only feebly ruled by morality, the greatest part of their existence takes place outside the moral sphere. Now, for the sentiment of duty to be fixed strongly in us, the circumstances in which we live must keep us awake. Naturally, we are not inclined to thwart and restrain ourselves; if, then, we are not invited, at each moment, to exercise this restraint without which there is no ethic, how can we learn the habit? If in the task that occupies almost all our time we follow no other rule than that of our well-understood interest, how can we learn to depend upon disinterestedness, on self-forgetfulness, on sacrifice? In this way, the absence of all economic discipline cannot fail to extend its effects beyond the economic world, and consequently weaken public morality.

But, the evil observed, what is its cause and what can be its remedy?

In the body of this work, we have especially insisted upon showing that the division of labor cannot be held responsible, as is sometimes unjustly charged; that it does not necessarily produce dispersion and incoherence, but that functions, when they are sufficiently in contact with one another, tend to stabilize and regulate themselves. But this explanation is incomplete. For, if it is true that social functions spontaneously seek to adapt themselves to one another, provided they are regularly in relationship, nevertheless this mode of adaptation becomes a rule of conduct only if the group consecrates it with its authority. A rule, indeed, is not only an habitual means of acting; it is, above all, *an obligatory means of acting*; which is to say, withdrawn from individual discretion. Now, only a constituted society enjoys the moral and material supremacy indispensable in making law for individuals, for the only moral personality above particular personalities is the one formed by collective life. It alone has continuity and the necessary perpetuity to maintain the rule beyond the ephemeral relations which daily incarnate it. Moreover, its role is not limited simply to forming into imperative principles the most general results of particular contracts; it intervenes in an active and positive manner in the formation of each rule. First, it is the arbiter naturally designed to settle interests in conflict, and to assign to each its suitable limits. Then it has the chief interest in order and peace; if anomy is an evil, it is above all because society suffers from it, being unable to live without cohesion and regularity. A moral or juridical regulation essentially expresses, then, social needs that society alone can feel; it rests in a state of opinion, and all opinion is a collective thing, produced by collective elaboration. For anomy to end, there must then exist, or be formed, a group which can constitute the system of rules actually needed.

Neither political society, in its entirety, nor the State can take over this function; economic life, because it is specialized and grows more specialized every day, escapes their competence and their action.[24] An occupational activity can be efficaciously regulated only by a group intimate enough with it to know its functioning, feel all its needs, and able to follow all their variations. The only one that could answer all these conditions is the one formed by all the agents of the same industry, united and organized into a single body. This is what is called the corporation or occupational group.

Now, in the economic order, the occupational group does not exist anymore than occupational ethics. Since the eighteenth century *rightfully* suppressed the old corporations, only fragmentary and incomplete attempts have been made to bring them back with new foundations. To be sure, individuals working at the same trade have relations with one another because of their similar occupation. Even competition puts them in relationship. But these relations have nothing ordered about them; they depend upon chance meetings, and have, very often, an entirely personal aspect. A particular tradesman is found in contact with some fellow-tradesman; this does not result from the industrial body of this or that specialty united for common action. In exceptional circumstances, the members of the same occupation come together as a unit to treat some question of general interest, but these meetings are only temporary. They do not survive the particular circumstances which bring them into being, and consequently the collective life of which they are the cause is more or less completely obliterated with them.

The only groups which have a certain permanence today are those called syndicates, composed of either employers or workmen. To be sure, there is, in this, a beginning of occupational organization, but still quite formless and rudimentary. For, first, a syndicate is a private association, without legal authority, deprived, consequently, of all

---

[24] We shall return to this point, p. 281 ff.

regulatory power. The number of syndicates is theoretically limitless, even in the interior of the same industrial category; and as each of them is independent of the others, if they do not federate or unify there is nothing intrinsic in them expressing the unity of the occupation in its entirety. Finally, the syndicates of employers and the syndicates of employees are distinct from each other, which is *legitimate and necessary*, but with no regular contact between them. There exists no common organization for their union where they can develop a common authority, fixing their mutual relations and commanding obedience, without a consequent loss of individuality. Consequently, it is always the law of the strongest which settles conflicts, and the state of war is continuous. Save for those of their acts which arise from common ethics, employers and workmen are, in relation to each other, in the same situation as two autonomous states, but of unequal power. They can form contracts, but these contracts express only the respective state of their military forces. They sanction a condition of fact; they cannot make it a condition of right.

For the establishment of an occupational ethic and law in the different economic occupations, the corporation, instead of remaining a confused aggregate, without unity, would have to become again a defined, organized group; in a word, a public institution. But any project of this sort runs afoul of a certain number of prejudices which must be forestalled or dissipated.

In the first place, the corporation has its historic past against it. Indeed, it is taken as being strictly solidary with our old political regime, and consequently considered unable to survive it. The point is made that to ask for a corporative organization for industry and commerce is to demand that we retrace the course of history. Such retrogression is correctly looked upon either as impossible or as abnormal.

This argument would carry weight if we proposed artificially to resuscitate the old corporation as it existed in the Middle Ages. But the problem is not presented in that fight. It is not a question of discovering whether the medieval institution can identically fit our contemporary societies, but whether the needs which it answered are not always present, although it must, in order to satisfy them, change according to the times.

Now, what precludes our seeing in the corporations a temporary organization, good only for someone epoch and determined civilization, is, at once, their venerable age and the manner in which they have developed in history. If they dated only from the Middle Ages, one could believe that, having been born with a political system, they must of necessity disappear with it. But, in reality, they have a much more ancient origin. Generally, they appear as soon as there are trades, which means as soon as industry ceases being purely agricultural. If they seem to have been unknown in Greece, at least up to the time of the Roman conquest, that is because trades, being looked down upon there, were carried on almost exclusively by strangers, and for that very reason found themselves outside the legal organization of the city.[25] But in Rome they date at least from the earliest times of the Republic; tradition even attributes their creation to king Numa.[26] It is true that for a long time they had to lead a rather humble existence, for historians and tablets speak of them but rarely, so that we know very little of the way in which they were organized. But from the time of Cicero, their number became more considerable, and they began to play a part in Roman society. From that moment, says Waltzing, "all the working classes seem possessed with the desire to multiply the occupational groups." The expanding movement continues apace, reaching, under the Empire, "an extension which, perhaps, has not been surpassed since, if one takes into account the economic differences."[27] All the categories of workmen, which were many, finally ended by forming themselves into constituencies, and it was the same with men who lived by commerce. At the same time, the character of these groups was changed; they ended by becoming part of the administrative machine. They fulfilled official functions; each occupation was looked upon as a public service whose corresponding corporation had obligations and responsibilities toward the State.[28]

This was the ruin of the institution. For this dependence upon the State was not long in degenerating into an intolerable servitude that emperors could maintain only by force. All sorts of methods were employed for preventing workmen from getting rid of the heavy obligations resulting from their occupation; they went so far as to recruit and force enrollment. Such a system evidently could only last as long as the political power was strong enough to impose it. That is why it did not survive the dissolution of the Empire. Besides, civil wars and invasions had destroyed commerce and industry; workmen profited

---

[25] See Hermann, *Lehrbuch der griechischen Antiquitäten*, vol. iv, 3rd ed., p. 398. Sometimes the worker, because of his occupation, was even deprived of the freedom of the city (*ibid.*, p. 392). We have yet to know whether, for want of an official and legal organization, there was not something clandestine about it. What is certain is that there were some corporations of merchants. (See Francotte, *L'Industrie dans la Grèce antique*, vol. ii, pp. 204 ff.)

[26] Plutarch, *Life of Numa*; Pliny, *Hist, nat.*, XXXIV. It is, to be sure, only a legend, but it proves that the Romans regarded their corporations as one of their oldest institutions.

[27] *Étude historique sur les corporations professionnelles chez les Romains*, vol. i, pp. 56-57.

[28] Certain historians believe that, from their very origin, corporations were related to the State. But it is quite certain, in any case, that their official character was otherwise developed during the Empire.

from these circumstances to flee the cities and scatter about in the country. Thus, the first centuries of our era produced a phenomenon which was to be repeated identically at the end of the eighteenth century. Corporative life was almost completely extinguished. Some few traces remained, in Gaul and in Germany in the cities of Roman origin. If, then, a theorist had taken stock of the situation, he would reasonably have concluded, as economists did later, that corporations had not, or at least no longer had, any reason for existing, that they had disappeared once and for all, and he would, no doubt, have treated any attempt to bring them back as retrogressive and unrealizable. But events would soon have refuted such a prophecy.

Indeed, after some time, the corporations began a new existence in all European societies. They endured to rise again in the eleventh and twelfth centuries. At that time, says Levasseur, "the workmen began to feel the need of combining and forming their first associations."[29] In any case, in the thirteenth century, they are once again flourishing, and they develop up to the day when a new decadence begins for them. So persistent an institution cannot depend upon a contingent and accidental existence. Still less possible is the admission that they may have been the product of some strange collective aberration. If from the origin of the city up to the zenith of the Empire, from the dawn of Christian societies up to modern times, they have been necessary, it is because they answer durable and profound needs. The fact that after having disappeared the first time they came into being themselves and in a new form especially removes all value from the argument which presents their violent disappearance at the end of the eighteenth century as a proof that they are no longer in harmony with the new conditions of collective existence. Moreover, the need which all great civilized societies feel to recall them to life is the surest symptom that this radical suppression was not a remedy, and that the reform of Turgot necessitates another that cannot be indefinitely postponed.

II

But if all corporative organization is not necessarily an historical anachronism, is there any reason for believing that it may play, in contemporary societies, the great role we have attributed to it? For, if it be indispensable, it is not because of the economic services it can render, but because of the moral influence it can have. What we especially see in the occupational group is a moral power capable of containing individual egos, of maintaining a spirited sentiment of common solidarity in the consciousness of all the workers, of preventing the law of the strongest from being brutally applied to

---

[29] *Les classes ouvrières en France jusqu'à la Révolution*, I, p. 194.

industrial and commercial relations. It is now thought to be unsuitable for such a role. Because it had its origin in short-lived interests, it appears that it can be used only for utilitarian ends, and the mementos left by corporations of the old regime seem only to confirm this impression. They are gratuitously represented in the future as they were during the last days of their existence, particularly busy in maintaining or increasing their privileges and their monopolies; and it cannot be seen how interests so narrowly occupational can have a favorable effect on the ethics of the body or its members.

But what has been true of certain corporations for a very short space of their development cannot be applied to all the corporative regime. Far from having acquired a sort of moral infirmity from its constitution, it has especially played a moral role during the major part of its history. This is particularly evident in the Roman corporations. "The corporations of workers," says Waltzing, "were, with the Romans, far from having an occupational character as pronounced as in the Middle Ages; we find there neither regulation of methods, nor imposed apprenticeship, nor monopoly; nor was their end to unite the necessary elements to exploit an industry."[30] To be sure, the association gave them more force in time of need for safeguarding their common interests. But that was only one of the useful consequences produced by the institution; that was not its *raison d'être*, its principal function. Above all, the corporation was a religious organization. Each one had its particular god whose cult was celebrated in a special temple when the means were available. In the same way as each family had its *Lar familiaris*; each city its *Genius publicus*, each organization had its protecting god, *Genius collegii.* Naturally, this occupational cult did not dispense with celebrations, with sacrifices and banquets in common. All sorts of circumstances were used as reasons for these joyful gatherings. Moreover, distribution of food-stuffs and money often took place at the community's expense. There have been questions as to whether the corporation had a sick-fund; if it regularly helped those members who were in need. Opinions on this point are divergent.[31] But what lends interest and import to this discussion is that these common banquets, more or less periodic, and the distribution accompanying them, often took the place of help, and formed a bureau of indirect assistance. Thus, the unfortunate knew they could count on this disguised aid. As corollary to this religious character, the organization of workmen was, at the same time, a burial society. United in a cult during their lives, like the *Gentiles*, the members of these corporations also wished to rest together after death. All the fairly rich corporations

---

[30] *Op. cit.*, I, p. 194.
[31] The majority of historians believe that certain organizations, at least, were mutual-aid societies.

had a collective *columbarium* where, when the organization had not the funds to buy a burial plot, there was at least the certainty that its members would have honorable burial at the expense of the common fund.

A common cult, common banquets, a common cemetery, all united together,—are these not all the distinctive characteristics of the domestic organization at the time of the Romans? Thus, it has been said that the Roman corporation was a "great family." "No word," says Waltzing, "better indicates the nature of the relations uniting the brotherhood, and a great many indications prove a great fraternity reigned in their midst."[32] The community of interests took the place of the community of blood. "The members looked upon themselves as brothers, even to the extent of calling themselves by that name." The most ordinary expression, as a matter of fact, was that of *sodales*, but even that word expresses a spiritual relationship implying a narrow fraternity. The protectors of the organization often took the names of father and mother. "A proof of the devotion the brothers had for their organization lies in the bequests and donations they made. There are also funereal monuments upon which are found: *Pius in collegio*, he was faithful towards his organization, as if one said, *Pius in suos*"[33] This familial life was so developed that Boissier makes it the principal aim of all the Roman corporations. "Even in the workers' corporations," he says, "there was association principally for the pleasure of living together, for finding outside oneself distractions from fatigue and boredom, to create an intimacy less restrained than the family, and less extensive than the city, and thus to make life easier and more agreeable."[34]

As Christian societies belong to a social type very different from the city-state, the corporations of the Middle Ages do not exactly resemble the Roman corporations. But they also constitute a moral environment for their members. "The corporation," says Levasseur, "united people of the same occupation by strong bonds. Rather often they were established in the parish house, or in a particular chapel and put themselves under the invocation of a saint who became the patron saint of all the community. . . . There they gathered, attended with great ceremony the solemn masses; after which the members of the brotherhood went, all together, to end their day in joyous feasting. In this way the corporations of the Middle Ages closely resembled those of Roman times."[35] The corporation, moreover, often used part of its budgetary funds for charity.

---

[32] *Op. cit.*, I, p. 330.
[33] *Op. cit.*, I, p. 331.
[34] *La Religion romaine*, II, pp. 287-288.
[35] *Op. cit.*, I, pp. 217-218.

Moreover, precise rules fixed the respective duties of employers and workmen, as well as the duties of employers toward each other, for each occupation. There are, to be sure, regulations not in accord with our present ideas, but judgment must be made according to the ethics of the time, since that is what the rules express. What is indisputable is that they are all inspired by zeal, not for individuals, but for corporative interest, whether poorly or well understood. Now the subordination of private utility to common utility, whatever it may be, always has a moral character, for it necessarily implies sacrifice and abnegation. In addition, a great many of these rules proceeded from moral sentiments still ours today.[36] The valet was protected from the caprices of his master who could not dismiss him at will. It is true that the obligation was reciprocal; but besides this reciprocity being just in itself, it is still more justified by reason of the important privileges the worker enjoyed then. Thus, masters were forbidden to negate his *right to work*, which allowed him to seek assistance from his neighbors, or even their wives. In short, as Levasseur says, "these regulations concerning the apprentices and workmen are worthy of consideration by historian and economist. They are not the work of a barbarous century. They carry the mark of worth-while minds and good, common sense, worthy of observation."[37] Finally, a system of rules was designed to guarantee occupational honesty. All sorts of precautions were taken to prevent the merchant or workman from deceiving the buyer, to compel him "to perform good, loyal work."[38] To be sure, a time came when the rules became uselessly complicated, when the masters were a great deal busier safeguarding their privileges than caring about the good name of the occupation and the honesty of their members. But there is no institution which, at some given moment, does not degenerate, either because it does not know how to change and mobilize anew, or because it develops unilaterally, overdoing some of its activities. This makes it unsuited to furnish the services with which it is charged. That is reason to seek its reformation, not to declare it forever useless, nor to destroy it.

Whatever it may be from this standpoint, the preceding facts sufficiently prove that the occupational group is not incapable of exerting moral action. The considerable place that religion took in life, in Rome as well as in the Middle Ages, makes particularly evident the true nature of its functions, for all religious community then constituted a moral milieu, in the same way as all moral discipline tended forcibly to take a religious form. And besides, this character of corporative

---

[36] *Op. cit.*, I, p. 221.—See, on the same moral character of the corporation in Germany, Gierke, *Das Deutsche Genossenschaftswesen*, I, p. 384; for England, Ashley, *An Introduction to English Economic History and Theory.*

[37] *Op. cit.*, p. 238.

[38] *Op. cit.*, pp. 240-261.

organization comes from very general causes that can be seen acting in other circumstances. When a certain number of individuals in the midst of a political society are found to have ideas, interests, sentiments, and occupations not shared by the rest of the population, it is inevitable that they will be attracted toward each other under the influence of these likenesses. They will seek each other out, enter into relations, associate, and thus, little by little, a restricted group, having its special characteristics, will be formed in the midst of the general society. But once the group is formed, a moral life appears naturally carrying the mark of the particular conditions in which it has developed. For it is impossible for men to live together, associating in industry, without acquiring a sentiment of the whole formed by their union, without attaching themselves to that whole, preoccupying themselves with its interests, and taking account of it in their conduct. This attachment has in it something surpassing the individual. This subordination of particular interests to the general interest is, indeed, the source of all moral activity. As this sentiment grows more precise and determined, applying itself to the most ordinary and the most important circumstances of life, it is translated into definitive formulae, and thus a body of moral rules is in process of establishment.

At the same time that this result is produced of itself and by the force of circumstances, it is useful and the feeling of its utility lends confirmation to it. Society is not alone in its interest in the formation of special groups to regulate their own activity, developing within them what otherwise would become anarchic; but the individual, on his part, finds joy in it, for anarchy is painful to him. He also suffers from pain and disorder produced whenever inter-individual relations are not submitted to some regulatory influence. It is not good for man to live with the threat of war in the midst of his immediate companions. This sensation of general hostility, the mutual defiance resulting from it, the tension it necessitates, are difficult states when they are chronic. If we love war, we also love the joys of peace, and the latter are of more worth as men are more profoundly socialized, which is to say (for the two words are synonymous) more profoundly civilized. Common life is attractive as well as coercive. Doubtless, constraint is necessary to lead man to surpass himself, to add to his physical nature another; but as he learns the charm of this new life, he contracts the need for it, and there is no order of activity in which he does not seek it passionately. That is why when individuals who are found to have common interests associate, it is not only to defend these interests, it is to associate, that is, not to feel lost among adversaries, to have the pleasure of communing, to make one out of many, which is to say, finally, to lead the same moral life together.

Domestic morality is not otherwise formed. Because of the prestige the family has in our eyes, it seems to us that if it has been, and if it is always, a school of devotion, of abnegation, the place *par excellence* of morality, it is because of quite particular, intrinsic characteristics found nowhere else. It is believed that consanguinity is an exceptionally powerful cause of moral relationship. But we have often had the occasion for showing[39] that consanguinity has not the extraordinary efficacy attributed to it. The proof is that in many societies the non-blood relations are found in numbers in the centre of the family; the so-called relationship is then contracted with great facility, and it has all the effects of a blood-tie. Inversely, it often happens that very near blood relations are, morally or juridically, strangers to each other; for example, the case of cognates in the Roman family. The family does not then owe its virtues to the unity of descent; it is quite simply a group of individuals who find themselves related to one another in the midst of political society by a particularly strong community of ideas, of sentiments and interests. Consanguinity facilitates this concentration, for it causes mutual adaptation of consciences. But a great many other factors come into play: material neighborhood, solidarity of interests, the need of uniting against a common danger, or simply to unite, are other powerful causes of relationship.

Now, they are not special to the family, but they are found, although in different forms, in the corporation. If, then, the first of these groups has played so considerable a role in the moral history of humanity, why should the second be incapable of doing the same? To be sure, there is always this difference between them, that members of a family live their lives together, while members of a corporation live only their occupational lives together. The family is a sort of complete society whose action controls our economic activity as well as our religious, political, scientific activities. Anything significant we do, even outside the house, acts upon it, and provokes appropriate reactions. The sphere of influence of a corporation is, in a sense, more restricted. Still, we must not lose sight of the increasingly important position the occupation takes in life as work becomes more specialized, for the field of each individual activity tends steadily to become delimited by the functions with which the individual is particularly charged. Moreover, if familial action extends everywhere, it can only be general; detail escapes it. Finally, the family, in losing the unity and indivisibility of former times, has lost with one stroke a great part of its efficacy. As it is today broken up with each generation, man passes a notable part of his existence far from all domestic influence.[40] The corporation has none of these disturbances; it is as continuous as life. The inferiority that it presents, in comparison with the family, has its compensation.

---

[39] See especially *Année sociologique*, I, pp. 313 ff.
[40] We have developed this idea in *Le Suicide*, p. 433.

If we find it necessary thus to bring together the family and the corporation, it is not simply to establish an instructive parallel between them, but because the two institutions are closely connected. This is observable in the history of Roman corporations. We have seen, indeed, that they were formed on the model of domestic society, of which they were at first only a new and enlarged form. But, the occupational group would not, at this point, recall the familial group, if there were not some bond of relation between them. And, indeed, the corporation has been, in a sense, the heir of the family. As long as industry is exclusively agricultural, it has, in the family and in the village, which is itself only a sort of great family, its immediate organ, and it needs no other. As exchange is not, or is very little, developed, the farmer's life does not extend outside the familial circle. Economic activity, having no consequences outside the family, is sufficiently regulated by the family, and the family itself thus serves as occupational group. But the case is no longer the same once trades exist. For to live by a trade, customers are necessary, and going outside the house to find them is necessary, as is having relations with competitors, fighting against them, coming to an understanding with them. In addition, trades demand cities, and cities have always been formed and recruited principally from the ranks of immigrants, individuals who have left their native homes. A new form of activity was thus constituted which burst from the old familial form. In order not to remain in an unorganized state, it was necessary to create a new form, which would be fitting to it; or otherwise said, it was necessary for a secondary group of a new kind to be formed. This is the origin of the corporation; it was substituted for the family in the exercise of a function which had first been domestic, but which could no longer keep this character. Such an origin does not allow us to attribute to it that sort of constitutional amorality which is generally gratuitously bestowed upon it. Just as the family has elaborated domestic ethics and law, the corporation is now the source of occupational ethics and law.

III

But to succeed in getting rid of all the prejudices, to show that the corporative system is not solely an institution of the past, it would be necessary to see what transformation it must and can submit to in order to adapt itself to modern societies, for evidently it cannot exist today as it did in the Middle Ages.

To treat this question systematically, it would be necessary first to establish in what manner the corporative regime has evolved in the past and what are the causes which have determined the principal variations it has gone through. "Being given the conditions in which European societies find themselves, one would be able to foresee fairly accurately what it must become. But for that, comparative studies, which have not yet been made, would be necessary. These can only be made as we proceed. However, we can perhaps see, in a most general way, what the development has been.

We have seen from the preceding that the corporation in Rome did not become what it later did in Christian societies. Its difference does not rest only in its more religious and less occupational character, but in the place it occupied in society. It was, indeed, at least in origin, an extra-social institution. The historian undertaking the study of Roman political organization in all its elements does not meet in the course of his analysis any fact manifesting the existence of corporations. They were not recognized in the Roman constitution as definite associations. In none of the electoral assemblies, in none of the army meetings, did the workers get together in organizations; the occupational group nowhere took part in public life as such, either in a body or through regular representatives. At most, there is a question as to three or four organizations that have been identified with certain of the centuries set up by Servius Tullius (*tignarii, aearii, tibicines, cornicines*); even there the fact is problematical.[41] And as for the other corporations, they were certainly outside the official organization of the Roman people.[42]

This unusual situation is, in some part, explained by the very conditions in which they were formed. They appear when trades begin to develop. Now, for a long time, trades were only an accessory and secondary form of the social activity of the Romans. Rome was essentially an agricultural and military society. As agricultural, it was divided into *gentes* and *curia*; the centurial assembly rather reflected the military organization. As for the industrial functions, they were too rudimentary to affect the political structure of the city.[43] Besides up to a late stage in Roman history, the trades were socially outlawed and were not allowed any regular place in the State. To be sure, there came a time when their social condition improved. But the manner in which this improvement was achieved is in itself significant. To succeed in having their interests respected, and to play a role in public life, the workers had to resort to irregular and extra-legal procedures. They

---

[41] It appears most likely that the centuries thus marked off did not comprise all the carpenters and blacksmiths, but only those manufacturing or repairing arms and war-machines. Dionysius of Halicarnassus formally tells us that workmen thus grouped had a purely military function, εἰς τὸν πόλεμὸν; these were not, therefore, guilds, properly speaking, but divisions of the army.

[42] All we say of the situation of the corporations entirely leaves aside the controversial question as to whether, originally, the State intervened in their formation. Even if they had been under State control from the very beginning (which does not appear likely) it still is true that they did not affect the political structure. That is what is important for us.

[43] If one probes deeper, their situation is even stranger. At Athens they are not only extra-social, but almost extra-legal.

triumphed over scorn only by means of intrigues, plots, and clandestine agitation.[44] This alone is the best proof that Roman society was not open to them. And if, later, they finally became an integral part of the State and of the administrative machine, it cannot be said that this was a glorious triumph for them, but rather a painful dependence. If they then became a part of the State, it was not to occupy the position which their social services might rightfully give them, but simply so that they could be more adroitly watched by the governmental power. "The corporation," says Levasseur, "became the chain which made them captives, and imperial power became more oppressive as their work became more difficult or more necessary to the State."[45]

Their place in the Middle Ages is quite another matter. There, as soon as the corporation appears, it appears as the normal mould for that part of the population called to play such a considerable role in the State: the bourgeoisie or the third estate. Indeed, for a long time, the bourgeoisie and tradespeople are one and the same. "The bourgeoisie in the thirteenth century," says Levasseur, "was exclusively composed of tradespeople. The class of magistrates and legists had scarcely begun to be formed; the scholars still belonged to the Church; the number of men receiving incomes from property was still restricted, because territorial property was then almost entirely in the hands of nobles. There remained to the commoner only the work of the shop and the counter; and it was by industry or commerce that they had conquered for themselves a place in the kingdom."[46] It was the same in Germany. Bourgeois and citizen were synonymous terms; and, moreover, we know that the German cities were formed about permanent markets, opened by a nobleman on a part of his domain.[47] The population grouping itself around these markets, which became the urban population, was then almost exclusively made up of workers and merchants. Thus, the word *forenses* or *mercatores* was used indifferently to designate the inhabitants of cities, and the *ius civile* or urban law is very often called *ius fori* or law of the market. The organization of trades and of commerce seems, then, to have been the primitive organization of the European bourgeoisie.

Thus, when the cities freed themselves from the seignorial power, when the commune was formed, the body of trades which had preceded and prepared this movement became the foundation of the communal constitution. Indeed, "in almost all the communes, the political system and the election of magistrates are founded on the division of citizens

---

[44] Waltzing, *op. cit.*, I, pp. 85 ff.
[45] *Op.* cit., I, p. 31.
[46] *Op.* cit., I, p. 191.
[47] See Rietschel, *Markt und Stadt in ihrem rechtlichen Verhältniss*, Leipzig, 1897, and all the work of Sohm on this question.

into bodies of trades."[48] Very often, votes were cast by bodies of trades, and elected, at the same time, the heads of the corporation and those of the commune. "At Amiens, the workers, for example, united every year to elect the mayors of each corporation; the elected mayors then named twelve sheriffs who named twelve others, and the sheriffship presented in its turn to the mayors of the corporations three persons from among whom they chose the mayor of the commune. ... In some cities, the method of election was still more complicated, but, in all, the political and municipal organization was narrowly restricted to the organization of work."[49] Just as the commune was an aggregate of trades-bodies, the trades-bodies were communes on a small scale, for the very reason that they had been the model of which the communal institution was the enlarged and developed form.

Now, we know from the history of our societies that the commune has become their corner-stone. Consequently, since it was a combination of corporations, and was formed on the style of a corporation, it is the latter, in the last analysis, which has served as foundation for all the political system which has issued from the communal movement. It has grown in importance and dignity. Whereas in Rome it began by being almost outside the normal framework, it has, on the contrary, served as elementary framework in our present societies. This is another reason for our refusing to see in it a sort of archaic institution, destined to disappear from history. For if, in the past, the role it played became more vital as commerce and industry developed, it is entirely unreasonable to believe that new economic progress can drive it out of existence. The opposite hypothesis seems more justified.[50]

But there is more knowledge to be gathered from the summary we have just made.

First of all, it shows us how the corporation has fallen into discredit for about two centuries, and, consequently, what it must become in order to take its place again among our public institutions. We have just seen, indeed, that in the form it had in the Middle Ages it was narrowly bound to the organization of the commune. This solidarity was without inconvenience as long as the trades themselves had a communal character. While, as originally, merchants and workers

---

[48] *Op. cit.*, I, p. 193.

[49] *Ibid.*, I, p. 183.

[50] It is true that, when trades are organized into castes, they soon take a place in social organization, as in the case of Indian society. But the caste is not the corporation. It is essentially a familial and religious group, not an occupational group. Each has its degree of peculiar religiousness. And as society is organized religiously, this religiousness, depending upon various causes, assigns to each caste a determined rank in the totality of the social system. But its economic role is nothing in this official situation. (Cf. Bouglé, *Remarques sur le régime des castes, Année Sociologique*, IV.)

had only the inhabitants of the city or its immediate environs for customers, which means as long as the market was principally local, the bodies of trades, with their municipal organization, answered all needs. But it was no longer the same once great industry was born. As it had nothing especially urban about it, it could not adapt itself to a system which had not been made for it. First, it does not necessarily have its centre in a city; it can even be established outside all pre-existing rural or urban agglomerations. It looks for that territory where it can best maintain itself and thrive. Thus, its field of action is limited to no determined region; its clientele is recruited everywhere. An institution so entirely wrapped up in the commune as was the old corporation could not then be used to encompass and regulate a form of collective activity which was so completely foreign to the communal life.

And, indeed, as soon as great industry appeared, it was found to be outside the corporative regime, and that was what caused the bodies of trades to do all in their power to prevent industry's progress. Nevertheless, it was certainly not freed of all regulation; in the beginning the State played a role analogous to that which the corporations played for small-scale commerce and urban trades. At the same time as the royal power accorded the manufacturers certain privileges, in return it submitted them to its control. That is indicated in the title of royal manufacturers. But as it is well known how unsuited the State is for this function, this direct control could not fail to become oppressive. It was almost impossible from the time great industry reached a certain degree of development and diversity; that is why classical economists demanded its suppression, and with good cause. But if the corporation, as it then existed, could not be adapted to this new form of industry, and if the State could not replace the old corporative discipline, it does not follow that all discipline would be useless thenceforward. It simply meant that the old corporation had to be transformed to continue to fill its role in the new conditions of economic life. Unfortunately, it had not enough suppleness to be reformed in time; that is why it was discarded. Because it did not know how to assimilate itself to the new life which was evolving, it was divorced from that life, and, in this way, it became what it was upon the eve of the Revolution, a sort of dead substance, a strange body which could maintain itself in the social organism only through inertia. It is then not surprising that a moment came when it was violently expelled. But to destroy it was not a means of giving satisfaction to the needs it had not satisfied. And that is the reason the question still remains with us, and has become still more acute after a century of groping and fruitless experience.

The work of the sociologist is not that of the statesman. We do not have to present in detail what this reform should be. It will be sufficient to indicate the general principles as they appear from the preceding facts.

What the experience of the past proves, above all, is that the framework of the occupational group must always have relations with the framework of economic life. It is because of this lack of relationship that the corporative regime disappeared. Since the market, formerly municipal, has become national and international, the corporations must assume the same extension. Instead of being limited only to the workers of a city, it must enlarge in such a way as to include all the members of the occupation scattered over the territory,[51] for in whatever region they are found, whether they live in the city or the country, they are all solidary, and participate in a common life. Since this common life is, in certain respects, independent of all territorial determinations, the appropriate organ must be created that expresses and regularizes its function. Because of these dimensions, such an organ would necessarily be in direct contact with the central organ of the collective life, for the rather important events which interest a whole category of industrial enterprises in a country necessarily have very general repercussions of which* the State cannot fail to take cognizance; hence it intervenes. Thus, it is not without reason that royal power tended instinctively not to allow great industry outside its control when it did appear. It was impossible for it not to be interested in a form of activity which, by its very nature, can always affect all society. But this regulatory action, if it is necessary, must not degenerate into narrow subordination, as happened in the seventeenth and eighteenth centuries. The two related organs must remain distinct and autonomous; each of them has its function, which it alone can take care of. If the function of making general principles of industrial legislation belongs to the governmental assemblies, they are incapable of diversifying them according to the different industries. It is this diversification which constitutes the proper task of the corporation.[52]

---

[51] We do not have to speak of international organization which, in consequence of the international character of the market, would necessarily develop above this national organization, for the latter alone can actually constitute a juridical institution. The first, under present European law, can result only in freely concluded arrangements between national corporations.

[52] This specialization could be made only with the aid of elected assemblies charged to represent the corporation. In the present state of industry, these assemblies, in the same way as tribunals charged with applying the occupational regulations, should evidently be comprised of representatives of employees and representatives of employers, as is already the case in the tribunals of skilled trades; and that, in proportions corresponding to the respective importance attributed by opinion to these two factors in production. But if it is necessary that both meet in the directing councils of the corporations, it is no less important that at the base of the corporative organization they form distinct and independent groups, for their interests are too often rival and antagonistic. To be able to go about their ways freely, they must go about their ways separately. The two groups thus constituted would then be able to appoint their representatives to the common assemblies.

This unitarian organization for a whole country in no way excludes the formation of secondary organs, comprising workers of the same region, or of the same locality, whose role would be to specialize still more the occupational regulation according to the local or regional necessities. Economic life would thus be regulated and determined without losing any of its diversity.

For that very reason, the corporative regime would be protected against that tendency towards immobility that it has often been charged with in the past, for it is a fault which is rooted in the narrowly communal character of the corporation. As long as it was limited to the city, it was inevitable for it to become a prisoner of tradition as the city itself. As, in a group so restricted, the conditions of life are almost invariable, habit exercises a terrific effect upon people, and even innovations are dreaded. The traditionalism of the corporations was thus only an aspect of the communal traditionalism, and had the same qualities. Then, once it was ingrained in the mores, it survived the causes which had produced and originally justified it. That is why, when the material and moral concentration of the country, and great industry which is its consequence, had opened minds to new desires, awakened new needs, introduced into the tastes and fashions a mobility heretofore unknown, the corporation, which was obstinately attached to its old customs, was unable to satisfy these new exigencies. But national corporations, by virtue of their dimension and complexity, would not be exposed to this danger. Too many diverse minds would be in action for stationary uniformity to be established. In a group formed of numerous and varied elements, new combinations are always being produced.[53] There would then be nothing rigid about such an organization, and it would consequently find itself in harmony with the mobile equilibrium of needs and ideas.

Besides, it must not be thought that the entire function of the corporation is to make rules and apply them. To be sure, where a group is formed, a moral discipline is formed too. But the institution of this discipline is only one of the many ways through which collective activity is manifested. A group is not only a moral authority which dominates the life of its members; it is also a source of life *sui generis*. From it comes a warmth which animates its members, making them intensely human, destroying their egotisms. Thus, in the past, the family was the legislator of law and ethics whose severity went to extremes of violence, at the same time that it was the place where one first learned to enjoy the effusions of sentiment. We have also seen how the corporation, in Rome and in the Middle Ages, awakened these same needs and sought to satisfy them. The corporations of the future will have a complexity of attributes still greater, by reason of their increased

---

[53] Book II, ch. iii, § 4.

growth. Around their proper occupational functions others which come from the communes or private societies will be grouping themselves. The functions of assistance are such that, to be well filled, they demand feelings of solidarity between assistants and assisted, a certain intellectual and moral homogeneity such as the same occupation produces. A great many educational institutions (technical schools, adult education, etc.) equally seem to have to find their natural environment in the corporation. It is the same for aesthetic life, for it appears in the nature of things that this noble form of sport and recreation develops side by side with the serious life which it serves to balance and relieve. In fact, there are even now syndicates which are at the same time societies of mutual aid; others found common houses where there are organized courses, concerts, and dramatic presentations. The corporative activity can thus assume the most varied forms.

There is even reason to suppose that the corporation will become the foundation or one of the essential bases of our political organization. We have seen, indeed, that if it first begins by being outside the social system, it tends to fix itself in it in proportion to the development of economic life. It is, therefore, just to say that if progress continues to be made in this direction, it will have to take a more prominent and more predominant place in society. It was formerly the elementary division of communal organization. Now that the commune, heretofore an autonomous organism, has lost its place in the State, as the municipal market did in the national market, is it not fair to suppose that the corporation also will have to experience a corresponding transformation, becoming the elementary division of the State, the fundamental political unity? Society, instead of remaining what it is today, an aggregate of juxtaposed territorial districts, would become a vast system of national corporations. From various quarters it is asked that elective assemblies be formed by occupations, and not by territorial divisions; and certainly, in this way, political assemblies would more exactly express the diversity of social interests and their relations. They would be a more faithful picture of social life in its entirety. But to say that the nation, in becoming aware of itself, must be grouped into occupations,—does not this mean that the organized occupation or corporation should be the essential organ of public life?

Thus the great gap in the structure of European societies we elsewhere point to[54] would be filled. It will be seen, indeed, how, as advances are made in history, the organization which has territorial groups as its base (village or city, district, province, etc.) steadily becomes effaced. To be sure, each of us belongs to a commune, or a department, but the bonds attaching us there became daily more fragile

---

[54] See pp. 181-182.

and more slack. These geographical divisions are, for the most part, artificial and no longer awaken in us profound sentiments. The provincial spirit has disappeared never to return; the patriotism of the parish has become an archaism that cannot be restored at will. The municipal or departmental affairs affect and agitate us in proportion to their coincidence with our occupational affairs. Our activity is extended quite beyond these groups which are too narrow for it, and, moreover, a good deal of what happens there leaves us indifferent. There is thus produced a spontaneous weakening of the old social structure. Now, it is impossible for this organization to disappear without something replacing it. A society composed of an infinite number of unorganized individuals, that a hypertrophied State is forced to oppress and contain, constitutes a veritable sociological monstrosity. For collective activity is always too complex to be able to be expressed through the single and unique organ of the State. Moreover, the State is too remote from individuals; its relations with them too external and intermittent to penetrate deeply into individual consciences and socialize them within. Where the State is the only environment in which men can five communal lives, they inevitably lose contact, become detached, and thus society disintegrates. A nation can be maintained only if, between the State and the individual, there is intercalated a whole series of secondary groups near enough to the individuals to attract them strongly in their sphere of action and drag them, in this way, into the general torrent of social life. We have just shown how occupational groups are suited to fill this role, and that is their destiny. One thus conceives how important it is, especially in the economic order, for them to emerge from that state of inconsistency and disorganization in which they have remained for a century, since these occupations today absorb the major part of our collective forces.[55]

Perhaps now we shall be better able to explain the conclusions we reached at the end of our book, *Le Suicide*.[56] We were already proposing there a strong corporative organization as a means of remedying the misfortune which the increase in suicides, together with many other symptoms, evinces. Certain critics have found that the

---

[55] We do not mean that the territorial divisions are destined to disappear entirely, but only that they will become of less importance. The old institutions never vanish before the new without leaving any traces of themselves. They persist, not only through sheer force of survival, but because there still persists something of the needs they once answered. The material neighborhood will always constitute a bond between men; consequently, political and social organization with a territorial base will certainly exist. Only, they will not have their present predominance, precisely because this bond has lost its force. Moreover, we have shown above, that even at the base of the corporation, there will always be found geographical divisions. Furthermore, between the diverse corporations of the same locality or region there will necessarily be special relations of solidarity which will, at all times, demand appropriate organization.

[56] *Le Suicide*, pp. 434 ff.

remedy was not proportionate to the extent of the evil, but that is because they have undervalued the true nature of the corporation, and the place to which it is destined in social life, as well as the grave anomaly resulting from its disappearance. They have seen only an utilitarian association whose effect would at best bring order to economic interests, whereas it must really be the essential element of our social structure. The absence of all corporative institution creates, then, in the organization of a people like ours, a void whose importance it is difficult to exaggerate. It is a whole system of organs necessary in the normal functioning of the common life which is wanting. Such a constitutive lack is evidently not a local evil, limited to a region of society; it is a malady *totius substantiae*, affecting all the organism. Consequently, the attempt to put an end to it cannot fail to produce the most far reaching consequences. It is the general health of the social body which is here at stake.

That does not mean, however, that the corporation is a sort of panacea for everything. The crisis through which we are passing is not rooted in a single and unique cause. To put an end to it, it is not sufficient to regulate it where necessary. Justice must prevail. Now, as we shall say further on, "as long as there are rich and poor at birth, there cannot be just contract," nor a just distribution of social goods.[57] But if the corporative reform does not dispense with the others, it is the first condition for their efficacy. Let us imagine that the primordial condition of ideal justice may be realized; let us suppose that men enter life in a state of perfect economic equality, which is to say, that riches have entirely ceased being hereditary. The problems in the environment with which we were struggling would not be solved by that. Indeed, there will always be an economic apparatus, and various agents collaborating in its functioning. It will then be necessary to determine their rights and duties, and that, for each form of industry. It will be necessary that in each occupation a body of laws be made fixing the quantity of work, the just remuneration of the different officials, their duties toward each other, and toward the community, etc. Life will be just as complex as ever. Because riches will not be transmitted any longer as they are today will not mean that the state of anarchy has disappeared, for it is not a question as to the ownership of riches, but as to the regulation of the activity to which these riches give rise. It will not regulate itself by magic, as soon as it is useful, if the necessary forces for the institution of this regulation have not been aroused and organized.

Moreover, new difficulties will arise which will remain insoluble without a corporative organization. Up to now, it was the family which, either through collective property or descendence, assured the

---

[57] See below, Book III, ch. ii.

continuity of economic life, by the possession and exploitation of goods held intact, or, from the time the old familial communism fell away, the nearest relatives received the goods of the deceased.[58] In the case of collective property, neither death nor a new generation changed the relations of things to persons; in the case of descent, the change was made automatically, and the goods, at no time, remained unowned and unused. But if domestic society cannot play this role any longer, there must be another social organ to replace its exercise of this necessary function. For there is only one way of preventing the periodic suspension of any activity: a group, perpetual as the family, must possess goods and exploit them itself, or, at the death of the owner, receive them and send them to some other individual holder to improve them. But as we have shown, the State is poorly equipped to supervise these very specialized economic tasks. There is, then, only the occupational group which can capably look after them. It answers, indeed, two necessary conditions; it is so closely connected with the economic life that it feels its needs, at the same time having a perpetuity at least equal to the family. But to fill this role, it must exist and be mature enough to take care of the new and complex role which devolves upon it.

If the problem of the corporation is not the only one demanding public attention, there is certainly none more urgent, for the others can be considered only when this has been solved. No modification, no matter how small, can be introduced into the juridical order, if one does not begin by creating the necessary organ for the institution of the new law. That is why it is vain to delay by seeking precisely what this law must be, for in the present state of knowledge, our approximation will be clumsy and always open to doubt. How much more important it is to put ourselves at once to work establishing the moral forces which alone can determine its realization!

Preface to the First Edition

This book is pre-eminently an attempt to treat the facts of the moral life according to the method of the positive sciences. But a use has been made of this method that distorts its meaning, and which we oppose. The moralists who deduce their doctrines, not from some *a priori* principle, but from some propositions borrowed from one or more of the positive sciences like biology, psychology, sociology, call their ethics scientific. We do not propose to follow this method. We do

---

[58] It is true that where a will is permitted the proprietor can determine the transmission of his property. But a will only gives the right to act contrary to the law of succession. This law is the norm according to which the transfers are made. These cases are very generally limited and are always exceptional.

not wish to extract ethics from science, but to establish the science of ethics, which is quite different. Moral facts are phenomena like others; they consist of rules of action recognizable by certain distinctive characteristics. It must, then, be possible to observe them, describe them, classify them, and look for the laws explaining them. That is what we shall do for certain of them. Perhaps it will be objected: What of the existence of liberty? But truly if that implies the negation of all determined law, it is an insurmountable obstacle, not only for the psychological and social, but for all sciences; for, as human wills are always connected with some external events, the existence of liberty makes determinism quite as unintelligible outside, as within us. However, no one would argue about the possibility of the physical and natural sciences. We claim the same right for our science.[59]

Thus understood, this science is not in conflict with any philosophy, since it has an entirely different basis. Possibly ethics may have some transcendental aim beyond experience; that is the concern of the metaphysician. Certainly it does develop in history and in the realm of historic causes; it has a function in our every-day life. Whatever it is at any given moment, the conditions in which men live do not permit its being otherwise, and the proof is that it changes as conditions change, and only then. It is no longer possible to believe that moral evolution consists in the development of the same idea, confused and uncertain with primitive man, little by little growing clearer and more precise with the spontaneous progress of knowledge. If the ancient Romans had not the wide conception of humanity we have today, it is not the result of an error due to the narrowness of their understanding, but simply that such ideas were incompatible with the nature of the Roman world. Our cosmopolitanism could no more appear there than a plant can grow on a soil incapable of feeding it; thus transplanted, it would die. If, on the other hand, it has since made its appearance, it is not as a consequence of philosophical discoveries; it is not because our minds have been opened to truths they scorned; the changes produced in the structure of societies have made necessary the change in customs. The moral law, then, is formed, transformed, and maintained in accordance with changing demands; these are the only conditions the science of ethics tries to determine.

Although we set out primarily to study reality, it does not follow that we do not wish to improve it; we should judge our researches to have no worth at all if they were to have only a speculative interest. If we separate carefully the theoretical from the practical problems, it is

---

[59] We have been reproached (Beudant, *Le Droit individuel et l'Etat*, p. 244) for having qualified this question of liberty as somewhat overnice. We meant nothing disdainful by the treatment. If we put the problem aside, it is solely because the solution that is given it, *whatever it may be*, can offer no obstacle to our investigation.

not to the neglect of the latter; but, on the contrary, to be in better position to solve them. However, it is the custom to reproach those who undertake to study ethics scientifically for their inability to formulate an ideal. It is said that their respect for the fact does not permit them to go beyond it; that they are able to observe accurately what is, but cannot supply rules of conduct for the future. We hope this book will at least do away with that prejudice; for we shall see that science can help us adjust ourselves, determining the ideal toward which we are heading confusedly. But we shall attain this ideal only after observing reality, and separating it from the ideal. But is it possible to proceed otherwise? Even the most excessive idealists cannot proceed in any other fashion; for the ideal rests on nothing if it does not keep its roots in reality. The essential difference is that they study reality in a very summary fashion, often even contenting themselves with setting up an ideal, an exalted desire of the heart, *that still is but a fact*, into a sort of imperative, before which they submit their reason, and ask us to submit ours.

Some will object that the method of observation lacks rules to judge the collected facts. But this rule grows out of the facts themselves, as we shall have opportunity to demonstrate. First of all, there is a state of moral health which science alone is able to determine competently; and, being nowhere wholly realized, it becomes an ideal as we seek to draw near it. Moreover, the conditions of that state change because societies are changing, and the gravest practical problems we have to solve consist precisely in determining anew the moral health, functionally, in relation to the changes which have occurred in the environment. Now, science, in furnishing us the law of variations through which moral health has already passed, permits us to anticipate those coming into being, which the new order of things demands. If we know in what sense the law of property evolves as societies become larger and denser, and if some new growth in size and density makes new modifications necessary, we shall be able to foresee them, and foreseeing them, will them beforehand. Finally, comparing the normal type with itself—a strictly scientific operation—we shall be able to find if it is not entirely in agreement with itself, if it contains contradictions, which is to say, imperfections, and seek to eliminate them or to correct them. This is a new objective that science offers to the human will. But one may say, if science foresees, it does not command. That is true. Science tells us simply what is necessary to life. But obviously, *the supposition, man wishes to live*, a very simple speculation, immediately transforms the laws science establishes into imperative rules of conduct. To be sure, it is then transformed into art; but the passage from science to art is made without a break. Even on the ultimate question, whether we ought to wish to live, we believe science is not silent.[60]

While the science of ethics does not make us indifferent or resigned spectators of reality, at the same time it does teach us to treat it with extreme prudence, imparting to us a conservative attitude. There has been good reason to upbraid certain theories which are thought to be scientific for being destructive and revolutionary; but they are scientific in name only. They construct, but they do not observe. They see in ethics, not a collection of facts to study, but a sort of revocable law-making which each thinker establishes for himself. Ethics as practiced is then considered only as a collection of habits, prejudices valuable only if they conform to the doctrine proposed; and as this doctrine is not induced from observation of the moral facts, but borrowed from outside sciences, it inevitably contradicts the existing moral order on more than one point. But we are less exposed to that danger, for ethics is for us a system of realized facts, bound up in the total world-system. Now, legerdemain does not change a fact, even when this is desirable. Besides, since it is bound up with other facts, it cannot be modified without the modification of other facts, and it is often quite difficult to calculate in advance the final result of this series of repercussions; thus the boldest mind becomes cautious before such risks. Finally, each vital fact—and a moral fact is vital—cannot endure if it is not of some use, if it does not answer some need; until the opposite is proved true, such vital facts are entitled to our respect. Doubtless there comes a time when everything is not all it ought to be, and that, consequently, will be the time to intervene. This is what we have just proved. But the intervention then is limited; it has for its object, not to make an ethic completely different from the prevailing one, but to correct the latter, or partially to improve it.

Thus, the antithesis between science and ethics, that formidable argument with which the mystics of all times have wished to cloud human reason, disappears. To govern our relations with men, it is not necessary to resort to any other means than those which we use to govern our relations with things; thought, methodically employed, is sufficient in either case. What reconciles science and ethics is the science of ethics, for at the same time that it teaches us to respect the moral reality, it furnishes us the means to improve it.

We believe, then, that the reading of this work can, and must be, approached without distrust and with no mental reservation. At the same time, the reader must expect to meet some propositions which will disrupt certain accepted ideas. As we feel the need of understanding, or of believing we understand, the reasons for our conduct, thought is applied to ethics before the latter has become the

---

[60] We shall treat the question later, Book II, ch. i.

object of science. A certain manner of representing and explaining to ourselves the principal facts of the moral life has thus become habitual to us; a manner, however, having nothing scientific about it, for, being formed by chance and without method, it results in summary superficial examinations, made in passing, as it were. If we do not free ourselves from these ready-made judgments, we cannot grasp the considerations which follow; science, here as elsewhere, supposes a complete freedom of mind. We must rid ourselves of that habit of seeing and judging which long custom has fixed in us; we must submit ourselves rigorously to the discipline of the methodical doubt. Such doubt is, however, not dangerous; for it has nothing to do with the moral reality, but with the explanation which incompetent and badly informed thought gives it.

We must be careful to admit no explanation that does not rest on authentic proofs. The methods we have used in giving the greatest possible exactness will thus be judged. To subject an order of facts to science, it is not sufficient to observe them carefully, to describe and classify them, but what is a great deal more difficult, we must also find, in the words of Descartes, *the way in which they are scientific*, that is to say, to discover in them some objective element that allows an exact determination, and if possible, measurement. We have tried to satisfy this condition of all science. It will be distinctly seen how we have studied social solidarity through the system of juridical rules; how, in the search for causes, we have put aside all that too readily lends itself to personal judgments and subjective appreciations, so as to reach certain rather profound facts of the social structure, capable of being objects of judgment, and, consequently, of science. At the same time, we must renounce the method too often followed by sociologists who, to prove their thesis, are content with citing without order and haphazardly a more or less impressive number of favorable facts, paying no attention to contradictory facts. We have insisted upon true experiences, that is to say, methodical comparisons. Nevertheless, no matter what precautions we take, it is quite certain that such attempts can only be very imperfect as yet; but as defective as they may be, they must be attempted. There is, indeed, only one way of establishing a science and that is by attempting it, but with method. Surely the attempt is impossible if there be a question as to the primary materials. But, on the other hand, it is a vain delusion to believe that the best way to prepare for the advent of a science is first to accumulate patiently all the materials it will use, for one can know what these needed materials are only if there is already some presentiment of its essence and its needs, consequent if it exists.

This work had its origins in the question of the relations of the individual to social solidarity. Why does the individual, while becoming more autonomous, depend more upon society? How can he be at once more individual and more solidary? Certainly, these two movements, contradictory as they appear, develop in parallel fashion. This is the problem we are raising. It appeared to us that what resolves this apparent antinomy is a transformation of social solidarity due to the steadily growing development of the division of labor. That is how we have been led to make this the object of our study.[61]

Introduction

THE PROBLEM

The division of labor is not of recent origin, but it was only at the end of the eighteenth century that social cognizance was taken of the principle, though, until then, unwitting submission had been rendered to it. To be sure, several thinkers from earliest times saw its importance;[62] but Adam Smith was the first to attempt a theory of it. Moreover, he adopted this phrase that social science later lent to biology.

Nowadays, the phenomenon has developed so generally it is obvious to all. We need have no further illusions about the tendencies of modern industry; it advances steadily towards powerful machines, towards great concentrations of forces and capital, and consequently to the extreme division of labor. Occupations are infinitely separated and specialized, not only inside the factories, but each product is itself a specialty dependent upon others. Adam Smith and John Stuart Mill still hoped that agriculture, at least, would be an exception to the rule, and they saw it as the last resort of small-scale industry. Although one must be careful not to generalize unduly in such matters, nevertheless it is hard to deny today that the principal branches of the agricultural industry are steadily being drawn into the general movement.[63] Finally, business itself is ingeniously following and reflecting in all its shadings the infinite diversity of industrial enterprises; and, while this evolution is realizing itself with unpremeditated spontaneity, the economists, examining its causes and appreciating its results, far from condemning or opposing it, uphold it as necessary. They see in it the supreme law of human societies and the condition of their progress.

But the division of labor is not peculiar to the economic world; we can observe its growing influence in the most varied fields of society.

---

[61] The question of social solidarity has already been studied in the second part of Marion's book *Solidarité morale*. But Marion has considered the problem from another angle; he is especially interested in establishing the reality of the phenomenon of solidarity.

[62] Aristotle, *Nichomachean Ethics*, E, 1133a, 16.

[63] *Journal des Economistes*, November 1884, p. 211.

The political, administrative, and judicial functions are growing more and more specialized. It is the same with the aesthetic and scientific functions. It is long since philosophy reigned as the science unique; it has been broken into a multitude of special disciplines each of which has its object, method, and thought. "Men working in the sciences have become increasingly more specialized."[64]

Before revealing the nature of the studies with which the most illustrious scholars have concerned themselves for two centuries, de Candolle observed that at the time of Leibnitz and Newton, it would have been necessary to write "almost always, two or three titles for each scholar; for instance, astronomer and physician, or mathematician, astronomer, and physician, or else to employ only general terms like philosopher or naturalist. Even that would not be enough. The mathematicians and naturalists were sometimes literary men or poets. Even at the end of the eighteenth century, these multiple titles would have been necessary to indicate exactly what such men as Wolff, Haller, Charles Bonnet had done in several categories of the arts and sciences. In the nineteenth century, this difficulty no longer exists, or at least is very rare."[65] Not only has the scholar ceased to take up different sciences simultaneously, but he does not even cover a single science completely any more. The ambit of his researches is restricted to a determined order of problems or even to a single problem. At the same time, the scientific function, formerly always allied with something more lucrative, like that of physician, priest, magistrate, soldier, has become more and more sufficient unto itself. De Candolle even foresees a day when the professions of scholar and teacher, still so intimately united, will finally separate.

The recent speculation in the philosophy of biology has ended by making us see in the division of labor a fact of a very general nature, which the economists, who first proposed it, never suspected. It is general knowledge since the works of Wolff, Von Baer, and Milne-Edwards, that the law of the division of labor applies to organisms as to societies; it can even be said that the more specialized the functions of the organism, the greater its development. This discovery has had the effect of immeasurably extending the scope of the division of labor, placing its origins in an infinitely distant past, since it becomes almost contemporaneous with the coming of life into the world. It is no longer considered only a social institution that has its source in the intelligence and will of men, but is a phenomenon of general biology whose conditions must be sought in the essential properties of organized matter. The division of labor in society appears to be no more than a particular form of this general process; and societies, in conforming to

----

[64] De Candolle, *Histoire des Sciences et des Savants*, 2nd ed., p. 263.
[65] *Loc. cit.*

that law, seem to be yielding to a movement that was born before them, and that similarly governs the entire world.

Such a fact evidently cannot be produced without profoundly affecting our moral constitution; for the development of man will be conceived in two entirely different ways, depending on whether we yield to the movement or resist it. At this point, an urgent question arises: Of these two directions, which must we choose? Is it our duty to seek to become a thorough and complete human being, one quite sufficient unto oneself; or, on the contrary, to be only a part of a whole, the organ of an organism? Briefly, is the division of labor, at the same time that it is a law of nature, also a moral rule of human conduct; and, if it has this latter character, why and in what degree? It is not necessary to show the gravity of this practical problem; for, whatever opinion one has about the division of labor, everyone knows that it exists, and is more and more becoming one of the fundamental bases of the social order.[66]

The moral conscience of nations is often posed with this problem, but confusedly, and does not succeed in solving anything. Two contradictory tendencies are present, and neither is able to assume a completely uncontested preponderance over the other.

Of course, it seems that opinion is steadily inclining towards making the division of labor an imperative rule of conduct, to present it as a duty. Those who shun it are not punished by a precise penalty fixed by law, it is true; but they are blamed. The time has passed when the perfect man was he who appeared interested in everything without attaching himself exclusively to anything, capable of tasting and understanding everything, finding means to unite and condense in himself all that was most exquisite in civilization. This general culture, formerly lavishly praised, now appears to us as a loose and flabby discipline.[67] To fight against nature we need more vigorous faculties and more productive strength. We want activity, instead of spreading itself over a large area, to concentrate and gain in intensity what it loses in extent. We distrust those excessively mobile talents that lend themselves equally to all uses, refusing to choose a special role and keep to it. We disapprove of those men whose unique care is to organize and develop all their faculties, but without making any definite use of them, and without sacrificing any of them, as if each man were sufficient unto himself, and constituted an independent

---

[66] Translator's Note: In the first edition, there follows at this point many additional pages of critical material, omitted in the later editions. This appears as an appendix to the translation.

[67] This passage has sometimes been interpreted as implying an absolute condemnation of all kinds of general culture. However, as is evident in the context, we are speaking only of the humanistic culture, truly a general culture, but not the only one possible.

world. It seems to us that this state of detachment and indetermination has something anti-social about it. The praiseworthy man of former times is only a dilettante to us, and we refuse to give dilettantism any moral value; we rather see perfection in the man seeking, not to be complete, but to produce; who has a restricted task, and devotes himself to it; who does his duty, accomplishes his work. "To perfect oneself," said Secrétan, "is to learn one's role, to become capable of fulfilling one's function. . . The measure of our perfection is no longer found in our complacence with ourselves, in the applause of a crowd, or in the approving smile of an affected dilettantism, but in the sum of given services and in our capacity to give more."[68] As unified, simple, and impersonal as the moral idea was, it grows more and more so while diversifying itself. We no longer think that the exclusive duty of man is to realize in himself the qualities of man in general; but we believe he must have those pertaining to his function. The following fact, among others, substantiates this opinion. Education is growing more and more specialized. We deem it more and more necessary not to submit children to a uniform culture, as if they were all to lead the same life; but to train them differently in the fight of the different functions they will be called upon to fill. Briefly, in one of its aspects, the categorical imperative of the moral conscience is assuming the following form: *Make yourself usefully fulfill a determinate function.*

But in the face of these facts, others can be cited contradicting them. If public opinion sanctions the division of labor, it is not without a sort of uneasiness and hesitation. While commanding men to specialize, it seems to fear they will specialize too much. Besides the maxims praising intensive work, there are others, no less prevalent, which call attention to its dangers. "It is a sad commentary," said Jean-Baptiste Say, "that we have come to the state where we never do anything more than make the eighteenth part of a pin; nor is it only the workman who lowers his natural dignity by wielding a file and hammer through his life; the same may be said of the man whose professional duties call into play the finest faculties of the mind."[69] Lemontey,[70] at the beginning of the nineteenth century, comparing the life of the modern workman to the free, bold life of the savage, found the second much more favorable than the first. Tocqueville is no less severe: "In so far as the principle of the division of labor receives a more complete application, the art progresses, the artisan retrogresses."[71] Generally, the maxim ordering us to specialize is refuted by the contradictory maxim commanding us all to realize the same ideal, and the latter is

---

[68] *Le Principe de la morale*, p. 189.
[69] *Traité d'économie politique*, Book I, ch. viii.
[70] *Raison ou Folie*, chapter on the influence of the division of labor.
[71] *La Democratie en Amerique*.

still far from having lost all its authority. Doubtless, in principle, this conflict ought to occasion no surprise. The moral life, as that of body and mind, answers different and even contradictory needs; it is thus natural that it be made up, in part, of antagonistic elements limiting and balancing each other. It is no less true that in such antagonism there is something to trouble the moral conscience of nations, for an explanation of such a contradiction must be given.

To put an end to this indecision, we shall not resort to the ordinary method of moralists, who, when they wish to decide the moral value of any precept, begin by putting forward a general formula of morality in order thus to confront the maxim in question with it. We know today what these summary generalizations are worth.[72] Asked at the beginning of a study before any observation of the facts, they do not propose to look at the facts, but to express an abstract principle of an ideal law completely established. They do not then give us a résumé of the essential characteristics that moral rules really present in a society, or in a determined social type; but they only express the manner in which the moralist represents the moral law. Under these circumstances, they are somewhat instructive, for they direct us to the moral tendencies coming to light at the moment considered. But they have only the interest of a fact, not of a scientific examination. There is no authority for seeing in the personal aspirations felt by a thinker, no matter how real they may be, an adequate expression of the moral reality. They manifest needs which are never anything but partial; they answer some particular, determined *desideratum* that conscience, suffering from this common illusion, erects into a last and final end. How often it happens to be of a morbid nature! We cannot then refer to them as objective criteria which permit an appreciation of the morality of practices.

We must eliminate these deductions that are generally used only to resemble an argument, and that justify, after the resolution, preconceived sentiments and personal impressions. The one way to succeed in objectively appreciating the division of labor is to study it first in itself, entirely speculatively, to look for its use, and upon what it depends, and finally, to form as adequate a notion as possible of it. That done, we shall be in a position to compare it with other moral phenomena, and see what relations it has with them. If we find that it plays a role similar to some other practice whose moral and normal character is undisputed; and that, if it does not fill this role in certain cases, it is because of abnormal deviations; and that its causes are also the determining conditions of other moral rules—then we shall be able to conclude that it must be classed among these last. And thus, without wishing to substitute ourselves for the moral conscience of societies,

---

[72] Translator's Note: See appendix for critical material found in first edition.

without pretending to make laws in their place, we shall be able to clarify the problem, and lessen its perplexities.

Our work, then, will be divided into three principal parts:

To determine the function of the division of labor, that is to say, what social need it satisfies.

To determine, then, the causes and conditions on which it is dependent.

Finally, as it would not have been the object of such grave accusations if it had not really deviated fairly often from the normal condition, we shall try to classify the principal abnormal forms it presents, so that they will not be confused with the others. Moreover, this study will be of interest, for, here, as in biology, pathology will help us more fully to understand physiology.

Moreover, if there has been so much talk about the moral value of the division of labor, it is not so much because it is not in agreement with a general formula of morality, as it is because facts have been neglected which we are going to meet. It has always been assumed that they were evident, as if, in order to know the nature, role, and causes of the division of labor, it would be sufficient to analyze the notion each of us has about them. Such a method does not permit of scientific conclusions; that is why the theory of the division of labor has made such little progress since Adam Smith. "His followers," said Schmoller, "had a dearth of worthy ideas, were obstinately attached to his examples and his remarks up to the day when the socialists enlarged the field of their observations and contrasted the division of labor in actual factories with that of the small shops of the eighteenth century. Even that way, the theory has not been developed in a profoundly systematic manner; the technological considerations or the observations of banal truth on the part of some economists could not make the development of these ideas particularly favorable."[73] To know what the division of labor is objectively it is not enough to develop the contents of the idea we have of it, but we must treat it as an objective fact, observe, compare; and we shall see that the result of these observations often differs from the one its intimate meaning suggests to us.[74]

---

[73] *La Division du travail étudiée au point de vue historique*, in *Revue d'econ. pol.*, 1889, p. 567.

[74] Since 1893, two works interested in the question here treated have come to our attention. First, the *Soziale Differenzierung* of Simmel, where it is not a question of the division of labor specifically, but of the process of individuation in general. Then there is the book of Bucher, *Die Entstehung der Wolkswirt-schaft*, in which several chapters are devoted to the division of economic labor.

Book One. The Function of the Division of Labor

CHAPTER ONE. THE METHOD FOR
DETERMINING THIS FUNCTION

The word *function* is used in two quite different senses. Sometimes it suggests a system of vital movements, without reference to their consequences; at others it expresses the relation existing between these movements and corresponding needs of the organism. Thus, we speak of the function of digestion, of respiration, etc.; but we also say that digestion has as its function the incorporation into the organism of liquid or solid substances designed to replenish its losses, that respiration has for its function the introduction of necessary gases into the tissues of an animal for the sustainment of life, etc. It is in the second sense that we shall use the term. To ask what the function of the division of labor is, is to seek for the need which it supplies. When we have answered this question, we shall be able to see if this need is of the same sort as those to which other rules of conduct respond whose moral character is agreed upon.

We have chosen this term because any other would be inexact or equivocal. We cannot employ *aim* or *object* and speak of the end of the division of labor because that would presuppose that the division of labor exists *in the light of results* which we are going to determine. The terms, "results" or "effects," would be no more satisfactory, because they imply no idea of correspondence. On the other hand, the term "role," or "function," has the great advantage of implying this idea, without prejudging the question as to how this correspondence is established, whether it results from an intentional and preconceived adaptation or an aftermath adjustment. What is important for our purposes is to establish its existence and the elements of its existence; not to inquire whether there has been a prior presentiment of it, nor even if it has been sensibly felt afterwards.

I

Nothing seems easier to determine, at first glance, than the role of the division of labor. Are not its effects universally recognized? Since it combines both the productive power and the ability of the workman, it is the necessary condition of development in societies, both intellectual and material development. It is the source of civilization. Besides, since we quite facilely assign an absolute value to civilization, we do not bethink ourselves to seek any other function for the division of labor.

Though it may truly have this effect, there would be in that nothing to amplify through discussion. But if it had no other, and did not serve any other purpose, there would be no reason to assign it a moral character.

In short, the services that it renders are very near to being foreign to the moral life, or at least have only indirect and remote relation to it. Although it may be common enough today to reply to the polemic of Rousseau with dithyrambs of opposite meaning, nevertheless there is no proof at all that civilization is a moral fact. To meet the problem, we cannot refer to concepts which are necessarily subjective; rather it would be necessary to employ a standard by which to measure the level of average morality, and to observe, thus, how it varies in proportion to the progress of civilization. Unfortunately, this standard of measurement is not forthcoming, but we do possess one for collective immorality. The average number of suicides, of crimes of all sorts, can effectively serve to mark the intensity of immorality in a given society. If we make this experiment, it does not turn out creditably for civilization, for the number of these morbid phenomena seems to increase as the arts, sciences, and industry progress.[75] Doubtless, there would be some inadvertence in concluding from this fact that civilization is immoral, but one can at least be certain that, if it has a positive and favorable influence on the moral life, it is quite weak.

But, if we analyze this badly defined complex called civilization, we find that the elements of which it is composed are bereft of any moral character whatever.

It is particularly true of the economic activity which always accompanies civilization. Far from serving moral progress, it is in the great industrial centres that crimes and suicides are most numerous. In any event, it evidently does not present the external indices by which we recognize moral facts. We have replaced stage coaches by railroads, sailboats by transatlantic liners, small shops by manufacturing plants. All this changed activity is generally considered useful, but it contains nothing morally binding. The artisan and the private *entrepreneur* who resist this general current and obstinately pursue their modest enterprises do their duty quite as well as the great manufacturer who covers a country with machines and places a whole army of workers under his command. The moral conscience of nations is in this respect correct; it prefers a little justice to all the industrial perfection in the world. No doubt industrial activities have a reason for existing. They respond to needs, but these needs are not moral.

The case is even stronger with art, which is absolutely refractory to all that resembles an obligation, for it is the domain of liberty. It is a luxury and an acquirement which it is perhaps lovely to possess, but which is not obligatory; what is superfluous does not impose itself. On

---

[75] Alexander von Oettingen, *Moralstatistik*, §§ 37 ff.; Tarde, *Criminalité comparée*, ch. ii. (For suicides, see *infra*, Book II, ch. 1, § 2.)

the other hand, morality is the least indispensable, the strictly necessary, the daily bread without which societies cannot exist. Art responds to our need of pursuing an activity without end, for the pleasure of the pursuit, whereas morality compels us to follow a determinate path to a definite end. Whatever is obligatory is at the same time constraining. Thus, although art may be animated by moral ideas or find itself involved in the evolution of phenomena which, properly speaking, are moral, it is not in itself moral. It might even be contended that in the case of individuals, as in societies, an intemperant development of the aesthetic faculties is a serious sign from a moral point of view.

Of all the elements of civilization, science is the only one which, under certain conditions, presents a moral character. That is, societies are tending more and more to look upon it as a duty for the individual to develop his intelligence by learning the scientific truths which have been established. At present, there are a certain number of propositions which we must all understand. We are not forced to inject ourselves into the industrial mêlée; we do not have to be artists, but everyone is now forced not to be ignorant. This obligation is, indeed, so strongly entrenched that, in certain societies, it is sanctioned not only by public opinion, but also by law. It is, moreover, not difficult to understand whence comes this special status accorded to science. Science is nothing else than conscience carried to its highest point of clarity. Thus, in order for society to live under existent conditions, the field of conscience, individual as well as social, must be extended and clarified. That is, as the environments in which they exist become more and more complex, and, consequently, more and more changeable, to endure, they must change often. On the other hand, the more obscure conscience is, the more refractory to change it is, because it does not perceive quickly enough the necessity for changing nor in what sense it must change. On the contrary, an enlightened conscience prepares itself in advance for adaptation. That is why intelligence guided by science must take a larger part in the course of collective life.

But the science which everybody is thus required to possess does not merit the name at all. It is not science; it is at most the common part and the most general. It is reduced, really, to a small number of indispensable propositions which are necessary for all to have only because they are within reach of everybody. Science, properly considered, is far above this common modicum. It does not encompass only what it is shameful not to know, but everything that it is possible to know. It does not ask of those who cultivate it only ordinary faculties that every man possesses, but special qualifications. Accordingly, being available only to an elite, it is not obligatory; it is a useful and a good thing, but it is not imperatively necessary for society to avail itself of it. It is advantageous to have; there is nothing immoral in not having acquired it. It is a field of action which is open to the initiative of all, but where none is forced to enter. We do not have to be scholars any more than we have to be artists. Science is, then, as art and industry, outside the moral sphere.[76]

So many controversies have taken place concerning the moral character of civilization because very often moralists have no objective criterion to distinguish moral facts from those not moral. We fall into the habit of qualifying as moral everything that has a certain nobility and some value, everything that is an object of elevated aspirations, and it is because of this overextension of the term that we have considered civilization as moral. But the domain of ethics is not so nebulous; it consists of all the rules of action which are imperatively imposed upon conduct, to which a sanction is attached, but no more. Consequently, since there is nothing in civilization which presents this moral criterion, civilization is morally indifferent. If, then, the division of labor had no other role than to render civilization possible, it would participate in the same moral neutrality.

It is because they have not seen any further function of the division of labor that the theories that have been proposed are inconsistent on this point. In short, though there exist a zone neutral to morals, the division of labor cannot be part of it.[77] If it is not good, it is bad; if it is not moral, it is immoral. If, then, it has no other use, one falls into irresolvable antinomies, for the greater economies that it offers are offset by moral inconveniences, and since it is impossible to separate these two heterogeneous and incomparable quantities, we could not decide which prevailed over the other, nor, consequently, take a position on the matter. We would invoke the primacy of morality as a sweeping condemnation of the division of labor. However, this *ultima ratio* is arrived at through a scientific *coup d'état*, and the evident necessity for specialization makes such a position untenable.

Moreover, if the division of labor does not fill any other role, not only does it not have a moral character, but it is difficult to see what reason for existence it can have. We shall see that, taken by itself, civilization has no intrinsic and absolute value; what makes it valuable is its correspondence to certain needs. But the proposition will be demonstrated later[78] that these needs are themselves results of the division of labor. Because the latter does not go forward without a demand for greater expenditure of energy, man is led to seek, as compensation, certain goods from civilization which, otherwise, would not interest him in the least. If, however, the division of labor replied to

---

[76] "The essential character of good compared with true is that of being obligatory. Truth, taken by itself, does not have this character." Janet, *Morale*, p. 139.

[77] For it is in opposition to a moral rule. See p. 54.

[78] Book II, chs. i and v.

no other needs than these, it would have no other function than to diminish the effects which it produces itself, or to heal the wounds which it inflicts. Under these conditions, we would have to endure it, but there would be no reason for desiring it since the services it would render would reduce its function to replenishing the losses that it caused.

All this leads us to seek some other function for the division of labor. Certain current facts put us on the road to a solution.

II

Everybody knows that we like those who resemble us, those who think and feel as we do. But the opposite is no less true. It very often happens that we feel kindly towards those who do not resemble us, precisely because of this lack of resemblance. These facts are apparently so contradictory that moralists have always vacillated concerning the true nature of friendship and have derived it sometimes from the former, sometimes from the latter. The Greeks had long ago posed this problem. "Friendship," says Aristotle, "causes much discussion. According to some people, it consists in a certain resemblance, and we like those who resemble us: whence the proverbs 'birds of a feather flock together' and 'like seeks like,' and other such phrases. Others, on the contrary, say that all who are alike are opposed to one another. Again, some men push their inquiries on these points higher and reason from a consideration of nature. So Euripides says,

> The earth by drought consumed doth love the rain,
> And the great heaven overcharged with rain,
> Doth love to fall in showers upon the earth.

Heraclitus, again, maintains that 'contrariety is expedient, and that the best agreement arises from things differing, and that all things come into being in the way of the principle of antagonism.'"[79]

These opposing doctrines prove that both types are necessary to natural friendship. Difference, as likeness, can be a cause of mutual attraction. However, certain differences do not produce this effect. We do not find any pleasure in those completely different from us. Spendthrifts do not seek the company of misers, nor moral and honest people that of hypocrites and pretenders; sweet and gentle spirits have no taste for sour and malevolent temperaments. Only certain kinds of differences attract each other. They are those which, instead of opposing and excluding, complement each other. As Bain says, there is a type of difference which repels, another which attracts, one which

---

[79] *Nichomachean Ethics*, VIII, 1, 1155a, 32.

leads to rivalry, another which leads to friendship. If one of two people has what the other has not, but desires, in that fact lies the point of departure for a positive attraction.[80] Thus it is that a theorist, a subtle and reasoning individual, often has a very special sympathy for practical men, with their quick sense and rapid intuitions; the timid for the firm and resolute, the weak for the strong, and conversely. As richly endowed as we may be, we always lack something, and the best of us realize our own insufficiency. That is why we seek in our friends the qualities that we lack, since in joining with them, we participate in some measure in their nature and thus feel less incomplete. So it is that small friendly associations are formed wherein each one plays a role conformable to his character, where there is a true exchange of services. One urges on, another consoles; this one advises, that one follows the advice, and it is this apportionment of functions or, to use the usual expression, this division of labor, which determines the relations of friendship.

We are thus led to consider the division of labor in a new light. In this instance, the economic services that it can render are picayune compared to the moral effect that it produces, and its true function is to create in two or more persons a feeling of solidarity. In whatever manner the result is obtained, its aim is to cause coherence among friends and to stamp them with its seal.

The history of conjugal society offers us an even more striking example of the same phenomenon.

Without doubt, sexual attraction does not come about except between individuals of the same type, and love generally asks a certain harmony of thought and sentiment. It is not less true that what gives to this relationship its peculiar character, and what causes its particular energy, is not the resemblance, but the difference in the natures which it unites. Precisely because man and woman are different, they seek each other passionately. However, as in the preceding instance, it is not a contrast pure and simple which brings about reciprocal feelings. Only those differences which require each other for their mutual fruition can have this quality. In short, man and woman isolated from each other are only different parts of the same concrete universal which they reform when they unite. In other words, the sexual division of labor is the source of conjugal solidarity, and that is why psychologists have very justly seen in the separation of the sexes an event of tremendous importance in the evolution of emotions. It has made possible perhaps the strongest of all unselfish inclinations.

Moreover, there may be greater or less division of labor; it can either affect only sexual organs and some secondary activities, or else

---

[80] *The Emotions and the Will.*

also extend to all organic and social functions. Thus, we can see in history that it has developed concomitant with conjugal solidarity.

The further we look into the past, the smaller becomes this difference between man and woman. The woman of past days was not at all the weak creature that she has become with the progress of morality. Prehistoric bones show that the difference between the strength of man and of woman was relatively much smaller than it is today.[81] Even now, during infancy and until puberty, the development of the two sexes does not differ in any appreciable way: the characteristics are quite feminine. If one admits that the development of the individual reproduces in its course that of the species, one may conjecture that the same homogeneity was found at the beginning of human evolution, and see in the female form the aboriginal image of what was the one and only type from which the masculine variety slowly detached itself. Travelers report, moreover, that in certain tribes of South America, man and woman, in structure and general appearance, present a similarity which is far greater than is seen elsewhere.[82] Finally, Dr. Lebon has been able to establish directly and with mathematical precision this original resemblance of the two sexes in regard to the preeminent organ of physical and psychic life, the brain. By comparing a large number of crania chosen from different races and different societies, he has come to the following conclusion: "The volume of the crania of man and woman, even when we compare subjects of equal age, of equal height and equal weight, show considerable differences in favor of the man, and this inequality grows proportionally with civilization, so that from the point of view of the mass of the brain, and correspondingly of intelligence, woman tends more and more to be differentiated from the male sex. The difference which exists, for example, between the average cranium of Parisian men of the present day and that of Parisian women is almost double that observed between male and female of ancient Egypt."[83] A German anthropologist, Bischoff, has arrived at the same result on this point.[84]

These anatomical resemblances are accompanied by functional resemblances. In the same societies, female functions are not very clearly distinguished from male. Rather, the two sexes lead almost the same existence. There is even now a very great number of savage people where the woman mingles in political life. That has been observed especially in the Indian tribes of America, such as the Iroquois, the Natchez;[85] in Hawaii she participates in myriad ways in

---

[81] Topinard, *Anthropologie*, p. 146.
[82] See Spencer, *Scientific Essays*, p. 300. Waitz, in his *Anthropologie der Naturvoelker*, i, p. 76, relates many facts of the same sort.
[83] *L'Homme et les societés*, II, p. 154.
[84] *Das Gehirngewicht des Menschen*, eine Studie, Bonn, 1880.
[85] Waitz, *Anthropologie*, III, pp. 101-102.

the men's lives,[86] as she does in New Zealand and in Samoa. Moreover, we very often observe women accompanying men to war, urging them on to battle and even taking a very active part. In Cuba, in Dahomey, they are as war-like as the men and battle at their side.[87] One of the distinctive contemporary qualities of woman, gentility, does not appear to pertain to her in primitive society. In certain animal species, indeed, the female prides herself on the contrary characteristic.

Thus, among the same peoples, marriage is in a completely rudimentary state. It is quite probable, if not absolutely demonstrated, that there was an epoch in the history of the family when there was no such thing as marriage. Sexual relations were entered into and broken at will without any juridical obligations linking the union. In any case, we see a family type which is relatively near ours where marriage is still only in a very indistinct, germinal state. This is the matriarchal family.[88] The relations of the mother to her children are very definite, but those of the two married people are very loose. The relation can be terminated at the will of the parties involved, or they can even contract to sustain the relation for a limited time.[89] Conjugal fidelity is not even required. Marriage, or what is so called, consists solely in obligations of restricted scope and often of short duration, which link the husband to the parents of the woman. It is thus reduced to a small thing. Thus, in a given society, the totality of juridical rules which constitute marriage only symbolize the state of conjugal solidarity. If this is very strong, the ties which bind the married people are numerous and complex, and, consequently, the matrimonial set of rules whose object is to define these ties is itself very highly developed. If, on the contrary, conjugal society lacks cohesion, if the relations between man and woman are unstable and intermittent, they cannot take a very determinate form, and, consequently, marriage is reduced to a small number of rules without rigor or precision. The state of marriage in societies where the two sexes are only weakly differentiated thus evinces conjugal solidarity which is itself very weak.

On the contrary, as we advance to modern times, we see marriage developing. The circle of ties which it creates extends further and further; the obligations that it sanctions multiply. The conditions under which it can be contracted, those under which it can be dissolved, are limited with a precision growing as the effects of such dissolution grow. The duty of fidelity gains order; first imposed on the woman only, it later becomes reciprocal. When the dowry appears, very complex rules fix the respective rights of each person according to his

---

[86] Waitz, *op. cit.*, VI, p. 121.

[87] Spencer, *Principles of Sociology*, III, p. 391.

[88] The matriarchal family certainly existed among the Germans.—See Dargun, *Mutterrecht und Raubehe in Germanischen Rechte*, Breslau, 1883.

[89] See especially, Smith, *Kinship and Marriage in Early Arabia*, p. 67.

or her appropriate fortune and that of the other. It suffices to take a bird's-eye view of our Codes to see what an important place marriage occupies. The union of two people has ceased to be ephemeral; it is no longer an external contact, temporary and partial, but an intimate association, lasting, often even indissoluble during the whole lifetime of the two parties.

It is certain that at the same time sexual labor is more and more divided. Limited first only to sexual functions, it slowly becomes extended to others. Long ago, woman retired from warfare and public affairs, and consecrated her entire life to her family. Since then, her role has become even more specialized. Today, among cultivated people, the woman leads a completely different existence from that of the man. One might say that the two great functions of the psychic life are thus dissociated, that one of the sexes takes care of the affective functions and the other of intellectual functions. In view of the fact that in certain classes women participate in artistic and literary life just as men, we might be led to believe, to be sure, that the occupations of the two sexes are becoming homogeneous. But, even in this sphere of action, woman carries out her own nature, and her role is very specialized, very different from that of man. Further, if art and letters begin to become feminine tasks, the other sex seems to permit it in order to give itself more specially to the pursuit of science. It might, then, be very well contended that this apparent return to primitive homogeneity is nothing else than the beginning of a new differentiation. Moreover, the functional differences are rendered materially visible by the morphological differences that they have determined. Not only are the height, weight, and the general form very dissimilar in men and women, but Dr. Lebon has shown, as we have seen, that with the progress of civilization the brain of the two sexes differentiates itself more and more. According to this observer, this progressive chart would be due both to the considerable development of masculine crania and to a stationary or even regressive state of female crania. "Thus," he says, "though the average cranium of Parisian men ranks among the greatest known crania, the average of Parisian women ranks among the smallest observed, even below the crania of the Chinese, and hardly above those of the women of New Caledonia."[90]

In all these examples, the most remarkable effect of the division of labor is not that it increases the output of functions divided, but that it renders them solidary. Its role in all these cases is not simply to embellish or ameliorate existing societies, but to render societies possible which, without it, would not exist. Permit the sexual division of labor to recede below a certain level and conjugal society would eventually subsist in sexual relations preeminently ephemeral. If the

---

[90] *Op. cit.*, p. 154.

sexes were not separated at all, an entire category of social life would be absent. It is possible that the economic utility of the division of labor may have a hand in this, but, in any case, it passes far beyond purely economic interests, for it consists in the establishment of a social and moral order *sui generis.* Through it, individuals are linked to one another. Without it, they would be independent. Instead of developing separately, they pool their efforts. They are solidary, but it is a solidarity which is not merely a question of the short time in which services are exchanged, but one which extends much further. Conjugal solidarity, for example, such as today exists among the most cultivated people, makes its action felt at each moment and in all the details of life. Moreover, societies created by the division of labor cannot fail to bear its mark. Since they have this special origin, they cannot resemble those determined by the attraction of like for like; they must be constituted in a different fashion, rest upon other foundations, appeal to other sentiments.

The social relations to which the division of labor gives birth have often been considered only in terms of exchange, but this misinterprets what such exchange implies and what results from it. It suggests two beings mutually dependent because they are each incomplete, and translates this mutual dependence outwardly. It is, then, only the superficial expression of an internal and very deep state. Precisely because this state is constant, it calls up a whole mechanism of images which function with a continuity that exchange does not possess. The image of the one who completes us becomes inseparable from ours, not only because it is frequently associated with ours, but particularly because it is the natural complement of it. It thus becomes an integral and permanent part of our conscience, to such a point that we can no longer separate ourselves from it and seek to increase its force. That is why we enjoy the society of the one it represents, since the presence of the object that it expresses, by making us actually perceive it, sets it off more. On the other hand, we will suffer from all circumstances which, like absence or death, may have as effect the barring of its return or the diminishing of its vivacity.

As short as this analysis is, it suffices to show that this mechanism is not identical with that which serves as a basis for sentiments of sympathy whose source is resemblance. Surely there can be no solidarity between others and us unless the image of others unites itself with ours. But when the union results from the resemblance of two images, it consists in an agglutination. The two representations become solidary because, being indistinct, totally or in part, they confound each other, and become no more than one, and they are solidary only in the measure which they confound themselves. On the contrary, in the case of the division of labor, they are outside each other and are linked only because they are distinct. Neither the sentiments nor the social relations which derive from these sentiments are the same in the two cases.

We are thus led to ask if the division of labor would not play the same role in more extensive groups, if, in contemporary societies where it has developed as we know, it would not have as its function the integration of the social body to assure unity. It is quite legitimate to suppose that the facts which we have just observed reproduce themselves here, but with greater amplitude, that great political societies can maintain themselves in equilibrium only thanks to the specialization of tasks, that the division of labor is the source, if not unique, at least principal, of social solidarity. Comte took this point of view. Of all sociologists, to our knowledge, he is the first to have recognized in the division of labor something other than a purely economic phenomenon. He saw in it "the most essential condition of social life," provided that one conceives it "in all its rational extent; that is to say, that one applies it to the totality of all our diverse operations of whatever kind, instead of attributing it, as is ordinarily done, to simple material usages." Considered in this light, he says, "it leads immediately to regarding not only individuals and classes, but also, in many respects, different peoples, as at once participating, following a definite path in a special degree, exactly determined, in a work, immense and communal, whose inevitable gradual development links actual cooperators to their predecessors and even to their successors. It is thus the continuous repartition of different human endeavors which especially constitutes social solidarity and which becomes the elementary cause of the extension and growing complication of the social organism."[91]

If this hypothesis were proved, the division of labor would play a role much more important than that which we ordinarily attribute to it. It would serve not only to raise societies to luxury, desirable perhaps, but superfluous; it would be a condition of their existence. Through it, or at least particularly through it, their cohesion would be assured; it would determine the essential traits of their constitution. Accordingly, although we may not yet be in position to resolve the question rigorously, we can, however, imply from it now that, if such is really the function of the division of labor, it must have a moral character, for the need of order, harmony, and social solidarity is generally considered moral.

But before seeing whether this common opinion is well founded, we must verify the hypothesis that we have just given forth concerning

---

[91] *Cours de philosophie positive*, IV, p. 425.—Analogous ideas are found in Schaeffle, *Bau und Leben des sozialen Koerpers*, II, *passim*, and Clément, *Science Sociale*, I, pp. 235 ff.

the role of the division of labor. Let us see if, in effect, in the societies in which we live, it is from this that social solidarity essentially derives.

III

But how shall we proceed to such verification?

We must not simply look to see if, in these types of society, there exists a social solidarity which comes from the division of labor. That is a self-evident truism, since in such societies the division of labor is highly developed and produces solidarity. Rather we must especially determine in what degree the solidarity that it produces contributes to the general integration of society, for it is only then that we shall know how far necessary it is, whether it is an essential factor of social cohesion, or whether, on the contrary, it is only an accessory and secondary condition. To reply to this question, we must compare this social link to others in order to measure how much credit is due to it in the total effect; and to that end, we must begin by classifying the different types of social solidarity.

But social solidarity is a completely moral phenomenon which, taken by itself, does not lend itself to exact observation nor indeed to measurement. To proceed to this classification and this comparison, we must substitute for this internal fact which escapes us an external index which symbolizes it and study the former in the light of the latter.

This visible symbol is law. In effect, despite its immaterial character, wherever social solidarity exists, it resides not in a state of pure potentiality, but manifests its presence by sensible indices. Where it is strong, it leads men strongly to one another, frequently puts them in contact, multiplies the occasions when they find themselves related. To speak correctly, considering the point our investigation has reached, it is not easy to say whether social solidarity produces these phenomena, or whether it is a result of them, whether men relate themselves because it is a driving force, or whether it is a driving force because they relate themselves. However, it is not, at the moment, necessary to decide this question; it suffices to state that the two orders of fact are linked and vary at the same time and in the same sense. The more solidary the members of a society are, the more they sustain diverse relations, one with another, or with the group taken collectively, for, if their meetings were rare, they would depend upon one another only at rare intervals, and then tenuously. Moreover, the number of these relations is necessarily proportional to that of the juridical rules which determine them. Indeed, social life, especially where it exists durably, tends inevitably to assume a definite form and to organize itself, and law is nothing else than this very organization in so far as it has greater stability and precision.[92] The general life of society cannot extend its sway without juridical life extending its sway at the same time and in direct relation. We can thus be certain of finding reflected in law all the essential varieties of social solidarity.

The objection may be raised, it is true, that social relations can fix themselves without assuming a juridical form. Some of them do not attain this degree of consolidation and precision, but they do not remain undetermined on that account. Instead of being regulated by law, they are regulated by custom. Law, then, reflects only part of social life and furnishes us with incomplete data for the solution of the problem. Moreover, it often happens that custom is not in accord with law; we usually say that it tempers law's severity, that it corrects law's formalism, sometimes, indeed, that it is animated by a different spirit. Would it not then be true that custom manifests other sorts of solidarity than that expressed in positive law?

This opposition, however, crops up only in quite exceptional circumstances. This comes about when law no longer corresponds to the state of existing society, but maintains itself, without reason for so doing, by the force of habit. In such a case, new relations which establish themselves in spite of it are not bereft of organization, for they cannot endure without seeking consolidation. But since they are in conflict with the old existing law, they can attain only superficial organization. They do not pass beyond the stage of custom and do not enter into the juridical life proper. Thus conflict ensues. But it arises only in rare and pathological cases which cannot endure without danger. Normally, custom is not opposed to law, but is, on the contrary, its basis. It happens, in truth, that on such a basis nothing may rear its head. Social relations ensue which convey a diffuse regulation which comes from custom; but they lack importance and continuity, except in the abnormal cases of which we were just speaking. If, then, there are types of social solidarity which custom alone manifests, they are assuredly secondary; law produces those which are essential and they are the only ones we need to know.

Shall we go further and say that social solidarity does not completely manifest itself perceptibly, that these manifestations are only partial and imperfect, that behind law and custom there is an internal state whence it derives, and that in order to know it truly we must intuit it without intermediaries?—But we can know causes scientifically only by the effects that they produce, and in order to determine their nature, science chooses from these effects only the most objective and most easily measurable. Science studies heat through the variations in volume which changes in temperature produce in bodies,

---

[92] See *infra*, Book III, ch. i.

electricity through its physico-chemical effects, force through movement. Why should social solidarity be an exception?

What remains of it divested of social forms? What gives it its specific characters is the nature of the group whose unity it assures; that is why it varies according to social types. It is not the same in the family and in political societies; we are not attached to our country in the same fashion as the Roman was to his city or the German to his tribe. But since these differences relate themselves to social causes, we can understand them only with reference to the differences that the social effects of solidarity present. If, then, we neglect the latter, all the varieties become indiscernible and we can no longer perceive what is common to all of them, that is, the general tendency to sociability, a tendency which is always and everywhere the same and is special to no particular social type. But this residue is only an abstraction, for sociability in itself is nowhere found. What exists and really lives are the particular forms of solidarity, domestic solidarity, occupational solidarity, national solidarity, yesterday's, today's, etc. Each has its proper nature; consequently, these general remarks, in every case, give only a very incomplete explanation of a phenomenon, since they necessarily omit the concrete and the vital.

The study of solidarity thus grows out of sociology. It is a social fact we can know only through the intermediary of social effects. If so many moralists and psychologists have been able to treat the question without following this procedure, it has been by circumventing the difficulty. They have eliminated from the phenomenon all that is peculiarly social in order to retain only the psychological germ whence it developed. It is surely true that solidarity, while being a social fact of the first order, depends on the individual organism. In order to exist, it must be contained in our physical and psychic constitution. One can thus rigorously limit oneself to studying this aspect. But, in that case, one sees only the most indistinct and least special aspect. It is not even solidarity properly speaking, but rather what makes it possible.

Moreover, this abstract study would not be very fertile in results. For, in its dependence upon a state of simple disposition in our psychic nature, Solidarity is much too indefinite to be comprehended easily. It is an intangible phenomenon which does not lend itself to observation. In order to assume a comprehensible form, certain social consequences must translate it overtly. Moreover, even in this indeterminate state, it depends upon social conditions which explain it and from which, consequently, it cannot be detached. That is why it is very rare that some sociological views do not find their way into these analyses of pure psychology. For example, we speak of the influence of the *gregarious state* on the formation of social sentiment in general[93]; or

---

[93] Bain, *The Emotions and the Will*, pp. 131 ff.

perhaps indicate in short compass the principal social relations on which sociability quite apparently depends.[94] Without doubt, these complementary considerations, introduced helter-skelter, with examples and following chance suggestions, will not suffice to elucidate very much of the social nature of solidarity. They show, at least, that the sociological point of view is incumbent even upon psychologists.

Our method has now been fully outlined. Since law reproduces the principal forms of social solidarity, we have only to classify the different types of law to find therefrom the different types of social solidarity which correspond to it. It is now probable that there is a type which symbolizes this special solidarity of which the division of labor is the cause. That found, it will suffice, in order to measure the part of the division of labor, to compare the number of juridical rules which express it with the total volume of law.

For this task, we cannot use the distinctions utilized by the jurisconsults. Created for practical purposes, they can be very useful from this point of view, but science cannot content itself with these empirical classifications and approximations. The most accepted is that which divides law into public and private; the first is for the regulation of the relations of the individual to the State, the second, of individuals among themselves. But when we try to get closer to these terms, the line of demarcation which appeared so neat at the beginning fades away. All law is private in the sense that it is always about individuals who are present and acting; but so, too, all law is public, in the sense that it is a social function and that all individuals are, whatever their varying titles, functionaries of society. Marital functions, paternal, etc., are neither delimited nor organized in a manner different from ministerial and legislative functions, and it is not without reason that Roman law entitled tutelage *munus publicum*. What, moreover, is the State? Where does it begin and where does it end? We know how controversial the question is; it is not scientific to make a fundamental classification repose on a notion so obscure and so badly analyzed.

To proceed scientifically, we must find some characteristic which, while being essential to juridical phenomena, varies as they vary. Every precept of law can be defined as a rule of sanctioned conduct. Moreover, it is evident that sanctions change with the gravity attributed to precepts, the place they hold in the public conscience, the role they play in society. It is right, then, to classify juridical rules according to the different sanctions which are attached to them.

They are of two kinds. Some consist essentially in suffering, or at least a loss, inflicted on the agent. They make demands on his fortune,

---

[94] Spencer, *Principles of Psychology*, Part VIII, ch. v.

or on his honor, or on his life, or on his liberty, and deprive him of something he enjoys. We call them repressive. They constitute penal law. It is true that those which are attached to rules which are purely moral have the same character, only they are distributed in a diffuse manner, by everybody indiscriminately, whereas those in penal law are applied through the intermediary of a definite organ; they are organized. As for the other type, it does not necessarily imply suffering for the agent, but consists only of *the return of things as they were*, in the reestablishment of troubled relations to their normal state, whether the incriminated act is restored by force to the type whence it deviated, or is annulled, that is, deprived of all social value. We must then separate juridical rules into two great classes, accordingly as they have organized repressive sanctions or only restitutive sanctions.[95] The first comprise all penal law; the second, civil law, commercial law, procedural law, administrative and constitutional law, after abstraction of the penal rules which may be found there.

Let us now seek for the type of social solidarity to which each of these two types corresponds.

CHAPTER TWO. MECHANICAL SOLIDARITY THROUGH LIKENESS

I

The link of social solidarity to which repressive law corresponds is the one whose break constitutes a crime. By this name we call every act which, in any degree whatever, invokes against its author the characteristic reaction which we term punishment. To seek the nature of this link is to inquire into the cause of punishment, or, more precisely, to inquire what crime essentially consists of.

Surely there are crimes of different kinds; but among all these kinds, there is, no less surely, a common element. The proof of this is

---

[95] Translator's Note: In the first edition the following footnote, omitted in the fifth (and I believe in the other editions) is found at this point:—

If this division is combined with the definition that we have given of purely moral rules [in the introduction to the first edition; see appendix to this translation], the following table is obtained, based on a complete classification of all obligatory rules of conduct:

Obligatory rules of conduct

With repressive sanctions	Diffuse (Common morality without juridical sanctions).
	Organized (Penal Law).
With restitutive sanctions.	

This table shows anew how difficult it is to separate the study of simply moral rules from the study of juridical rules.

that the reaction which crimes call forth from society, in respect of punishment, is, save for differences of degree, always and ever the same. The unity of effect shows the unity of the cause. Not only among the types of crime provided for legally in the same society, but even among those which have been or are recognized and punished in different social systems, essential resemblances assuredly exist. As different as they appear at first glance, they must have a common foundation, for they everywhere affect the moral conscience of nations in the same way and produce the same result. They are all crimes; that is to say, acts reprised by definite punishments. The essential properties of a thing are those which one observes universally wherever that thing exists and which pertain to it alone. If, then, we wish to know what crime essentially is, we must extract the elements of crimes which are found similar in all criminological varieties in different social systems. None must be neglected. The juridical conceptions of the most inferior societies are no less significant than those of the most elevated societies; they are not less instructive. To omit any would expose us to the error of finding the essence of crime where it is not. Thus, the biologist would have given vital phenomena a very inexact definition, if he had disdained to observe mono-cellular organisms, for, solely from the contemplation of organisms of higher type, he would have wrongly concluded that life essentially consists in organization.

The method of finding this permanent and pervasive element is surely not by enumerating the acts that at all times and in every place have been termed crimes, observing, thus, the characters that they present. For if, as it may be, they are actions which have universally been regarded as criminal, they are the smallest minority, and, consequently, such a method would give us a very mistaken notion, since it would be applied only to exceptions.[96] These variations of

---

[96] It is this method which Garafalo has followed. No doubt, he seems to renounce it when he realizes the impossibility of drawing up a list of acts universally punished (*Criminologie*, p. 5), which is excessive. But he finally reverts to it, since, in sum, natural crime is, for him, that which runs counter to the sentiments which are everywhere at the basis of penal law; that is to say, the invariable part of the moral sense and that alone. But why would a crime which ran counter to some particular sentiment in certain social systems be less a crime than others? Garafalo is thus led to refuse the name of crime to those acts which have been universally recognized as crimes in certain social systems, and accordingly, to retrace artificially the elements of criminality. The result is that his notion of crime is singularly incomplete. It is vacillating because its author does not trouble himself to enter into a comparison of all social systems, but excludes a great number that he treats as abnormal. One can say of a social fact that it is abnormal relative to the type of the species, but a species cannot be abnormal. The two words cannot be joined. As interesting as is Garafalo's attempt to arrive at a scientific notion of a delict, it has not been made with a method sufficiently exact and precise. This is shown by the expression *natural delict* which he uses. Are not all delicts natural? It seems probable that here is a return to Spencer's doctrine, which treats social life as truly natural only in industrial societies. Unfortunately, nothing is more incorrect.

repressive law prove at the same time that the constant characteristic could not be found among the intrinsic properties of acts imposed or prohibited by penal rules, since they present such diversity, but rather in the relations that they sustain with some condition external to them.

It has been thought that this relation is found in a sort of antagonism between these actions and great social interests, and it has been said that penal rules announce the fundamental conditions of collective life for each social type. Their authority thus derives from their necessity. Moreover, as these necessities vary with societies, the variability of repressive law would thus be explained. But we have already made ourselves explicit on this point. Besides the fact that such a theory accords too large a part in the direction of social evolution to calculation and reflection, there are many acts which have been and still are regarded as criminal without in themselves being harmful to society. What social danger is there in touching a tabooed object, an impure animal or man, in letting the sacred fire die down, in eating certain meats, in failure to make the traditional sacrifice over the graves of parents, in not exactly pronouncing the ritual formula, in not celebrating certain holidays, etc.? We know, however, what a large place in the repressive law of many peoples ritual regimentation, etiquette, ceremonial, and religious practices play. We have only to open the Pentateuch to convince ourselves, and as these facts normally recur in certain social types, we cannot think of them as anomalies or pathological cases which we can rightly neglect.

Even when a criminal act is certainly harmful to society, it is not true that the amount of harm that it does is regularly related to the intensity of the repression which it calls forth. In the penal law of the most civilized people, murder is universally regarded as the greatest of crimes. However, an economic crisis, a stock-market crash, even a failure, can disorganize the social body more severely than an isolated homicide. No doubt murder is always an evil, but there is no proof that it is the greatest of evils. What is one man less to society? What does one lost cell matter to the organism? We say that the future general security would be menaced if the act remained unpunished; but if we compare the significance of the danger, real as it is, and that of the punishment, the disproportion is striking. Moreover, the examples we have just cited show that an act can be disastrous to society without incurring the least repression. This definition of crime is, then, completely inadequate.

Shall we say, in modifying it, that criminal acts are those which *seem* harmful to the society that represses them, that penal rules express, not the conditions which are essential to social life, but those which *appear* such to the group which observes them? But such an explanation explains nothing, for it does not show why, in so large a number of cases, societies are mistaken and have imposed practices which by themselves were not even useful. Surely this pretended solution of the problem reduces itself to a veritable truism, for if societies thus oblige each individual to obey their rules, it is evidently because they believe, wrongly or rightly, that this regular and punctual obedience is indispensable to them. That is why they hold to it so doggedly. The solution then amounts to saying that societies judge these rules necessary because they judge them necessary. What we must find out is why they consider them so necessary. If this sentiment had its cause in the objective necessity of penal prescriptions, or, at least, in their utility, it would be an explanation. But that is contradicted by the facts; the question remains entirely unresolved.

However, this last theory is not without some foundation; it is with reason that it seeks in certain states of the subject the constitutive conditions of criminality. In effect, the only common characteristic of all crimes is that they consist—except some apparent exceptions with which we shall deal later—in acts universally disapproved of by members of each society. We ask ourselves these days whether this reprobation is rational, whether it would not be wiser to see in crime only a malady or an error. But we need not enter upon these discussions; we seek to determine what is or has been, not what ought to be. Thus, the reality of the fact that we have just established is not contestable; that is, that crime shocks sentiments which, for a given social system, are found in all healthy consciences.

It is not possible otherwise to determine the nature of these sentiments, to define them in terms of the function of their particular objects, for these objects have infinitely varied and can still vary.[97] Today, there are altruistic sentiments which present this character most markedly; but there was a time, not far distant from ours, when religious, domestic, and a thousand other traditional sentiments had exactly the same effects. Even now, negative sympathy for another does not, as Garafalo wishes, alone produce this result. Do we not have the same aversion, in times of peace, for the man who betrays his country as for the robber or the murderer? In a country where monarchical sentiment is still strong, do crimes against *lèse-majesté* not call forth general indignation? In democratic countries, are injuries to the people not inveighed against? We cannot thus draw up a list of sentiments whose violation constitutes a crime; they distinguish themselves from others only by this trait, that they are common to the average mass of individuals of the same society. So the rules which prohibit these acts and which penal law sanctions are the only ones to

---

[97] We do not see what scientific reason Garafalo has for saying that the moral sentiments actually acquired by the civilized part of humanity constitute a morality "not susceptible of loss, but of a continually growing development" (p. 9). What permits him thus to limit the changes that will come about in one sense or another?

which the famous juridical axiom *ignorance of the law is no excuse* is applied without fiction. As they are graven in all consciences, everybody knows them and feels that they are well founded. It is at least true of the normal state. If we come upon adults who do not know these fundamental rules or do not recognize their authority, such ignorance or insubmissiveness is an undeniable sign of pathological perversion. Or, if it happens that a penal disposition exists for a long time although opposed by all, it is because of very exceptional circumstances, consequently, abnormal; and such a state of affairs can never long endure.

This explains the particular manner in which penal law is codified. Every written law has a double object: to prescribe certain obligations, and to define the sanctions which are attached to them. In civil law, and more generally in every type of law with restitutive sanctions, the legislator takes up and solves the two questions separately. He first determines the obligation with all possible precision, and it is only later that he stipulates the manner in which it should be sanctioned. For example, in the chapter of the French civil code which is devoted to the respective duties of married persons, the rights and obligations are announced in a positive manner; but no mention is made of what happens when these duties are violated by one or the other. We must go otherwheres to find this sanction. Sometimes it is totally lacking. Thus, article 214 of the civil code orders the wife to live with her husband; we deduce from that that the husband can force her to remain in the conjugal domicile, but this sanction is nowhere formally indicated. Penal law, on the contrary, sets forth only sanctions, but says nothing of the obligations to which they correspond. It does not command respect for the life of another, but kills the assassin. It does not say, first off, as does civil law: Here is the duty; but rather, Here is the punishment. No doubt, if the action is punished, it is because it is contrary to an obligatory rule, but this rule is not expressly formulated. There can be only one reason for this, which is that the rule is known and accepted by everybody. When a law of custom becomes written and is codified, it is because questions of litigation demand a more definite solution. If the custom continues to function silently, without raising any discussion or difficulties, there is no reason for transforming it. Since penal law is codified only to establish a graduated scale of punishments, it is thus the scale alone which can lend itself to doubt. Inversely, if rules whose violation is punished do not need a juridical expression, it is because they are the object of no contest, because everybody feels their authority.[98]

It is true that sometimes the Pentateuch does not set forth sanctions, though, we shall see, it contains little more than penal

---

[98] Cf. Binding, *Die Normen und ihre Uebertretung*, I, pp. 6 ff., Leipzig, 1872.

dispositions. This is the case with the Ten Commandments as they are found formulated in chapter XX of *Exodus* and chapter V of *Deuteronomy.* But the Pentateuch, although it has the function of a code, is not, however, a code properly speaking. Its object is not to unite in a single system and to make precise the penal rules of the Jewish people; it is so far from being a codification that the various parts of which it is composed seem not to have been formulated in the same epoch. It is above all a résumé of all sorts of traditions by which the Jews explained to their satisfaction and in their fashion the genesis of the world, of their society, and of their principal social practices. If, then, it prescribes duties which assuredly were sanctioned by punishments, they were not ignored or unknown to the Jews, nor was it necessary to make them manifest. On the contrary, since the book is only a tissue of national legends, we can rest assured that everything that it contains was engraven in every conscience. It was essentially a problem of reproducing and stabilizing the popular beliefs on the origins of these precepts, on the historical circumstances in which they were believed to have been promulgated, on the sources of their authority. Thus, from this point of view, the determination of punishment becomes something accessory.[99]

It is for this reason that the functioning of repressive justice tends to remain more or less diffuse. In very different social systems, it does not function through the means of a special magistracy, but the whole society participates in a rather large measure. In primitive societies, where, as we shall see, law is wholly penal, it is the assembly of the people which renders justice. This was the case among the ancient Germans.[100] In Rome, while civil affairs were given over to the praetor, criminal matters were handled by the people, first by the curile comites, and then, beginning with the law of the Twelve Tables, by the centurial comites. Until the end of the republic, even though in fact it had delegated its powers to permanent commissions, the people remained, in principle, the supreme judge of this type of process.[101] In Athens, under the legislation of Solon, criminal jurisdiction partly rested in the 'Ηλιαία, a vast assemblage which nominally comprised all the citizens over the age of thirty.[102] Then, among Germano-Latin peoples, society, in the person of the jury, intervened in the exercise of these same

---

[99] The only true exceptions to this particularity of penal law are produced when the act is committed by the public authority which created the delict. In this case, the duty is generally defined independently of the sanction; we will later consider the cause of this exception.

[100] Tacitus, *Germania*, ch. xii.

[101] Cf. Walter, *Histoire de la procédure civile et du droit criminel chez les Romains*, tr. fr. § 829; Rein, *Criminalrecht der Roemer*, p. 63.

[102] Cf. Gilbert, *Handbuch der Griechischen Staatsalterthümer*, I, p. 138, Leipzig, 1881.

functions. The diffused state in which this part of judicial power is thus found would be inexplicable, if the rules whose observation it assured, and, consequently, the sentiments to which these rules corresponded, were not imminent in all consciences. It is true that, in other cases, the power is wielded by a privileged class or by particular magistrates. But these facts do not lessen the demonstrative value of the preceding, for, simply because collective sentiments are enforced only through certain intermediaries, it does not follow that they have ceased to be collective while localizing themselves in a restricted number of consciences. This delegation may be due either to the very great multiplicity of affairs which necessitate the institution of special functionaries, or to the very great importance assumed by certain persons or certain classes and which makes them the authorized interpreters of collective sentiments.

But we have not defined crime when we say that it consists in an offense to collective sentiments, for there are some among these which can be offended without there being a crime. Thus, incest is the object of quite general aversion, and yet it is an act that is only immoral. It is in like case with the reflections upon a woman's honor accruing from promiscuous intercourse outside of marriage, from the fact of total alienation of her liberty at another's hands, or of accepting such alienation from another. The collective sentiments to which crime corresponds must, therefore, singularize themselves from others by some distinctive property; they must have a certain average intensity. Not only are they engraven in all consciences, but they are strongly engraven. They are not hesitant and superficial desires, but emotions and tendencies which are strongly ingrained in us. The proof of this is the extreme slowness with which penal law evolves. Not only is it modified more slowly than custom, but it is the part of positive law most refractory to change. Observe, for example, what has been accomplished in legislation since the beginning of the nineteenth century in the different spheres of juridical life; the innovations in the matter of penal law are extremely rare and restricted compared to the multitude of new dispositions introduced into the civil law, commercial law, administrative law, and constitutional law. When we compare the penal law which the Twelve Tables set up in Rome with that which we find there in the classical epoch, the changes that are observable are small indeed compared to those induced in the civil law during the same period. From the time of the Twelve Tables, says Mainz, the principal crimes and delicts are constituted: "During ten generations, the catalogue of public crimes had added to it only some few laws which punished thievery, brigandage, and perhaps the *plagium*"[103] As for private delicts, we encounter only two new ones: rapine (*actio*

---

[103] *Esquisse historique du droit criminel de l'ancienne Rome*, in *Nouvelle Revue historique du droit français et étranger*, 1882, pp. 24 and 27.

bonorum vi raptorum) and damage unjustly caused (*damnum injuria datum*). The same phenomenon is universally found. In lower societies, law, as we shall see, is almost exclusively penal; it is likewise very stationary. Generally, religious law is always repressive; it is essentially conservative. This fixity of penal law evinces the resistive force of the collective sentiments to which it corresponds. Inversely, the very great plasticity of purely moral rules and the relative rapidity of their evolution show the smaller force of the sentiments at their base; either they have been more recently acquired and have not yet had time to penetrate deeply into consciences, or they are in process of losing strength and moving from depth to surface.

One last addition is still necessary in order to make our definition exact. If, in general, the sentiments which purely moral sanctions protect, that is to say, diffuse sanctions, are less intense and less solidly organized than those which punishment, properly called, protects, nevertheless there are exceptions. Thus, there is no reason for believing that the average filial piety or even the elementary forms of compassion for the most apparent evils today consist of sentiments more superficial than those concerning property or public authority. The wayward son, however, and even the most hardened egotist are not treated as criminals. It is not sufficient, then, that the sentiments be strong; they must be precise. In effect, each of them is relative to a very definite practice. This practice can be simple or complex, positive or negative, that is to say, consist in action or abstention, but it is always determined. It is a question of doing or not doing this or that, of not killing, not wounding, of pronouncing such a formula, of going through such a rite, etc. On the contrary, sentiments such as filial love or charity are vague aspirations towards very general objects. So penal laws are remarkable for their neatness and precision, while purely moral rules are generally somewhat nebulous. Their inchoate nature very often even makes it difficult to render them in a short formula. We may quite generally say that a man ought to work, that he ought to have pity on others, etc., but we cannot determine in what fashion or in what measure. There is room here, consequently, for variations and nuances. On the other hand, since the sentiments which are incarnate in penal rules are determined, they have a much greater uniformity. As they cannot be understood in different ways, they are ever the same.

We are now in a position to come to a conclusion.

The totality of beliefs and sentiments common to average citizens of the same society forms a determinate system which has its own life; one may call it the *collective* or *common conscience*. No doubt, it has not a specific organ as a substratum; it is, by definition, diffuse in every reach of society. Nevertheless, it has specific characteristics which make it a distinct reality. It is, in effect, independent of the particular conditions in which individuals are placed; they pass on and it remains. It is the same in the North and in the South, in great cities and in small, in different professions. Moreover, it does not change with each generation, but, on the contrary, it connects successive generations with one another. It is, thus, an entirely different thing from particular consciences, although it can be realized only through them. It is the psychical type of society, a type which has its properties, its conditions of existence, its mode of development, just as individual types, although in a different way. Thus understood, it has the right to be denoted by a special word. The one which we have just employed is not, it is true, without ambiguity. As the terms, collective and social, are often considered synonymous, one is inclined to believe that the collective conscience is the total social conscience, that is, extend it to include more than the psychic life of society, although, particularly in advanced societies, it is only a very restricted part. Judicial, governmental, scientific, industrial, in short, all special functions are of a psychic nature, since they consist in systems of representations and actions. They, however, are surely outside the common conscience. To avoid the confusion[104] into which some have fallen, the best way would be to create a technical expression especially to designate the totality of social similitudes. However, since the use of a new word, when not absolutely necessary, is not without inconvenience, we shall employ the well-worn expression, collective or common conscience, but we shall always mean the strict sense in which we have taken it.

We can, then, to resume the preceding analysis, say that an act is criminal when it offends strong and defined states of the collective conscience.[105]

The statement of this proposition is not generally called into question, but it is ordinarily given a sense very different from that which it ought to convey. We take it as if it expressed, not the essential property of crime, but one of its repercussions. We well know that crime violates very pervasive and intense sentiments, but we believe that this' pervasiveness and this intensity derive from the criminal character of the act, which consequently remains to be defined. We do not deny that every delict is universally reproved, but we take as agreed that the reprobation to which it is subjected results from its delictness.

---

[104] The confusion is not without its dangers. Thus, we sometimes ask if the individual conscience varies as the collective conscience. It all depends upon the sense in which the word is taken. If it represents social likenesses, the variation is inverse, as we shall see. If it signifies the total psychic life of society, the relation is direct. It is thus necessary to distinguish them.

[105] We shall not consider the question whether the collective conscience is a conscience as is that of the individual. By this term, we simply signify the totality of social likenesses, without prejudging the category by which this system of phenomena ought to be defined.

But we are hard put to say what this delictness consists of. In immorality which is particularly serious? I wish such were the case, but that is to reply to the question by putting one word in place of another, for it is precisely the problem to understand what this immorality is, and especially this particular immorality which society reproves by means of organized punishment and which constitutes criminality. It can evidently come only from one or several characteristics common to all criminological types. The only one which would satisfy this condition is that opposition between a crime, whatever it is, and certain collective sentiments. It is, accordingly, this opposition which makes crime rather than being a derivative of crime. In other words, we must not say that an action shocks the common conscience because it is criminal, but rather that it is criminal because it shocks the common conscience. We do not reprove it because it is a crime, but it is a crime because we reprove it. As for the intrinsic nature of these sentiments, it is impossible to specify them. They have the most diverse objects and cannot be encompassed in a single formula. We can say that they relate neither to vital interests of society nor to a minimum of justice. All these definitions are inadequate. By this alone can we recognize it: a sentiment, whatever its origin and end, is found in all consciences with a certain degree of force and precision, and every action which violates it is a crime. Contemporary psychology is more and more reverting to the idea of Spinoza, according to which things are good because we like them, as against our liking them because they are good. What is primary is the tendency, the inclination; the pleasure and pain are only derivative facts. It is just so in social life. An act is socially bad because society disproves of it. But, it will be asked, are there not some collective sentiments which result from pleasure and pain which society feels from contact with their ends? No doubt, but they do not all have this origin. A great many, if not the larger part, come from other causes. Everything that leads activity to assume a definite form can give rise to habits, whence result tendencies which must be satisfied. Moreover, it is these latter tendencies which alone are truly fundamental. The others are only special forms and more determinate. Thus, to find charm in such and such an object, collective sensibility must already be constituted so as to be able to enjoy it. If the corresponding sentiments are abolished, the most harmful act to society will not only be tolerated, but even honored and proposed as an example. Pleasure is incapable of creating an impulse out of whole cloth; it can only link those sentiments which exist to such and such a particular end, provided that the end be in accord with their original nature.

There are, however, some cases where the preceding does not explain. There are some actions which are more severely repressed than they are strongly reproved by general opinion. Thus, a coalition of functionaries, the encroachment of judicial authority on administrative authority, religious functions on civil functions, are the object of a repression which is not in accord with the indignation that they arouse in consciences. The appropriation of public goods leaves us quite indifferent, and yet is punished quite severely. It may even happen that the act punished may not directly hurt any collective sentiment. There is nothing in us which protests against fishing and hunting out of season, or against overloaded conveyances on the public highway. But there is no reason for separating these delicts from others; every radical distinction[106] would be arbitrary, since they all present, in different degree, the same external criterion. No doubt, in any of these examples, the punishment does not appear unjust. But if it is not enforced by public opinion, such opinion, left to itself, would either not object to it at all, or show itself less insistent. Thus, in all cases of this type, delictness does not come about, or does not entirely derive from the vivacity of the collective sentiments which are offended, but comes from some other cause.

It is surely true that once a governmental power is instituted, it has, by itself, enough force to attach a penal sanction spontaneously to certain rules of conduct. It is capable, by its own action, of creating certain delicts or of increasing the criminological value of certain others. So, all the actions that we have just cited present this common character of being directed against some administrative organ of social life. Must we then admit that there are two kinds of crimes coming from two different causes? Such an hypothesis cannot be considered. As numerous as the varieties are, crime is everywhere essentially the same, since it everywhere calls forth the same effect, in respect of punishment, which, if it can be more or less intense, does not by that change its nature. But the same fact cannot have two causes, unless this duality is only apparent, and basically they are one. The power of reaction which is proper to the State ought, then, to be of the same sort as that which is diffused throughout society.

And where would it come from? From the depth of the interests which the State cares for and which demand protection in a very special way? But we know that the subversion of even deep interests does not alone suffice to determine the penal reaction; it must still be felt in a very decided way.

How does it come about that the least damage done to a governmental organ is punished, although many much more severe disorders in other social organs are reparable only civilly? The smallest injury to the police power calls forth a penalty, while even repeated

---

[106] We have only to notice how Garafalo distinguishes what he calls true crimes from others (p. 45); it is but a personal judgment which does not rest upon any objective characteristic.

violation of contracts, or constant lack of correctness in economic relations only asks amends for the loss. Doubtless, the system of direction plays an eminent role in social life, but there are others whose interest is of great importance, yet whose functioning is not assured in this fashion. If the brain have its importance, the stomach is an organ which is likewise essential, and the sicknesses of one are menaces to life just as those of the other. Why is this privilege accorded to what is sometimes called the social brain?

The difficulty resolves itself easily if we notice that, wherever a directive power is established, its primary and principal function is to create respect for the beliefs, traditions, and collective practices; that is, to defend the common conscience against all enemies within and without. It thus becomes its symbol, its living expression in the eyes of all. Thus, the life which is in the collective conscience is communicated to the directive organ as the affinities of ideas are communicated to the words which represent them, and that is how it assumes a character which puts it above all others. It is no longer a more or less important social function; it is the collective type incarnate. It participates in the authority which the latter exercises over consciences, and it is from there that it draws its force. Once constituted, however, without freeing itself from the source whence it flows and whence it continues to draw its sustenance, it nevertheless becomes an autonomous factor in social life, capable of spontaneously producing its own movements without external impulsion, precisely because of the supremacy which it has acquired. Since, moreover, it is only a derivation from the force which is imminent in the collective conscience, it necessarily has the same properties and reacts in the same manner, although the latter does not react completely in unison. It repulses every antagonistic force as would the diffuse soul of society, although the latter does not feel this antagonism, or rather, does not feel it so directly. That is, it considers as criminal, actions which shock it without, however, shocking the collective sentiments in the same degree. But it is from these latter that it receives all the power which permits it to create crimes and delicts. Besides, not coming from without or arising from nothing, the following facts, which will be amply developed in the rest of this work, confirm this explanation. The extent of the activity which the governmental organ exercises over the number and the qualification of criminal acts depends on the force it receives. That can be measured either by the extent of the authority which it exercises over citizens, or by the degree of gravity recognized in crimes directed against it. But we shall see that it is in lower societies that this authority is greatest and this gravity most elevated, and moreover, that it is in these same social types that the collective conscience has the most power.[107]

---

[107] Moreover, when the fine constitutes the whole punishment, since it is only a

Thus, we must always return to this last; that is whence, directly or indirectly, comes all criminality. Crime is not simply the disruption even of serious interests; it is an offense against an authority in some way transcendent. But, from experience, there is no moral force superior to the individual save collective force.

There is, moreover, a way of checking up on the result at which we have just arrived. What characterizes crime is that it determines punishment. If, then, our definition of crime is exact, it ought to explain all the characteristics of punishment. We shall proceed to this verification.

But first we must find out what these characteristics are.

II

In the first place, punishment consists of a passionate reaction. This character is especially apparent in less cultivated societies. In effect, primitive peoples punish for the sake of punishing, make the culpable suffer particularly for the sake of making him suffer and without seeking any advantage for themselves from the suffering which they impose. The proof of this is that they seek neither to strike back justly nor to strike back usefully, but merely to strike back. It is thus that they punish animals which have committed a wrong act,[108] or even inanimate beings which have been its passive instrument.[109] When punishment is applied only to people, it often extends further than the culpable and reaches the innocent, his wife, his children, his neighbors, etc.[110] That is because the passion which is the soul of punishment ceases only when exhausted. If, therefore, after it has destroyed the one who has immediately called it forth, there still remains force within it, it expands in quite mechanical fashion. Even when it is quite tempered and attends only to the culpable, it makes its presence felt by the tendency to surpass in severity the action against which it is reacting. That is whence come the refinements of pain added to capital punishment. Even in Rome the thief not only had to return the stolen object, but also pay retribution of double and quadruple the amount.[111] Moreover, is not the very general punishment of the *lex talionis* a satisfaction accorded to the passion for vengeance?

---

reparation whose amount is fixed, the action is on the limits of penal law and restitutive law.

[108] See *Exodus*, xxi, 28; *Leviticus, xx,* 16.

[109] For example, the instrument which has aided in the perpetration of murder.—See Post, *Bausteine für eine allegemeine Rechtswissenschaft,* I, pp. 230-231.

[110] See *Exodus, xx,* 4 and 5; *Deuteronomy,* xii, 12-18; Thonissen, *Etudes sur l'histoire du droit criminel,* I, p. 70 and pp. 178 ff.

[111] Walter, op. *cit,* § 793.

But today, it is said, punishment has changed its character; it is no longer to avenge itself that society punishes, it is to defend itself. The pain which it inflicts is in its hands no longer anything but a methodical means of protection. It punishes, not because chastisement offers it any satisfaction for itself, but so that the fear of punishment may paralyze those who contemplate evil. This is no longer choler, but a reflected provision which determines repression. The preceding observations could not then be made general; they would deal only with the primitive form of punishment and would not extend to the existing form.

But to justify such a radical distinction between these two sorts of punishment, it is not enough to state them in view of their employment of different ends. The nature of a practice does not necessarily change because the conscious intentions of those who apply it are modified. It might, in truth, still play the same role as before, but without being perceived. In this case, why would it transform only in that aspect which better explains its effects? It adapts itself to new conditions of existence without any essential changes. It is so with punishment.

It is an error to believe that vengeance is but useless cruelty. It is very possible that, in itself, it consists of a mechanical and aimless reaction, in an emotional and irrational movement, in an unintelligent need to destroy; but, in fact, what it tends to destroy was a menace to us. It consists, then, in a veritable act of defense, although an instinctive and unreflective one. We avenge ourselves only upon what has done us evil, and what has done us evil is always dangerous. The instinct of vengeance is, in sum, only the instinct of conservation exacerbated by peril. Thus, vengeance is far from having had the negative and sterile role in the history of mankind which is attributed to it. It is a defensive weapon which has its worth, but it is a rude weapon. As it has no realization of the services which it automatically renders, it cannot, in consequence, regulate itself; but it responds somewhat haphazardly to blind causes which urge it on and without anything moderating its activities. Today, since we better understand the end to be attained, we better know how to utilize the means at our disposal; we protect ourselves with better means and, accordingly, more efficiently. But, in the beginning, this result was obtained in a rather imperfect manner. Between the punishment of today and yesterday, there is no chasm, and consequently it was not necessary for the latter to become something other than itself to accommodate itself to the role that it plays in our civilized societies. The whole difference derives from the fact that it now produces its effects with a much greater understanding of what it does. But, although the individual or social conscience may not be without influence upon the reality that it clarifies, it has not the power to change its nature. The internal structure of phenomena remains the same, whether they be conscious of it or not. We thus reach the conclusion that the essential elements of punishment are the same as of old.

And in truth, punishment has remained, at least in part, a work of vengeance. It is said that we do not make the culpable suffer in order to make him suffer; it is none the less true that we find it just that he suffer. Perhaps we are wrong, but that is not the question. We seek, at the moment, to define punishment as it is or has been, not as it ought to be. It is certain that this expression of public vindication which finds its way again and again into the language of the courts is not a word taken in vain. In supposing that punishment can really serve to protect us in the future, we think that it ought to be above all an *expiation* of the past. The proof of this lies in the minute precautions we take to proportion punishment as exactly as possible to the severity of the crime; they would be inexplicable if we did not believe that the culpable ought to suffer because he has done evil and in the same degree. In effect, this gradation is not necessary if punishment is only a means of defense. No doubt, there would be danger for society in having the gravest acts considered simple delicts; but it would be greater, in the majority of cases, if the second were considered as the first. Against an enemy, we cannot take too much precaution. Shall we say that the authors of the smallest misdeeds have natures less perverse, and that to neutralize their evil instincts less stringent punishments will suffice? But if their motives are less vicious, they are not on that account less intense. Robbers are as strongly inclined to rob as murderers are to murder; the resistance offered by the former is not less than that of the latter, and consequently, to control it, we would have recourse to the same means. If, as has been said, it was solely a question of putting down a noxious force by an opposing force, the intensity of the second would be measured solely by the intensity of the first, without the quality of the latter entering into the consideration. The penal scale would then encompass only a small number of degrees. Punishment would vary only as the criminal is more or less hardened, and not according to the nature of the criminal act. An incorrigible robber would be treated as an incorrigible murderer. But, in fact, if it were shown that a misdoer was definitely incurable, we would feel bound not to chastise him unduly. This is proof that we are faithful to the principle of retaliation, although we apply it in a more elevated sense than heretofore. We no longer measure in so material and gross a manner either the extent of the deed or of the punishment; but we always think that there ought to be an equation between the two terms, whether or not we benefit from this balance. Punishment, thus, remains for us what it was for our fathers. It is still an act of vengeance since it is an expiation. What we avenge, what the criminal expiates, is the outrage to morality.

There is, indeed, a punishment where this passionate character is more manifest than elsewhere. It is the disgrace which doubles the majority of punishments and which grows with them. Very often it serves no purpose. What good is it to disgrace a man who ought no longer to live in a society of his peers and who has superabundantly proved by his conduct that the most redoubtable threats are not sufficient to intimidate him? Disgrace is called upon when there is no other punishment, or as complement to a quite feeble material punishment. In the latter case it metes out double punishment. We can even say that society has recourse to legal chastisement only when the others are insufficient; but then why maintain them? They are a sort of supplementary, aimless aid, and can have no other cause for being other than the need of compensating evil with evil. It is a product of instinctive, irresistible sentiments, which often extend to the innocent. It is thus that the place of crime, the instruments which have served it, the relatives of the culpable, sometimes participate in the opprobrium in which the criminal is involved. But the causes which determine this diffuse repression are the same as those of the organized repression which accompany the former. It is sufficient, moreover, to see how punishment functions in courts, in order to understand that its spirit is completely passionate, for it is to these passions that both prosecutor and defense-attorney address themselves. The latter seeks to excite sympathy for the defendant, the former to awaken the social sentiments which have been violated by the criminal act, and it is under the influence of these contrary passions that the judge pronounces sentence.

Thus, the nature of punishment has not been changed in essentials. All that we can say is that the need of vengeance is better directed today than heretofore. The spirit of foresight which has been aroused no longer leaves the field so free for the blind action of passion. It contains it within certain limits; it is opposed to absurd violence, to unreasonable ravaging. More clarified, it expands less on chance. One no longer sees it turn against the innocent to satisfy itself. But it nevertheless remains the soul of penality. We can thus say that punishment consists in a passionate reaction of graduated intensity.[112]

But whence comes this reaction? From the individual or from society?

Everybody knows that it is society that punishes, but it might be held that this is not by design. What puts beyond doubt the social

---

[112] Moreover, this is what those who find the idea of expiation unintelligible themselves recognize, for their conclusion is that, to be put in harmony with their doctrine, the traditional conception of punishment must be totally transformed and reformed from top to bottom. This is because it rests and has always rested upon the principle which they oppose. See Fouillée, *Science Sociale*, pp. 307 ff.

character of punishment is that, once pronounced, it cannot be lifted except by the government in the name of society. If it were a satisfaction given to particular persons, they would always be the judges of its remission. We cannot conceive of a privilege imposed unless its beneficiary could renounce it. If it is society alone that employs the repression, that is because it is attacked when individuals are, and the attack directed against it is repressed by punishment.

We can cite cases, however, where the execution of punishment depends upon the desires of particular people. In Rome, certain misdeeds were punished in a manner to profit the wronged party, who could renounce it or make it an object of compromise; such were robbery unseen, rapine, slander, damage unjustly caused.[113] These delicts, which were called private (*delicta privata*), were different from crime properly speaking, whose repression was pursued in the name of the city. We find the same distinction in Greece and among the Hebrews.[114] Among more primitive peoples punishment sometimes seems still more completely private, as the custom of the *vendetta* would seem to prove. These societies are composed of elementary aggregations of quasi-familial character, and are easily described by the word *clans*. But when an attack has been made by one or several members of a clan against another clan, it is the latter which itself punishes the offense to which it has been subjected.[115] What seemingly increases the importance of these facts is that it has very often been contended that the *vendetta* was primitively the unique form of punishment. But, then, it would have first consisted in acts of private vengeance. But if today society is armed with the right to punish, it can be, it seems, only because of a sort of delegation of individuals. It is only their representative. It guards their interest for them, probably because it guards them better, but these interests are not properly its own. According to this principle, they would avenge themselves. Now it is society which avenges them, but as penal law could not have changed its nature according to this simple transfer, there would be nothing social about it. If society appears to play a preponderant role in it, it is only as a substitute for individuals.

But, as common as this theory is, it is contrary to facts better established. Not a single society can be instanced where the *vendetta* has been the primitive form of punishment. On the contrary, it is certain that penal law was essentially religious in its origin. It is an evident fact in India and Judea, since the law which was practiced there was considered revealed.[116] In Egypt, the ten books of Hermes, which

---

[113] Rein, *op. cit.*, p. 111.

[114] Among the Hebrews, robbery, violation of trust, abuse of confidence, and assault were treated as private delicts.

[115] See especially Morgan, *Ancient Society*, p. 76, London, 1870.

[116] In Judea, the judges were not priests, but every judge was the representative of

contained the criminal law with all other laws relative to the government of the State, were called sacerdotal, and Élien affirms that, from earliest times, the Egyptian priests exercised judicial power.[117] The case was the same in ancient Germany.[118] In Greece, justice was considered as an emanation from Zeus, and the sentiment a vengeance from God.[119] In Rome, the religious origins of penal law are clearly shown both by old traditions,[120] and by archaic practices which persisted until a late date, and by the juridical terminology itself.[121] But religion is an essentially social phenomenon. Far from pursuing only personal ends, it exercises, at all times, a constraint upon the individual. It forces him into practices which subject him to small or large sacrifices which are painful to him. He must take from his goods the offerings that he is compelled to present to the divinity; he must take time from his work or play in which to observe rites; he must impose upon himself every sort of privation which is demanded of him, even to renounce life if the gods ordain. Religious life consists entirely in abnegation and disinterestedness. If, then, in primitive societies, criminal law is religious law, we can be sure that the interests it serves are social. It is their own offenses that the gods avenge by punishment and not those of particular persons. But offenses against the gods are offenses against society.

Thus, in lower societies, the most numerous delicts are those which relate to public affairs; delicts against religion, against custom, against authority, etc. We need only look at the Bible, the laws of Manou, at the monuments which remain of the old Egyptian law to see the relatively small place accorded to prescriptions for the protection of individuals, and, contrariwise, the luxuriant development of repressive legislation concerning the different forms of sacrilege, the omission of certain religious duties, the demands of ceremonial, etc.[122] At the same time, these crimes are the most severely punished. Among the Jews, the most abominable attacks are those against religion.[123] Among the ancient Germans, only two crimes were punished by death according to Tacitus: treason and desertion.[124] According to Confucius and Meng-

---

God, the man of God. (*Deuteronomy*, i, 17; *Exodus*, xxii, 28.) In India, it was the king who judged, but this function was regarded as essentially religious. (Manou, VIII, v, 303-311.)

[117] Thonissen, *Etudes sur l'histoire du droit criminel, I*, p. 107.

[118] Zoepfl, *Deutsche Rechtsgeschichte*, p. 909.

[119] "It is the son of Saturn," says Hesiod, "who has given justice to men." (*Works and Days*, V, 279 and 280.) "When mortals commit . . . wrong acts, Zeus in his wisdom metes out proper punishment." *Ibid.*, V, 266. Cf. *Iliad*, XVI, 384 ff.

[120] Walter, *op. cit.*, § 788.

[121] Rein, *op. cit.*, pp. 27-36.

[122] See Thonissen, *passim*.

[123] Munck, *Palestine*, p. 216.

[124] *Germania*, XII.

Tseu, impiety is a greater crime than murder.[125] In Egypt, the smallest sacrilege was punished by death.[126] In Rome, the height of criminality is found in the *crimen perduellionis.*[127]

But then, what of the private punishments of which we gave some examples above? They have a mixed nature and invoke at the same time the repressive sanction and the restitutive sanction. It is thus that the private delict of Roman law represents a sort of intermediary between crime properly called and the purely civil breach. It has traits of both and is marginal on the confines of the two domains. It is a delict in the sense that the sanction fixed by law does not simply consist in a restoration of things to their original state; the delinquent is forced not only to repair the damage he has caused, but he must also expiate the deed. But it is not completely a delict since, if it is society that metes out punishment, it is not society that is mistress of its application. It is a right that it confers on the wronged party who alone freely exercises it.[128] Moreover, the *vendetta* is evidently a punishment which society recognizes as legitimate, but which it leaves to particular persons to inflict. These facts only confirm what we have said of the nature of penality. If this sort of intermediate sanction is in part a private thing, in the same degree it is not a punishment. The penal character is less pronounced as the social character is more effaced, and inversely. It is far from true that private vengeance is the prototype of punishment; it is, on the contrary, only an imperfect punishment. Far from attacks against persons being the first which were reprised, in origin they are only on the threshold of penal law. They are raised in the scale of criminality only as society is more fully distressed by them, and this operation, which we do not have to describe, is not reducible simply to a transfer. On the contrary, the history of this penality is only a continuous series of encroachments by society upon the individual, or rather on elementary groups that it contains within its scope, and the result of these encroachments is to displace individual law more and more by social law.[129]

But the above characteristics appertain quite as well to diffuse repression which follows simply immoral actions as they do to legal

---

[125] Plath, *Gesetz und Recht in alten China*, pp. 69 and 70, 1865.

[126] Thonissen, *op. cit., I*, p. 145.

[127] Walter, *op. cit.*, § 803.

[128] However, what accentuates the penal character of the private delict is that it implies infamy, a true public punishment. (See Rein, *op. cit.*, p. 916, and Bouvy, *De l'infamie en droit romain*, p. 35.)

[129] In every case, it is important to notice that the *vendetta* is an eminently collective thing. It is not the individual who avenges himself, but his clan. Later, it is to the clan or to the family that restitution is made.

repression. What distinguishes legal repression is, we have said, that it is organized; but in what does this organization consist?

When we think of penal law as it functions in our own societies, we consider it as a code where very definite punishments are attached to equally definite crimes. The judge is given a certain latitude in the application to each particular case of these general dispositions, but in its essential lineaments, punishment is predetermined for each category of delictuous acts. This planned organization does not, however, constitute punishment, for there are societies where punishment exists without being fixed in advance. There is in the Bible a number of prohibitions which are as imperative as possible, but which are not sanctioned by any expressly formulated punishment. There is no doubt about their penal character, for, if the texts are silent as to the punishment, yet they express such a horror of the act that we cannot for a moment suppose that it went unpunished.[130] There is every reason for believing, then, that this silence of the law comes simply from the undetermined nature of the repression. And, in effect, many instances in the Pentateuch teach us that there were acts whose criminal value was incontestable, yet whose punishment was established only by the judge who applied it. Society knew well enough that it was in the presence of a crime, but the penal sanction which should have been attached to it was not yet determined.[131] Moreover, even among punishments which are enunciated by the legislator, there are a great many which are not specified with precision. Thus, we know that there were different sorts of punishment which were not put on the same level, and moreover, in a great number of cases the texts speak only of death in a general manner, without saying what kind of death ought to be inflicted. According to Maine, the case was the same in primitive Rome; the *crimina* were prosecuted before the assembly of the people who fixed with their sovereign will the punishment according to a law, at the same time as they established the reality of the fact incriminated.[132] Besides, even until the sixteenth century, the general principle of penality "is that the application was left to the discretion of the judge, *arbitrio et officio judicis*. . . . Only, a judge was not permitted to invent punishments other than those which were customary."[133] Another result of this power of the judge was to make

---

[130] *Deuteronomy*, vi, 25.

[131] "And while the children of Israel were in the wilderness, they found a man gathering sticks upon the sabbath day. And they that found him gathering sticks brought him unto Moses and Aaron, and unto all the congregation. And they put him in ward, *because it had not been declared what should be done to him.*" *Numbers*, xv, 32-34. Another time, it was a question of a man who had blasphemed against the name of the Lord. He was arrested, but they did not know what to do with him. Moses himself did not know and went to consult the Lord. (*Leviticus*, xxiv, 12-16.)

[132] *Ancient Law*

[133] Du Boys, *Histoire du droit criminel des peuples modernes*, VI, p. 11.

entirely dependent upon his judgment even the qualification of the criminal act, which, consequently, was itself not determined.[134]

It is not, then, in the regulation of punishments that the distinctive organization of this type of repression consists. It is, moreover, not in the institution of criminal procedure. The facts that we have just cited show quite well that that remained faulty for a long time. The only organization which meets us everywhere that there is punishment properly so called is that resident in the establishment of a tribunal. In whatever manner it is composed, whether it comprises all the people, or only a select number, whether or not it follows a regular procedure as much in the instruction of the affair as in the application of the punishment, because the infraction, instead of being judged by each, is submitted to the consideration of a constituted body, because the collective, reaction has a definite organ as an intermediary, it ceases to be diffuse; it is organized. The organization will be more complete the moment it exists.

Punishment consists, then, essentially in a passionate reaction of graduated intensity that society exercises through the medium of a body acting upon those of its members who have violated certain rules of conduct.

Thus, the definition we have given of crime quite easily explains all these characteristics of punishment.

III

Every strong state of conscience is a source of life; it is an essential factor of our general vitality. Consequently, everything that tends to enfeeble it wastes and corrupts us. There results a troubled sense of illness analogous to that which we feel when an important function is suspended or lapses. It is then inevitable that we should react energetically against the cause that threatens us with such diminution, that we strain to do away with it in order to maintain the integrity of our conscience.

In the first class of causes which produce this result, we must put the representation of a contrary state. A representation is not simply a mere image of reality, an inert shadow projected by things upon us, but it is a force which raises around itself a turbulence of organic and psychical phenomena. Not only does the nervous current which accompanies the ideation radiate to the cortical centres around the point where it originated and pass from one plexus to the next, but it gains a foothold in the motor centres where it determines movements, in the sensorial centres where it arouses images, sometimes excites

---

[134] Du Boys, *ibid.*, p. 14.

beginnings of illusions and may even affect vegetative functions.[135] This foothold is as much more considerable as the representation is itself more intense, as the emotional element is more developed. Thus, the representation of a sentiment contrary to ours acts in us in the same sense and in the same manner as the sentiment for which it is a substitute. It is as if it had itself become part of our conscience. It has, in truth, the same affinities, although less lively; it tends to evoke the same ideas, the same movements, the same emotions. It sets up a resistance to the play of our personal sentiment and, accordingly, enfeebles it by directing a great part of our energy in an opposing direction. It is as if a strange force were introduced by nature to upset the free functioning of our psychic life. That is why a conviction opposed to ours cannot manifest itself in our presence without troubling us; that is because, at the same time, it penetrates us, and finding itself in conflict with everything that it encounters, causes real disorders. Of course, in so far as the conflict ensues only between abstract ideas, there is nothing disastrous about it, because there is nothing deep about it. The realm of ideas is at the same time the most elevated and the most superficial in conscience, and the changes which it undergoes, not having any extended repercussions, have only feeble effects upon us. But when it is a question of a belief which is dear to us, we do not, and cannot, permit a contrary belief to rear its head with impunity. Every offense directed against it calls forth an emotional reaction, more or less violent, which turns against the offender. We inveigh against it, we work against it, we will to do something to it, and the sentiments so evolved cannot fail to translate themselves into actions. We run away from it, we hold it at a distance, we banish it from our society, etc.

We do not pretend, of course, that every strong conviction is necessarily intolerant. The current observation suffices to show the contrary. But external causes neutralize those whose effects we have just analyzed. For example, there can be a general sympathy between adversaries which sets bounds to their antagonism and attenuates it. But this sympathy must be stronger than this antagonism; otherwise it would not survive. Or else the two parties, face to face, turn from the conflict realizing that it solves nothing and content themselves with the retention of their former situations. They tolerate each other, not being able to conquer. The reciprocal tolerance which puts an end to religious wars is often of this nature. In all these cases, if the conflict of sentiments does not engender its natural consequences, that is not because it does not harbor them; it is because it is hindered in their production.

Moreover, they are useful as well as necessary. Besides arising from the causes producing them, they contribute to their maintenance.

---

[135] See Maudsley, *Physiologie de esprit*, tr. fr. p. 270.

All violent emotions really appeal to supplementary forces which come to render to the attacked sentiment the energy which the contradiction extorts from it. It has been sometimes said that choler was useless because it was only a destructive passion, but that is to see only one of its aspects. In fact, it consists of a superexcitation of latent and disposable forces which come to the aid of our personal sentiment in the face of the dangers by re-enforcing them. In a state of peace, the sentiment is not sufficiently armed for conflict. It would be in danger of succumbing if the passionate reserves were not available at the desired moment. Choler is nothing else than the mobilization of these reserves. It may even come about that the aid so evoked being more than needed, the discussion may have as its result the greater affirmation of our convictions, rather than their weakening.

But we know what degree of energy a belief or a sentiment can take solely because it is felt by the same community of men in relation with one another; the causes of this phenomenon are now well known.[136] Even as contrary states of conscience enfeeble themselves reciprocally, identical states of conscience, in exchanging, re-enforce one another. While the first detract, the second add. If anyone expresses before we do an idea which we have already thought of, the representation that we gain from it contributes to our own idea, superimposes itself, confounds itself with it, communicates to it whatever vitality it has. From this fusion grows a new idea which absorbs its predecessors and which, accordingly, is more vivid than each of those taken separately. That is why, in large assemblies, an emotion can acquire such violence. It is because the vivacity with which it is produced in each conscience has repercussions in all the others. It is not even necessary for us to experience a collective sentiment by ourselves, through our individual nature alone, for it to assume such an intensity for us, for what we add to it is after all a little thing. It suffices that we be not occupied refractorily to it, so that, penetrating from outside with a force that its origin gives it, it may impose itself upon us. Since, therefore, the sentiments which crime offends are, in any given society, the most universally collective that there are; since they are, indeed, particularly strong states of the common conscience, it is impossible for them to tolerate contradiction. Particularly if this contradiction is not purely theoretical, if it affirms itself not only by words, but by acts—when it is thus carried to its maximum, we cannot avoid rising against it passionately. A simple restitution of the troubled order would not suffice for us; we must have a more violent satisfaction. The force against which the crime comes is too intense to react with very much moderation. Moreover, it cannot do so without enfeebling itself, for it is thanks to the intensity of the

---

[136] See Espinas, *Sociétés animales, passim.*

reaction that it keeps alive and maintains itself with the same degree of energy.

We can thus explain a character of this reaction that has often seemed irrational. It is certain that at the bottom of the notion of expiation there is the idea of a satisfaction accorded to some power, real or ideal, which is superior to us. When we desire the repression of crime, it is not we that we desire to avenge personally, but to avenge something sacred which we feel more or less confusedly outside and above us. This something we conceive of in different ways according to the time and the place. Sometimes it is a simple idea, as morality, duty; most often we represent it in the form of one or several concrete beings: ancestors, divinity. That is why penal law is not alone essentially religious in origin, but indeed always retains a certain religious stamp. It is because the acts that it punishes appear to be attacks upon something transcendent, whether being or concept. It is for this very reason that we explain to ourselves the need for a sanction superior to a simple reparation which would content us in the order of purely human interests.

Assuredly, this representation is illusory. It is ourselves that we, in a sense, avenge, ourselves that we satisfy, since it is within us and in us alone that the offended sentiments are found. But this illusion is necessary. Since these sentiments have exceptional force because of their collective origin, their universality, their permanence, and their intrinsic intensity, they separate themselves radically from the rest of our conscience whose states are much more feeble. They dominate us; they are, so to speak, something superhuman, and, at the same time, they bind us to objects which are outside of our temporal life. They appear to us as an echo in us of a force which is foreign to us, and which is superior to that which we are. We are thus forced to project them outside ourselves, to attribute what concerns them to some exterior object. We know today how partial alienations of personality thus come about. This mirage is so inevitable that, under one form or another, it will grow until a repressive system appears. For, if this did not follow, we would not need collective sentiments of more than mediocre intensity, and in that case there would no longer be such a thing as punishment. Shall we say that the error will dissipate itself as soon as men are conscious of it? But we hardly know that the sun is an immense globe; we see it only as a disc of a few inches. This information can teach us to interpret our sensations; it cannot change them. Besides, the error is only partial. Since these sentiments are collective it is not us they represent in us, but society. Thus, in avenging them, it is surely society and not ourselves that we avenge, and moreover, it is something superior to the individual. It is thus wrong for us to seize upon this quasi-religious character of expiation and consider it as a sort of parasitic hypostatization. It is, on the contrary, an integral element of punishment. No doubt, it expresses its nature in a somewhat metaphorical manner, but the metaphor is not without truth.

Moreover, we know that the penal reaction is not uniform in all cases since the emotions which determine it are not always the same. They are, in effect, more or less lively according to the vivacity of the offended sentiment, and also according to the gravity of the offense suffered. A strong state reacts more than a feeble state, and two states of the same intensity react unequally according as they are more or less violently opposed. These variations are produced of necessity, and, moreover, they have their uses, since it is right that the appeal of forces be related to the importance of the danger. Were they too feeble, it would be insufficient; too violent, it would be a useless loss. Since the gravity of the criminal act varies in relation to the same factors, the proportionality that we observe everywhere between crime and punishment establishes itself with mechanical spontaneity, without there being any necessity for making learned suppositions for its calculation. What gives crimes grades is also that which gives punishments grades. The two scales cannot, consequently, fail to correspond, and this correspondence, to be necessary, must be useful at the same time.

As for the social character of this reaction, it comes from the social nature of the offended sentiments. Because they are found in all consciences, the infraction committed arouses in those who have evidence of it or who learn of its existence the same indignation. Everybody is attacked; consequently, everybody opposes the attack. Not only is the reaction general, but it is collective, which is not the same thing. It is not produced isolatedly in each one, but with a totality and a unity, nevertheless variable, according to the case. In effect, while opposite sentiments oppose each other, similar sentiments attract each other, and as strongly do they attract as they themselves are intense. As contradiction is an exasperating danger, it adds to their attractive force. Never do we feel the need of the company of our compatriots so greatly as when we are in a strange country; never does the believer feel so strongly attracted to his co-religionists as during periods of persecution. Of course, we always love the company of those who feel and think as we do, but it is with passion, and no longer solely with pleasure, that we seek it immediately after discussions where our common beliefs have been greatly combated. Crime brings together upright consciences and concentrates them. We have only to notice what happens, particularly in a small town, when some moral scandal has just been committed. They stop each other on the street, they visit each other, they seek to come together to talk of the event and to wax indignant in common. From all the similar impressions which are exchanged, from all the temper that gets itself expressed, there emerges a unique temper, more or less determinate according to the circumstances, which is everybody's without being anybody's in particular. That is the public temper.

Moreover, it alone has a specific use. In fact, the sentiments thus in question derive all their force from the fact that they are common to everybody. They are strong because they are uncontested. What adds the peculiar respect of which they are the object is that they are universally respected. But crime is possible only if this respect is not truly universal. Consequently, it implies that they are not absolutely collective. Crime thus damages this unanimity which is the source of their authority. If, then, when it is committed, the consciences which it offends do not unite themselves to give mutual evidence of their communion, and recognize that the case is anomalous, they would be permanently unsettled. They must re-enforce themselves by mutual assurances that they are always agreed. The only means for this is action in common. In short, since it is the common conscience which is attacked, it must be that which resists, and accordingly the resistance must be collective.

It remains for us to say why it is organized.

This last character will be explained if we realize that organized repression is not opposed to diffuse repression, but is distinguished from it only by a difference of degree; the reaction has more unity. The very great intensity and the very definite nature of the sentiments which punishment properly so called avenges, clearly accounts for this more perfect unification. If the traversed state is feeble, or if it is traversed only feebly, it can only determine a feeble concentration of outraged consciences. On the contrary, if it is strong, if the offense is serious, the whole group attacked masses itself in the face of the danger and unites, so to speak, in itself. They no longer are content with exchanging impressions when they find the occasion, of approaching each other here or there according to chance or the convenience of meeting, but the agitation which has gradually gained ground violently pushes all those who are alike towards one another and unites them in the same place. This material contraction of the aggregate, while making the mutual penetration of spirits more intimate, also makes all group-movements easier. The emotional reactions of which each conscience is the theatre are thus in most favorable condition for unification. If they were too diverse, however, whether in quality or in quantity, a complete fusion between these partially heterogeneous and irreducible elements would be impossible. But we know that the sentiments which determine them are very definite, and consequently very uniform. They participate in the same uniformity, and, accordingly, quite naturally lose themselves in one another, compounding in a unique resultant which serves as their substitute and which is exercised, not by each alone, but by the social body so constituted.

Many facts tend to prove that such was, historically, the genesis of punishment. We know that, in origin, the assembly of the people in their entirety functioned as the tribunal. If we look at the examples we just cited from the Pentateuch,[137] we shall observe these things as we have just described them. As soon as the news of a crime gets abroad, the people unite, and although the punishment may not be predetermined, the reaction is unified. In certain cases, indeed, the people themselves executed the sentence collectively as soon as it had been pronounced.[138] Thus, when the assembly became incarnated in the person of a chief, he became, totally or in part, the organ of penal reaction, and the organization guided itself conformably to the general laws of all organic development.

Thus, the nature of collective sentiments accounts for punishment, and, consequently, for crime. Moreover, we see anew that the power of reaction which is given over to governmental functionaries, once they have made their appearance, is only an emanation of that which has been diffuse in society since its birth. The one is only the reflex of the other. The extent of the first varies with that of the second. Let us add, moreover, that the institution of this power serves to maintain the common conscience itself. For it would be enfeebled if the organ which represents it did not partake of that which inspired it and the particular authority that it exercises. But it cannot participate in it unless all the acts which offend it are opposed and combated as those which offend the collective conscience, even though the collective conscience is not directly affected.

IV

Thus, the analysis of punishment confirms our definition of crime. We began by establishing inductively that crime consisted essentially in an act contrary to strong and defined states of the common conscience. We have just seen that all the qualities of punishment ultimately derive from this nature of crime. That is because the rules that it sanctions express the most essential social likenesses.

Thus we see what type of solidarity penal law symbolizes. Everybody knows that there is a social cohesion whose cause lies in a certain conformity of all particular consciences to a common type which is none other than the psychic type of society. In these conditions, not only are all the members of the group individually

---

[137] See above, footnote 131.

[138] See Thonissen, *Etudes*, etc. II, pp. 30 and 232. The witnesses of a crime sometimes play a preponderant role in the execution.

attracted to one another because they resemble one another, but also because they are joined to what is the condition of existence of this collective type; that is to say, to the society that they form by their union. Not only do citizens love each other and seek each other out in preference to strangers, but they love their country. They will it as they will themselves, hold to it durably and for prosperity, because, without it, a great part of their psychic lives would function poorly. Inversely, society holds to what they present in the way of fundamental resemblances because that is a condition of its cohesion. There are in us two consciences: one contains states which are personal to each of us and which characterize us, while the states which comprehend the other are common to all society.[139] The first represent only our individual personality and constitute it; the second represent the collective type and, consequently, society, without which it would not exist. When it is one of the elements of this latter which determines our conduct, it is not in view of our personal interest that we act, but we pursue collective ends. Although distinct, these two consciences are linked one to the other, since, in sum, they are only one, having one and the same organic substratum. They are thus solidary. From this results a solidarity *sui generis*, which, born of resemblances, directly links the individual with society. We shall be better able to show in the next chapter why we propose to call it mechanical. This solidarity does not consist only in a general and indeterminate attachment of the individual to the group, but also makes the detail of his movements harmonious. In short, as these collective movements are always the same, they always produce the same effects. Consequently, each time that they are in play, wills move spontaneously and together in the same sense.

It is this solidarity which repressive law expresses, at least whatever there is vital in it. The acts that it prohibits and qualifies as crimes are of two sorts. Either they directly manifest very violent dissemblance between the agent who accomplishes them and the collective type, or else they offend the organ of the common conscience. In one case as in the other, the force that is offended by the crime and which suppresses it is thus the same. It is a product of the most essential social likenesses, and it has for its effect the maintenance of the social cohesion which results from these likenesses. It is this force which penal law protects against all enfeeblement, both in demanding from each of us a minimum of resemblances without which the individual would be a menace to the unity of the social body, and in imposing upon us the respect for the symbol which expresses and

---

[139] To simplify the exposition, we hold that the individual appears only in one society. In fact, we take part in several groups and there are in us several collective consciences; but this complication changes nothing with regard to the relation that we are now establishing.

summarizes these resemblances at the same time that it guarantees them.

We thus explain why acts have been so often reputed criminal and punished as such without, in themselves, being evil for society. That is, just as the individual type, the collective type is formed from very diverse causes and even from fortuitous combinations. Produced through historical development, it carries the mark of circumstances of every kind which society has gone through in its history. It would be miraculous, then, if everything that we find there were adjusted to some useful end. But it cannot be that elements more or less numerous were there introduced without having any relation to social utility. Among the inclinations and tendencies that the individual has received from his ancestors, or which he has formed himself, many are certainly of no use, or cost more than they are worth. Of course, the majority are not harmful, for being, under such conditions, does not mean activity. But there are some of them remaining without any use, and those whose services are most incontestable often have an intensity which has no relation to their utility, because it comes to them, in part, from other causes. The case is the same with collective passions. All the acts which offend them are not dangerous in themselves, or, at least, are not as dangerous as they are made out to be. But, the reprobation of which these acts are the object still has reason for existing, whatever the origin of the sentiments involved, once they are made part of a collective type, and especially if they are essential elements, everything which contributes to disturb them, at the same time disturbs social cohesion and compromises society. It was not at all useful for them to be born, but once they have endured, it becomes necessary that they persist in spite of their irrationality. That is why it is good, in general, that the acts which offend them be not tolerated. Of course, reasoning in the abstract, we may well show that there is no reason for a society to forbid the eating of such and such a meat, in itself inoffensive. But once the horror of this has become an integral part of the common conscience, it cannot disappear without a social link being broken, and that is what sane consciences obscurely feel.[140]

The case is the same with punishment. Although it proceeds from a quite mechanical reaction, from movements which are passionate and in great part non-reflective, it does play a useful role. Only this role is not where we ordinarily look for it. It does not serve, or else only

---

[140] That does not mean that it is necessary to conserve a penal rule because, at some given moment, it corresponded to some collective sentiment. It has a *raison d'être* only if this latter is living and energetic. If it has disappeared or been enfeebled, nothing is vainer or worse than trying to keep it alive artificially or by force. It can even be that it was necessary to combat a practice which was common, but is no longer so, and opposes the establishment of new and necessary practices. But we need not enter into this casuistical problem.

serves quite secondarily, in correcting the culpable or in intimidating possible followers. From this point of view, its efficacy is justly doubtful and, in any case, mediocre. Its true function is to maintain social cohesion intact, while maintaining all its vitality in the common conscience. Denied so categorically, it would necessarily lose its energy, if an emotional reaction of the community did not come to compensate its loss, and it would result in a breakdown of social solidarity. It is necessary, then, that it be affirmed forcibly at the very moment when it is contradicted, and the only means of affirming it is to express the unanimous aversion which the crime continues to inspire, by an authentic act which can consist only in suffering inflicted upon the agent. Thus, while being the necessary product of the causes which engender it, this suffering is not a gratuitous cruelty. It is the sign which witnesses that collective sentiments are always collective, that the communion of spirits in the same faith rests on a solid foundation, and accordingly, that it is repairing the evil which the crime inflicted upon society. That is why we are right in saying that the criminal must suffer in proportion to his crime, why theories which refuse to punishment any expiatory character appear as so many spirits subversive of the social order. It is because these doctrines could be practiced only in a society where the whole common conscience would be nearly gone. Without this necessary satisfaction, what we call the moral conscience could not be conserved. We can thus say without paradox that punishment is above all designed to act upon upright people, for, since it serves to heal the wounds made upon collective sentiments, it can fill this role only where these sentiments exist, and commensurately with their vivacity. Of course, by warning already disturbed spirits of a new enfeeblement of the collective soul, it can even stop attacks from multiplying, but this result, however useful, is only a particular counter blow. In short, in order to form an exact idea of punishment, we must reconcile the two contradictory theories which deal with it: that which sees it as expiation, and that which makes it a weapon for social defense. It is certain that it functions for the protection of society, but that is because it is expiatory. Moreover, if it must be expiatory, that does not mean that by some mystical virtue pain compensates for the error, but rather that it can produce a socially useful effect only under this condition.[141]

The result of this chapter is this: there exists a social solidarity which comes from a certain number of states of conscience which are common to all the members of the same society. This is what repressive

---

[141] In saying that punishment, such as it is, has a *raison d'être* we do not intend to suggest that it is perfect and incapable of betterment. It is very evident, on the contrary, that having been produced, in great part, by very mechanical causes, it can be but very imperfectly adjusted to its role. The matter is only a question of justification in the large.

law materially represents, at least in so far as it is essential. The part that it plays in the general integration of society evidently depends upon the greater or lesser extent of the social life which the common conscience embraces and regulates. The greater the diversity of relations wherein the latter makes its action felt, the more also it creates links which attach the individual to the group; the more, consequently, social cohesion derives completely from this source and bears its mark. But the number of these relations is itself proportional to that of the repressive rules. In determining what fraction of the juridical system penal law represents, we, at the same time, measure the relative importance of this solidarity. It is true that in such a procedure we do not take into account certain elements of the collective conscience which, because of their smaller power or their indeterminateness, remain foreign to repressive law while contributing to the assurance of social harmony. These are the ones protected by punishments which are merely diffuse. But the same is the case with other parts of law. There is not one of them which is not complemented by custom, and as there is no reason for supposing that the relation of law and custom is not the same in these different spheres, this elimination is not made at the risk of having to alter the results of our comparison.

CHAPTER THREE. ORGANIC SOLIDARITY DUE TO THE DIVISION OF LABOR

I

The very nature of the restitutive sanction suffices to show that the social solidarity to which this type of law corresponds is of a totally different kind.

What distinguishes this sanction is that it is not expiatory, but consists of a simple *return in state.* Sufferance proportionate to the misdeed is not inflicted on the one who has violated the law or who disregards it; he is simply sentenced to comply with it. If certain things were done, the judge reinstates them as they would have been. He speaks of law; he says nothing of punishment. Damage-interests have no penal character; they are only a means of reviewing the past in order to reinstate it, as far as possible, to its normal form. Tarde, it is true, has tried to find a sort of civil penality in the payment of costs by the defeated party.[142] But, taken in this sense, the word has only a metaphorical value. For punishment to obtain, there would at least have to be some relation between the punishment and the misdeed, and for that it would be necessary for the degree of gravity of the misdeed to be firmly established. In fact, however, he who loses the litigation pays the

---

[142] Tarde, *Criminalité comparée,* p. 113.

damages even when his intentions were pure, even when his ignorance alone was his culpability. The reasons for this rule are different from those offered by Tarde: given the fact that justice is not rendered gratuitously, it appears equitable for the damages to be paid by the one who brought them into being. Moreover, it is possible that the prospect of such costs may stop the rash pleader, but that is not sufficient to constitute punishment. The fear of ruin which ordinarily follows indolence or negligence may keep the negotiant active and awake, though ruin is not, in the proper sense of the word, the penal sanction for his misdeeds.

Neglect of these rules is not even punished diffusely. The pleader who has lost in litigation is not disgraced, his honor is not put in question. We can even imagine these rules being other than they are without feeling any repugnance. The idea of tolerating murder arouses us, but we quite easily accept modification of the right of succession, and can even conceive of its possible abolition. It is at least a question which we do not refuse to discuss. Indeed, we admit with impunity that the law of servitudes or that of usufructs may be otherwise organized, that the obligations of vendor and purchaser may be determined in some other manner, that administrative functions may be distributed according to different principles. As these prescriptions do not correspond to any sentiment in us, and as we generally do not scientifically know the reasons for their existence, since this science is not definite, they have no roots in the majority of us. Of course, there are exceptions. We do not tolerate the idea that an engagement contrary to custom or obtained either through violence or fraud can bind the contracting parties. Thus, when public opinion finds itself in the presence of such a case, it shows itself less indifferent than we have just now said, and it increases the legal sanction by its censure. The different domains of the moral life are not radically separated one from another; they are, rather, continuous, and, accordingly, there are among them marginal regions where different characters are found at the same time. However, the preceding proposition remains true in the great majority of cases. It is proof that the rules with a restitutive sanction either do not totally derive from the collective conscience, or are only feeble states of it. Repressive law corresponds to the heart, the centre of the common conscience; laws purely moral are a part less central; finally, restitutive law is born in very ex-centric regions whence it spreads further. The more it becomes truly itself, the more removed it is.

This characteristic is, indeed, made manifest by the manner of its functioning. While repressive law tends to remain diffuse within society, restitutive law creates organs which are more and more specialized: consular tribunals, councils of arbitration, administrative tribunals of every sort. Even in its most general part, that which pertains to civil law, it is exercised only through particular functionaries: magistrates, lawyers, etc., who have become apt in this role because of very special training.

But, although these rules are more or less outside the collective conscience, they are not interested solely in individuals. If this were so, restitutive law would have nothing in common with social solidarity, for the relations that it regulates would bind individuals to one another without binding them to society. They would simply be happenings in private life, as friendly relations are. But society is far from having no hand in this sphere of juridical life. It is true that, generally, it does not intervene of itself and through its own movements; it must be solicited by the interested parties. But, in being called forth, its intervention is none the less the essential cog in the machine, since it alone makes it function. It propounds the law through the organ of its representatives.

It has been contended, however, that this role has nothing properly social about it, but reduces itself to that of a conciliator of private interests; that, consequently, any individual can fill it, and that, if society is in charge of it, it is only for commodious reasons. But nothing is more incorrect than considering society as a sort of third-party arbitrator. When it is led to intervene, it is not to put to rights some individual interests. It does not seek to discover what may be the most advantageous solution for the adversaries and does not propose a compromise for them. Rather, it applies to the particular case which is submitted to it general and traditional rules of law. But law is, above all, a social thing and has a totally different object than the interest of the pleaders. The judge who examines a request for divorce is not concerned with knowing whether this separation is truly desirable for the married parties, but rather whether the causes which are adduced come under one of the categories foreseen by the law.

But better to appreciate the importance of social action, we must observe it, not only at the moment when the sanction is applied, when the troubled relation is adjudicated, but also when it is instituted.

It is, in effect, necessary either to establish or to modify a number of juridical relations which this law takes care of and which the consent of the interested parties suffices neither to create nor to change. Such are those, notably, which concern the state of the persons. Although marriage is a contract, the married persons can neither form it nor break it at their pleasure. It is the same with all the other domestic relations and, with stronger reason, with all those which administrative law regulates. It is true that obligations properly contractual can be entered into and abrogated solely through the efforts of those desiring them. But it must not be forgotten that, if the contract has the power to bind, it is society which gives this power to it. Suppose that society did not sanction the obligations contracted for. They become simply promises which have no more than moral authority.[143] Every contract thus supposes that behind the parties implicated in it there is society very ready to intervene in order to gain respect for the engagements which have been made. Moreover, it lends this obligatory force only to contracts which have in themselves a social value, which is to say, those which conform to the rules of law. We shall see that its intervention is sometimes even more positive. It is present in all relations which restitutive law determines, even in those which appear most completely private, and its presence, though not felt, at least in normal circumstances, is none the less essential.[144]

Since rules with restitutive sanctions are strangers to the common conscience, the relations that they determine are not those which attach themselves indistinctly everywhere. That is to say, they are established immediately, not between the individual and society, but between restricted, special parties in society whom they bind. But, since society is not absent, it must be more or less directly interested, it must feel the repercussions. Thus, according to the force with which society feels them, it intervenes more or less concomitantly and more or less actively, through the intermediary of special organs charged with representing it. These relations are, then, quite different from those which repressive law regulates, for the latter attach the particular conscience to the collective conscience directly and without mediation; that is, the individual to society.

But these relations can take two very different forms: sometimes they are negative and reduce themselves to pure abstention; sometimes they are positive and co-operative. To the two classes of rules which determine these, there correspond two sorts of social solidarity which we must distinguish.

II

The negative relation which may serve as a type for the others is the one which unites the thing to the person.

Things, to be sure, form part of society just as persons, and they play a specific role in it. Thus it is necessary that their relations with the social organism be determined. We may then say that there is a solidarity of things whose nature is quite special and translates itself outside through juridical consequences of a very particular character.

The jurisconsults distinguish two kinds of rights: to one they give the name real; to the other, that of personal. The right of property, the

---

[143] And even this moral authority comes from custom, which is to say, from society.

[144] We must restrict ourselves to general indications, common to all the forms of restitutive law. Otherwheres will be found (Book I, ch. vii) numerous proofs of this truth for the part of this law which corresponds to the solidarity which the division of labor produces.

pledge, pertains to the first type; the right of credit to the second. What characterizes real rights is that only they give a preferential and successoral right. Thus, the right that I have in the thing excludes anyone else from coming to usurp what is mine. If, for example, a thing has been successively hypothecated to two creditors, the second pledge can in no wise restrain the rights of the first. Moreover, if my debtor alienates the thing in which I have a right of hypothecation, that is in no wise attacked, but the third party is held either to pay me or to lose what he has acquired. But for this to come about, it is necessary that the bond of law unite me directly and without the mediation of any other person to the thing determinate of my juridical personality. This privileged situation is, then, the consequence of the solidarity proper to things. On the other hand, when the right is personal, the person who is obligated to me can, in contracting new obligations, give me co-creditors whose right is equal to mine, and although I may have as security all the goods of my debtor, if he alienates them, they come out of my security and patrimony. The reason for this is that there is no special relation between these goods and me, but between the person of their owner and my own person.[145]

Thus we see what this real solidarity consists of; it directly links things to persons, but not persons among themselves. In a strict sense, one can exercise a real right by thinking one is alone in the world, without reference to other men. Consequently, since it is only through the medium of persons that things are integrated in society, the solidarity resulting from this integration is wholly negative. It does not lead wills to move toward common ends, but merely makes things gravitate around wills in orderly fashion. Because real rights are thus limited, they do not cause conflicts; hostility is precluded, but there is no active coming together, no consensus. Suppose an agreement of this kind were as perfect as possible; the society in which it exists—if it exists alone—will resemble an immense constellation where each star moves in its orbit without concern for the movements of neighboring stars. Such solidarity does not make the elements that it relates at all capable of acting together; it contributes nothing to the unity of the social body.

From the preceding, it is easy to determine what part of restitutive law this solidarity corresponds to: it is the body of real rights. But from the definition which has been given of them, it comes about that the law of property is the most perfect example of them. In effect, the most complete relation which can exist between a thing and a person is that

---

[145] It has sometimes been said that the quality of fatherhood, that of son, etc. were the object of real rights. (See Ortolan, *Instituts*, I, p. 660.) But these qualities are only abstract symbols of divers rights, some real (right of father over fortune of his minor children, for example), others personal.

which makes the former entirely dependent upon the latter. But this relation is itself very complex, and the different elements which go to make it up can become the object of many secondary real rights as well, such as usufruct, servitudes, usage, and habitation. We can then summarily say that real rights comprise the law of property in its different forms (literary, artistic, industrial, mobile, immobile) and its different modalities such as the second book of the French Civil Code regulates. In addition to this book, the French law recognizes four other real rights, but they are only auxiliary and eventual substitutes for personal rights: these are lien, pledge, gift, and hypothecation (articles 2071-2203). It is proper to add to them all that relates to the law of succession, wills, and, consequently, absence, since it creates, when declared, a sort of provisory succession. In effect, an inheritance is a thing or group of things in which the inheriting parties or the legatees have a real right, which may be acquired, *ipso facto* upon the decease of the owner, or may be available only by judicial act, as happens with indirect heirs and legatees of particular station. In all these cases, the juridical relation is directly established, not between one person and another, but between a person and a thing. The case is the same with testamentary donation, which is only the exercise of the real right which the owner has over his goods, or at least that portion of them which are disposable.

But there are relations of persons to persons which, though not real, are nevertheless as negative as the preceding and express a solidarity of the same nature.

In the first place, there are those which the exercise of actual real rights occasion. It is inevitable that the functioning of these should sometimes call forth the very persons of their detainers. For example, when a thing is added to another, the one who is reputedly owner of the first by that act becomes the owner of the second; only "he must pay to the other the value of the thing appropriated" (article 566). This obligation is evidently personal. Likewise, every owner of a separating wall who wishes to raise it must pay to the co-proprietor the loss accruing from the change (article 658). An individual legatee is obliged to address himself to the residuary legatee in order to obtain the deliverance of the thing bequeathed, although he may have the right to it from the death of the testator (article 1014). But the solidarity which these relations express does not differ from that of which we have just been speaking. They have been set up only to repair or prevent an injury. If the detainer of each real right could always exercise it without ever going beyond its limits, each would remain unto himself, and there would be no place for any juridical commerce. But, in fact, it endlessly happens that the different rights impinge on one another so that we cannot invoke one without encroaching upon others which limit it. For instance, the thing in which I have a right is found in someone else's hands; such is the case in a legacy. In another case, I cannot enjoy my right without harming someone else; such is the case with certain servitudes. These relations are then necessary in repairing wrong, if it has been done, or in preventing it; but there is nothing positive about them. They do not cause the people whom they put in contact with one another to concur; they do not demand any co-operation; but they simply restore or maintain, in the new conditions which are produced, this negative solidarity whose circumstances have troubled its functioning. Far from uniting, their task is rather to separate what has been united through the force of things, to re-establish the limits which have been transgressed and replace each in its proper sphere. They are so well identified with the relations of a thing to a person that the codifiers did not make a place apart for them, but have treated them just as they treated real rights.

Finally, the obligations which arise from a delict or quasi-delict have exactly the same character.[146] In truth, they force each to repair the damage which his fault has caused to the legitimate interests of another. They are thus personal, but the solidarity to which they correspond is evidently wholly negative, since they consist, not in serving, but in not harming. The link whose break they sanction is altogether external. The only difference there is between these relations and the preceding is that, in one case, the break comes from a fault, and in the other, from circumstances determined and foreseen by the law. But the troubled order is the same; it results, not in concurrence, but in pure abstention.[147] Moreover, those rights whose violation gives rise to these obligations are themselves real, for I am owner of my body, of my health, of my honor, of my reputation, in the same respect and in the same manner as I own the material things which are mine.

In short, the rules relative to real rights and to personal relations which are established in their turn form a definite system which has as its function, not to attach different parts of society to one another, but, on the contrary, to put them outside one another, to mark cleanly the barriers which separate them. They do not correspond to a positive social link. The very expression of negative solidarity which we have used is not perfectly exact. It is not a true solidarity, having its own existence and its special nature, but rather the negative side of every species of solidarity. The first condition of total coherence is that the parties who compose it should not interfere with one another through

---

[146] Art. 1382-1386 of the French Civil Code.—One might join together here the articles on the repetition of the improper.

[147] The contracting party that fails to keep his engagements is, himself, held to indemnify the other party. But, in this case, the damage-interests serve as sanction with a positive link. It is not for having erred that the violator of the contract pays, but for not having carried out the stated promise.

discordant movements. But this external accord does not make for cohesion; on the contrary, it supposes it. Negative solidarity is possible only where there exists some other of a positive nature, of which it is at once the resultant and the condition.

In effect, the rights of individuals, as much in themselves as in things, can be determined only thanks to some compromise and some mutual concessions, for everything which is accorded to some is necessarily abandoned by the others. It has sometimes been said that we can deduce the normal extent of the development of the individual from the concept of human personality (Kant), or from the notion of the individual organism (Spencer). That is possible, although the rigor of the rationalizations may be very contestable. In any event, what is certain is that in historical reality it is not on these abstract considerations that the moral order has been founded. In fact, in order that man might recognize the rights of others, not only logically, but in the practical workaday world, it was necessary that he consent to limit his rights, and, consequently, this mutual limitation could be made only in a spirit of agreement and accord. But, if we suppose a multitude of individuals without previous links between them, what reason could there have been to induce them to make these reciprocal sacrifices? The need for living in peace? But peace by itself is not a thing more desirable than war. War has its interest and its advantages. Have there not been some peoples and, at all times, some individuals in whom it was a passion? The instincts to which it responds are not less strong than those which peace satisfies. Doubtless, fatigue can for a time put an end to hostilities, but this bare armistice cannot be more durable than the temporary lassitude which occasions it. The case is even stronger in respect of the conclusions due solely to the triumph of force; they are as provisory and precarious as the treaties which put an end to international wars. Men have need of peace only as they are already united by some tie of sociability. In this case, the sentiments which incline them towards each other quite naturally moderate the urgings of egoism; and, from another standpoint, the society which envelops them, not being able to live except on condition of not being at every instant embroiled in conflicts, urges on them, and obliges them to make, necessary concessions.

It is true that we sometimes see independent societies agreeing to determine their respective rights over things, that is to say, their territories. But really, the extreme instability of these relations is the best proof that negative solidarity cannot alone suffice. If today, among cultivated peoples, it seems to have more force, if that part of international law which regulates what we might call the real rights of European societies has more authority than heretofore, it is because the different nations of Europe are much less independent of one another, because, in certain respects, they are all part of the same society, still incoherent, it is true, but becoming more and more self-conscious. What we call the equilibrium of Europe is a beginning of the organization of this society.

It is customary to distinguish carefully justice from charity; that is, simple respect for the rights of another from every act which goes beyond this purely negative virtue. We see in the two sorts of activity two independent layers of morality: justice, in itself, would only consist of fundamental postulates; charity would be the perfection of justice. The distinction is so radical that, according to partisans of a certain type of morality, justice alone would serve to make the functioning of social life good; generous self-denial would be a private virtue, worthy of pursuit by a particular individual, but dispensable to society. Many even look askance at its intrusion into public life. We can see from what has preceded how little in accord with the facts this conception is. In reality, for men to recognize and mutually guarantee rights, they must, first of all, love each other, they must, for some reason, depend upon each other and on the same society of which they are a part. Justice is full of charity, or, to employ our expressions, negative solidarity is only an emanation from some other solidarity whose nature is positive. It is the repercussion in the sphere of real rights of social sentiments which come from another source. There is nothing specific about it, but it is the necessary accompaniment of every type of solidarity. It is met with forcefully wherever men live a common life, and that comes from the division of social labor or from the attraction of like for like.

III

If, from restitutive law, we take away the rules of which we have just spoken, what remains constitutes a system, no less definite, which comprises domestic law, contract-law, commercial law, procedural law, administrative law, and constitutional law. The relations which are regulated by it are of a totally different character from the preceding ones; they express a positive union, a co-operation which derives, in essentials, from the division of labor.

The questions which domestic law resolves can be put under two headings:

1. How are the different domestic functions assigned? What is it to be a husband, a father, a legitimate child, a guardian?

2. What is the normal type for these functions and their relations?

It is to the first of these questions that the dispositions respond which determine the qualities and conditions required to contract marriage, the necessary formalities for the validation of marriage, the conditions of legitimate filiation, natural and adoptive, and the manner in which a guardian must be chosen.

It is, on the other hand, to the second question that the chapters respond which govern the respective rights and duties of the couple, the state of their relations in case of divorce, annulment of marriage, separation from bed and board, the *patria potestas*, the effects of adoption, the administration of guardianship and its relation with the ward, the role of the family council as against the first and the second, and the role of the relatives in cases of interdiction and judicial counsel.

Thus this part of civil law has for its object the determination of the manner in which the different familial functions are distributed, and what they ought to be in their mutual relations; that is to say, it expresses the particular solidarity which unites the members of a family in accordance with the division of domestic labor. It is true that we are not accustomed to view the family in this light. We believe, most often, that what brings about its cohesion is exclusively the community of sentiments and beliefs. There are, to be sure, so many things common to members of the familial group that the special character of tasks which devolve upon each of them easily escapes us. That is what made Comte say that the domestic union excluded "all thought of direct and continuous co-operation to a definite goal."[148] But the juridical organization of the family, of which we have just related the essential lines, shows the reality of these functional differences and their importance. The history of the family, from its very origins, is only an uninterrupted movement of dissociation in the course of which diverse functions, at first undivided and confounded one with another, have been little by little separated, constituted apart, apportioned among the relatives according to sex, age, relations of dependence, in a way to make each of them a special functionary of domestic society.[149] Far from being only an accessory and secondary phenomenon, this division of familial labor, on the contrary, dominates the entire development of the family.

The relation of the division of labor to contract-law is not less distinct.

In effect, the contract is, *par excellence*, the juridical expression of co-operation. There are, to be sure, contracts of benevolence, where only one of the parties is bound. If I give something unconditionally to somebody else, if I gratuitously take upon myself a trust or a commission, there result precise and determined obligations which I must perform. Properly speaking, however, there is no union between the contracting parties, since there are duties on one side only. But co-operation is not absent from the case; it is merely gratuitous or unilateral. What is a gift, for example, but an exchange without

---

[148] *Court de philosophie positive*, IV, p. 419.
[149] For further consideration on this point, see Book I, ch. vii of this work.

reciprocal obligations? These types of contracts are, then, only a variety of contracts truly co-operative.

Moreover, they are very rare, for it is very exceptional for acts of kindness to come under legal surveillance. As for the other contracts, which constitute the great majority, the obligations to which they give rise are correlative or reciprocal obligations, or events already effectuated. The involvement of one party results either from involvement assumed by the other, or from some service already rendered by the latter.[150] But this reciprocity is possible only where there is co-operation, and that, in its turn, does not come about without the division of labor. To co-operate, in short, is to participate in a common task. If this is divided into tasks qualitatively similar, but mutually indispensable, there is a simple division of labor of the first degree. If they are of a different character, there is a compound division of labor, specialization properly called.

This latter form of co-operation is, moreover, in great part, that which contract most generally expresses. The only one which has any other signification is the contract of society, and perhaps also the marriage-contract, in so far as it determines the contributive part of married people in the expenses of the household. Still, for this to be so, the contract of society must put all those associated on the same level, their shares must be identical, and their functions the same. Such a case is never exactly presented in matrimonial relations, in the conjugal division of labor. Over against these rare types, let us put the multiplicity of contracts which have as their object the adjustment of special, different functions to one another: contracts between buyer and seller, contracts of exchange, contracts between employers and workers, between tenant and landlord, between lender and borrower, between depositary and depositor, between inn-keeper and traveler, between principal and agent, between the creditor and the security of the debtor. In general fashion, the contract is the symbol of exchange. Thus, Spencer has not without justice qualified as a physiological contract the exchange of materials which is made at every instant between the different organs of the living body.[151] Thus it is clear that exchange always presupposes some division of. labor more or less developed. It is true that the contracts of which we have just been speaking still have a somewhat general character. But one must not forget that law deals only in generalities, in the great lines of social relations, those which are found identical in the different spheres of collective life. Thus, each of these types of contract implies a multitude of others, more particular, of which it is the common imprint and which it regulates in one sweep, but where the relations established are

---

[150] For example, in the case of a loan at interest.
[151] In his work on ethics.

between very special functions. Thus, in spite of the relative simplicity of this scheme, it suffices to make clear the extreme complexity of the facts which it encompasses.

This specialization of function is, indeed, more immediately apparent in the commercial code which regulates, pre-eminently, the contracts special to business: contracts between commission-agent and principal, between carrier and shipper, between the holder of a letter of exchange and the drawer, between the owner of a ship and his creditors, between the first and the captain and crew, between the granter of a charter and the charterer, between the lender and the borrower in gross, between the insurer and the insured. Even here, however, there is a large gap between the generality relative to the juridical prescriptions and the diversity of the particular functions whose relations they govern, as the important place given to custom in commercial law amply proves.

When the commercial code does not regulate contracts properly speaking, it determines what certain special functions ought to be, as those of the agent of exchange, of the broker, of the captain, of the adjudicator in case of bankruptcy, in order to assure the solidarity of all the parties involved in the commercial field.

Procedural law—which takes care of criminal, civil, or commercial procedure—plays the same role in the judicial scheme. The sanctions of juridical rules of all sorts can be applied only thanks to the interplay of a certain number of functions, of magistrates, of defense counsel, of prosecutors, of jurors, of plaintiffs and defendants, etc. Procedure fixes the way in which they must come into play and relate themselves. It announces what they must be and what part each plays in the general life of the organ.

It seems to us that in a rational classification of juridical rules procedural law ought to be considered only as a variety of administrative law. We do not see any radical difference separating the administration of justice from the rest of administration. Whatever it may be in this view, administrative law, properly called thus, regulates functions badly defined as administrative,[152] just as the preceding does for judicial functions. It determines their normal type and their relations either one with another, or with the diffuse functions of society. We would only have to drop a certain number of rules which are generally

---

[152] We are keeping the expression currently employed, but it will have to be defined, and we do not feel in position to do that. It seems to us, in the large, that these functions are those which are immediately placed under the action of governmental centres. But many distinctions would be necessary.

put under this rubric, because they have a penal character.[153] Finally, constitutional law does the same thing for governmental functions.

Some may be astonished to see united in the same class administrative and political law and what we ordinarily call private law. But, first of all, this unification imposes itself if we take as basis for the classification the nature of sanctions, and it does not seem to us possible to do otherwise if we wish to proceed scientifically. Moreover, in order completely to separate the two sorts of law, it would be necessary to admit that there is really a private law, whereas we believe that all law is public, because all law is social. All the functions of society are social, as all the functions of the organism are organic. Economic functions have the same character as the others. Moreover, even among the most diffuse, there are none which are not, in greater or lesser degree, under the supervision of action by governmental bodies. From this point of view, there is only a difference of degree between them.

To sum up: the relations governed by co-operative law with restitutive sanctions and the solidarity which they express, result from the division of social labor. We have explained, moreover, that, in general, co-operative relations do not convey other sanctions. In fact, it is in the nature of special tasks to escape the action of the collective conscience, for, in order for a thing to be the object of common sentiments, the first condition is that it be common, that is to say, that it be present in all consciences and that all can represent it in one and the same manner. To be sure, in so far as functions have a certain generality, everybody can have some idea of them. But the more specialized they are, the more circumscribed the number of those cognizant of each of them. Consequently, the more marginal they are to the common conscience. The rules which determine them cannot have the superior force, the transcendent authority which, when offended, demands expiation. It is also from opinion that their authority comes, as is the case with penal rules, but from an opinion localized in restricted regions of society.

Moreover, even in the special circles where they apply and where, consequently, they are represented in people, they do not correspond to very active sentiments, nor even very often to any type of emotional state. For, as they fix the manner in which the different functions ought to concur in diverse combinations of circumstances which can arise, the objects to which they relate themselves are not always present to consciences. We do not always have to administer guardianship,

---

[153] And also those concerning the real rights of moral persons in the administrative order, for the relations they determine are negative.

trusteeship,[154] or exercise the rights of creditor or buyer, etc., or even exercise them in such and such a condition. But the states of conscience are strong only in so far as they are permanent. The violation of these rules reaches neither the common soul of society in its living parts, nor even, at least not generally, that of special groups, and, consequently, it can determine only a very moderate reaction. All that is necessary is that the functions concur in a regular manner. If this regularity is disrupted, it behooves us to re-establish it. Assuredly, that is not to say that the development of the division of labor cannot be affective of penal law. There are, as we already know, administrative and governmental functions in which certain relations are regulated by repressive law, because of the particular character which the organ of common conscience and everything that relates to it has. In still other cases, the links of solidarity which unite certain social functions can be such that from their break quite general repercussions result invoking a penal sanction. But, for the reason we have given, these counter-blows are exceptional.

This law definitely plays a role in society analogous to that played by the nervous system in the organism. The latter has as its task, in effect, the regulation of the different functions of the body in such a way as to make them harmonize. It thus very naturally expresses the state of concentration at which the organism has arrived, in accordance with the division of physiological labor. Thus, on different levels of the animal scale, we can measure the degree of this concentration according to the development of the nervous system. Which is to say that we can equally measure the degree of concentration at which a society has arrived in accordance with the division of social labor according to the development of co-operative law with restitutive sanctions. We can foresee the great services that this criterion will render us.

IV

Since negative solidarity does not produce any integration by itself, and since, moreover, there is nothing specific about it, we shall recognize only two kinds of positive solidarity which are distinguishable by the following qualities:

1. The first binds the individual directly to society without any intermediary. In the second, he depends upon society, because he depends upon the parts of which it is composed.

2. Society is not seen in the same aspect in the two cases. In the first, what we call society is a more or less organized totality of beliefs

---

[154] That is why the law which governs the relations of domestic functions is not penal, although these functions are very general.

and sentiments common to all the members of the group: this is the collective type. On the other hand, the society in which we are solidary in the second instance is a system of different, special functions which definite relations unite. These two societies really make up only one. They are two aspects of one and the same reality, but none the less they must be distinguished.

3. From this second difference there arises another which helps us to characterize and name the two kinds of solidarity.

The first can be strong only if the ideas and tendencies common to all the members of the society are greater in number and intensity than those which pertain personally to each member. It is as much stronger as the excess is more considerable. But what makes our personality is how much of our own individual qualities we have, what distinguishes us from others. This solidarity can grow only in inverse ratio to personality. There are in each of us, as we have said, two consciences: one which is common to our group in its entirety, which, consequently, is not ourself, but society living and acting within us; the other, on the contrary, represents that in us which is personal and distinct, that which makes us an individual.[155] Solidarity which comes from likenesses is at its maximum when the collective conscience completely envelops our whole conscience and coincides in all points with it. But, at that moment, our individuality is nil. It can be born only if the community takes smaller toll of us. There are, here, two contrary forces, one centripetal, the other centrifugal, which cannot flourish at the same time. We cannot, at one and the same time, develop ourselves in two opposite senses. If we have a lively desire to think and act for ourselves, we cannot be strongly inclined to think and act as others do. If our ideal is to present a singular and personal appearance, we do not want to resemble everybody else. Moreover, at the moment when this solidarity exercises its force, our personality vanishes, as our definition permits us to say, for we are no longer ourselves, but the collective life.

The social molecules which can be coherent in this way can act together only in the measure that they have no actions of their own, as the molecules of inorganic bodies. That is why we propose to call this type of solidarity mechanical. The term does not signify that it is produced by mechanical and artificial means. We call it that only by analogy to the cohesion which unites the elements of an inanimate body, as opposed to that which makes a unity out of the elements of a living body. What justifies this term is that the fink which thus unites the individual to society is wholly analogous to that which attaches a thing to a person. The individual conscience, considered in this light, is a simple dependent upon the collective type and follows all of its

---

[155] However, these two consciences are not in regions geographically distinct from us, but penetrate from all sides.

movements, as the possessed object follows those of its owner. In societies where this type of solidarity is highly developed, the individual does not appear, as we shall see later. Individuality is something which the society possesses. Thus, in these social types, personal rights are not yet distinguished from real rights.

It is quite otherwise with the solidarity which the division of labor produces. Whereas the previous type implies that individuals resemble each other, this type presumes their difference. The first is possible only in so far as the individual personality is absorbed into the collective personality; the second is possible only if each one has a sphere of action which is peculiar to him; that is, a personality. It is necessary, then, that the collective conscience leave open a part of the individual conscience in order that special functions may be established there, functions which it cannot regulate. The more this region is extended, the stronger is the cohesion which results from this solidarity. In effect, on the one hand, each one depends as much more strictly on society as labor is more divided; and, on the other, the activity of each is as much more personal as it is more specialized. Doubtless, as circumscribed as it is, it is never completely original. Even in the exercise of our occupation, we conform to usages, to practices which are common to our whole professional brotherhood. But, even in this instance, the yoke that we submit to is much less heavy than when society completely controls us, and it leaves much more place open for the free play of our initiative. Here, then, the individuality of all grows at the same time as that of its parts. Society becomes more capable of collective movement, at the same time that each of its elements has more freedom of movement. This solidarity resembles that which we observe among the higher animals. Each organ, in effect, has its special physiognomy, its autonomy. And, moreover, the unity of the organism is as great as the individuation of the parts is more marked. Because of this analogy, we propose to call the solidarity which is due to the division of labor, organic.

At the same time, this chapter and the preceding furnish us with the means to calculate the part which remains to each of these two social links in the total common result which they concur in producing through their different media. We know under what external forms these two types of solidarity are symbolized, that is to say, what the body of juridical rules which corresponds to each of them is. Consequently, in order to recognize their respective importance in a given social type, it is enough to compare the respective extent of the two types of law which express them, since law always varies as the social relations which it governs.[156]

---

[156] To make these ideas precise, we develop in the following table, the classification of juridical rules which is found implicit in this chapter and the preceding:

CHAPTER FOUR. FURTHER PROOF OF THE PRECEDING

Because of the importance of the results of the preceding investigation, it will be well, before going further, to confirm them once more. This added verification is the more useful in that it will give us the opportunity for establishing a law which, while serving as proof, will also serve to clarify what is to follow.

If the two types of solidarity which we have just distinguished really have the juridical expression that we have suggested, the preponderance of repressive law over co-operative law ought to be just as great as the collective type is more pronounced and as the division of labor is more rudimentary. Inversely, commensurate with the development of individual types and the specialization of tasks, the proportion between the two types of law ought to become reversed. The reality of this relationship can be shown experimentally.

I

The more primitive societies are, the more resemblances there are among the individuals who compose them. Even Hippocrates in his work, *De Aere et Locis*, had said that the Scythians had an ethnic type, and not personal types. Humboldt remarks in his *Neuspanien*[157] that

---

I. Rules with Organized Repressive Sanction
(A classification of these rules will be found in chapter five)

II. Rules with Restitutive Sanction Determining

Negative or Abstentive Relations	Of the thing with the person	Law of property in its various forms (movable, immovable, etc.) Various modalities of the law of property (servitudes, usufruct, etc.)
	Of persons with persons	Determined by the normal exercise of real rights Determined by the violation of real rights
Positive Relations of Co-operation	Between domestic functions	
	Between diffuse economic functions	Contractual relations in general Special contracts
	Of administrative functions	Between themselves With governmental functions With diffuse functions of society
	Of governmental functions	Between themselves With administrative functions With diffuse political functions

---

[157] I, p. 116.

among barbarous peoples there is found a physiognomy peculiar to the horde rather than individual physiognomies. And the fact has been confirmed by a great many observers. "Even as the Romans found among the ancient Germans very great resemblances, so-called savages have the same effect upon a civilized European. In truth, the lack of experience may often be the principal cause which determines such a judgment from a traveler; . . . however, this inexperience could hardly produce this result if the differences to which civilized man is accustomed in his natal environment were not really more important than those that he meets with among primitive peoples. Well-known and often cited is the phrase of Ulloa that one who has seen an aboriginal American has seen all aboriginal Americans."[158] On the other hand, among civilized peoples, two individuals are distinguishable from each other at a glance, and no preparation is needed for such an observation.

Dr. Lebon has been able to establish in objective fashion this homogeneity growing proportionally as one goes back to origins. He has compared the crania indigenous to different races and different societies, and has found "that the differences in cranial volume existing among individuals of the same race . . . are as great as the race is more elevated in the scale of civilization. After grouping the cranial volumes of each race in progressive series, being careful to establish comparisons only in series numerous enough for the terms to be reliable in gradual fashion, I have found that the difference in volume between the greatest male adult cranium and the smallest is roughly 200 cubic centimeters in the case of the gorilla, 280 in the case of the pariahs of India, 310 among the Australians, 350 among the ancient Egyptians, 470 in the case of twelfth-century Parisians, 600 among modern Parisians, and 700 among the Germans."[159] There are even some peoples where the differences are non-existent. "The Andamans and the Todas are all alike. We can almost say the same for the Greenlanders. Five Patagonian crania that Broca has in his laboratory are identical."[160]

There is no doubt that the organic likenesses correspond to psychic likenesses. "It is certain," says Waitz, "that this great physical resemblance of the natives derives essentially from the absence of all strong psychic individuality, and from the state of inferiority of intellectual culture in general. The homogeneity of characters (*Gemüthseigenschaften*) is incontestable in the case of negroid peoples. In upper Egypt, the slave-trader appraises a slave according to his place of birth and not according to his individual character, for long

---

[158] Waitz, *Anthropologie der Naturvoelker*, I, pp. 75-76.
[159] *Les Sociétés*, p. 193.
[160] Topinard, *Anthropologie*, p. 393.

experience has taught him that the differences between individuals of the same tribe are insignificant beside those which are due to race. It is because of this that Nubas and Gallas are considered very faithful, northern Abyssinians treacherous and perfidious, the majority of others good domestic slaves, but not employable for manual labor; those of Fertit savage and prompt in wreaking vengeance."[161] Thus, originality is not simply very rare there, but it has no place. Everybody professes and practices, without demurring, the same religion; schisms and dissents are unknown; they would not be tolerated. But, at this time, religion comprises all, extends to all. It contains in a confused mass, besides beliefs properly religious, morality, law, the principles of political organization, and even science, or at least what passes for it. Religion even regulates details of private life. Consequently, to say that religious consciences are identical there—and this identity is absolute—is to imply that, save for the sensations pertaining to the organism and to the states of the organism, all individual consciences are composed of practically the same elements. Even sensible impressions themselves do not offer great diversity, because of the physical resemblances which individuals present.

It is a very prevalent notion, however, that civilization has for its aim the growth of social similitudes. "As human associations extend," says Tarde, "the diffusion of ideas following a regular geometric progression is more marked."[162] According to Hale,[163] it is an error to attribute to primitive peoples a certain uniformity of character, and he gives as proof the fact that the yellow and black races of the Pacific, who live side by side, are more sharply distinguished one from the other than two European peoples. Indeed, are not the differences which separate a Frenchman from an Englishman or a German less today than heretofore? In almost all European societies, law, morality, customs, even fundamental political institutions are nearly identical. We can equally notice that in the midst of the same country we no longer find today the same contrasts that we used to find. Social life no longer varies, or no longer varies so much from one province to another. In unified countries such as France, it is nearly the same in all regions, and this leveling is at its maximum among the cultivated classes.[164]

But these facts do not weaken our position at all. Certainly different societies tend to resemble each other more, but that is not the same as saying that the individuals who compose them do so. There is now less distance than heretofore between the Frenchman and the

---

[161] *Op. cit.*, I, p. 77.—Cf. *ibid.*, p. 446.

[162] *Lois de l'imitation*, p. 19.

[163] *Ethnography and philology of the United States*, p. 13, Philadelphia, 1846.

[164] That is what makes Tarde say: "The traveller who traverses several European countries observes more differences among the classes of people who have remained faithful to their old customs than among those of the higher classes." *Op. cit.*, p. 59.

Englishman, generally speaking, but that does not stop the contemporary Frenchmen from differing among themselves more than the Frenchmen of yesteryear. Indeed, it is even true that each province tends to lose its distinctive feature, but that does not deny that each individual partakes more and more of what is personal to him. The Norman is less different from the Gascon, the Gascon from the Lorrainian and the Provençal; they no longer have little in common with the traits common to all Frenchmen, but the diversity which the last, taken as a unit, present, continues to grow. For, if some provincial types which used to exist tend to merge with others and disappear, there remains, in their place, a very considerable number of individual types. There are no longer as many differences as there are great regions, but there are almost as many as there are individuals. Inversely, where each province has its personality, it is not the same in individuals. In relation to each other, they can be very heterogeneous, and yet be formed only of similar elements. This is the spectacle presented by political societies. Indeed, in the biological world, the protozoans are so greatly distinct from each other that it is impossible to classify them in species;[165] and yet, each is composed of perfectly homogeneous matter.

This opinion reposes, then, on a confusion of individual types and collective types, as provincial or national. It is surely true that civilization tends to render the second nugatory, but we wrongly conclude that it has the same effect upon the first, and that the uniformity becomes general. Far from the two types varying with each other, we shall see that the effacement of one is the necessary condition for the appearance of the other.[166] But there is never more than a restricted number of collective types in the midst of the same society, for it can comprise only a small number of races and regions different enough to produce such dissimilarities. On the other hand, individuals are susceptible to infinite diversification. The diversity is as great as the individual types are more highly developed.

The preceding likewise applies to occupational types. There are reasons for believing that they lose their old distinction, that the chasm which used to separate occupations, and particularly certain of them, is in process of being filled in. But what is certain is that in the interior of each occupation the differences are growing. Each individual is more and more acquiring his own way of thinking and acting, and submits less completely to the common corporate opinion. Moreover, if, from occupation to occupation, the differences are less marked, they are, in any case, more numerous, for occupational types have themselves been multiplied as labor has come to be more and more divided. If they no

---

[165] See Perrier, *Transformisme*, p. 235.

[166] See below, Book II, chs. ii and iii.—What we say there can serve at the same time to explain and confirm the facts that we are here establishing.

longer distinguish themselves from one another except through slight differences of emphasis, at least the emphases are more varied. The diversity is not, then, even from this point of view, less, although it may no longer manifest itself through violent and sharp contrasts.

We can rest assured, then, that the more one goes back in history, the greater the homogeneity. On the other hand, the further one approaches to the highest social types, the greater the development of the division of labor. Let us now see how the two forms of law that we have distinguished vary in different steps of the social scale.

II

As far as we can judge of the state of law in very inferior societies, it appears to be entirely repressive. "The savage," says Lubbock, "is in no part free. Throughout the entire world, the daily life of the savage is regulated by a number of customs (as imperious as laws), complicated and very importunate, of prohibitions and interdictions. Numerous severe rules, although not written, encompass all the acts of his life."[167] We know, of course, the extreme facility, among primitive peoples, with which ways of acting become transformed into traditional practices, and how great among them the force of tradition is. Ancestral customs are granted respect in such degree that their derogation leads to punishment.

But such observations necessarily lack precision, for nothing is as difficult to comprehend as these undulating customs. For our investigation to be conducted methodically, we must carry it, as far as possible, into the region of written laws.

The four last books of the Pentateuch, *Exodus, Leviticus, Numbers, Deuteronomy*, represent the oldest monument of this kind that we have.[168] In these four or five thousand verses, there is a relatively small number wherein laws which can rigorously be called other than repressive are set down. They relate to the following objects:

Law of property: Law of redemption; Jubilee;—Property of the Levites (*Leviticus*, xxv, 14-25, 29-34, and xxvii, 1-34).

Domestic law: Marriage (*Deuteronomy*, xxi, 11-14; xxiii, 5; xxv, 5-10; *Leviticus*, xxi, 7, 13, 14); Law of succession (*Numbers*, xxvii, 8-11 and xxvi, 8; *Deuteronomy*, xxi, 15-17);—Enslavement of natives

---

[167] Lubbock, *Les Origines de la civilisation*, p. 440. Cf. Spencer, *Principles of Sociology*, p. 435.

[168] We do not have to give our opinion on the real antiquity of the work—it is sufficient that it refer to a society of very inferior type—nor on the relative antiquity of the parts which compose it, for, from our point of view, they present the same character. We think of them as one.

and foreigners (*Deuteronomy*, xv, 12-17; *Exodus*, xxi, 2-11; *Leviticus*, xix, 20; xxv, 39-44; xxxvi, 44r-54).

Loans and wages: (*Deuteronomy*, xv, 7-9; xxiii, 19-20; xxiv, 6 and 10-13; xxv, 15).

Quasi-delicts: (*Exodus*, xxi, 18-33 and 33-35; xxii, 6 and 10-17).[169] *Organization of public functions*: Functions of priests (*Numbers*, x); of Levites (*Numbers*, iii and iv); of Elders (*Deuteronomy*, xxi, 19; xxii, 15; xxv, 7; xxi, 1; *Leviticus*, iv, 15); of Judges (*Exodus*, xviii, 25; *Deuteronomy*, i, 15-17).

Restitutive law—co-operative law in particular—holds a very minor position. Moreover, among the rules that we have just cited, many are not as foreign to penal law as appears at first glance, for they all bear the mark of religion. They all come, in the same degree, from the divinity; to violate them is to offend the divinity, and such offenses are sins which must be expiated. The Testament does not distinguish between commandments, but all of them consist of divine words which cannot be disobeyed with impunity. "If thou wilt not observe to do all the words of this law that are written in this book, that thou mayest fear this glorious and fearful name, *The Lord Thy God*; Then the Lord will make thy plagues wonderful, and the plagues of thy seed, even great plagues, and of long continuance, and sore sicknesses, and of long continuance."[170] The failure, even through error, to follow some precept, constitutes a sin and demands expiation.[171] Some threats of this kind, about whose penal nature there can be no doubt even directly sanction some of the rules that we have attributed to restitutive law. After deciding that a divorced woman could not be taken back by her husband, if, after remarriage, she obtained another divorce, the text adds: "For that is abomination before the Lord: *and thou shalt not cause the land to sin*, which the Lord thy God giveth thee for an inheritance."[172] Moreover, there is the verse in which the manner that wages ought to be paid is regulated: "At his day thou shalt give him his hire, neither shall the sun go down upon it; for he is poor, and setteth his heart upon it: *lest he cry against thee unto the Lord, and it be sin unto thee.*"[173] The indemnities which quasi-delicts give rise to are equally presented as veritable expiations. Thus we read in *Leviticus*: "And he that killeth any man shall surely be put to death. And he that killeth a beast shall make it good; beast for beast . . . breach for breach,

---

[169] All of the verses here brought together (less those referring to public functions) number 135.

[170] *Deuteronomy*, xxviii, 58-59.—Cf. *Numbers*, xv, 30-31.

[171] *Leviticus*, iv.

[172] *Deuteronomy*, xxiv, 4.

[173] *Deuteronomy*, xxv, 15.

eye for eye, tooth for tooth."[174] Reparation for damage caused seems to be assimilated into punishment for murder and to be regarded as an application of the *lex talionis*.

It is true that there is a certain number of precepts whose sanction is not specifically indicated; but we already know that it is certainly a penal sanction. The nature of the expressions employed is sufficient proof of this. Moreover, tradition teaches us that a corporal punishment was inflicted upon those who violated a negative precept, when the law did not formally stipulate such punishment.[175] In brief, in varying degree, all Hebrew law, such as we find it in the Pentateuch, bears an essentially repressive stamp. This is more marked in some spots, more latent in others, but its presence is felt everywhere. Because all the prescriptions that it lays down are commandments from God, placed, so to speak, under his direct suzerainty, they all owe to this origin an extraordinary prestige which renders them sacrosanct. Thus, when they are violated, public conscience does not content itself with a simple reparation, but demands expiation which avenges it. Since what gives penal law its peculiar character is the extraordinary authority of the rules which it sanctions, and since men have never known nor imagined any authority higher than that which the believer vests in God, law which is agreed to be the word of God himself cannot fail to be essentially repressive. We have even been able to say that all penal law is more or less religious, for its very soul is the sentiment of respect for a force superior to the individual man, for a power in some way transcendent, under some symbol which it makes penetrate into consciences, and this sentiment is also at the basis of all religiosity. That is why, in general fashion, repression dominates all law in lower societies. It is because religion completely pervades juridical life, as it does, indeed, all social life.

Indeed, this character is still very marked in the laws of Manou. We have only to look at the high rank accorded criminal justice in the system of national institutions. "To help the King in his duties," says Manou, "God made him the guiding genius of punishment, the protector of all living beings, the administrator of justice, his very son, whose essence is wholly divine. It is the fear of punishment which makes all mobile and immobile creatures do their duty and accomplish their tasks . . . Punishment rules humanity; punishment protects humanity. Punishment works while the world sleeps; punishment is justice, say the wise men. ... All classes would be torn asunder, all

---

[174] xxiv, 17, 18, 20.
[175] See Munck, *Palestine*, p. 216.—Seiden, *De Synedriis*, pp. 889-903, enumerates, following Maimonides, all the precepts which fall into this category.

barriers would be broken, there would be only confusion in the universe if punishment no longer held its sway."[176]

The law of the Twelve Tables refers to a society already much more advanced,[177] and much nearer to us, than was the Hebrew. The proof of this is that Roman society arrived at the city-type only after passing through the stage of society at which the Jews remained fixed, and going beyond it. We shall have further proof of this later.[178] Moreover, other facts serve as evidence for this short advance. First of all, we find in the law of the Twelve Tables all the principal germs of our actual law, whereas there is nothing common between Hebraic law and our law.[179] Accordingly, the law of the Twelve Tables is absolutely laic. If in primitive Rome some legislators such as Numa were thought to have received their inspiration from heaven, and if, accordingly, law and religion were then intimately linked, this alliance was certainly terminated at the time when the Twelve Tables were drawn up, for this juridical monument has been presented from its very inception as a wholly human work supervising only human relations. We find there some few dispositions concerning religious ceremonies, but they seem rather to partake of the quality of sumptuary laws. This more or less complete state of dissociation which we find between law and religion is one of the best signs by which we can recognize whether a society is more or less developed than another.[180]

Thus, criminal law no longer occupies the whole field. The rules sanctioned by punishments and those which have only restitutive sanctions are now very distinct from each other. Restitutive law is separated from repressive law which formerly absorbed it; it now has its own characteristics, its peculiar structure, its own individuality. It exists as a distinct juridical species, with special organs, and a special procedure. Co-operative law itself makes its appearance. We find in the Twelve Tables a domestic law and a contract-law.

---

[176] *Lois de Manou*, trans. Loiseleur, VII, v. 14-24.

[177] In speaking of one social type as being more advanced than another, we do not mean to suggest that the different social types are stages in one and the same ascending linear series, more or less elevated according to their historical places. It is, rather, certain that, if the genealogical table of social types could be completely drawn up, it would resemble a tufted tree, with a single trunk, to be sure, but with diverging branches. However, in spite of this tendency, the distance between two types is measurable; they are higher or lower. Surely we have the right to say of a type that it is above another when it began with the form of the latter and yet has gone above it. Such is certainly the case with a more elevated branch or bough.

[178] See Book I, ch. vi, 2.

[179] Contract-law, the law of wills, guardianship, adoption, etc. are things unknown in the Pentateuch.

[180] Cf. Walter, *op. cit.*, §§ 1 and 2; Voigt, *Die XII Tafeln*, I, p. 43.

Penal law, however, while losing its primitive preponderance, still remains great. In the 115 fragments of this law which Voigt has collated, there are only 66 which can be called restitutive; 49 have a distinct penal accent.[181] Consequently, penal law is not far from occupying half of the code that has come down to us. Moreover, what we have left can give us only a very incomplete idea of the importance which repressive law had at the time it was drawn up. For there are parts which were devoted to this type of law which must have been the most easily lost. It is to the jurisconsults of the classical epoch that we owe, almost exclusively, the redemption of the fragments, but they were much more interested in the problems of civil law than in those of criminal law. The latter does not easily lend itself to the delicious controversies which have always occupied the attentions of jurists. This general indifference towards it must have shrouded in darkness a good part of the ancient penal law of Rome. Moreover, even the authentic, complete text of the law of the Twelve Tables certainly did not contain all of it. For it spoke neither of religious crimes, nor domestic crimes, which were each judged by particular tribunals, nor of offenses against custom. We must take account, too, of the delay which penal law encounters in being codified. As it is engraven in all consciences, men do not see the need of writing it down in order to make it known. For all these reasons, we have the right to presume that, even in the fourth century in Rome, penal law still represented the greater part of juridical rules.

This preponderance is still more certain and evident if we compare it, not to all restitutive law, but only to that part of this law which corresponds to organic solidarity. At this time, there is small evidence that domestic law is already very advanced. Procedure, being cumbersome, is neither varied nor complex. Contract-law is only just being born. "The small number of contracts which ancient law recognizes," says Voigt, "contrasts in most striking fashion with the multitude of obligations which arise from the delict."[182] As for public law, besides still being very simple, it has, in large part, a penal character because it bears a religious stamp.

Beginning with this epoch, repressive law loses its relative importance. On the one hand, even supposing that it has not regressed in a great number of instances, that many acts which in origin were regarded as criminal had not ceased to be punished—and the contrary is certain for what concerns religious delicts—at least it has not perceptively grown. We know that from the time of the Twelve Tables the principal criminological types of Roman law were settled. On the

---

[181] Ten (which are sumptuary laws) make no express mention of a sanction, but there is no doubting their penal character.

[182] *XII Tafeln*, II, p. 448.

other hand, contract-law, procedure, public law, were further and further extended. As we advance, we see the infrequent and meager formulas that the law of the Twelve Tables comprised on these different points developing and multiplying until they became the voluminous systems of the classical epoch. Domestic law itself becomes complicated and diversified, as to primitive civil law there is added, little by little, praetorian law.

The history of Christian society offers us another example of the same phenomenon. Maine had already conjectured that, in comparing the different primitive laws, we would find the place of penal law to be as great as the societies were ancient.[183] The facts confirm this assumption.

The Salic law relates to a society less developed than was Rome in the fourth century. For although, as the latter, it had advanced beyond the social type at which the Hebrew people stopped, it was, however, less completely advanced. The traces are very much apparent, as we shall show later. Hence, penal law had a much greater importance there. In the 293 articles of which the text of the Salic law is composed, as Waitz has edited it,[184] there are only 25 (about 9%) which do not have a repressive character. They are those which relate to the constitution of the Frankish family.[185] Contract has not yet been divorced from penal law, for the refusal to execute the contractual engagement on the fixed day is subject to a penalty. Still the Salic law contains only a part of the penal law of the Franks, since it concerns only the crimes or the delicts for which a settlement is permitted. But there were certainly some which could not be bought off. If we consider that the *Lex* contained not one word about crimes against the State, nor about military crimes, nor religious crimes, then the preponderance of repressive law will appear even more considerable.[186]

There is already less repressive law in the law of the Burgundians which is more recent. In 311 articles, we have counted 98, that is, nearly one-third, which have no penal character. But this growth takes place particularly in domestic law, which is complicated in its relation to the law of things as well as its relation to the law of persons. Contract-law is not much more developed here than in the Salic law.

Finally, the law of the Visigoths, which is still more recent, and which concerns a still more cultivated people, evinces new progress in the same direction. Although penal law still predominates here, restitutive law has almost equal importance. We find here, in fact, a

---

[183] *Ancient Law.*
[184] *Das Alte Recht der Salischen Franken*, Kiel, 1846.
[185] Tit. xliv, xiv, xlvi, lix, lx, lxii.
[186] Cf. Thonissen, *Procédure de la loi salique*, p. 244.

complete code of procedure (Books I and II), a matrimonial and domestic law already highly developed (Book III, i and vi; Book IV). Finally, for the first time, a whole book, the fifth, is devoted to business transactions.

The absence of codification does not permit us to observe with the same precision this double development in all the course of our history, but it is incontestable that it followed the same direction. From this epoch, in fact, the juridical catalogue of crimes and delicts is already very complete. On the other hand, domestic law, contract-law, procedure, public law, are developed without interruption, and it is thus that the relation between the two parts of law that we have compared is finally found reversed.

Repressive law and co-operative law vary, then, exactly as the theory, which finds itself thus confirmed, foresaw. It is true that this predominance of repressive law in lower societies has sometimes been attributed to some other cause. It has been explained "by the habitual violence in the societies which begin to write their laws. The legislator has divided his work in proportion to the frequency of certain accidents of barbarous life."[187] Maine, who gives this explanation, does not find it complete. In reality, it is not only incomplete; it is false. First of all, it makes law an artificial creation of the legislator, since it would have been instituted to contradict public customs and react against them. But such a contention is today no longer tenable. Law expresses customs, and if it acts against them, it is with a force that it has borrowed from them. Where acts of violence are frequent, they are tolerated; their delictuous character is in inverse proportion to their frequency. Thus, among lower peoples, crimes against persons are more ordinary than in civilized societies. Thus, they are in the last degree of the penal scale. We can almost say that the attacks are as severely punished as they are rare. Moreover, what makes the state of penal law plethoric is not that our crimes today are the object of more extended provisions, but there exists a luxuriant criminality, peculiar to those societies, and which their pretended violence cannot account for: delicts against religious faith, against ritual, against ceremonial, against traditions of all sorts, etc. The real reason for this development of repressive rules is that at this moment in the evolutionary scheme the collective conscience is extensive and strong, since labor has not yet been divided.

These principles having been set up, the conclusion forthwith emerges from them.

---

[187] *Ancient Law.*

CHAPTER FIVE. PROGRESSIVE PREPONDERANCE OF ORGANIC SOLIDARITY; ITS CONSEQUENCES

I

It is enough to take a bird's-eye view of our Codes to see what a reduced place repressive law occupies in comparison with co-operative law. What is the former along side of the vast system formed by domestic law, contract-law, commercial law, etc.? The totality of relationships which come under penal regulation represent only the smallest fraction of general life; and, consequently, the ties which bind us to society and which come from the community of beliefs and sentiments are much less numerous than those which result from the division of labor.

It is true, as we have already remarked, that the common conscience and the solidarity which it produces are not entirely expressed by penal law. The former creates other ties than those whose break it punishes. There are some weaker and vaguer states of the collective conscience which make their action felt through the intermediary of custom, public opinion, without any legal sanction attaching to them, and which, moreover, contribute to the strength of social cohesion. But neither does co-operative law express all the links which the division of labor brings about, for it likewise gives us only a schematic representation from every part of life. In a multitude of cases, the relations of mutual dependence which unite the divided functions are regulated only by usage, and these unwritten rules certainly surpass in number those which are projections of repressive law, for they must be as diverse as the social functions themselves. The relation between them is, then, the same as that between the two types of law which they complement, and consequently, we can disregard them without modifying the calculated result.

If, however, we were to state this relation only in our actual societies and at the precise moment of their history at which we have arrived, one might think that it was due to temporary or, perhaps, pathological causes. But we have just seen that the closer a social type approaches ours, the more dominant cooperative law becomes. On the other hand, penal law has a greater place the further removed it is from our present organization. It is thus that this phenomenon is linked, not to some accidental and more or less morbid cause, but to the structure of our societies in their very essentials, since it develops further as the structure becomes more determined. Thus, the law that we established in our preceding chapter is doubly useful. Besides confirming the principles upon which our conclusion rests, it permits us to establish the generality of this conclusion.

But from this comparison alone we cannot yet deduce what part organic solidarity plays in the general cohesion of society. In effect, what makes the individual more or less strictly attached to his group is not only the greater or lesser multiplicity of the points of attachment, but also the variable intensity of the forces which hold him attached there. Accordingly, the ties which result from the division of labor, while being more numerous, would be weaker than the others, and the superior force of the latter would compensate for their numerical inferiority. But the contrary is the truth.

What truly measures the relative force of two social ties is the unequal facility with which they break down. The less resistant is evidently that one which breaks down under the less strain. But it happens that in lower societies, where solidarity rests solely, or nearly so, upon resemblances, breaks are more frequent and easier to bring about. In the beginning, as Spencer says, although man must unite himself in a group, he is not obliged to remain united to the same group. The Kalmucks and the Mongols abandon their chief when they find his authority oppressive, and pass on to others. The Abipones leave their chief without asking his permission and without incurring his displeasure, and they migrate with their family wherever they please.[188] In South Africa the Balondas migrate ceaselessly from one part of the country to the other. MacCulloch noticed the same phenomenon among the Koukis. Among the Germans every man who loved fighting could place himself under the military command of a chief of his own choosing. "Nothing was more ordinary and nothing seemed more legitimate. A man would arise in mid-assembly; he would announce that he was going to make an expedition to some place, against some enemy. Those who had confidence in him and who desired booty acclaimed him as their chief and followed him. . . . The social tie was too weak to hold men back from the temptations of a life of wandering and gain."[189] Waitz, in speaking generally of lower societies, says that, even where a directive power is established, each individual retains enough independence so that he may, at any moment, separate from his chief, "and rise up against him, if he is powerful enough for that, without such an act being considered criminal."[190] Even where the government is a despotism, says the same author, each man always has the liberty to secede with his family. Would not the rule according to which the Roman, made prisoner by the enemy, ceased to be part of the city, also be explained by the facility with which the social tie could be broken?

---

[188] *Principles of Sociology*, III, p. 381.

[189] Fustel de Coulanges, *Histoire des Institutions politiques de l'ancienne France*, Part I, p. 352.

[190] *Anthropologie*, etc., Part I, pp. 359-360.

It is quite otherwise as labor becomes divided. The different parts of the aggregate, because they fill different functions, cannot easily be separated. In the words of Spencer, if we separated from Middlesex its surrounding district, all operations would cease in a few days, due to shortage of materials. Separate the district where cotton is manufactured from Liverpool and other centres, and industry ceases, since the population will perish. Separate the mining populations from the neighboring populations which found metal or make clothing by machinery, and they would die socially, since they would die individually. Of course, when a civilized society undergoes a division such that one of its parts lives deprived of a central agency exercising its authority, it will not delay in setting up another, but it runs great risk of dissolution, and before reorganization reconstitutes a sufficient authority, it is exposed, for some time, to disorder and weakness.[191] It is for this reason that violent annexations, otherwise so frequent, more and more become delicate operations with uncertain success. Today, to detach a province from a country is to detach one or several organs of an organism. The life of the annexed region is profoundly troubled, separated as it is from the essential organs upon which it depends; but such mutilations and such troubles necessarily determine durable grief whose memory is not effaceable. Even for an isolated individual, it is not an easy thing to change nationalities, in spite of the very great likeness between different civilizations.[192] The opposite fact would not be less manifest. The more feeble solidarity is, that is to say, the more the social tie is loosened, the easier it ought to be for foreign elements to become part of societies. But, among lower peoples, naturalization is the most simple process in the world. Among the Indians of North America, every member of the clan has the right to introduce new members into it with a view to adopting them. Captives taken in war are either put to death or adopted into the clan. The women and children-prisoners are usually the object of clemency. Adoption does not confer only the tribal rights (clan-rights), but even the nationality of the tribe.[193] We know how easily Rome, in its early days, accorded the right of citizenship to homeless and conquered peoples.[194] It is particularly by such incorporations that primitive societies grow. For them to be thus penetrable, there could not be a very strong sense of their own unity or their own personality.[195] The contrary phenomenon

---

[191] *Principles of Sociology*, II, p. 54.

[192] We shall even see, in Chapter VII, that the tie which binds the individual to his family is just as strong, more difficult to break, as domestic labor is more divided.

[193] Morgan, *Ancient Society*, p. 80.

[194] Dionysius of Halicarnassus, I, 9.—Cf. Accarias, *Précis de droit romain*, I, §51.

[195] This fact is not at all irreconcilable with the fact that, in these societies, the stranger is an object of repulsion. He inspires such sentiments in so far as he remains a stranger. What we are saying is that he easily drops this stranger-quality in becoming

is observable where functions are specialized. The stranger, no doubt, can be provisionally introduced into the society, but the process by which he is assimilated and naturalized is long and complex. It is no longer possible without assent from the group, solemnly made manifest and brought about under special conditions.[196]

It may appear astonishing that a tie which binds the individual to the community by absorbing him into it can be broken or made with such facility. But what makes a social tie rigid is not what gives it resistive force. Because the parts of the aggregate, when united, only move together, it does not follow that they are obliged either to remain united or to perish. On the contrary, since they do not need each other, as each contains within himself all that social life consists of, he can go and carry it elsewhere. This can be done so much the more easily when the secessions are made by bands, for the individual is then constituted in such a way that he can only move with a band, even in order to separate himself from his group. On its part, society demands from each of its members, in so far as they are part of it, a uniformity of beliefs and practices. But as it can lose a certain number of its members without the economy of its internal life being disturbed, because social work is very little divided, it does not strongly oppose these departures. Indeed, where solidarity derives solely from resemblances, whoever does not deviate too much from the collective type is, without opposition, incorporated into the aggregate. There are no reasons for opposing him, and, indeed, if there are places vacant, there is good reason for accepting him. But where society is made up of a system of differentiated parts which mutually complement each other, new elements cannot be grafted upon the old without upsetting this equilibrium, without altering these relationships, and, accordingly, the organism resists intrusions which cannot produce anything but disturbance.

II

Not only, in a general way, does mechanical solidarity link men less strongly than organic solidarity, but also, as we advance in the scale of social evolution, it grows ever slacker.

The force of social links which have this origin vary with respect to the three following conditions:

1. The relation between the volume of the common conscience and that of the individual conscience. The links are as strong as the first more completely envelops the second.

---

naturalized.
   [196] We shall see, in Chapter VII, that the intrusions of strangers into familial society are as easily made as domestic work is less divided.

2. The average intensity of the states of the collective conscience. The relation between volumes being equal, it has as much power over the individual as it has vitality. If, on the other hand, it consists of only feeble forces, it can but feebly influence the collective sense. It will the more easily be able to pursue its own course, and solidarity will be less strong.

3. The greater or lesser determination of these same states. That is, the more defined beliefs and practices are, the less place they leave for individual divergencies. They are uniform moulds into which we all, in the same manner, couch our ideas and our actions. The *consensus* is then as perfect as possible; all consciences vibrate in unison. Inversely, the more general and indeterminate the rules of conduct and thought are, the more individual reflection must intervene to apply them to particular cases. But it cannot awaken without upheavals occurring, for, as it varies from one man to another in quality and quantity, everything that it produces has the same character. Centrifugal tendencies thus multiply at the expense of social cohesion and the harmony of its movements.

On the other hand, strong and defined states of the common conscience are the roots of penal law. But we are going to see that the number of these is less today than heretofore, and that it diminishes, progressively, as societies approach our social type. It is thus that the average intensity and the mean degree of determination of collective states have themselves diminished. From this fact, it is true, we cannot conclude that the total extent of the common conscience has narrowed, for it may be that the region to which penal law corresponds has contracted, and that the remainder have dilated. It can have fewer strong and defined states, and retaliate with a very great number of others. But this growth, if it is real, is altogether equivalent to that which is produced in the individual conscience, for the latter has, at least, grown in the same proportions. If there are more things common to all, there are many more that are personal to each. There is, indeed, every reason for believing that the latter have increased more than the former, for the differences between men have become more pronounced in so far as they are more cultivated. We have just seen that special activities are more developed than the common conscience. It is, therefore, at least probable that, in each particular conscience, the personal sphere is much greater than the other. In any case, the relation between them has at most remained the same. Consequently, from this point of view, mechanical solidarity has gained nothing, even if it has not lost anything. If, on the other hand, we discover that the collective conscience has become more feeble and vaguer, we can rest assured that there has been an enfeeblement of this solidarity, since, in respect of the three conditions upon which its power of action rests, two, at least, are losing their intensity, while the third remains unchanged.

To prove this, it would avail us nothing to compare the number of rules with repressive sanctions in different social types, for the number of rules does not vary exactly with the sentiments the rules represent. The same sentiment can, in effect, be offended in several different ways, and thus give rise to several rules without diversifying itself in so doing. Because there are now more ways of acquiring property, there are also more ways of stealing, but the sentiment of respect for the property of another has not multiplied itself proportionally. Because individual personality has developed and comprehends more aspects, there are more attacks possible against it, but the sentiment that they offend is always the same. It is necessary for us, then, not to number the rules, but to group them in classes and sub-classes, according as they relate to the same sentiment or to different sentiments, or to different varieties of the same sentiment. We shall thus constitute criminological types and their essential varieties, whose number is necessarily equal to that of strong and defined states of the common conscience. The more numerous the latter are, the more criminal types there ought to be, and, consequently, the variations of the one should exactly reflect the variations of the other. To make these ideas precise, we have united in the following table the principal types and their varieties which have been found in different kinds of society. It is quite evident that such a classification will be neither complete nor perfectly rigorous. For the conclusion that we wish to draw, however, it has a very sufficient exactitude. Surely it encompasses all the actual criminological types; we risk omitting only some which have disappeared. But as we wish to demonstrate capably the fact that their number has diminished, these omissions add fuel to our proposition.

RULES FORBIDDING ACTS CONTRARY TO COLLECTIVE SENTIMENTS

I

Having General Objects

Religious sentiments
- Positive (imposing the practice of the religion)
- Negative [196]
  - Relative to beliefs about divinity
  - Relative to worship
  - Relative to the organs of worship { Sanctuaries / Priests

National sentiments
- Positive (Positive civic obligations)
- Negative (Treason, civil war, etc.)

Domestic sentiments
- Positive
  - Paternal and filial
  - Conjugal
  - Of kinship in general
- Negative — The same

Sentiments relative to sexual relations
- Forbidden unions
  - Incest
  - Sodomy
  - Misalliances
- Prostitution
- Public decency
- Respect for minors

Sentiments relative to work
- Begging
- Vagabondage
- Intoxication [197]
- Penal regulation of work

Traditional diverse sentiments
- Relative to certain occupational usages
- Relative to burial
- Relative to food
- Relative to dress
- Relative to ceremonial
- Relative to usages of all sorts

Sentiments relative to the organ of the common conscience
- In so far as they are directly offended
  - Lèse-majesté
  - Plots against constituted authority
  - Outrages, violence against authority
  - Rebellion
- Indirectly [198]
  - Encroachment of private individuals on public functions
  - — Usurpations —
  - Public falsification
  - Impersonation of functionaries and diverse occupational misdeeds
  - Frauds to the detriment of the State
  - Disobedience of all sorts (administrative contraventions)

197 198 199

---

[197] The sentiments which we call positive are those which impose positive actions,

II

Having Individual Objects

Sentiments relative to the person of the individual	Murder, assault — suicide	
	Individual liberty { Physical Moral (Pressure in the exercise of civil rights)	
	Honor { Injuries, calumnies False witness	
Relative to the possessions of the individual	Robbery — swindling, abuse of confidence Diverse frauds	
Sentiments relative to the mass of individuals in respect of their persons or their goods	Counterfeiting — bankruptcy Arson Brigandage — pillage Public health	

III

It is enough to glance at this table to see that a large number of criminological types have progressively disappeared.

Today, the regulation of domestic life has almost entirely lost all penal character. We must except only adultery and bigamy. Still, adultery occupies a very exceptional place in the list of crimes, since the husband has the right to excuse the condemned wife. As for the duties of the other members of the family, they no longer have any repressive sanction. It was not always thus. The decalogue makes filial piety a social obligation. Thus, assault upon a parent,[200] or speaking evil of a parent,[201] or disobeying one's father[202] was punishable by death.

In the Athenian city-state, which, though similar in appearance to the Roman city-state, represents a more primitive type, legislation on this point was the same. Failure to perform familial duties gave rise to a special complaint, the γραφὴ κακώσεως. "Those who maltreated or insulted their parents or their superiors, who did not furnish them with means of existence which they required, who did not see to it that they

---

as the practice of the faith. The negative sentiments demand only abstinence. Between them there are only differences of degree. These differences, however, are important, for they mark out two moments in their development.

[198] It is probable that other ideas enter into reprobation of intoxication, notably the distaste which the state of degradation in which the intoxicated naturally finds himself inspires.

[199] We put in this class the acts which owe their criminal character to the power of reaction proper to the organ of the common conscience, at least in part. An exact separation between these two subclasses is, however, very difficult to make rules which is found implicit in this chapter and the preceding:

[200] *Exodus*, xxi, 17.—Cf. *Deuteronomy*, xxvii, 16.

[201] *Exodus*, xxi, 15.

[202] *Ibid.*, xxi, 18-21.

were given funerals in keeping with the dignity of their families . . . could be prosecuted by the γραφὴ κακώσεως."[203] The duties of relatives towards an orphan were sanctioned by actions of the same kind. But the obviously smaller penalties which were meted out to these delicts show that the corresponding sentiments did not have the same force or the same determination in Athens that they had in Judea.[204]

In Rome, a new regression even more defined is observed. The only familial obligations that penal law consecrates are those which link a client to his patron and conversely.[205] As for other domestic misdeeds, they are no longer punished except by the father of the family acting as disciplinarian. To be sure, the authority which he had permitted him to deal with them severely, but when he employs his power thus, he is not a public functionary, a magistrate charged with enforcing respect for the general law of the State in his house; but he is acting as a private citizen.[206] These sorts of infraction tend to become purely private affairs in which society has no interest. So domestic functions, little by little, are taken from the central part of the common conscience.[207]

Like has been the evolution of sentiments relative to the relations of the sexes. In the Pentateuch, sins against custom occupy a considerable place. A multitude of acts are treated as crimes which our laws no longer countenance as such: defilement of the fiancée (*Deuteronomy*, xxii, 23-27), union with a woman-slave (*Leviticus*, xix, 20-22), deception on the part of a deflowered girl who presents herself as a virgin at marriage (*Deuteronomy*, xxii, 13-21), sodomy (*Leviticus*, xviii, 22), bestiality (*Exodus*, xxii, 19), prostitution (*Leviticus*, xix, 29), and more specially prostitution of daughters of priests (*ibid.*, xxi, 19), incest, of which *Leviticus* (ch. xvii) lists no less than seventeen cases. All these crimes, moreover, are punished very severely; for the most part, by death. They are already less numerous in Athenian law, which

---

[203] Thonissen, *Droit pénal de la République athénienne*, p. 288.

[204] The punishment was not determined, but seems to have consisted in degradation. (See Thonissen, *op. cit.*, p. 291.)

[205] *Patronus, si clienti fraudem fecerit, sacer esto*, says the law of the Twelve Tables.—In the early life of the city, penal law was less foreign to domestic life. A *lex regia*, which tradition ascribes to Romulus, punished the child who had maltreated his parents (Festus, p. 230, see *Plorare*).

[206] See Voigt, *XII Tafeln*, II, p. 273.

[207] It may astonish some to hear talk of a regression of domestic sentiments among the Romans, the original home of the patriarchal family. We can only state the facts; what explains them is that the formation of the patriarchal family had taken from public life a host of elements, constituted as a sphere of private activity, a sort of interior conscience. A source of variations is thus opened which until then had not existed. From the day when familial life is taken from the jurisdiction of social action and put into the home, it varies from home to home, and domestic sentiments have lost their uniformity and their determination.

no longer punishes any but paid pederasty, pandering, intercourse with a pure woman-citizen outside of marriage, finally, incest, although we are badly informed on the constitutive characteristics of the incestuous act. The punishments were generally less severe. In the Roman city, the situation is very much the same, although all this part of legislation is more undetermined. We might say that it has lost its importance. "Pederasty, in the primitive city," says Rein, "without being provided for by law, was punished by the people, the censors, or by the head of the family with death, a penalty, or infamy."[208] The case was much the same with *stuprum* or illegitimate intercourse with a matron. The father had the right to punish his daughter; the people punished the same crime on complaint of the aediles by exacting a penalty or banishment.[209] It even seems that the repression of these delicts may be already, in part, a domestic and private affair. Today these sentiments no longer have any place in penal law except in two instances: when they are publicly offended, or the attack made upon the person of a minor, incapable of self-defense.[210]

The class of penal rules that we have put under the heading *diverse traditions* represents, in reality, a multitude of distinct criminological types, corresponding to different collective sentiments. But they have all, or nearly all, disappeared. In simple societies where tradition is all-powerful and where nearly everything is held in common, the most puerile usages become, by force of habit, imperative duties. At Tonkin, there are a host of failures to conform to conventions which are more severely punished than serious attacks on society.[211] In China, the doctor who has not correctly made out his prescription is punished.[212] The Pentateuch is filled with restrictions of the same kind. Without considering a very great number of semi-religious practices whose origin is evidently historical and all of whose force comes from tradition, food,[213] dress,[214] a thousand details of economic life are submitted to very extended regulation.[215] Such was still the case up to a certain point in the Greek city-states. "The State," says Fustel de Coulanges, "exercised its tyranny over the smallest things. At Locris, the law forbade men to drink pure wine. It was the usual thing for dress to be fixed invariably by the laws of each city-state. The laws of Sparta

---

[208] *Criminalrecht der Roemer*, p. 865.

[209] *Ibid.*, p. 869.

[210] We put under this rubric neither rape, nor violation, where other elements enter in. They are acts of violence more than acts of indecency.

[211] Post, *Bausteine*, I, p. 226.

[212] Post, *ibid.*—The case was the same in ancient Egypt. (See Thonissen, *Etudes sur l'histoire du droit criminel des peuples anciens*, I, p. 149.)

[213] *Deuteronomy*, xiv, 3 ff.

[214] *Ibid.*, xxii, 5, 11, 12, and xiv, 1.

[215] "Thou shalt not sow thy vineyard with two kinds of seed" (*ibid.*, xxii, 9).— "Thou shalt not plow with an ox and an ass together" (*ibid.*, 10).

regulated the coiffure of women, and the Athenian laws forbade carrying more than three dresses on a journey. In Rhodes, the law forbade shaving; at Byzantium, the law punished anyone who even possessed a razor. In Sparta, on the contrary, it forced every man to shave his mustache."[216] But the number of these delicts is already smaller. In Rome, we find no more than a few sumptuary prescriptions relative to women. In our time, we believe, it would be difficult to find any in our law.

But much the most important loss penal law suffered is that due to the total, or almost total, disappearance of religious crimes. Thus, a world of sentiments ceased to count among the strong and defined states of the common conscience. No doubt, when we remain content to compare our legislation on this matter with that of inferior social types taken in bulk, this regression appears so marked that we may doubt its normalcy and its durability. But when we closely follow the development of the facts, we see that this elimination has been regularly progressive. We see it become more and more complete as we advance from one social type to another, and it is consequently impossible for it to be due to some passing and fortuitous accident.

We could not enumerate all the religious crimes which the Pentateuch marks out and represses. The Jew had to obey all the commandments of the Law on pain of suppression. "But the soul that doeth aught with a high hand, whether he be home-born or a sojourner, the same blasphemeth Jehovah; and that soul shall be cut off from among his people."[217] Under this ruling, he was not only held not to do anything forbidden, but also to do everything ordered, such as having himself and his kin circumcised, of celebrating the sabbath, feast-days, etc. We do not need to recall how numerous these prescriptions are and with what terrible punishments they are sanctioned.

In Athens, the place of religious criminality was still very great. There was a special writ, the γραφὴ ἀσεβείας, designed to deal with attacks against the national religion. Its sphere was certainly very extensive. "From all appearances, Attic law did not clearly define crimes and delicts which were qualified as ἀσέβεια, so that a large place was left to the discretion of the judge."[218] The list, however, was certainly shorter than in Hebrew law. Moreover, they are all, or nearly all, delicts of action, not of abstention. The principal ones that are cited are, in effect, the following: the denial of beliefs relating to the gods to their existence, to their role in human affairs; the profanation of feast-days, of sacrifices, of games, of temples and altars; the violation of the right of asylum, failure to show respect to the dead, the omission or

---

[216] *Cite antique*, p. 266.

[217] *Numbers*, xv, 30.

[218] Meier and Schoemann, *Der attische Process*, 2nd ed., p. 367.

alteration of ritual practices by the priest, initiating the vulgar into the mysteries, plucking the sacred olives, frequenting of temples by people who have been forbidden to enter.[219] The crime consisted, then, not in not celebrating the cult, but in disturbing it by positive acts or words.[220] There is no proof that the introduction of new divinities needed to be regularly authorized and was treated as an impiety, although the natural elasticity of this accusation permitted such an interpretation of the case.[221] It is evident, moreover, that the religious conscience had to be less intolerant in the land of the sophists and of Socrates than in a theocratic society such as the Hebrew. In order for philosophy to be born and develop there, it was necessary for traditional beliefs not to be so strong that they prevented its hatching.

In Rome, there is even less prescription of individual consciences. Fustel de Coulanges has justly insisted upon the religious character of Roman society, but compared to earlier peoples, the Roman State was much less penetrated with religious feeling.[222] Political functions, very early separated from religious functions, subordinated them. "Thanks to this preponderance of the political principle and to the political character of the Roman religion, the State did not lend its authority to religion except in so far as the attacks directed against it also menaced statehood indirectly. The religious beliefs of foreign States and of foreigners living in the Roman Empire were tolerated, if they were kept within bounds and did not tread upon the State's authority."[223] But the State intervened if its citizens turned towards strange divinities, and, by that, weakened the national religion. "However, this point was treated less as a question of law than as an interest of high administration, and action was taken against them according to the exigency of the circumstances, by edicts of warning and prohibition or by punishments ranging up to death."[224] The religious processes certainly did not have as much importance in Roman criminal justice as they had in Athens. We do not find any juridical institution there which recalls the γραφή ἀσεβείας.

Not only are crimes against religion more clearly determined and less numerous, but many of them have descended one or several degrees. The Romans did not put them all on the same level, but

---

[219] we reproduce the list of Meier and Schoemann, *op. cit.*, p. 368. Cf. Thonissen, *op. cit.*) ch. ii.

[220] Fustel de Coulanges says, it is true, that according to a text of Pollux (viii, 46), the celebration of feast-days was obligatory. But the text cited speaks of a positive profanation, and not of abstention.

[221] Meier and Schoemann, *op. cit.*, p. 369.—Cf. *Dictionnaire des Antiquités*, art. *Asebeia*.

[222] Fustel de Coulanges himself admits that this character was much more marked in the Athenian city-state (*La Cité*, ch. xviii, last lines).

[223] Rein, *op. cit.*, pp. 887-888.

[224] Walter, *op. cit.*, § 804.

distinguished *scelera expiabilia* from *scelera inexpiabilia.* The first required only an expiation which consisted of a sacrifice offered to the gods.[225] No doubt, this sacrifice was a punishment in the sense that the State could enforce its accomplishment, because the act which the guilty one had done contaminated society and might incur the wrath of the gods. But it is a punishment of an entirely different character from death, confiscation, exile, etc. Yet these faults, so easily redeemable, were the ones that Athenian law punished with the greatest severity. They were:

1. Profanation of any *locus sacer*;
2. Profanation of any *locus religiosus*;
3. Divorce in case of marriage *per confarreationem*;
4. The coming of a male issue from such a marriage;
5. Exposure of a dead person to the rays of the sun;
6. The accomplishment without bad intention of some one of the *scelera inexpiabilia.*

In Athens, profanation of temples, any troubling of religious ceremonies, sometimes even the smallest infraction of ritual[226] were punished with death.

In Rome, there were real punishments only against attacks which were both very serious and intentional. The only *scelera inexpiabilia* were really the following:

1. All intentional failure of duty on the part of functionaries to take care of the auspices or to accomplish the *sacra*, or, even more, their profanation;
2. The doing of a *legis actio* by a magistrate on a forbidden day, and that intentionally;
3. The intentional profanation of *feriae* by acts forbidden in such cases;
4. Incest committed by a vestal or with a vestal.[227]

Christianity has often been reproached for its intolerance. From this point of view, however, it realized considerable progress over preceding religions. The religious conscience of Christian societies, even at the time when the faith was at its height, called forth a penal reaction only when it was attacked by some infamous action, when one

---

[225] Marquardt, *Roemische Staatsverfassung*, 2nd ed., vol. III, p. 185.

[226] For evidence of these facts, see Thonissen, *op. cit.*, p. 187.

[227] According to Voigt, *XII Tafeln*, I, pp. 450-455.—Cf. Marquardt, *Roemische Alterthümer*, VI, p. 248.—We put aside one or two *scelera* which had a lay character, as well as religious, and we count as such only those which are direct offenses against divine things.

attacked it openly. Separated from temporal life much more completely than it was at Rome, it could no longer impose the same authority and had to hem itself in more with a defensive attitude. It no longer demanded repression of infractions of minor import as those we have just spoken of, but only those that menaced some one of its fundamental principles, and the number of these was not great, for the faith, in becoming spiritual, more general and more abstract, became, at the same time, simplified. Sacrilege, of which blasphemy is only one variety, heresy under various forms, are hereafter considered the only religious crimes.[228] The list continues to diminish, thus evincing that the strong and defined sentiments themselves became less numerous. How could it be otherwise? Everybody knows that the Christian religion is the most idealistic that has ever existed. Thus, it is made up of articles of faith which are very broad and very general, rather than of particular beliefs and determined practices. That is how it comes about that the dawn of free thought under Christianity was relatively precocious. Since its origin, different schools have been founded, and even opposing sects. Hardly had Christian societies begun to organize themselves in the Middle Ages than scholasticism appeared, the first systematic effort of free thought, the first source of differences. The rights of discussion are from the first recognized. It is not necessary to show that its development since then has served to accentuate this. It thus comes about that religious criminality ended by completely departing, or almost completely departing, from penal law.

IV

Thus, there are a number of criminological types which have progressively disappeared without any compensation, for no new ones replaced those which disappeared. If we prohibit begging, Athens punished idleness.[229] There is no society where attacks against national sentiments or national institutions have ever been tolerated. Their repression seems to have been greater heretofore; consequently, there is reason for believing that the corresponding sentiments have been weakened. The crime of *lèse-majesté*, if heretofore widely applied, tends more and more to disappear.

---

[228] Du Boys, *op. cit.*, VI, pp. 62 ff. Still it is necessary to notice that the severity with which religious crimes were treated is a late development. In the ninth century, sacrilege is still relievable by paying thirty livres (Du Boys, V, p. 231). An ordinance of 1226, for the first time, sanctioned the death-penalty for heretics. We can thus see that the enforcement of punishments against crimes is an abnormal phenomenon, due to exceptional circumstances, and that it did not partake of the normal development of Christianity.

[229] Thonissen, *op. cit.*, p. 363.

It has sometimes been said, however, that crimes against the individual person were not known among lower peoples, that robbery and murder were even respected there. Lombroso has recently tried to take up this thesis. He holds "that crime, with the savage, is not an exception, but the general rule . . . that it is not considered a crime by anybody."[230] But, in support of this position, he cites only some rare, equivocal facts interpreted uncritically. Thus, he is forced to identify robbery with the practice of communism or with international brigandage.[231] But, because property is common to all the members of the group, it does not at all follow that the law relating to robbery was recognized. Robbery can exist only in so far as there is property.[232] Moreover, because one society does not find pillaging upon neighboring nations revolting, we cannot conclude that it tolerates the same practices in its internal relations and does not protect its nationals from one another. But it is internal brigandage with impunity that we must establish. There is, it is true, a text of Diodorus and another of Aulus Gellius[233] which would make one believe that such license existed in ancient Egypt. But these texts are contradicted by everything that we know of Egyptian civilization: "How can we admit," Thonissen very justly says, "tolerance of robbery in a country where . . . the laws pronounced the sentence of death upon him who lived by illicit gain; where the simple alteration of weight or size was punishable by the loss of both hands?"[234] We can seek by means of conjectures[235] to put together the facts that writers have inexactly reported to us, but the inexactitude of their recital is undoubted.

As for the homicides of which Lombroso speaks, they are always done under exceptional circumstances. They are so many acts of war, so many religious sacrifices or the result of the absolute power that a barbarous despot exercises over his subjects, or a father over his children. But what must be shown is the absence of any rule which, in principle, proscribes murder. Among these particularly extraordinary examples there is not one which conduces to such a conclusion. The fact that under special conditions there is a departure from this rule does not prove that it does not exist. Do we not, indeed, meet with such exceptions even in contemporary societies? Is a general who sends a

---

[230] *L'homme criminel*, French trans., p. 36.

[231] "Even among civilized peoples," says Lombroso, in support of his thesis, "it took a long time to establish private property" (p. 36).

[232] This must not be forgotten in judging certain ideas of primitive peoples concerning robbery. Where communism is recent, the link between the thing and the person is still weak; that is to say, the right of an individual in a thing is not as strong as it is today, nor, accordingly, are the attacks against this right so serious. It is not that robbery is so much tolerated; it does not exist where private property is non-existent.

[233] Diodorus, I, 39; Aulus Gellius, *Nodes Atticae*, XI, 18.

[234] Thonissen, *Études*, etc., I, 168.

[235] The conjectures are very simple. (See Thonissen and Tarde, *Criminalité*, p. 40.)

regiment to certain death in order to save the rest of the army acting otherwise than the priest who sacrifices a victim to appease the national god? Are not people killed in war? Does not the husband who puts to death an adulterous wife enjoy, in certain cases, a relative impunity, if not an absolute? The sympathy with which murderers and robbers are sometimes treated is not more demonstrative. Individuals can admire the courage of a man without, in principle, tolerating his act.

Besides, the conception which is at the base of this doctrine is contradictory in its terms. It supposes, in effect, that primitive peoples are devoid of all morality. But from the moment that men form a society, as rudimentary as it may be, there are of necessity rules which govern their relations, and, consequently, an ethic which, while it does not resemble ours, nonetheless exists. Moreover, if there is one rule common to all these moral precepts, it is certainly that which forbids attacks upon the person, for men who resemble each other cannot live together without each manifesting to his fellows a sympathy which opposes every act of a kind to make them suffer.[236]

What there is of truth in this theory is, first, that the laws protective of the person sometimes overlook a part of the population, such as children and slaves. Second, it is legitimate to believe that this protection is now assured with a more jealous care, and, consequently, that the collective sentiments which correspond to it have become stronger. But there is nothing in these facts which invalidates our conclusion. If all the individuals who make up society are today equally protected, no matter what their status, this tempering of customs is due, not to the appearance of a really new penal rule, but to the extension of an old one. In the beginning, it was forbidden to make an attempt upon the life of members of the group; but this did not apply to children and slaves. Now that we no longer make this distinction, some acts which were not criminal have become punishable. But that is simply because there are more persons in society, and not because there are more collective sentiments. It is not they which have multiplied, but the objects to which they relate themselves. If, however, there is place for admitting that the respect of society for the individual has become stronger, it does not follow that the central region of the common conscience is more extended. No new elements have entered, since this sentiment has always existed and has always had enough energy not to tolerate its abrogation. The only change that has been produced is that an old element has become more intense. But this simple growth of

---

[236] This proposition does not contradict that other, often enunciated in this work, that, at this moment of evolution, the individual personality does not exist. That which makes it imperfect is the psychic personality, and especially the superior psychic personality. But individuals always have a distinct organic life, and this suffices to give birth to this sympathy, although it becomes stronger when personality is more developed.

strength cannot compensate for the multiple, serious losses that we have observed.

Thus, viewed in the large, the common conscience consists less and less of strong, determined sentiments. Thus it comes about that the average intensity and mean degree of determination of collective states are always diminishing, as we have stated. Even the very restrained growth that we have just observed only serves to confirm this result. It is, indeed, remarkable that the only collective sentiments that have become more intense are those which have for their object, not social affairs, but the individual. For this to be so, the individual personality must have become a much more important element in the life of society, and in order for it to have acquired this importance, it is not enough for the personal conscience of each to have grown in absolute value, but also to have grown more than the common conscience. It must have been emancipated from the yoke of the latter, and, consequently, the latter must have fallen from its throne and lost the determinate power that it originally used to exercise. In short, if the relation between these two had remained the same, if both had developed in volume and vitality in the same proportions, the collective sentiments which relate to the individual would themselves also have remained the same. Above all, they would not be the only ones that had grown. For they depend uniquely on the social value of the individual factor, and that, in its turn, is determined, not by the absolute development of this factor, but by the relative extent of the part which relates to it in the totality of social phenomena.

V

We could further verify this proposition by proceeding with a method that we shall only briefly indicate.

We do not actually possess any scientific notion of what religion is. To obtain this, we would have to treat the problem by the same comparative method that we have applied to the question of crime, and that is an effort which has not yet been made. It has often been said that religion was, at each moment of history, the totality of beliefs and sentiments of all sorts relative to the relations of man with a being or beings whose nature he regarded as superior to his own. But such a definition is manifestly inadequate. In effect, there is a multitude of rules, either of conduct or of thought, which are certainly religious, and which, moreover, apply to relations of an entirely different sort. Religion forbids the Jews eating certain meats and orders them to dress in a certain fixed way. It imposes such and such an opinion concerning the nature of man and things, concerning the origin of the world. It often governs even juridical, moral, and economic relations. Its sphere of action extends, then, beyond the commerce of man with the divine.

We know for certain, moreover, that a religion without God exists.[237] This alone should be sufficient to show that we no longer have the right to define religion in terms of the idea of God. Finally, if the extraordinary authority that the believer vests in the divinity can account for the particular prestige of everything religious, it remains to be explained how men have been led to attribute such an authority to a being who, in the opinion of the world, is in many cases, if not always, a product of their imagination. Nothing comes from nothing; this force must have come to him from somewhere, and, consequently, this formula does not get to the heart of the matter.

But this element aside, the sole characteristic that all ideas such as religious sentiments equally present seems to be that they are common to a certain number of people living together, and that, besides, they have an average intensity that is quite elevated. It is, indeed, a constant fact that, when a slightly strong conviction is held by the same community of men, it inevitably takes on a religious character. It inspires in consciences the same reverential respect as beliefs properly religious. It is, thus, very probable—this brief exposition, of course, is not rigorous proof—that religion corresponds to a region equally very central in the common conscience. It remains, it is true, to circumscribe this region, to distinguish it from that to which penal law corresponds, and with which, moreover, it is often either wholly or in part confused. These questions are left to study, but their solution does not directly affect the highly probable conjecture that we have just made.

But, if there is one truth that history teaches us beyond doubt, it is that religion tends to embrace a smaller and smaller portion of social life. Originally, it pervades everything; everything social is religious; the two words are synonymous. Then, little by little, political, economic, scientific functions free themselves from the religious function, constitute themselves apart and take on a more and more acknowledged temporal character. God, who was at first present in all human relations, progressively withdraws from them; he abandons the world to men and their disputes. At least, if he continues to dominate it, it is from on high and at a distance, and the force which he exercises, becoming more general and more indeterminate, leaves more place to the free play of human forces. The individual really feels himself less *acted upon*; he becomes more a source of spontaneous activity. In short, not only does not the domain of religion grow at the same time and in the same measure as temporal life, but it contracts more and more. This regression did not begin at some certain moment of history, but we can follow its phases since the origins of social evolution. It is, thus, linked to the fundamental conditions of the development of societies, and it shows that there is a decreasing number of collective

---

[237] Buddhism (see article on Buddhism in the *Encyclopédie des sciences religeuses*).

beliefs and sentiments which are both collective enough and strong enough to take on a religious character. That is to say, the average intensity of the common conscience progressively becomes enfeebled.

This proof has an advantage over the preceding; it permits us to establish that the same law of regression applies to the representative element of the common conscience quite as completely as to the affective element. Through penal law, we can reach only phenomena of sensibility, whereas religion comprehends, besides sentiments, ideas and doctrines.

The decrease in the number of proverbs, adages, dicta, etc. as societies develop, is another proof that the collective representations move towards indetermination.

Among primitive peoples, formulas of this type are very numerous. The greater part of the races of west Africa, as Ellis says, possess an abundant collection of proverbs; there is at least one for each circumstance of life, a fact which is common to the majority of peoples who have made little progress in civilization.[238] Advanced societies are somewhat fertile in this regard only during the early years of their existence. Later, not only do they not produce any new proverbs, but the old ones die out little by little, lose their proper acceptation and end even by no longer being communicated. The proof of this is that it is particularly in lower societies that they find their most fertile field, and that today they are found maintained only in the least elevated classes.[239] But a proverb is a condensed statement of a collective idea or sentiment relative to a determined category of objects. It is, indeed, impossible that there be some beliefs and sentiments of this character without their being fixed in this form. As every thought tends towards an expression adequate to it, if it is common to a certain number of individuals, it necessarily ends by being enclosed in a formula which is equally common to them. Every function which endures makes an organ in its own image. It is thus wrong to explain the decline of proverbs by speaking of our realistic taste and our scientific temper. We do not carry over into conversational language such a care for precision nor such a disdain for images. On the contrary, we find a great deal of relish in the old proverbs which have come down to us. Moreover, the image is not an inherent element in the proverb; it is one of the means, but not the only one, by which collective thought condenses itself. These short formulas end, however, by becoming much too narrow to encompass the diversity of individual sentiments. Their unity no longer has any relation to the divergences which are existent. Thus, they manage to maintain themselves only by assuming a

---

[238] *The Ewe-Speaking Peoples of the Slave Coast*, p. 258, London, 1890.

[239] Wilhelm Borchardt, *Die Sprichwörtlichen Redensarten*, XII, Leipzig, 1888.—Cf. v. Wyss, *Die Sprichwörter bei den Roemischen Komikern*, Zurich, 1889.

very general signification, and ultimately disappear. The organ atrophies because the function is no longer exercised; that is to say, because there are fewer quite defined collective representations to enclose in a determined form.

Thus, everything tends to prove that the evolution of the common conscience takes place in the manner we have indicated. Truly, it progresses less than individual consciences. In any case, it becomes feebler and vaguer in its entirety. The collective type loses its background, its forms become more abstract and more indecisive. No doubt, if this decadence were, as has often been believed, an original product of our most recent civilization and a unique happening in the history of societies, we might ask if it will endure. But, in reality, it has pursued this course in an uninterrupted manner since the most distant times. That is what we are showing. Individualism, free thought, dates neither from our time, nor from 1789, nor from the Reformation, nor from scholasticism, nor from the decline of Graeco-Latin polytheism or oriental theocracies. It is a phenomenon which begins in no certain part, but which develops without cessation all through history. Assuredly, this development is not straightforward. New societies which replace old social types never begin their careers where their predecessors left off. How could that be possible? What the child continues is not the old age or mature age of its parents, but their own infancy. If, then, we wish to reckon the course that has been run, we must consider successive societies at the same epoch of their life. We must compare Christian societies of the Middle Ages with primitive Rome, the latter with the original Greek city-state, etc. We find, then, that this progress, or, if one wishes, this regression, is accomplished, so to speak, without a break in continuity. This is an inevitable law against which it would be absurd to inveigh.

This is not to say, however, that the common conscience is threatened with total disappearance. Only, it more and more comes to consist of very general and very indeterminate ways of thinking and feeling, which leave an open place for a growing multitude of individual differences. There is even a place where it is strengthened and made precise: that is the way in which it regards the individual. As all the other beliefs and all the other practices take on a character less and less religious, the individual becomes the object of a sort of religion. We erect a cult in behalf of personal dignity which, as every strong cult, already has its superstitions. It is thus, if one wishes, a common cult, but it is possible only by the ruin of all others, and, consequently, cannot produce the same effects as this multitude of extinguished beliefs. There is no compensation for that. Moreover, if it is common in so far as the community partakes of it, it is individual in its object. If it turns all wills towards the same end, this end is not social. It thus occupies a completely exceptional place in the collective conscience. It is still from society that it takes all its force, but it is not to society that it attaches us; it is to ourselves. Hence, it does not constitute a true social fink. That is why we have been justly able to reproach the theorists who have made this sentiment exclusively basic in their moral doctrine, with the ensuing dissolution of society. We can then conclude by saying that all social links which result from likeness progressively slacken.

This law, in itself, is already enough to show the tremendous grandeur of the role of the division of labor. In sum, since mechanical solidarity progressively becomes enfeebled, life properly social must decrease or another solidarity must slowly come in to take the place of that which has gone. The choice must be made. In vain shall we contend that the collective conscience extends and grows stronger at the same time as that of individuals. We have just proved that the two terms vary in a sense inverse to each other. Social progress, however, does not consist in a continual dissolution. On the contrary, the more we advance, the more profoundly do societies reveal the sentiment of self and of unity. There must, then, be some other social link which produces this result; this cannot be any other than that which comes from the division of labor.

If, moreover, one recalls that even where it is most resistant, mechanical solidarity does not link men with the same force as the division of labor, and that, moreover, it leaves outside its scope the major part of phenomena actually social, it will become still more evident that social solidarity tends to become exclusively organic. It is the division of labor which, more and more, fills the role that was formerly filled by the common conscience. It is the principal bond of social aggregates of higher types.

This is a function of the division of labor a good deal more important than that ordinarily assigned to it by economists.

CHAPTER SIX. PROGRESSIVE PREPONDERANCE OF ORGANIC SOLIDARITY; ITS CONSEQUENCES (*Continued*)

I

Thus, it is an historical law that mechanical solidarity which first stands alone, or nearly so, progressively loses ground, and that organic solidarity becomes, little by little, preponderant. But when the way in which men are solidary becomes modified, the structure of societies cannot but change. The form of a body is necessarily transformed when the molecular affinities are no longer the same. Consequently, if the preceding proposition is correct, there ought to be two social types which correspond to these two types of solidarity.

If we try to construct intellectually the ideal type of a society whose cohesion was exclusively the result of resemblances, we should have to conceive it as an absolutely homogeneous mass whose parts were not distinguished from one another. Consequently, they would have no arrangement; in short, it would be devoid of all definite form and all organization. It would be the veritable social protoplasm, the germ whence would arise all social types. We propose to call the aggregate thus characterized, *horde.*

It is true that we have not yet, in any completely authentic fashion, observed societies which, in all respects, complied with this definition. What gives us the right to postulate their existence, however, is that lower societies, those which are most closely akin to primitivity, are formed by a simple repetition of aggregates of this kind. We find an almost perfectly pure example of this social organization among the Indians of North America. Each Iroquois tribe, for example, contains a certain number of partial societies (the largest ones comprise eight) which present all the characteristics we have just mentioned. The adults of both sexes are on a plane of equality. The sachems and chiefs, who are at the head of these groups and by whose council the common affairs of the tribe are administered, do not enjoy any superiority. Kinship itself is not organized, for we cannot give this name to the distribution of the mass in generations. In the late epoch when we observed these peoples, there were, indeed, some special obligations which bound the child to its maternal relatives, but these relations come to very little and are not sensibly distinguishable from those which bind the child to other members of society. Originally, all persons of the same age were kin in the same degree.[240] In other cases, we are even nearer the horde. Fison and Howitt describe Australian tribes which consist of only two such divisions.[241]

We give the name *clan* to the horde which has ceased to be independent by becoming an element in a more extensive group, and that of *segmental societies with a clan-base* to peoples who are constituted through an association of clans. We say of these societies that they are segmental in order to indicate their formation by the repetition of like aggregates in them, analogous to the rings of an earthworm, and we say of this elementary aggregate that it is a clan, because this word well expresses its mixed nature, at once familial and political. It is a family in the sense that all the members who compose it are considered as kin of one another, and they are, in fact, for the most part consanguineous. The affinities that the community of blood brings about are principally those which keep them united. Moreover, they

---

[240] Morgan, *Ancient Society*, pp. 62-122.
[241] *Kamilaroi and Kurnai.* This state has, however, been passed through by the Indian societies of America. (See Morgan, *op. cit.*)

sustain relations with one another that we can term domestic, since we also find them in societies whose familial character is uncontested: I mean collective punishment, collective responsibility, and, as soon as private property makes its appearance, mutual inheritance. But, on the other hand, it is not a family in the proper sense of the word, for, in order to partake of it, it is not necessary to have any definite relations of consanguinity with other members of the clan. It is enough to present an external criterion which generally consists in using the same name. Although this sign is thought to denote a common origin, such a civil state really constitutes a proof which is not very demonstrative and very easy to imitate. Thus, the clan contains a great many strangers, and this permits it to attain dimensions such as a family, properly speaking, never has. It often comprises several thousand persons. Moreover, it is the fundamental political unity; the heads of clans are the only social authorities.[242]

We can thus qualify this organization as politico-familial. Not only has the clan consanguinity as its basis, but different clans of the same people are often considered as kin to one another. Among the Iroquois, they treat each other, according to circumstances, as brothers or as cousins.[243] Among the Jews, who present, as we shall see, the most characteristic traits of the same social organization, the ancestor of each of the clans which compose the tribe is believed to be descended from the tribal founder, who is himself regarded as one of the sons of the father of the race. But this denomination has the inconvenience, in comparison with the preceding, of not putting in relief that which gives the peculiar structure to these societies.

But, in whatever manner we name it, this organization, just as the horde, of which it is only an extension, carries with it no other solidarity than that derived from likenesses, since the society is formed of similar segments and these in their turn enclose only homogeneous elements. No doubt, each clan has its own features and is thereby distinguished from others, but also the solidarity is proportionally more feeble as they are more heterogeneous, and inversely. For segmental organization to be possible, the segments must resemble one another; without that, they would not be united. And they must differ; without this, they would lose themselves in each other and be effaced.

---

[242] If, in its pure state, as we at least believe, the clan is made up of an undivided family which is confused, later particular families, distinct from one another, appear on the foundation of primitive homogeneity. But this appearance does not alter the essential traits of the social organization that we are describing; that is why this is no place to stop. The clan remains the political unity, and as families are similar and equal, society remains formed of similar and homogeneous segments, although, besides these primitive segments, new segmentations begin to appear, but of the same kind.

[243] Morgan, *op.cit.*, p. 90.

According to the societies, the two contrary necessities are satisfied in different proportions, but the social type remains the same.

Now we are leaving the domain of pre-history and conjecture. Not only is there nothing hypothetical about this social type, but it is almost the most common among lower societies, and we know that they are the most numerous. We have already seen that it was general in America and in Australia. Post shows that it is very frequent among the African negroes.[244] The Hebrews remained in it to a late date, and the Kabyles never passed beyond it.[245] Thus, Waitz, wishing to characterize the structure of these peoples in a general way, people whom he calls *Naturvoelker*, gives the following picture in which will be found the general lines of the organization that we have just described: "As a general rule, families live one beside the other in great independence, and little by little develop a grouping of small societies [clans][246] which have no definite constitution, so long as internal conflicts or an external danger, such as war, does not lead one or several men to disengage themselves from the mass and become leaders. Their influence, which rests peculiarly on their personal titles, only extends and has sway within marked limits set forth by the confidence and patience of the others. Every adult remains in the eyes of such a chief in a state of complete independence. That is why such people, without any other internal organization, are held together only by external circumstances and through the habit of common life."[247]

The disposition of the clans in the interior of the society, and, accordingly, its configuration, can, of course, vary. Sometimes, they are simply juxtaposed so as to form a linear series; such is the case among many of the Indian tribes of North America.[248] Sometimes—and this is a mark of a more elevated organization—each of them is involved in a much greater group which, formed by the union of several clans, has its own life and a special name. Each of these groups, in its turn, can be involved with several others in another aggregate still more extensive, and from this series of successive involvements there results the unity of the total society. Thus, among the Kabyles, the political unity is the clan, constituted in the form of a village (*djemmaa or thaddart*); several *djemmaa* form a tribe (*arch'*), and several tribes form the confederation (*thak' ebilt*), the highest political society that the Kabyles know. The same is true among the Hebrews; the clan (which is so erroneously

---

[244] *Afrikanische Jurisprudenz,* I.

[245] See Hanoteau and Letourneux, *La Kabylie et les Coutumes kabyles,* II, and Masqueray, *Formation des cités chez les populations sedentaires de l'Algérie,* ch. v.

[246] Waitz erroneously presents the clan as derivative from the family. The contrary is the case. Even if this description is important because of the competency of its author, it lacks some precision.

[247] *Anthropologie,* I, p. 359.

[248] Morgan, *op. cit.,* pp. 153 ff.

translated as the *family*) is a vast society which encompasses thousands of persons, descended, according to tradition, from the same ancestor.[249] A certain number of *families* composed the tribe and the union of the twelve tribes formed the totality of the Hebrew people.

These societies are such typical examples of mechanical solidarity that their principal physiological characteristics come from it.

We know that, in them, religion pervades the whole social life, but that is because social life is made up almost exclusively of common beliefs and of common practices which derive from unanimous adhesion a very particular intensity. Retracing by analysis of only classical texts until an epoch completely analogous to that of which we are speaking, Fustel de Coulanges has discovered that the early organization of these societies was of a familial nature, and that, moreover, the primitive family was constituted on a religious base. But he has mistaken the cause for the effect. After setting up the religious idea, without bothering to establish its derivation, he has deduced from it social arrangements,[250] when, on the contrary, it is the latter that explain the power and nature of the religious idea. Because all social masses have been formed from homogeneous elements, that is to say, because the collective type was very developed there and the individual type in a rudimentary state, it was inevitable that the whole psychic life of society should take on a religious character.

Thus does communism arise, a quality so often noted among these peoples. Communism, in effect, is the necessary product of this special cohesion which absorbs the individual in the group, the part in the whole. Property is definitive only of the extension of the person over things. Where the collective personality is the only one existent, property also must be collective. It will become individual only when the individual, disengaging himself from the mass, shall become a being personal and distinct, not only as an organism, but also as a factor in social life.[251]

---

[249] Thus, the tribe of Reuben, which comprised in all *f out families*, consisted of, according to *Numbers* (xxvi, 7), more than forty-three thousand adults above twenty years. (Cf. *Numbers*, ch. iii, 15 ff.; *Joshua*, vii, 14.—Munck, *Palestine*, pp. 116, 125, 191.)

[250] "We have established the history of a belief. It is set up; human society is constituted. It modifies itself; society goes through a series of revolutions. It disappears; society undergoes a change" (*Cite antique*, end).

[251] Spencer has already said that social evolution, just as universal evolution, begins in a stage of more or less perfect homogeneity. But this proposition does not in any wise resemble the one that we have just been developing. For Spencer, a society that was perfectly homogeneous would not truly be a society, for homogeneity is by nature unstable, and society is essentially a coherent whole. The social role of homogeneity is completely secondary; it may look towards an ulterior co-operation, but it is not a specific source of social life. At times, Spencer seems to see in societies such as we have just been describing only an ephemeral juxtaposition of independent individuals, the zero of social life. We have, on the contrary, just seen that they have a very strong collective

This type can even be modified without the nature of social solidarity undergoing any change. In fact, primitive peoples do not all present this absence of centralization that we have just observed. There are some, on the contrary, subservient to an absolute power. The division of labor has then made its appearance among them. But in this case, the tie which binds the individual to the chief is identical with that which in our days attaches the thing to the person. The relations of a barbarous despot with his subjects, as that of a master with his slaves, of a father of a Roman family with his children, is not to be distinguished from the relations of an owner with the object he possesses. In these relations there is none of the reciprocity which the division of labor produces. They have with good reason been called unilateral.[252] The solidarity that they express remains mechanical. The whole difference is that it links the individual, not more directly to the group, but to the image of the group. But the unity of the whole is, as before, exclusive of the individuality of its parts.

If this early division of labor, important as it otherwise is, does not result in making social solidarity tractable, as might be expected, that is because of the particular conditions in which it is realized. It is a general law that the eminent organ of every society participates in the nature of the collective being that it represents. Where society has a religious and, so to speak, superhuman character, whose source we have just shown to lie in the constitution of the common conscience, it necessarily transmits itself to the chief who directs it and who is thus elevated above the rest of men. Where individuals are in simple dependence upon the collective type, they quite naturally become dependent upon the central authority in which it is incarnated. Indeed, the right of property which the community exercises over things in an undivided way passes intact into the superior personality who finds himself thus constituted. The properly professional services which the latter renders are little things in comparison with the extraordinary power with which he is invested. If, in some types of society, the directive power has so much authority, it is not, as has been said, because they have a more special need of energetic direction, but this authority emanates entirely from the common conscience, and it is great because the common conscience itself is highly developed. Suppose that the common conscience is very feeble or that it only embraces a small part of social life; the necessity for a supreme

---

life, although *sui generis*, which manifests itself not in exchanges and contracts, but in a great abundance of common beliefs and common practices. These aggregates are coherent, not in spite of their homogeneity, but because of their homogeneity. Not only is the community not too weak; but we may even say that it alone exists. Moreover, these societies have a definite type which comes from their homogeneity. We cannot treat them as negligible quantities.

[252] See Tarde, *Lois de l'imitation*, pp. 402-412.

regulative function will not be less. The rest of society, however, will not be stronger than he who is entrusted with inferior authority. That is why solidarity is still mechanical where the division of labor is not highly developed. It is, indeed, under these conditions that mechanical solidarity reaches its maximum power, for the action of the common conscience is stronger when it is exercised, not in a diffuse manner, but through the medium of a defined organ.

There is, then, a social structure of determined nature to which mechanical solidarity corresponds. What characterizes it is a system of segments homogeneous and similar to each other.

II

Quite different is the structure of societies where organic solidarity is preponderant.

They are constituted, not by a repetition of similar, homogeneous segments, but by a system of different organs each of which has a special role, and which are themselves formed of differentiated parts. Not only are social elements not of the same nature, but they are not arranged in the same manner. They are not juxtaposed linearily as the rings of an earthworm, nor entwined one with another, but co-ordinated and subordinated one to another around the same central organ which exercises a moderating action over the rest of the organism. This organ itself no longer has the same character as in the preceding case, for, if the others depend upon it, it, in its turn, depends upon them. No doubt, it still enjoys a special situation, and, if one chooses so to speak of it, a privileged position, but that is due to the nature of the role that it fills and not to some cause foreign to its functions, nor to some force communicated to it from without. Thus, there is no longer anything about it that is not temporal and human. Between it and other organs, there is no longer anything but differences in degree. It is thus that, in the animal kingdom, the pre-eminence of the nervous system over the other systems is reduced to the right, if one may speak thus, of receiving a choicer nourishment and of having its fill before the others. But it has need of them, just as they have need of it.

This social type rests on principles so different from the preceding that it can develop only in proportion to the effacement of that preceding type. In effect, individuals are here grouped, no longer according to their relations of lineage, but according to the particular nature of the social activity to which they consecrate themselves. Their natural milieu is no longer the natal milieu, but the occupational milieu. It is no longer real or fictitious consanguinity which marks the place of each one, but the function which he fills. No doubt, when this new organization begins to appear, it tries to utilize the existing organization and assimilate it. The way in which functions are divided thus follows,

as faithfully as possible, the way in which society is already divided. The segments, or at least the groups of segments united by special affinities become organs. It is thus that the clans which together formed the tribe of the Levites appropriated sacerdotal functions for themselves among the Hebrew people. In a general way, classes and castes probably have no other origin nor any other nature; they arise from the multitude of occupational organizations being born amidst the pre-existing familial organization. But this mixed arrangement cannot long endure, for between the two states that it attempts to reconcile, there is an antagonism which necessarily ends in a break. It is only a very rudimentary division of labor which can adapt itself to those rigid, defined moulds which were not made for it. It can grow only by freeing itself from the framework which encloses it. As soon as it has passed a certain stage of development, there is no longer any relation either between the immutable number of segments and the steady growth of functions which are becoming specialized, or between the hereditarily fixed properties of the first and the new aptitudes that the second calls forth.[253] The social material must enter into entirely new combinations in order to organize itself upon completely different foundations. But the old structure, so far as it persists, is opposed to this. That is why it must disappear.

The history of these two types shows, in effect, that one has progressed only as the other has retrogressed.

Among the Iroquois, the social constitution with a clan-base is in a state of purity, and the same is true of the Hebrews as we see them in the Pentateuch, except for the slight alteration that we have just noted. Thus, the organized type exists neither in the first nor in the second, although we can perhaps see the first stirrings of it in Jewish society.

The case is no longer the same among the Franks in their Salic law. It presents itself with its own characteristics, disengaged from all compromise. We find among these people, besides a central authority, stable and regular, a whole system of administrative functions, as well as judicial. Moreover, the existence of a contract-law, still, it is true, very poorly developed, is proof that economic functions themselves are beginning to be divided and organized. Thus, the politico-familial constitution is seriously undermined. To be sure, the last social molecule, the village, is still only a transformed clan. The proof of this is that, among the inhabitants of the same village, there are relations which are evidently of a domestic nature and which, in every case, are characteristic of the clan. All the members of the village have, in the absence of relatives, properly so designated, an hereditary right over one another.[254] A text found among the *Capita extravagantia legis*

---

[253] We shall see the reasons for this below, Book II, ch. iv.

[254] See Glasson, *Le droit de succession dans les lois barbares*, p. 19. It is true that

salicae (art. 9) tells us, indeed, that in case of murder committed in the village, the neighbors were collectively solidary. Moreover, the village is a much more hermetically closed system to the outside and more sufficient unto itself than would be a simple territorial circumscription, for nothing can be established there without unanimous consent, express or tacit, from all the inhabitants.[255] But, under this form, the clan has lost some of its essential characteristics. Not only has all remembrance of a common origin disappeared, but it has been almost completely stripped of any political importance. The political unit is the *Hundred*. "The population," says Waitz, "lived in villages, but it divided itself into Hundreds which, in peace and in war, formed the unity which served as a foundation for all relations."[256]

In Rome, this double movement of progression and retrogression also takes place. The Roman clan is the *gens*, and it is certain that the *gens* was the basis of the old Roman constitution. But, from the founding of the Republic, it has almost completely ceased to be a public institution. It is no longer either a definite territorial unity, as the village among the Franks, or a political unit. We find it neither in the configuration of territory, nor in the structure of the assemblies of the people. The *comitia curiata*, where it played a social role,[257] are replaced by the *comitia centuriata*, or by the *comitia tributa*, which were organized on quite different lines. It is no longer anything but a private association which is maintained by force of habit, but which is destined to disappear, because it no longer corresponds to anything in Roman life. But also, since the time of the Twelve Tables, the division of labor was much further advanced in Rome than among the preceding peoples and the organized structure more highly developed. There are already to be found there important corporations of functionaries (senators, equites, a pontifical college, etc.), workmen's groups,[258] at the same time that the notion of the lay state gets clear.

Thus, we find justification for the hierarchy that we have just established according to other criteria, less methodical, between the social types that we have previously compared. If we could say that the Hebrews of the Pentateuch appeared to be a social type less elevated than the Franks of the Salic law, and that the latter, in their turn, were below the Romans of the Twelve Tables, then there is a general law: the more the segmental organization with a clan-base is manifest and

---

the fact is contested by Fustel de Coulanges, despite the explicit statement of the text upon which Glasson relies.

[255] See the heading *De Migrantibus* of the Salic Law.

[256] *Deutsche Verfassungsgeschichte*, 2nd ed., II, p. 317.

[257] In the comitia, the voting was done by curia, that is, by a group of *gentes*. There is a text which even seems to say that in the interior of each curia there was voting by *gentes*. (Gell., XV, 27, 4.)

[258] Marquardt, *Privat Leben der Roemer*, II, p. 4.

strong among a people, the more inferior is their social type. It can elevate itself to a higher state only after freeing itself from this first stage. It is for the same reason that the Athenian city, while appearing to be exactly the same type as the Roman city, is, however, a more primitive type. The politico-familial organization disappeared much less quickly there. It persisted there almost until Athens' decadence.[259]

But the organized type cannot subsist alone in a pure state once the clan has disappeared. The organization with a clan-base is really only a species of a larger genus, the segmental organization. The distribution of society into similar compartments corresponds to persisting necessities, even in new societies where social life is being established, but which produce their effects in another form. The bulk of the population is no longer divided according to relations of consanguinity, real or fictive, but according to the division of territory. The segments are no longer familial aggregates, but territorial circumscriptions.

It is through a slow evolution, however, that the passage from one to another is made. When remembrance of common origin is extinct, when the domestic relations which derive from it—but as we have seen, often survive it—have themselves disappeared, the clan no longer has any conception of itself other than as a group of individuals who occupy the same territory. It becomes, properly speaking, the village. Thus it is that all peoples who have passed beyond the clan-stage are organized in territorial districts (counties, communes, etc.) which, just as the Roman *gens* came to take part in the curia, connected themselves with other districts of similar nature, but vaster, sometimes called the Hundred, sometimes the assembly, sometimes the ward, which, in their turn, are often enveloped by others, still more extensive (shire, province, department), whose union formed the society.[260] The envelopment can, however, be more or less hermetic; the ties which bind the widest districts can be more or less strong, as in the centralized countries of contemporary Europe, or loose, as in simple confederations. But the structural principle is the same, and that is why mechanical solidarity persists even in the most elevated societies.

But even as it is no longer preponderant, the arrangement by segments is no longer, as in the preceding, the unique framework, nor even the essential framework of society. In the first place, territorial

---

[259] Until Cleisthenes, and two centuries later, Athens lost her independence. Moreover, even after Cleisthenes, the Athenian clan, the γένος, while having totally lost its political character, retained a very strong organization. (Cf. Gilbert, *op. cit.*, I, pp. 142 and 200.)

[260] We do not wish to imply that territorial districts are only a reproduction of old familial arrangements. This new mode of grouping results, on the contrary, at least in part, from new causes which disturb the old. The principal of these causes is the growth of cities which become the centre of concentration of population (see below, Book II, ch. ii, 1). But whatever the origins of this arrangement may be, it is segmental.

divisions have something artificial about them. The ties which result from cohabitation are not as profoundly affective of the heart of men as are those arising from consanguinity. Thus, they have a much smaller resistive power. When a person is born into a clan, he can in no way ever change the fact of his parentage. The same does not hold true of changing from a city or a province. No doubt, the geographical distribution generally coincides, in the large, with a certain moral distribution of population. Each province, each territorial division, has its peculiar customs and manners, a life peculiar unto itself. It therefore exercises over the individuals who are affected by it an attraction which tends to keep itself alive, and to repel all opposing forces. But, in the case of the same country, these differences would be neither very numerous, nor very firmly marked out. The segments are each more exposed to the others. And in truth, since the Middle Ages, "after the formation of cities, foreign artisans moved about as easily and as far as did merchants."[261] The segmental organization lost its distinction.

It loses more and more ground as societies develop. It is a general law that partial aggregates which participate in a larger aggregate see their individuality becoming less and less distinct. With the disappearance of the familial organization, local religions disappear without returning. Yet they persist in local customs. Little by little, they join together and unite at the same time that dialects and jargons begin to resolve themselves into one and the same national language, at the same time that regional administration loses its autonomy. Some have seen in this fact a simple consequence of the law of imitation.[262] But it is rather a leveling analogous to that which is produced between liquid masses put into communication. The partitions which separate the various cells of social life, being less thick, are more often broken through. Their permeability becomes greater as they are traversed more. Accordingly, they lose their cohesion, become progressively effaced, and, in the same measure, confound themselves. But local diversities can maintain themselves only in so far as diversity of environments continues to exist. Territorial divisions are thus less and less grounded in the nature of things, and, consequently, lose their significance. We can almost say that a people is as much more advanced as territorial divisions are more superficial.

On the other hand, at the same time that the segmental organization is thus effaced, occupational organization comes out of its torpor more and more completely. In the beginning, it is true, it establishes itself only within the limits of the simplest segments without extending beyond them. Each city and its immediate environs form a group in the

---

[261] Schmoller, *La division du travail étudiée au point de vue historique*, in *Révue d''écon. pol.* 1890, p. 145.

[262] See Tarde, *Les Lois de l'imitation*, passim.

interior of which work is divided, but seeks to be sufficient unto itself. "The city," says Schmoller, "becomes as far as possible the ecclesiastical centre, the political and military centre of the surrounding villages. It tries to develop all the industries necessary for the supplying of the country, by seeking to concentrate commerce and transportation in its territory."[263] At the same time, in the interior of the city, the inhabitants are grouped according to their occupations. Each body of workers is like a city which leads its own life.[264] This is the state in which the cities of antiquity remained until a comparatively late date, and where Christian societies started. But the latter grew out of this stage very early. Since the fourteenth century, the inter-regional division of labor has been developing: "Each city, in its beginnings, had as many drapers as it needed. But the makers of grey cloth of Basle succumbed, even before 1362, to the competition of the Alsatians. In Strasburg, Frankfort, Leipzig, the spinning of wool is ruined about 1500. . . . The character of industrial universality of cities of former times found itself irreparably destroyed."

Since then the movement has been extended. "In the capital, today more than heretofore, the active forces of the central government, arts, literature, large credit-operations concentrate themselves; in the great seaports are concentrated, more than ever, all importing and exporting. Hundreds of small commercial places, trafficking in cattle and wheat, prosper and grow. Whereas previously each city had its ramparts and moats, now great fortresses are erected for the protection of the whole country. Like the capital, the chief places of each province grow through the concentration of provincial administration, by provincial establishments, collections, and schools. The insane and the sick of certain types, who were heretofore dispersed, are banded together from every province and every department into a single enclosure. Different cities always tend towards certain specialties, so that we now distinguish university-cities, government-cities, manufacturing cities, cities of commerce, of shipping, of banking. In certain points or certain regions, large industries are concentrated: machine-construction, spinning, textile-manufacture, tanneries, furnaces, a sugar industry supplying the whole country. Special schools have been established, the working-class population adapts itself there, the construction of machines is concentrated there, while the means of communication and the organization of credit accommodate themselves to particular circumstances."[265]

---

[263] *Op. cit.*, p. 144.

[264] See Levasseur, *Les classes ouvrières en France jusqu'à la Révolution*, I, p. 195.

[265] Schmoller, *La division du travail étudiée au point de vue historique*, pp. 145-148.

To be sure, in certain measure, this occupational organization was forced to adapt itself to the one which had existed before it, as it had earlier adapted itself to the familial organization. That is apparent from the description which has preceded. It is, moreover, a very general fact that new institutions first fall into the mould of old institutions. Territorial circumscriptions tend to specialize themselves like tissues, organs, or different parts, just as the clans before them. But, just like the latter, they are incapable of continuing this role. In fact, a city always circumscribes either different organs or parts of different organs; and inversely, there are not many organs which may be completely comprised within the limits of a determined district, no matter how far it extends. It almost always runs beyond them. Indeed, although very often the most highly solidary organs tend to come closer to each other, nevertheless, in general, their material proximity very inexactly reflects the more or less great intimacy of their relations. Certain of them are very distant, although they are directly dependent upon each other. Others are near, yet their relations are only mediate and distant. The manner of human grouping which results from the division of labor is thus very different from that which expresses the partition of the population in space. The occupational environment does not coincide with the territorial environment any more than it does with the familial environment. It is a new framework which substitutes itself for the others; thus the substitution is possible only in so far as the others are effaced.

If this social type is nowhere observable in its absolute purity; if, indeed, organic solidarity is nowhere come upon wholly alone, at least it disengages itself more and more from all mixture, just as it becomes more and more preponderant. This predominance is much more rapid and complete at the very moment when this structure affirms itself more strongly, the other having become more indistinct. The very defined segment that the clan formed is replaced by territorial circumscription. In its origin, at least, the latter corresponded, although in a vague and only proximate way, to the real moral division of the population. But it slowly loses this character and becomes an arbitrary, conventional combination. But in the degree that these barriers are broken down, they are rebuilt by systems of organs much more highly developed. If, then, social evolution rests upon the action of these same determinate causes,—and we shall later see that this hypothesis is the only one conceivable,—we may be permitted to predict that this double movement will continue in the same path, and that a day will come when our whole social and political organization will have a base exclusively, or almost exclusively, occupational.

Moreover, the investigations which are to follow[266] will prove that this occupational organization is not today everything that it ought to be; that abnormal causes have prevented it from attaining the degree of development which our social order now demands. We may judge by that what importance it must have in the future.

III

The same law holds of biological development.

We know today that lower animals are formed of similar segments, composed either of irregular masses, or in linear series. Indeed, at the lowest rung of the ladder, the elements are not only alike, they are still in homogeneous composition. We generally call them *colonies*. But this expression, which is certainly not without equivocation, does not signify that these associations are not individual organisms, for "every colony whose members have a continuity of tissues is, in reality, an individual."[267] What characterizes the individuality of any given aggregate is the existence of operations effectuated in common by all parts. Thus, among the members of a colony, nutritive materials are taken in common, making impossible any movement except through movements of the totality, in order for the colony not to be dissolved. Moreover, the egg, issuing from one of the associated segments, reproduces, not this segment, but the entire colony of which it is a part. "Between colonies of polyps and the most elevated animals, there is, from this point of view, no difference."[268] What makes such a total, radical separation impossible is that there are no organisms, as centralized as they may be, which do not present, in different degrees, some colonial constitution. We find traces up through the vertebrates, in their skeletal composition, in their urogenital make-up, etc. Particularly is proof rendered by their embryonic development of their being nothing else than modified colonies.[269]

There is, thus, in the animal world an individuality "which is produced apart from a whole combination of organs."[270] But, it is identical with that of societies that we have termed segmental. Not only is the structural plan evidently the same, but the solidarity is of the same kind. Since the parts which make up an animal colony are mechanically attached to each other, they can act only as a whole, at least if they remain united. Activity is here collective. In a society of polyps, since all stomachs work together, an individual cannot eat without other individuals eating. It is, says Perrier, communism in

---

[266] See below, in this book, ch. vii, § 2, and Book III, ch. i.

[267] Perrier, *Le Transformisme*, p. 159.

[268] Perrier, *Colonies animales*, p. 778.

[269] *Ibid.*, Book IV, ch. v, vi, vii.

[270] *Ibid.*, p. 779.

every meaning of the word.[271] A member of a colony, particularly when it is irresolute, cannot contract itself without dragging into its movement the polyps to which it is joined, and the movement communicates itself from place to place.[272] In a worm, each annule depends upon the others very rigidly, and that is so even though it can detach itself without danger.

But, even as the segmental type becomes effaced as we advance in the scale of social evolution, the colonial type disappears in so far as we go up in the scale of organisms. Already impaired among the earthworms, although still very apparent, it becomes almost imperceptible among the molluscs, and ultimately only the analysis of a scholar can find any traces of it among the vertebrates. We do not have to show the analogies between the type which replaces the preceding one and that of organic societies. In one case as in the other, the structure derives from the division of labor and its solidarity. Each part of the animal, having become an organ, has its proper sphere of action where it moves independently without imposing itself upon others. But, from another point of view, they depend more upon one another than in a colony, since they cannot separate without perishing. Finally, in organic evolution as in social evolution, the division of labor begins by utilizing the framework of segmental organization, but ultimately frees itself and develops autonomously. If, in fact, the organ is sometimes only a transformed segment, that is an exception.[273]

In sum, we have distinguished two kinds of solidarity; we have just learned that there exist two social types which correspond to them. Even as the solidarities develop in inverse ratio to each other, of the two corresponding social types, one regresses while the other progresses, and the latter is that fixed by the division of labor. Besides confirming what has preceded, this result succeeds in showing us the total importance of the division of labor. Just as it is it which, for the most part, makes coherent the societies in which we live, so also does it determine the constitutive traits of their structure, and every fact presages that, in the future, its role, from this point of view, will become ever greater.

IV

The law that we have established in the last two chapters has been able by a quality, but by a quality only, to recall to us the dominating tendency in Spencer's sociology. With him, we have said that the place

---

[271] *Transformisme*, p. 167.
[272] *Colonies animales*, p. 771.
[273] See *Colonies animales*, pp. 763 ff.

of the individual in society, of no account in its origins, becomes greater with civilization. But this incontestable fact is presented to us under an aspect totally different from that of English philosophy, so that, ultimately, our conclusions are opposed to his more than they are in agreement.

First of all, according to him, this absorption of the individual into the group would be the result of force and of an artificial organization necessitated by the state of war in which lower societies chronically live. It is especially in war that union is necessary to success. A group can defend itself against another group or subject it to itself only by acting together. It is necessary for all the individual forces to be concentrated in a permanent manner in an indissoluble union. But the only means of producing this concentration instantaneously is by instituting a very strong authority to which individuals are absolutely submissive. It is necessary that, as the will of a soldier finds itself suspended in executing the will of his superior, so too does the will of citizens find itself curtailed by that of the government.[274] Thus, it is an organized despotism which would annihilate individuals, and since this organization is essentially military, it is through militarism that Spencer defines these types of society.

We have seen, on the contrary, that this effacement of the individual has as its place of origin a social type which is characterized by a complete absence of all centralization. It is a product of that state of homogeneity which distinguishes primitive societies. If the individual is not distinct from the group, it is because the individual conscience is hardly at all distinguishable from the collective conscience. Spencer and other sociologists with him seem to have interpreted these distant facts in terms of very modern ideas. The very pronounced contemporary sentiment that each of us has of his own individuality has led them to believe that personal rights cannot be restrained to this point except by a coercive organization. We cling to them so firmly that they find it inconceivable for man to have willingly abandoned them. In fact, if in lower societies so small a place is given to individual personality, that is not because it has been restrained or artificially suppressed. It is simply because, at that moment of history, *it did not exist.*

Moreover, Spencer himself realizes that, of these societies, many have a constitution so little military and authoritarian that he qualifies them as democratic.[275] He wishes, however, to see in them the first symptoms of the future which he calls industrial. To that end, it is necessary for him to misconceive the fact that here as in those where there is submission to a despotic government, the individual has no

---

[274] *Principles of Sociology*, II, p. 153.
[275] *Principles of Sociology*, pp. 154-155.

sphere of action proper to him, as the general institution of communism proves.. Indeed, the traditions, prejudices, the collective usages of all sorts, are not any the less burdensome to him than would be a constituted authority. Thus, we can term them democratic only by distorting the ordinary sense of the word. Moreover, if they were really impressed with the precocious individualism that is attributed to them, we would come to the strange conclusion that social evolution has tried, from the very first, to produce the most perfect types, since, as he says, no governmental force exists at first except that of the common will expressed in the assembled horde.[276] Would not the movement of history then be circular and would progress consist in anything but a return to the past?

In a general way, it is easy to understand why individuals will not be submissive except to a collective despotism, for the members of a society can be dominated only by a force which is superior to them, and there is only one which has this quality: that is the group. Any personality, as powerful as it might be, would be as nothing against a whole society; the latter can carry on in spite of it. That is why, as we have seen, the force of authoritarian governments does not come from authorities themselves, but from the very constitution of society. If, however, individualism was at this point congenital with humanity, we cannot see how primitive peoples could so easily subject themselves to the despotic authority of a chief, wherever necessary. The ideas, customs, institutions would have opposed such a radical transformation. But all this is explained once we have taken cognizance of the nature of these societies, for then the change is no longer as great as it seems. Individuals, instead of subordinating themselves to the group, were subordinated to that which represented it, and as the collective authority, when it was diffuse, was absolute, that of the chief, who is only its organized incarnation, naturally took on the same character.

Rather than dating the effacement of the individual from the institution of a despotic authority, we must, on the contrary, see in this institution the first step made towards individualism. Chiefs are, in fact, the first personalities who emerge from the social mass. Their exceptional situation, putting them beyond the level of others, gives them a distinct physiognomy and accordingly confers individuality upon them. In dominating society, they are no longer forced to follow all of its movements. Of course, it is from the group that they derive their power, but once power is organized, it becomes autonomous and makes them capable of personal activity. A source of initiative is thus opened which had not existed before then. There is, hereafter, someone

---

[276] *Ibid.*, III, pp. 426-427.

who can produce new things and even, in certain measure, deny collective usages. Equilibrium has been broken.[277]

Our insistence upon this point was made in order to establish two important propositions.

In the first place, whenever we find ourselves in the presence of a governmental system endowed with great authority, we must seek the reason for it, not in the particular situation of the governing, but in the nature of the societies they govern. We must observe the common beliefs, the common sentiments which, by incarnating themselves in a person or in a family, communicate such power to it. As for the personal superiority of the chief, it plays only a secondary role in this process. It explains why the collective force is concentrated in his hands rather than in some others, but does not explain its intensity. From the moment that this force, instead of remaining diffuse, becomes delegated, it can only be for the profit of the individuals who have already otherwise evinced some superiority. But if such superiority suggests the sense in which the current is directed, it does not create the current. In Rome if the father of a family enjoys absolute power, it is not because he is the oldest, or the wisest, or the most experienced, but because, according to the circumstances in which the Roman family was placed, he incarnated the old familial communism. Despotism, at least when it is not a pathological, decadent phenomenon, is nothing else than transformed communism.

In the second place, we see from what precedes how false is the theory which makes egotism the point of departure for humanity, and altruism only a recent conquest.

What gives this hypothesis authority in the eyes of certain persons is that it appears to be the logical consequence of the principles of Darwinism. In the name of the dogma of struggle for existence and natural selection, they paint for us in the saddest colors this primitive humanity whose hunger and thirst, always badly satisfied, were their only passions; those sombre times when men had no other care and no other occupation than to quarrel with one another over their miserable nourishment. To react against those retrospective reveries of the philosophy of the eighteenth century and also against certain religious doctrines, to show with some force that the paradise lost is not behind us and that there is in our past nothing to regret, they believe we ought to make it dreary and belittle it systematically. Nothing is less scientific than this prejudice in the opposite direction. If the hypotheses of Darwin have a moral use, it is with more reserve and measure than in other sciences. They overlook the essential element of moral life, that is, the moderating influence that society exercises over its members,

---

[277] We find here confirmation of a previously enunciated proposition which makes governmental power an emanation of the inherent life of the collective conscience.

which tempers and neutralizes the brutal action of the struggle for existence and selection. Wherever there are societies, there is altruism, because there is solidarity.

Thus, we find altruism from the beginning of humanity and even in a truly intemperate form. For these privations that the savage imposes upon himself in obedience to religious tradition, the abnegation with which he sacrifices his life when society demands such sacrifice, the irresistible desire of the widow of India to follow her husband to the grave, of the Gaul not to survive the head of his clan, of the old Celt to free his companions from useless trouble by voluntary death,—is not all this altruism? Shall we treat these practices as superstitions? What matter, so long as they evince an aptitude for surrendering oneself? And where do superstitions begin and end? It would be very difficult to reply and to give a scientific answer to this question. Is it not also a superstition of ours to feel affection for the places in which we have lived, and for the persons with whom we have had durable relations? And is not this power of attachment the mark of a sane moral constitution? To speak rigorously, our whole sensible life is made up of superstitions, since it precedes and dominates judgment more than it depends upon it.

Scientifically, conduct is egotistical in the measure that it is determined by sentiments and representations which are exclusively personal. If, then, we remember to what extent in lower societies the conscience of the individual is wrapped in the collective conscience, we may even be led to believe that it is a thing totally different from the individual himself, that it is completely altruistic, as Condillac would say. This conclusion, however, would be exaggerated, for there is a sphere of psychic life which, however developed the collective type may be, varies from one man to another and remains peculiar with each. It is that which is formed by representations, by sentiments and tendencies which relate to the organism and to the state of the organism. It is the world of internal and external sensations and the movements which are directly linked to them. This first foundation of all individuality is inalienable and does not depend upon any social state. Thus, one must not say that altruism is born from egotism. Such a derivation would be possible only through a *creatio ex nihilo*. But, to speak rigorously, these two sides of conduct are found present from the beginning in all human consciences, for there cannot be things which do not reflect both of these aspects, the one relating to the individual alone and the other relating to the things which are not personal to him.

All that we can say is that, among savages, this inferior part of ourselves represents a more considerable fraction of total life, because this total has a smaller extent, since the higher spheres of the psychic life are less developed there. It thus has greater relative importance and, accordingly, greater sway over the will. But, on the other hand, with respect to what goes beyond this circle of physical necessities, the primitive conscience, to use a strong expression of Espinas, is completely outside of itself. Contrariwise, among the civilized, egotism is introduced in the midst of higher representations. Each of us has his opinions, his beliefs, his personal aspirations, and holds to them. It is even mingled with altruism, for it happens that we have a way of our own of being altruistic which clings to our personal character, to the texture of our spirit, and which we refuse to cast off. Of course, we must not conclude that the place of egotism has become greater throughout the whole of life, for we must take account of the fact that the whole conscience has been extended. It is none the less true that individualism has developed in absolute value by penetrating into regions which originally were closed to it.

But this individualism, the fruit of an historical development, is not at all that which Spencer described. The societies that he calls industrial do not resemble organized societies any more than military societies resemble segmental societies with a familial base. That is what we shall see in the following chapter.

CHAPTER SEVEN. ORGANIC SOLIDARITY AND CONTRACTUAL SOLIDARITY

I

It is true that in the industrial societies that Spencer speaks of, just as in organized societies, social harmony comes essentially from the division of labor.[278] It is characterized by a co-operation which is automatically produced through the pursuit by each individual of his own interests. It suffices that each individual consecrate himself to a special function in order, by the force of events, to make himself solidary with others. Is this not the distinctive sign of organized societies?

But if Spencer has justly noted what the principal cause of social solidarity in higher societies is, he has misunderstood the manner in which this cause produces its effect, and, accordingly, misunderstood the nature of the latter.

In short, for him, industrial solidarity, as he calls it, presents the two following characters:

Since it is spontaneous, it does not require any coercive force either to produce or to maintain it. Society does not have to intervene to assure the harmony which is self-established. Spencer says that each man can maintain himself through his work, can exchange his produce for the goods of another, can lend assistance and receive payment, can

---

[278] *Principles of Sociology*, III, pp. 332 ff.

enter into some association for pursuing some enterprise, small or large, without obeying the direction of society in its totality.[279] The sphere of social action would thus grow narrower and narrower, for it would have no other object than that of keeping individuals from disturbing and harming one another. That is to say, it would have only a negative regulative force.

Under these conditions, the only remaining link between men would be that of an absolutely free exchange. As Spencer says, all industrial affairs take place through the medium of free exchange, and this relation becomes predominant in society in so far as individual activity becomes dominant.[280] But the normal form of exchange is the contract. That is why in proportion to the decline of militarism and the ascendancy of industrialism, power as the gateway to authority becomes of less importance and free activity increases, and the relationship of contract becomes general. Finally, in the fully developed industrial type, this relationship becomes universal.[281]

By that, Spencer does not mean that society always rests on an implicit or formal contract. The hypothesis of a social contract is irreconcilable with the notion of the division of labor. The greater the part taken by the latter, the more completely must Rousseau's postulate be renounced. For in order for such a contract to be possible, it is necessary that, at a given moment, all individual wills direct themselves toward the common bases of the social organization, and, consequently, that each particular conscience pose the political problem for itself in all its generality. But that would make it necessary for each individual to leave his special sphere, so that all might equally play the same role, that of statesman and constituents. Thus, this is the situation when society makes a contract: if adhesion is unanimous, the content of all consciences is identical. Then, in the measure that social solidarity proceeds from such a cause, it has no relation with the division of labor.

Nothing, however, less resembles the spontaneous, automatic solidarity which, according to Spencer, distinguishes industrial societies, for he sees, on the contrary, in this conscious pursuit of social ends the characteristic of military societies.[282] Such a contract supposes that all individuals are able to represent in themselves the general conditions of the collective life in order to make a choice with knowledge. But Spencer understands that such a representation goes beyond the bounds of science in its actual state, and, consequently, beyond the bounds of conscience. He is so convinced of the vanity of reflection when it is applied to such matters that he wishes to take them

---

[279] *Ibid.*, III, p. 808.
[280] *Principles of Sociology*, II, p. 160.
[281] *Ibid.*, III, p. 813.
[282] *Ibid.*, III, pp. 332 ff.—See also *Man versus the State*.

away even from the legislator, to say nothing of submitting them to public opinion. He believes that social life, just as all life in general, can naturally organize itself only by an unconscious, spontaneous adaptation under the immediate pressure of needs, and not according to a rational plan of reflective intelligence. He does not believe that higher societies can be built according to a rigidly drawn program.

Thus, the conception of a social contract is today difficult to defend, for it has no relation to the facts. The observer does not meet it along his road, so to speak. Not only are there no societies which have such an origin, but there is none whose structure presents the least trace of a contractual organization. It is neither a fact acquired through history nor a tendency which grows out of historical development. Hence, to rejuvenate this doctrine and accredit it, it would be necessary to qualify as a contract the adhesion which each individual, as adult, gave to the society when he was born, solely by reason of which he continues to live. But then we would have to term contractual every action of man which is not determined by constraint.[283] In this light, there is no society, neither present nor past, which is not or has not been contractual, for there is none which could exist solely through pressure. We have given the reason for this above. If it has sometimes been thought that force was greater previously than it is today, that is because of the illusion which attributes to a coercive regime the small place given over to individual liberty in lower societies. In reality, social life, wherever it is normal, is spontaneous, and if it is abnormal, it cannot endure. The individual abdicates spontaneously. In fact, it is unjust to speak of abdication where there is nothing to abdicate. If this large and somewhat warped interpretation is given to this word, no distinction can be made between different social types, and if we understand by type only the very defined juridical tie which the word designates, we can be sure that no tie of this kind has ever existed between individuals and society.

But if higher societies do not rest upon a fundamental contract which sets forth the general principles of political life, they would have, or would be considered to have, according to Spencer, the vast system of particular contracts which link individuals as a unique basis. They would depend upon the group only in proportion to their dependence upon one another, and they would depend upon one another only in proportion to conventions privately entered into and freely concluded. Social solidarity would then be nothing else than the spontaneous accord of individual interests, an accord of which contracts are the natural expression. The typical social relation would be the economic, stripped of all regulation and resulting from the entirely free initiative

---

[283] This is what Fouillée does in opposing contract to pressure. (*Science sociale*, p. 8.)

of the parties. In short, society would be solely the stage where individuals exchanged the products of their labor, without any action properly social coming to regulate this exchange.

Is this the character of societies whose unity is produced by the division of labor? If this were so, we could with justice doubt their stability. For if interest relates men, it is never for more than some few moments. It can create only an external link between them. In the fact of exchange, the various agents remain outside of each other, and when the business has been completed, each one retires and is left entirely on his own. Consciences are only superficially in contact; they neither penetrate each other, nor do they adhere. If we look further into the matter, we shall see that this total harmony of interests conceals a latent or deferred conflict. For where interest is the only ruling force each individual finds himself in a state of war with every other since nothing comes to mollify the egos, and any truce in this eternal antagonism would not be of long duration. There is nothing less constant than interest. Today, it unites me to you; tomorrow, it will make me your enemy. Such a cause can only give rise to transient relations and passing associations. We now understand how necessary it is to see if this is really the nature of organic solidarity.

In no respect, according to Spencer, does industrial society exist in a pure state. It is a partially ideal type which slowly disengages itself in the evolutionary process, but it has not yet been completely realized. Consequently, to rightly attribute to it the qualities we have just been discussing, we would have to establish systematically that societies appear in a fashion as complete as they are elevated, discounting cases of regression.

It is first affirmed that the sphere of social activity grows smaller and smaller, to the great advantage of the individual. But to prove this proposition by real instances, it is not enough to cite, as Spencer does, some cases where the individual has been effectively emancipated from collective influence. These examples, numerous as they may be, can serve only as illustrations, and are, by themselves, devoid of any demonstrative force. It is very possible that, in this respect, social action has regressed, but that, in other respects, it has been extended, and that, ultimately, we are mistaking a transformation for a disappearance. The only way of giving objective proof is not to cite some facts taken at random, but to follow historically, from its origins until recent times, the way in which social action has essentially manifested itself, and to see whether, in time, it has added or lost volume. We know that this is law. The obligations that society imposes upon its members, as inconsequential and unenduring as they may be, take on a juridical form. Consequently, the relative dimensions of this system permit us to measure with exactitude the relative extent of social action.

But it is very evident that, far from diminishing, it grows greater and greater and becomes more and more complex. The more primitive a code is, the smaller its volume. On the contrary, it is as large as it is more recent. There can be no doubt about this. To be sure, it does not result in making the sphere of individual activity smaller. We must not forget that if there is more regulation in life, there is more life in general. This is sufficient proof that social discipline has not been relaxing. One of its forms tends, it is true, to regress, as we have already seen, but others, much richer and much more complex, develop in its place. If repressive law loses ground, restitutive law, which originally did not exist at all, keeps growing. If society no longer imposes upon everybody certain uniform practices, it takes greater care to define and regulate the special relations between different social functions, and this activity is not smaller because it is different.

Spencer would reply that he had not insisted upon the diminution of every kind of control, but only of positive control. Let us admit this distinction. Whether it be positive or negative, the control is none the less social, and the principal question is to understand whether it has extended itself or contracted. Whether it be to command or to deny, to say *Do this* or *Do not do that*, if society intervenes more, we have not the right to say that individual spontaneity suffices more and more in all spheres. If the rules determining conduct have multiplied, whether they be imperative or prohibitive, it is not true that it depends more and more completely on private initiative.

But has this distinction itself any foundation? By positive control, Spencer means that which commands action, while negative control commands only abstention. As he says: A man has a piece of land; I cultivate it for him either wholly or in part, or else I impose upon him either wholly or in part the way in which he should cultivate it. This is a positive control. On the other hand, I give him neither aid nor advice about its cultivation; I simply do not molest my neighbor's crop, or trespass upon my neighbor's land, or put rubbish on his clearing. This is a negative control. The difference is very marked between ordering him to follow, as a citizen, a certain course, or suggesting means for the citizen to employ, and, on the other hand, not disturbing the course which some citizen is pursuing.[284] If such is the meaning of these terms, then positive control is not disappearing.

We know, of course, that restitutive law is growing. But, in the large majority of cases, it either points out to a citizen the course he ought to pursue, or it interests itself in the means that this citizen is employing to attain his end. It answers the two following questions for each juridical relation: (1) Under what conditions and in what form does it normally exist? (2) What are the obligations it entails? The

---

[284] *Moral Essays*, p. 194 note.

determination of the form and the conditions is essentially positive, since it forces the individual to follow a certain procedure in order to attain his end. As for the obligations, if they only forbid, in principle, our troubling another person in the exercise of his functions, Spencer's thesis would be true, at least in part. But they consist most often in the statement of services of a positive nature.

On this point we must go into some detail.

II

It is quite true that contractual relations, which originally were rare or completely absent, multiply as social labor becomes divided. But what Spencer seems to have failed to see is that non-contractual relations develop at the same time.

First, let us examine that part of law which is improperly termed private, and which, in reality, regulates diffuse social functions, or what may be called the visceral life of the social organism.

In the first place, we know that domestic law, as simple as it was in the beginning, has become more and more complex. That is to say, that the different species of juridical relations to which family life gives rise are much more numerous than heretofore. But the obligations which result from this are of an eminently positive nature; they constitute a reciprocity of rights and duties. Moreover, they are not contractual, at least in their typical form. The conditions upon which they are dependent are related to our personal status which, in turn, depends upon birth, on our consanguineous relations, and, consequently, upon facts which are beyond volition.

Marriage and adoption, however, are sources of domestic relations, and they are contracts. But it rightly happens that the closer we get to the most elevated social types, the more also do these two juridical operations lose their properly contractual character.

Not only in lower societies, but in Rome itself until the end of the Empire, marriage remains an entirely private affair. It generally is a sale, real among primitive people, later fictive, but valid only through the consent of the parties duly attested. Neither solemn formalities of any kind nor intervention by some authority were then necessary. It is only with Christianity that marriage took on another character. The Christians early got into the habit of having their union consecrated by a priest. An act of the emperor Leo the Philosopher converted this usage into a law for the East. The Council of Trent sanctioned it likewise for the West. From then on, marriage ceased to be freely contracted, and was concluded through the intermediary of a public power, the Church, and the role that the Church played was not only that of a witness, but it was she and she alone who created the juridical tie which until then the wills of the participants sufficed to establish.

We know how, later, the civil authority was substituted in this function for the religious authority, and how at the same time the part played by society and its necessary formalities was extended.[285]

The history of the contract of adoption is still more instructive.

We have already seen with what facility and on what a large scale adoption was practiced among the Indian tribes of North America. It could give rise to all the forms of kinship. If the adopted was of the same age as the adopting, they became brothers and sisters; if the adopted was already a mother, she became the mother of the one who adopted her.

Among the Arabs, before Mohammed, adoption often served to establish real families.[286] It frequently happened that several persons would mutually adopt one another. They then became brothers and sisters, and the kinship which united them was just as strong as if they had been descended from a common origin. We find the same type of adoption among the Slavs. Very often, the members of different families became brothers and sisters and formed what is called a confraternity (*probatinstvo*). These societies were contracted for freely and without formality; agreement was enough to establish them. Moreover, the tie which binds these elective brothers is even stronger than that which results from natural fraternity.[287]

Among the Germans, adoption was probably quite as easy and frequent. Very simple ceremonies were enough to establish it.[288] But in India, Greece, and Rome, it was already subordinated to determined conditions. The one adopting had to be of a certain age, could not stand in such relation to the age of the adopted that it would be impossible to be his natural father. Ultimately, this change of family became a highly complex juridical operation which necessitated the intervention of a magistrate. At the same time, the number of those who could enjoy the right of adoption became more restricted. Only the father of a family or a bachelor *sui juris* could adopt, and the first could, only if he had no legitimate children.

In our current law the restrictive conditions have been even more multiplied. The adopted must be of age, the adopting must be more than fifty years of age, and have long treated the adopted as his child. We must notice that, thus limited, it has become a very rare event. Before the appearance of the French Code, the whole procedure had almost completely fallen into disuse, and today it is, in certain countries such as Holland and lower Canada, not permitted at all.

---

[285] Of course, the case is the same for the dissolution of the conjugal bond.

[286] Smith, *Marriage and Kinship in Early Arabia*, p. 135. Cambridge, 1885.

[287] Krauss, *Sitte und Branch der Südslaven*, ch. xxxi.

[288] Viollet, *Précis de l'histoire du droit français*, p. 402.

At the same time that it became more rare, adoption lost its efficacy. In the beginning, adoptive kinship was in all respects similar to natural kinship. In Rome, the similarity was still very great. It was no longer, however, a perfect identity.[289] In the sixteenth century, the adopted no longer has the right of succession if the adoptive father dies intestate.[290] The French Code has re-established this right, but the kinship to which the adoption gives rise does not extend beyond the adopting and the adopted.

We see how insufficient the traditional explanation is, which attributes this custom of adoption among ancient societies to the need of assuring the perpetuity of the ancestral cult. The peoples who have practiced it in the greatest and freest manner, as the Indians of America, the Arabs, the Slavs, had no such cult, and, furthermore, at Rome and Athens, where domestic religion was at its height, this law is for the first time submitted to control and restrictions. If it was able to satisfy these needs, it was not established to satisfy them, and, inversely, if it tends to disappear, it is not because we have less desire to perpetuate our name and our race. It is in the structure of actual societies and in the place which the family occupies that we must seek the determining cause for this change.

Another proof of the truth of this is that it has become even more impossible to leave a family by an act of private authority than to enter into it. As the kinship-tie does not result from a contract, it cannot be broken as a contract can. Among the Iroquois, we sometimes see a part of a clan leave to go to join a neighboring clan.[291] Among the Slavs, a member of the Zadruga who is tired of the common life can separate himself from the rest of the family and become a juridical stranger to it, even as he can be excluded by it.[292] Among the Germans, a ceremony of some slight complexity permitted every Frank who so desired to completely drop off all kinship-obligations.[293] In Rome, the son could not leave the family of his own will, and by this sign we recognize a more elevated social type. But the tie that the son could not break could be broken by the father. Thus was emancipation possible. Today neither the father nor the son can alter the natural state of domestic relations. They remain as birth determines them.

In short, at the same time that domestic obligations become more numerous, they take on, as is said, a public character. Not only in early times do they not have a contractual origin, but the role which contract plays in them becomes ever smaller. On the contrary, social control over the manner in which they form, break down, and are modified,

---

[289] Accarias, *Précis de droit romain*, I, pp. 240 ff.
[290] Viollet, *op. cit.*, p. 406.
[291] *Ancient Society*, p. 81.
[292] Krauss, *op. cit.*, pp. 113 ff.
[293] *Salic Law*, LX.

becomes greater. The reason lies in the progressive effacement of segmental organization. The family, in truth, is for a long time a veritable social segment. In origin, it confounds itself with the clan. If, later, it becomes distinguished from the clan, it is as a part of the whole. It is a product of a secondary segmentation of the clan, identical with that which has given birth to the clan itself, and when the latter has disappeared, it still keeps the same quality. But everything segmental tends to be more and more reabsorbed into the social mass. That is why the family is forced to transform itself. Instead of remaining an autonomous society along side of the great society, it becomes more and more involved in the system of social organs. It even becomes one of the organs, charged with special functions, and, accordingly, everything that happens within it is capable of general repercussions. That is what brings it about that the regulative organs of society are forced to intervene in order to exercise a moderating influence over the functioning of the family, or even, in certain cases, a positively arousing influence.[294]

But it is not only outside of contractual relations, it is in the play of these relations themselves that social action makes itself felt. For everything in the contract is not contractual. The only engagements which deserve this name are those which have been desired by the individuals and which have no other origin except in this manifestation of free will. Inversely, every obligation which has not been mutually consented to has nothing contractual about it. But wherever a contract exists, it is submitted to regulation which is the work of society and not that of individuals, and which becomes ever more voluminous and more complicated.

It is true that the contracting parties can, in certain respects, arrange to act contrary to the dispositions of the law. But, of course, their rights in this regard are not unlimited. For example, the agreement of the parties cannot make a contract valid if it does not satisfy the conditions of validity required by law. To be sure, in the great majority of cases, a contract is no longer restricted to determined forms. Still it must not be forgotten that there are in our Codes solemn contracts. But if law no longer has the formal exigencies of yesterday, it subjects contracts to obligations of a different sort. It refuses all obligatory force to engagements contracted by an incompetent, or without object, or

---

[294] For example, in cases of guardianship, of interdiction, where public authority sometimes intervenes officially. The progress of this regulatory action does not deny the regression, mentioned above, of collective sentiments which concern the family. On the contrary, the first phenomenon supposes the other, for, in order for the sentiments to diminish or become enfeebled, the family must have had to cease to confound itself with society and constitute itself as a sphere of personal action, distinct from the common conscience. But this transformation was necessary in its becoming an organ of society, since, as an organ, it is an individualized part of society.

with illicit purpose, or made by a person who cannot sell, or transacted over an article which cannot be sold. Among the obligations which it attaches to various contracts, there are some which cannot be changed by any stipulation. Thus, a vendor cannot fail in his obligation to guarantee the purchaser against any eviction which results from something personal to the vendor (art. 1628); he cannot fail to repay the purchase-price in case of eviction, whatever its origin, provided that the buyer has not known of the danger (art. 1629), nor to set forth clearly what is being contracted for (art. 1602). Indeed, in a certain measure, he cannot be exempt from guaranteeing against hidden defects (arts. 1641 and 1643), particularly when known. If it is a question of fixtures, it is the buyer who must not profit from the situation by imposing a price too obviously below the real value of the thing (art. 1674), etc. Moreover, everything that relates to proof, the nature of the actions to which the contract gives a right, the time in which they must be begun, is absolutely independent of individual transactions.

In other cases social action does not manifest itself only by the refusal to recognize a contract formed in violation of the law, but by a positive intervention. Thus, the judge can, whatever the terms of the agreement, grant a delay to a debtor (arts. 1184, 1244, 1655, 1900), or even oblige the borrower to restore the article to the lender before the term agreed upon, if the latter has pressing need of it (art. 1189). But what shows better than anything else that contracts give rise to obligations which have not been contracted for is that they "make obligatory not only what there is expressed in them, but also all consequences which equity, usage, or the law imputes from the nature of the obligation" (art. 1135). In virtue of this principle, there must be supplied in the contract "clauses pertaining to usage, although they may not be expressed therein" (art. 1160).

But even if social action should not express itself in this way, it would not cease to be real. This possibility of derogating the law, which seems to reduce the contractual right to the role of eventual substitute for contracts properly called, is, in the very great majority of cases, purely theoretical. We can convince ourselves of this by showing what it consists in.

To be sure, when men unite in a contract, it is because, through the division of labor, either simple or complex, they need each other. But in order for them to co-operate harmoniously, it is not enough that they enter into a relationship, nor even that they feel the state of mutual dependence in which they find themselves. It is still necessary that the conditions of this co-operation be fixed for the duration of their relations. The rights and duties of each must be defined, not only in view of the situation such as it presents itself at the moment when the contract is made, but with foresight for the circumstances which may arise to modify it. Otherwise, at every instant, there would be conflicts and endless difficulties. We must not forget that, if the division of labor makes interests solidary, it does not confound them; it keeps them distinct and opposite. Even as in the internal workings of the individual organism each organ is in conflict with others while co-operating with them, each of the contractants, while needing the other, seeks to obtain what he needs at the least expense; that is to say, to acquire as many rights as possible in exchange for the smallest possible obligations.

It is necessary therefore to pre-determine the share of each, but this cannot be done according to a preconceived plan. There is nothing in the nature of things from which one can deduce what the obligations of one or the other ought to be until a certain limit is reached. Every determination of this kind can only result in compromise. It is a compromise between the rivalry of interests present and their solidarity. It is a position of equilibrium which can be found only after more or less laborious experiments. But it is quite evident that we can neither begin these experiments over again nor restore this equilibrium at fresh expense every time that we engage in some contractual relation. We lack all ability to do that. It is not at the moment when difficulties surge upon us that we must resolve them, and, moreover, we can neither foresee the variety of possible circumstances in which our contract will involve itself, nor fix in advance with the aid of simple mental calculus what will be in each case the rights and duties of each, save in matters in which we have a very definite experience. Moreover, the material conditions of life oppose themselves to the repetition of such operations. For, at each instant, and often at the most inopportune, we find ourselves contracting, either for something we have bought, or sold, somewhere we are traveling, our hiring of one's services, some acceptance of hostelry, etc. The greater part of our relations with others is of a contractual nature. If, then, it were necessary each time to begin the struggles anew, to again go through the conferences necessary to establish firmly all the conditions of agreement for the present and the future, we would be put to rout. For all these reasons, if we were linked only by the terms of our contracts, as they are agreed upon, only a precarious solidarity would result.

But contract-law is that which determines the juridical consequences of our acts that we have not determined. It expresses the normal conditions of equilibrium, as they arise from themselves or from the average. A résumé of numerous, varied experiences, what we cannot foresee individually is there provided for, what we cannot regulate is there regulated, and this regulation imposes itself upon us, although it may not be our handiwork, but that of society and tradition. It forces us to assume obligations that we have not contracted for, in the exact sense of the word, since we have not deliberated upon them, nor even, occasionally, had any knowledge about them in advance. Of course, the initial act is always contractual, but there are consequences, sometimes immediate, which run over the limits of the contract. We co-operate because we wish to, but our voluntary co-operation creates duties for us that we did not desire.

From this point of view, the law of contracts appears in an entirely different light. It is no longer simply a useful complement of individual conventions; it is their fundamental norm. Imposing itself upon us with the authority of traditional experience, it constitutes the foundation of our contractual relations. We cannot evade it, except partially and accidentally. The law confers its-rights upon us and subjects us to duties deriving from such acts of our will. We can, in certain cases, abandon them or change them for others. But both are none the less the normal type of rights and duties which circumstance lays upon us, and an express act is necessary for their modification. Thus, modifications are relatively rare. In principle, the rule applies; innovations are exceptional. The law of contracts exercises over us a regulative force of the greatest importance, since it determines what we ought to do and what we can require. It is a law which can be changed only by the consent of the parties, but so long as it is not abrogated or replaced, it guards its authority, and, moreover, a legislative act can be passed only in rare cases. There is, then, only a difference of degree between the law which regulates the obligations which that contract engenders and those which fix the other duties of citizens.

Finally, besides this organized, defined pressure which law exercises, there is one which comes from custom. In the way in which we make our contracts and in which we execute them, we are held to conform to rules which, though not sanctioned either directly or indirectly by any code, are none the less imperative. There are professional obligations, purely moral, which are, however, very strict. They are particularly apparent in the so-called liberal professions, and if they are perhaps less numerous in others, there is place for demanding them, as we shall see, if such demand is not the result of a morbid condition. But if this action is more diffuse than the preceding, it is just as social. Moreover, it is necessarily as much more extended as the contractual relations are more developed, for it is diversified like contracts.

In sum, a contract is not sufficient unto itself, but is possible only thanks to a regulation of the contract which is originally social. It is implied, first, because it has for its function much less the creation of new rules than the diversification in particular cases of pre-established rules; then, because it has and can have the power to bind only under certain conditions which it is necessary to define. If, in principle, society lends it an obligatory force, it is because, in general, the accord of particular wills suffices to assure, with the preceding reservations, the harmonious coming together of diffuse social functions. But if it conflicts with social purposes, if it tends to trouble the regular operation of organs, if, as is said, it is not just, it is necessary, while depriving it of all social value, to strip it of all authority as well. The role of society is not, then, in any case, simply to see passively that contracts are carried out. It is also to determine under what conditions they are executable, and if it is necessary, to restore them to their normal form. The agreement of parties cannot render a clause just which by itself is unjust, and there are rules of justice whose violation social justice prevents, even if it has been consented to by the interested parties.

A regulation whose extent cannot be limited in advance is thus necessary. A contract, says Spencer, has for its object assuring the worker the equivalent of the expense which his work has cost him.[295] If such is truly the role of a contract, it will never be able to fulfill it unless it is more minutely regulated than it is today, for it surely would be a miracle if it succeeded in bringing about this equivalence. In fact, it is as much the gain which exceeds the expense, as the expense which exceeds the gain, and the disproportion is often striking. But, replies a whole school, if the gains are too small, the function will be abandoned for others. If they are too high, they will be sought after and this will diminish the profits. It is forgotten that one whole part of the population cannot thus quit its task, because no other is accessible to it. The very ones who have more liberty of movement cannot replace it in an instant. Such revolutions always take long to accomplish. While waiting, unjust contracts, unsocial by definition, have been executed with the agreement of society, and when the equilibrium in this respect has been reestablished, there is no reason for not breaking it for another.

There is no need for showing that this intervention, under its different forms, is of an eminently positive nature, since it has for its purpose the determination of the way in which we ought to co-operate. It is not it, it is true, which gives the impulse to the functions concurring, but once the concourse has begun, it rules it. As soon as we have made the first step towards cooperation, we are involved in the regulative action which society exercises over us. If Spencer qualified this as negative, it is because, for him, contract consists only in exchange. But, even from this point of view, the expression he employs is not exact. No doubt, when, after having an object delivered, or profiting from a service, I refuse to furnish a suitable equivalent, I take from another what belongs to him, and we can say that society, by obliging me to keep my promise, is only preventing an injury, an indirect aggression. But if I have simply promised a service without having previously received remuneration, I am not less held to keep my engagement. In this case, however, I do not enrich myself at the

---

[295] In his work on ethics.

expense of another; I only refuse to be useful to him. Moreover, exchange, as we have seen, is not all there is to a contract. There is also the proper harmony of functions concurring. They are not only in contact for the short time during which things pass from one hand to another; but more extensive relations necessarily result from them, in the course of which it is important that their solidarity be not troubled.

Even the biological comparisons on which Spencer willingly bases his theory of free contract are rather the refutation of it. He compares, as we have done, economic functions to the visceral life of the individual organism, and remarks that the latter does not directly depend upon the cerebro-spinal system, but upon a special system whose principal branches are the great sympathetic and the pneumo-gastric. But if from this comparison he is permitted to induce, with some probability, that economic functions are not of a kind to be placed under the immediate influence of the social brain, it does not follow that they can be freed of all regulative influences, for, if the great sympathetic is, in certain measure, independent of the brain, it dominates the movements of the visceral system just as the brain does those of the muscles. If, then, there is in society a system of the same kind, it must have an analogous action over the organs subject to it.

What corresponds to it, according to Spencer, is this exchange of information which takes place unceasingly from one place to another through supply and demand, and which, accordingly, stops or stimulates production.[296] But there is nothing here which resembles a regulatory action. To transmit a new movement is not to command movements. This function pertains to the afferent nerves, but it has nothing in common with that of the nerve-ganglia. It is the latter which exercise the domination of which we have been speaking. Interposed in the path of sensations, it is exclusively through their mediation that the latter reflect themselves in movements. Very probably, if the study were more advanced, we would see that their role, whether they are central or not, is to assure the harmonious concourse of the functions that they govern, which would at every instant be disorganized if it had to vary with each variation of the excitatory impressions. The great social sympathetic must, then, comprise, besides a system of roads for transmission, organs truly regulative which, charged to combine the intestinal acts as the cerebral ganglion combines the external acts, would have the power either to stop the excitations, or to amplify them, or to moderate them according to need.

This comparison induces us to think that the regulative action to which economic life is actually submitted is not what it should normally be. Of course, it is not nil; we have just shown that. Either it is diffuse, or else it comes directly from the State. We will with

---

[296] *Moral Essays*, p. 187.

difficulty find in contemporary societies regulative centres analogous to the ganglia of the great sympathetic. Assuredly, if this doubt had no other basis than the lack of symmetry between the individual and society, it would not merit any attention. But it must not be forgotten that up until recent times these intermediary organizations existed; they were the bodies of workers. We do not have to discuss here their advantages or disadvantages. Moreover, it is difficult to be objective about such discussion, for we cannot settle questions of practical utility without regard to personal feelings. But because of this fact alone, that an institution has been necessary to societies for centuries, it appears improbable that it should all at once fall away. No doubt, societies have changed, but it is legitimate to presume *a priori* that the changes through which they have passed demand less a radical destruction of this type of organization than a transformation. In any case, we have not lived under present conditions long enough to know if this state is normal and definitive or simply accidental and morbid. Even the uneasiness which is felt during this epoch in this sphere of social life does not seem to prejudge a favorable reply. We shall find in the rest of this work other facts which confirm this presumption.[297]

III

Finally, there is administrative law. We give this name to the totality of rules which determine, first, the functions of the central organ and their relations; then, the functions of the organs which are immediately subordinate to the first, their relations with one another, their relations with the first and with the diffuse functions of society. If we again borrow biological terminology which, though metaphorical, is none the less useful, we may say that these rules determine the way in which the cerebro-spinal system of the social organism functions. This system, in current parlance, is designated by the name, State.

There is no contesting the fact that social action which is thus expressed has a positive nature. In effect, its object is to fix the manner in which these special functions must co-operate. In certain respects, it even imposes such co-operation, for these various organs can be held together only with help imperatively demanded of each citizen. But, according to Spencer, this regulative system would be regressing as the industrial type gains sway over the military type, and finally the functions of the State would be reduced solely to administering justice.

The reasons employed in support of this proposition, however, are remarkably poor; they consist almost completely of a short comparison between England and France, and between England of yesterday and

---

[297] See Book III, ch. i.—See particularly the preface [to the second edition—G. S.] where we have expressed ourselves more explicitly on this point.

today. It is from this that Spencer claims to induce his general law of historical development.[298] The standards of proof, however, are not different in sociology from those in other sciences. To prove an hypothesis is not to show that it accounts very well for certain facts considered appropriate; one must make experiments with method. It must be shown that the phenomena between which we are establishing a relation either concur universally, or cannot exist one without the other, or that they vary in the same sense and in direct relationship. But some few examples thrown together in helter-skelter fashion do not constitute proof.

These facts taken by themselves do not prove anything of the kind. All that they prove is that the place of the individual becomes greater and the governmental power becomes *less absolute*. But there is no contradiction in the fact that the sphere of individual action grows at the same time as that of the State, or that the functions which are not made immediately dependent upon the central regulative system develop at the same time as it. Moreover, a power can be at once absolute and very simple. Nothing is less complex than the despotic government of a barbarian chief. The functions he fills are rudimentary and not very numerous. That is because the directive organ of social life can absorb all these in itself, without on that account being very highly developed if social life itself is not very highly developed. This organ exerts an exceptional force upon the rest of society, because there is nothing to hold it in check or to neutralize it. But it can very well happen that it takes up more volume at the same time that other organs are formed which balance it. It suffices on this account that the total volume of the organism be increased. No doubt, the action that it exerts under these conditions is no longer of the same nature, but the points at which it exercises its power have multiplied, and if it is less violent, it still imposes itself quite as formally. Acts of disobedience to constituted authority are no longer treated as sacrilegious, nor, consequently, repressed with the same severity. But they are not tolerated any the more, and these orders are more numerous and govern very different types. But the question which is posed is that of finding out, not if the coercive power which this regulative system dispenses is more or less intense, but whether this system itself has become more or less voluminous.

Once the problem has been thus formulated, there can be no doubt as to the solution. History surely shows, in very systematic fashion, that administrative law is as much more developed as societies approach a more elevated type. On the other hand, the farther back to origins we go, the more rudimentary is this type of law. The ideal State of Spencer is really the primitive form of the State. In fact, the only functions

---

[298] *Principles of Sociology*, III, pp. 822-834.

which normally pertain to the State in English philosophy are those relating to justice and to war, in the measure at least to which war is necessary. In lower societies, the State does not effectively play any other role. To be sure, these functions are not there conceived as they are now, but they are no different because of that. The whole tyrannical intervention which Spencer notes there is only one of the ways in which judicial power is exercised. In repressing attacks against religion, etiquette, against traditions of all sorts, the State fills the same office that judges do today when they protect the lives and property of individuals. But these duties become more and more numerous and varied as we approach higher social types. The very organ of justice, which is originally very simple, more and more moves towards differentiation. Various tribunals grow up, distinct magistracies are set up, the respective role of each is determined through its relations with others. A multitude of functions which were diffuse become concentrated. The care of educating the young, of protecting the public health, of presiding over the ways of administering public aid, of administering the means of transport and communication, little by little move over into the sphere of the central organ. Accordingly, the central organ develops and, at the same time, it progressively extends a more compact system over the whole surface of the territory, a system more and more complex with ramifications which displace or assimilate pre-existing local organs. Statistical services keep it informed of everything important that goes on in the organism. The system of international relations, that is, diplomacy, takes on greater and greater proportions. As institutions, such as great credit-establishments, are formed, having a general interest because of their dimensions and proportional multiplicity of function, the State exercises a moderating influence over them. Finally, even the military system, whose regression Spencer affirms, seems to develop and centralize itself in an uninterrupted manner.

This evolution is proved by so many evidences from historical fact that we do not think it necessary to go into any further detail in proof of it. If we compare tribes devoid of all central authority with centralized tribes, and the latter to the city, the city to feudal societies, feudal societies to present societies, we follow, step by step, the principal stages of development whose general march we have just traced. It is thus contrary to all method to regard the present dimensions of the governmental organ as a symptom of social illness, due to a concourse of accidental circumstances. Everything forces us to see in it a normal phenomenon, which holds even of the structure of higher societies, since it progresses in a perfectly continuous way, as societies tend to approach this type.

We can, moreover, show, at least in the large, how this results from the very progress of the division of labor and from the transformation which effects the passage of societies from a segmental type to an organized type.

As each segment has its life peculiar to it, it forms a small society within the great, and has, consequently, its own regulative organs, just as the great society. But their vitality is necessarily proportional to the intensity of this local life. They cannot fail to weaken when it is itself weakened. But we know that this enfeeblement is produced with the progressive effacement of segmental organization. The central organ, finding less resistance before it, since the forces which held it in check have lost their energy, develops and takes unto itself these functions, similar to those which it exercises, but which can no longer be held by those who formerly held them. These local organs, instead of holding to their individuality and remaining diffuse, become confounded in the central system which grows accordingly, grows in proportion to the vastness of society and the completeness of the fusion. That is to say, it is as much more voluminous as societies are of a more elevated type.

This phenomenon is produced with mechanical necessity, and, moreover, it is useful, for it corresponds to the new state of things. In the measure that society ceases to be formed by a repetition of similar segments, the regulative system must itself cease to be formed by a repetition of segmental, autonomous organs. We do not wish to imply, however, that the State normally absorbs into itself all the regulative organs of society no matter what they are, but only those which are of the same type as its own; that is to say, those which preside over life in general. As for those which take care of special functions, such as economic functions, they are outside its sphere of influence. It can even produce among them coalescence of the same kind, but not between them and it, or at least, if they are within the power of superior authorities, they remain distinct from them. Among the vertebrates, the cerebro-spinal system is very highly developed. It has influence over the great sympathetic, but it permits this latter great autonomy.

In the second place, when society is made up of segments, whatever is produced in one of the segments has as little chance of re-echoing in the others as the segmental organization is strong. The cellular system naturally lends itself to the localization of social events and their consequents. Thus it happens that in a colony of polyps one of the individuals can be sick without the others feeling it. This is no longer true when society is made up of a system of organs. According to their mutual dependence, what strikes one strikes the others, and thus every change, even slightly significant, takes on a general interest.

This generalization is further validated by two other circum stances. The more divided labor is, the less each social organ consists of distinct parts. As large-scale industry is substituted for small, the number of different enterprises grows less. Each has more relative importance, because it represents a greater fraction of the whole.

Whatever happens therein has much more extensive social repercussions. The closing of a small shop causes very little trouble, which is felt only within small compass. The failure of a great industrial company results, on the contrary, in public distress. Moreover, as the progress of the division of labor demands a very great concentration of the social mass, there is between the different parts of the same tissue, of the same organ, or the same system, a more intimate contact which makes happenings much more contagious. A movement in one part rapidly communicates itself to others. We need only look at how speedily a strike becomes general today in the same body of workers. But distress of some general scope cannot be produced without affecting the higher centres. These, being badly affected, are forced to intervene, and this intervention is more frequent as the social type is more elevated. But, on that account, it is necessary that they be organized. They must extend their ramifications in all directions in such a way as to be in relation with different regions of the organism, also in such manner as to hold in immediate dependence certain organs whose free play would, on occasion, have exceptionally grave repercussions. In short, since their functions become more numerous and complex, it is necessary for the organ which serves as their foundation to develop, just as the body of juridical rules which determine them.

To the reproach often leveled against him for contradicting his own doctrine by admitting that the development of the higher centres has been accomplished in a sense inverse in societies and organisms, Spencer replies that the different variations of the organ are linked to corresponding variations of the function. According to him, the essential role of the cerebrospinal system would be to regulate the relations of the individual with the outside world, to combine movements either for grasping booty or escaping the enemy.[299] As a system of attack and defense, it is naturally very voluminous among the most elevated organisms where the external relations are themselves very developed. Such is the case in military societies which live in a state of chronic hostility with their neighbors. On the contrary, among industrial peoples war is the exception; social interests are principally of an internal order; the external regulative system, no longer having the same reason for existence, necessarily regresses.

But this explanation rests on a double error.

First, every organism, whether or not it has predatory instincts, lives in an environment with which it has relations as much more numerous as it is more complex. If, then, the relations of hostility diminish in the measure that societies become more pacific, they are replaced by others. Industrial peoples have a commerce developed differently from that which lower peoples have with one another, as

---

[299] *Moral Essays*, p. 179.

bellicose as they are. We are speaking, not of the commerce which is established between individuals, but of that which unites social bodies together. Each society has general interests to defend against other societies, if not through force of arms, at least through negotiations, coalitions, treaties.

Moreover, it is not true that the brain presides over only external relations. Not only can it modify the state of the organs through means wholly internal, but even when it acts externally, it exercises its action within. Even the most internal viscera cannot function without the aid of materials which come from without, and as the brain sovereignly takes care of these materials, it thus has an influence over the total organism at all times. The stomach, it is said, has nothing to do with this order, but the presence of food is enough to excite peristaltic movements. If food is present, however, the brain has willed it, and the food is there in the quantity that it has fixed and the quality it has chosen. It does not command the beatings of the heart, but it can, by appropriate treatment, retard or accelerate them. There are not many tissues which do not undergo some one of the disciplines that it imposes, and the empire that it rules is as much more extensive and profound as the animal is of a more elevated type. Its true role is presiding, not only over relations from without, but over the totality of life. Its function is as complex as life itself is rich and concentrated. The same is true of societies. The governmental organ is more or less considerable, not because the people are more or less pacific, but rather because its growth is proportional to the progress of the division of labor, societies comprising more different organs the more intimately solidary they are.

IV

The following propositions sum up the first part of our work. Social life comes from a double source, the likeness of consciences and the division of social labor. The individual is socialized in the first case, because, not having any real individuality, he becomes, with those whom he resembles, part of the same collective type; in the second case, because, while having a physiognomy and a personal activity which distinguishes him from others, he depends upon them in the same measure that he is distinguished from them, and consequently upon the society which results from their union.

The similitude of consciences gives rise to juridical rules which, with the threat of repressive measures, impose uniform beliefs and practices upon all. The more pronounced this is, the more completely is social life confounded with religious life, and the nearer to communism are economic institutions.

The division of labor gives rise to juridical rules which determine the nature and the relations of divided functions, but whose violation calls forth only restitutive measures without any expiatory character. Each of these bodies of juridical rules is, moreover, accompanied by a body of purely moral rules. Where penal law is very voluminous, common morality is very extensive; that is to say, there is a multitude of collective practices placed under the protection of public opinion. Where restitutive law is highly developed, there is an occupational morality for each profession. In the interior of the same group of workers, there exists an opinion, diffuse in the entire extent of this circumscribed aggregate, which, without being furnished with legal sanctions, is rendered obedience. There are usages and customs common to the same order of functionaries which no one of them can break without incurring the censure of the corporation.[300] This morality is distinguished from the preceding by differences analogous to those which separate the two corresponding types of law. It is localized in a limited region of society. Moreover, the repressive character of the sanctions attaching to it is much less accentuated. Professional misdeeds call forth reprobation much more feeble than attacks against public morality.

The rules of occupational morality and justice, however, are as imperative as the others. They force the individual to act in view of ends which are not strictly his own, to make concessions, to consent to compromises, to take into account interests higher than his own. Consequently, even where society relies most completely upon the division of labor, it does not become a jumble of juxtaposed atoms, between which it can establish only external, transient contacts. Rather the members are united by ties which extend deeper and far beyond the short moments during which the exchange is made. Each of the functions that they exercise is, in a fixed way, dependent upon others, and with them forms a solidary system. Accordingly, from the nature of the chosen task permanent duties arise. Because we fill some certain domestic or social function, we are involved in a complex of obligations from which we have no right to free ourselves. There is, above all, an organ upon which we are tending to depend more and more; this is the State. The points at which we are in contact with it multiply as do the occasions when it is entrusted with the duty of reminding us of the sentiment of common solidarity.

Thus, altruism is not destined to become, as Spencer desires, a sort of agreeable ornament to social life, but it will forever be its fundamental basis. How can we ever really dispense with it? Men cannot live together without acknowledging, and, consequently,

---

[300] This censure, moreover, just as all moral punishment, is translated into external movements (discipline, dismissal of employees, loss of relations, etc.).

making mutual sacrifices, without tying themselves to one another with strong, durable bonds. Every society is a moral society. In certain respects, this character is even more pronounced in organized societies. Because the individual is not sufficient unto himself, it is from society that he receives everything necessary to him, as it is for society that he works. Thus is formed a very strong sentiment of the state of dependence in which he finds himself. He becomes accustomed to estimating it at its just value, that is to say, in regarding himself as part of a whole, the organ of an organism. Such sentiments naturally inspire not only mundane sacrifices which assure the regular development of daily social life, but even, on occasion, acts of complete self-renunciation and wholesale abnegation. On its side, society learns to regard its members no longer as things over which it has rights, but as co-operators whom it cannot neglect and towards whom it owes duties. Thus, it is wrong to oppose a society which comes from a community of beliefs to one which has a co-operative basis, according only to the first a moral character, and seeing in the latter only an economic grouping. In reality, co-operation also has its intrinsic morality. There is, however, reason to believe, as we shall see later, that in contemporary societies this morality has not yet reached the high development which would now seem necessary to it.

But it is not of the same nature as the other. The other is strong only if the individual is not. Made up of rules which are practiced by all indistinctly, it receives from this universal, uniform practice an authority which bestows something superhuman upon it, and which puts it beyond the pale of discussion. The co-operative society, on the contrary, develops in the measure that individual personality becomes stronger. As regulated as a function may be, there is a large place always left for personal initiative. A great many of the obligations thus sanctioned have their origin in a choice of the will. It is we who choose our professions, and even certain of our domestic functions. Of course, once our resolution has ceased to be internal and has been externally translated by social consequences, we are tied down. Duties are imposed upon us that we have not expressly desired. It is, however, through a voluntary act that this has taken place. Finally, because these rules of conduct relate, not to the conditions of common life, but to the different forms of professional activity, they have a more temporal character, which, while lessening their obligatory force, renders them more accessible to the action of men.

There are, then, two great currents of social life to which two types of structure, not less different, correspond.

Of these currents, that which has its origin in social similitudes first runs on alone and without a rival. At this moment, it confounds itself with the very life of society; then, little by little, it canalizes, rarefies, while the second is always growing. Indeed, the segmental structure is more and more covered over by the other, but without ever completely disappearing.

We have just established the reality of this relation of inverse variation. We shall find the causes for it in the following book.

Book Two. Causes and Conditions

CHAPTER ONE. THE PROGRESS OF THE DIVISION OF LABOR AND OF HAPPINESS

What causes have brought about the progress of the division of labor?

To be sure, this cannot be a question of finding a unique formula which takes into account all the possible modalities of the division of labor. Such a formula does not exist. Each particular circumstance depends upon particular causes that can only be determined by special examination. The problem we are raising is less vast. If one takes away the various forms the division of labor assumes according to conditions of time and place, there remains the fact that it advances regularly in history. This fact certainly depends upon equally constant causes which we are going to seek.

These causes cannot consist in an anticipated idea of the effects the division of labor produces in its contribution towards maintaining societies in equilibrium. That is a repercussion too remote to be understood by everyone. Most are unaware of it. In any case, it could only have become evident when the division of labor was already greatly advanced.

According to the most widely disseminated theory, it has its origin in man's unceasing desire to increase his happiness. It is known, indeed, that the more work is specialized, the higher the yield. The resources put at our disposal are more abundant and also of better quality. Science is perfected and more expeditious; works of art are more numerous and refined; industry produces more, and its products are nearer perfect. Now, man has need of all these things. It would seem, then, that he must be so much happier as he possesses more, and, consequently, that he may be naturally incited to look for them.

That granted, there is a simple explanation of the regularity with which the division of labor progresses. It is said to be sufficient that a net-work of circumstances, easy to imagine, may have warned man of some of these advantages, causing him to seek their further extension, and the greatest possible profit. The division of labor would then advance under the influence of exclusively individual and psychological causes. To propound its theory, it would not be necessary to observe societies and their structures. The simplest and most fundamental instinct of the human heart would be sufficient to account for it. It is the need of happiness which would urge the individual to specialize more and more. To be sure, as all specialization supposes the simultaneous presence of several individuals and their co-operation, it is not possible without a society. But in place of being its determinate cause, society would only be the means through which it is realized, the necessary material in the organization of the divided work. It would even be an effect of the phenomenon rather than its cause. Is it not endlessly repeated that the need for co-operation has given birth to societies? They would then be formed so that work could be divided, rather than work being divided for social reasons.

This explanation is classic in political economy. Moreover, it appears so simple and so evident that it is unconsciously admitted by a host of thinkers whose opinions are altered by it. That is why it is necessary to examine it first of all.

I

Nothing is less evident than the so-called axiom on which it rests.

No rational limit can be assigned to the productive power of work. To be sure, it depends upon technique, capital, etc. But these obstacles are never anything but provisional, as experience proves, and each generation pushes ever further back the boundary which stopped the preceding generation. Even were it to achieve a maximum one day that it could not surpass—gratuitous supposition—at least, it certainly has a field of immense development behind it. If, then, as is supposed, happiness increased regularly with it, it would also have to be able to increase indefinitely, or at least the increases to which it is susceptible would have to be proportionate to the other's advances. If it increased proportionally as agreeable stimuli become more numerous and more intense, it would be quite natural for man always to seek to produce more to enjoy still more. But, as a matter of fact, our capacity for happiness is very limited.

Indeed, it is a truth generally recognized today that pleasure accompanies neither the very intense states of conscience, nor those very feeble. There is pain when the functional activity is insufficient, but excessive activity produces the same effects.[301] Certain psychologists believe that pain is bound to a too intense nervous vibration.[302] Pleasure is, then, situated between these two extremes. This proposition is, besides, a corollary of the law of Weber and Fechner. If the mathematical formula these experimenters have given it

---

[301] Spencer, *Principles of Psychology*, I, p. 283; Wundt, *Physiological Psychology*, I, ch. x, § 1.

[302] Richet. See his article *Douleur* in *Dictionnaire encyclopédique des sciences médicales*.

is of questionable exactitude, they have removed doubt from at least one point. It is that the variations of intensity through which a sensation can pass are comprised within two limits. If the stimulus is too feeble, it is not felt; but if it surpasses a certain degree, the increases produce less and less effect, until they cease to be felt. Now, this law is equally true of the quality of sensation that is called pleasure. It was even formulated for pleasure and pain long before it was for other elements of sensation. Bernouilli applied it directly to the most complex sentiments, and Laplace, interpreting it in the same sense, gave it the form of a relation between physical fortune and moral fortune.[303] The gamut of variations through which the intensity of the same pleasure can run is thus limited.

Furthermore, if the states of conscience whose intensity is moderated are generally agreeable, they do not all present conditions equally favorable to the production of pleasure. In the region of the lower limit, the changes through which agreeable activity passes are too small in absolute value to determine sentiments of pleasure of great energy. On the other hand, when it approaches the point of indifference, that is, its maximum, the magnitude developed has too feeble a relative value. A man who has very little capital cannot easily increase it in proportions sufficient to change his condition perceptibly. That is why first economies carry so little joy with them; they are too petty to improve the situation. The insignificant advantages procured do not compensate for the privations they have cost. In the same way, a man whose fortune is excessive finds pleasure only in exceptional beneficence, for he measures its importance by what he already has. It is quite otherwise with average fortunes. Here, both the absolute size and the relative size of the variations are in best condition for production of pleasure, for they are sufficiently important, and yet it is not necessary for them to be extraordinary to be estimated at their worth. The standard serving to measure their value is not yet so high as to result in strong depreciation. The intensity of an agreeable stimulus can then increase *usefully* only between limits still more closely related than we first said, for it can only produce its full effect in the interval which corresponds to the average part of the agreeable activity. Above and below that, pleasure still exists, but it is not proportional to the cause producing it, whereas, in the limited zone, the least oscillations are felt and appreciated. Nothing of the energy of the stimulus converted into pleasure is lost.[304]

What we have just said of the intensity of each stimulus could be repeated of their number. They cease to be agreeable when they are too

---

[303] Laplace, *Théorie analytique des probabilités*, Paris, 1847, pp. 187, 432.— Fechner, *Psychophysik*, I, p. 236.
[304] Cf. Wundt, *loc. cit.*

many or too few, as when they surpass or do not attain a certain degree of vivacity. It is not without reason that human experience sees the condition of happiness in the *golden mean.*

If, then, the division of labor had really advanced only to increase our happiness, it would have arrived at its extreme limit a long time ago, as well as the civilization resulting from it, and both would have stopped. For to have man lead this temperate existence most favorable to pleasure, it was not necessary indefinitely to accumulate stimuli of all sorts. A moderate development would have been sufficient to assure individuals the sum-total of pleasures of which they were capable. Humanity would have rapidly come to a state from which it would not have emerged That is what happened to animals; most have not changed for centuries, because they have arrived at this state of equilibrium.

Other considerations lead to the same conclusion. It cannot absolutely be said that every agreeable state is useful, that pleasure and utility always vary in the same sense and same relation. Nevertheless, an organism pleased with things injurious to it evidently could not exist. It can then be accepted as a very general truth that pleasure is not linked to harmful states; which is to say that, in the large, happiness coincides with a healthy state. Only beings tainted with some physiological or psychological perversion find joy in morbidity. But health consists in a mean activity. It implies, in effect, a harmonious development of all functions, and functions can develop harmoniously only by virtue of moderating one another, by being mutually contained within certain limits beyond which sickness begins and pleasure ceases. As for a simultaneous growth of all faculties, it is possible for a given being only in very restricted measure, marked by the congenital state of the individual.

One thus understands what limits human happiness. It is the constitution of man, taken at each moment of history. Being given his temperament, the degree of attained physical and moral development, there is a maximum of happiness as well as a maximum of activity that cannot be surpassed. This is scarcely denied when it is a question of the organism. Everyone recognizes that the needs of the body are limited, and that, consequently, physical pleasure cannot increase indefinitely. But it is said that spiritual functions are exceptions. "No pain to chastise and repress . . . the most energetic impulses of devotion and charity, the passionate and enthusiastic search for truth and beauty. Hunger is satisfied with a determined quantity of food; reason cannot be satisfied with a determined quantity of knowledge."[305]

---

[305] Rabier, *Leçons de philosophie*, I, p. 479.

This overlooks that conscience, as the organism, is a system of functions which sets up an equilibrium, and that, moreover, it is linked to an organic substratum of the state upon which it depends. It is said there is a degree of fight that the eyes cannot support, but that there is never too much fight for reason. Too much knowledge, however, can be acquired only by an exaggerated development of the higher nervous centres, which itself cannot be produced without being accompanied by painful distress. There is then a maximum limit that cannot be surpassed with impunity, and as it varies with the average brain, it was particularly low at the beginning of humanity. Consequently, the limit was quickly attained. But understanding is only one of our faculties. It can increase beyond a certain point only to the detriment of the practical faculties, disrupting sentiments, beliefs, customs, with which we live, and such a rupture of equilibrium cannot take place without troublesome consequences. The followers of the crudest religion find pleasure in a rudimentary cosmogony and philosophy that is taught them which we must rise above without any compensation if we are to succeed in inculcating into them our scientific doctrines, no matter how unquestionable the latter's superiority. At each moment of history and in the conscience of each individual there is a determined place for clear ideas, reflected opinions, in short, for science, beyond which it cannot normally extend.

It is the same with morality. Each people has its morality which is determined by the conditions in which it lives. Another, therefore, cannot be inculcated, be it ever so elevated, without disorganization as consequence, and such troubles cannot but be painfully felt by the particular individuals. But the morality of each society, taken in and of itself, does it not allow an indefinite development of its charged virtues? Not at all. To act morally is to do one's duty, and all duty is limited. It is limited by other duties. One cannot give oneself too completely to others without abandoning oneself. One cannot develop personality to excess without developing egotism. On the other hand, the aggregate of our duties is itself limited by other exigencies of our nature. If it is necessary that certain forms of conduct be submitted to this imperative regulation characteristic of morality, there are others, on the contrary, naturally refractory, yet essential. Morality cannot excessively govern industrial, commercial functions, etc. without paralyzing them, and nevertheless they are vital. Thus, to consider wealth as immoral is not less deadly an error than to see in wealth the good *par excellence.* There can, then, be excesses of morality from which morality, indeed, is the first to suffer, for as its immediate object is to govern our temporal life, it cannot turn us from that temporal life without relinquishing the material to which it is applied.

The aesthetico-moral activity, it is true, seems freed of all control and limitation because it is not regulated. But, as a matter of fact, it is narrowly circumscribed by activity properly moral, for it can surpass a certain standard only to the detriment of morality. If we expend too much of our energy on the superfluous, there no longer remains enough for the necessary. When the place of the imagination in morality is made too great, obligatory tasks are necessarily neglected. All discipline appears intolerable when one is used to acting only under rules of one's own making. Too much idealism and moral elevation often deprives a man of the taste to fulfill his daily duties.

In general, the same may be said of all aesthetic activity; it is healthy only if moderated. The need of playing, acting without end and for the pleasure of acting, cannot be developed beyond a certain point without depriving oneself of serious life. Too great an artistic sensibility is a sickly phenomenon which cannot become general without danger to society. The limit beyond which excess begins is, of course, variable, according to the people or the social environment. It begins so much sooner as society is less advanced, or the environment less cultivated. The workingman, if he is in harmony with his conditions of existence, is and must be closed to pleasures normal to the man of letters, and it is the same with the savage in relation to civilized man.

If it is thus with the cultivation of the mind, with still stronger reason is it so of material luxury. There is, then, a normal intensity of all our needs, intellectual, moral, as well as physical, which cannot be exaggerated. At each moment of history, our thirst for science, art, and well-being is defined as are our appetites, and all that goes beyond this standard leaves us indifferent or causes us suffering. That is too often forgotten in comparing the happiness of our ancestors with our own. We reason as if all our pleasures could have been theirs. Then, thinking of all the refinements of civilization enjoyed by us and which they knew nothing about, we are inclined to pity their lot. We forget they were not qualified to enjoy them. If they were so greatly tormented by the desire to increase the productive power of work, it was not to achieve goods without value to them. To appreciate these goods, they would have had to contract tastes and habits they did not have, which is to say, to change their nature.

That is indeed what they have done, as the history of the transformations through which humanity has passed shows. For the need of greater happiness to account for the development of the division of labor, it would then be necessary for it also to be the cause of the changes progressively wrought in human nature, and for men to have changed in order to become happier.

But, even supposing that these transformations have had such a result, it is impossible that they were produced for that, and, consequently, they depend upon another cause.

Indeed, a change of existence, whether it be sudden or prepared, always brings forth a painful crisis, for it does violence to acquired instincts which oppose it. All the past holds us back, even though the most beautiful vistas appear before us. It is always a laborious operation to pull up the roots of habits that time has fixed and organized in us. It is possible that sedentary life offers more chances for happiness than nomadic life, but when this latter life has been led for centuries, it cannot easily be cast aside. Again, no matter how simple these transformations may be, an individual life is not sufficient to accomplish them. A generation is not enough to cast aside the work of generations, to put a new man in the place of the old. In the present state of our societies, work is not only useful, it is necessary; everyone feels this, and this necessity has been felt for a long time. Nevertheless, those who find pleasure in regular and persistent work are still few and far between. For most men, it is still an insupportable servitude. The idleness of primitive times has not lost its old attractions for them. These metamorphoses then cost a great deal for a long time without accomplishing anything. The generations inaugurating them do not receive the fruits, if there are any, because they come late. They have only the pain. Consequently, it is not the expectation of a greater happiness which drags them into such enterprises.

But, in fact, is it true that the happiness of the individual increases as man advances? Nothing is more doubtful.

II

Assuredly, there is a host of pleasures open to us today that more simple natures knew nothing about. But, on the other hand, we are exposed to a host of sufferings spared them, and it is not at all certain that the balance is to our advantage. Thought, to be sure, is a source of joy which can be very intense, but, at the same time, how much joy does it trouble! For a solved problem, how many questions are raised without solution! For a cleared-up doubt, how many mysteries come to disconcert! Indeed, if the savage knows nothing of the pleasures of bustling life, in return, he is immune to boredom, that monster of cultivated minds. His life runs on quietly without perpetually feeling the need of filling the shortest moments with numerous hurried facts. Let us not forget, besides, that work is still for most men a punishment and a scourge.

It will be said that with civilized people life is more varied, and variety is necessary to pleasure. But at the same time as there is a greater mobility, civilization carries with it more uniformity, for it has imposed upon man monotonous and continuous labor. The savage goes from one occupation to another, according to the circumstances and needs affecting him. The civilized man devotes himself entirely to a task which is always the same, and offering less variety as it is more greatly restricted. Organization necessarily implies an absolute regularity in habits, for a change cannot take place in an organ's function without the whole organism being affected by repercussions. From that angle, our life leaves least to chance at the same time that, by its greater instability, it takes away from enjoyment a part of the security it needs.

It is true that our nervous system, having become more delicate, is accessible to feeble stimuli that did not affect the less refined system of our ancestors. But, in addition, a great many stimuli formerly agreeable have become too strong for us, and, consequently, painful. If we are open to more pleasures, we are also open to more pain. On the other hand, if it is true, all things being equal, that suffering produces a more profound effect upon the organism than joy,[306] that a disagreeable stimulus produces more pain than an agreeable stimulus of the same intensity produces pleasure, this greater sensibility might well be more unfavorable than favorable to happiness. In fact, extremely refined nervous systems live in pain and end by attaching themselves to it. Is it not very remarkable that the fundamental cult of the most civilized religions is that of human suffering? Doubtless, for life to maintain itself, it is necessary, today as before, that in average circumstances pleasures exceed pains. But it is not certain that the excess has become greater.

Finally, there is no proof that this excess ever is a measure of happiness. To be sure, in these obscure and still badly studied questions, one can affirm nothing with certainty. But it appears fairly certain that happiness is something besides a sum of pleasures. It is a general and constant state accompanying the regular activity of all our organic and psychical functions. Thus, continuous activities, as those of respiration and circulation, do not yield positive enjoyment. But our good humor and spirits depend especially upon them. All pleasure is a sort of crisis; it is born, lasts a moment, and dies. Life, on the contrary, is continuous. What gives it its fundamental attraction must be continuous like itself. Pleasure is local; it is a limited affection of a point in the organism or conscience. Life resides neither here nor there, but everywhere. Our attachment for it must then be rooted in some equally general cause. In short, what happiness expresses is not the momentary state of a particular function, but the health of physical and moral life in its entirety. As pleasure accompanies the normal exercise of intermittent functions, it is indeed an element of happiness, and as much more important as these functions take greater parts in life. But it is not happiness; it can raise or lower the level only in restricted fashion, for it clings to ephemeral causes; happiness rests in permanent

---

[306] See Hartmann, *Philosophy of the Unconscious.*

dispositions. For local accidents to be able to affect this fundamental base of our sensibility profoundly, they would have to be repeated with an exceptional frequency and consistency. Most often, on the contrary, pleasure depends upon happiness. According to whether we are happy or sad, all things attract or sadden us. There is good reason for saying we carry our happiness within ourselves.

But, this being so, there is no longer any reason for asking whether happiness grows with civilization. It is the index of the state of health. Now, the health of a species is no more complete because that species happens to be of a higher type. A healthy mammifer is in no better health than a protozoan equally healthy. It must then be the same with happiness. It does not become greater because activity becomes richer, but it is the same wherever it is healthy. The most simple and the most complex being enjoy the same happiness if they equally realize their natures. The normal savage can be quite as happy as the normal civilized man.

Thus, the savages are quite as content with their lot as we can be with ours. This perfect contentment is even one of the distinctive traits of their character. They desire nothing more than they have, and have no wish to change their condition. "The inhabitant of the North," says Waitz, "does not look to the South to improve his position, and the inhabitant of a warm and unhealthy country does not aspire to leave it for a more favorable climate. In spite of the numerous maladies and evils of all sorts to which the inhabitant of Darfur is exposed, he loves his country, and not only does not emigrate but longs to return if he is in a foreign country. ... As a general rule, whatever the material misfortune of a people, it does not prevent the consideration of that country as the best in the world, its kind of life the most fecund with regard to pleasures, and looking to themselves as the first of all peoples. This conviction generally is the conviction of the Negro peoples."[307] Thus, in exploited countries, as so many in America, the natives firmly believe that the whites left their country only to come to seek happiness in America. The example is cited of young savages that unrest caused to leave their country in search of happiness, but they are very rare exceptions.

It is true that observers have sometimes painted the life of lower societies in quite different colors. But that is because they have taken their own impressions for that of the natives. But an existence which appears intolerable to us can be quite satisfying for men of a different physical and moral constitution. For example, when, from infancy on, one is accustomed to risking his life at every moment, and, consequently, to reckon it for nothing, what is death? To pity the lot of primitive peoples, it is not enough to establish that hygiene is badly

---

[307] Waitz, *Anthropologie* I, p. 346.

observed there, that police protection is wanting. The individual alone is competent to appreciate his happiness. He is happy if he feels happy. But, "from the inhabitant of Tierra del Fuego up to the Hottentot, man, in the natural state, lives satisfied with himself and his lot."[308] How much more rare contentment is in Europe! These facts explain the statement of a person of experience: "There are situations in which a thinking man feels himself inferior to the one whom nature alone has raised, in which he asks himself if his most solid convictions are worth more than the narrow prejudices which are enduring."[309]

But here is more objective proof. The only experimental fact proving that life is generally good is that the great mass of men prefer it to death. To be so, in the average life, happiness must prevail over unhappiness. If the relations were reversed, neither the attachment of men to life, nor its continuance jostled by the facts at each moment, could be understood. Pessimists, it is true, explain the persistence of this phenomenon by the illusions of hope. According to them, if, in spite of the deceptions of experience, we hold on to life, it is because we are wrongly hoping that the future will make up for the past. But even admitting that hope is sufficient to explain the love of life, it does not explain itself. It has not miraculously descended from heaven into our hearts, but it has had to be formed, as all sentiments, within the action of the facts. If, then, men have learned to hope, if, under a blow of misfortune, they have acquired the habit of turning their eyes toward the future, and of awaiting compensations for their present sufferings, it is because they see that these compensations are frequent, that the human organism is at once too supple and too resistant to be easily beaten into despondency, that the moments won by misfortune were exceptional, and that, generally, the balance ended by returning to its former state. Consequently, whatever may be the part of hope in the genesis of the instinct of conservation, the latter is a piercing witness of the relative bounty of life. For the same reason, where it loses either its energy, or its generality, one can be certain that life itself loses its attractions, that evil increases, or the causes of suffering increase, or the resistive force of individuals is reduced. If, then, we possess an objective and measurable fact translating the variations of intensity through which this sentiment passes in societies, we shall be able with one stroke to measure those of the average unhappiness in these same environments. This fact is the number of suicides. In the same way as the relative rarity of voluntary deaths is the best proof of the power and universality of this instinct, the fact that they increase proves it is losing ground.

---

[308] Waitz, *loc. cit.*, p. 347.
[309] Cowper Rose, *Four Years in Southern Africa*, p. 173, 1829.

But suicide scarcely appears except with civilization. [It is very rare in lower societies, or] [310] at least the only kind one observes there, [sometimes][311] in chronic state, presents very particular characteristics of a special type whose symptomatic value is not the same. It is not an act of despair but of abnegation. If with the ancient Danes, or the Celts, or Thracians, the old man at an advanced age put an end to his life, it was because it was his duty to free his companions from a useless burden. If the widow of the Indian did not survive her husband, nor the Gaul the chief of his clan, if the Buddhist has himself torn on the wheels of the carriage carrying his idol, it is because moral or religious prescriptions demand it. In all these circumstances, man kills himself, not because he judges life bad, but because the ideal to which he is attached demands the sacrifice. These voluntary deaths are therefore no more suicides, in the common sense of the word, than the death of a soldier or a doctor exposing himself knowingly because of duty.

On the contrary, the true suicide, the sad suicide, is in the endemic state with civilized peoples. He is even distributed geographically like civilization. On the charts of suicides, there is seen a very dark spot over all the central region of Europe between 47 and 57 degrees latitude and 20 and 40 degrees longitude. That space is the favorite place for suicide; according to Morselli's expression, it is the suicidogenous zone of Europe. There also are found the countries where scientific, artistic, economic activities are carried to their maximum: Germany and France. On the contrary, Spain, Portugal, Russia, the Slav people of the South are relatively immune. Italy, born yesterday, is still somewhat safe, but its immunity is lost as it advances. England alone is an exception. Still, we are badly informed as to the exact degree of its suicidal rate. In the interior of each country, one observes the same relation. Everywhere suicide rages more fiercely in the cities than in the country. Civilization is concentrated in the great cities, suicide likewise. It has even been viewed sometimes as a contagious disease which has as the sources of irradiation the capitals and important cities, and which, from there, spreads over the rest of the country. Finally, in all Europe, Norway excepted, the figures for suicides have steadily increased for a century.[312] According to one calculation, it has tripled from 1821 to 1880.[313] The march of civilization cannot be gauged with the same precision, but it is known how rapid its advance has been during that time.

The proofs could be multiplied. The classes of population furnish suicide a quota proportionate to their degree of civilization.

---

[310] Translator's Note: Not in fifth edition. Found in first edition.

[311] Translator's Note: Not in fifth edition. Found in first edition.

[312] See the Tables of Morselli.

[313] Oettingen, *Moralstatistik*, p. 742, Erlangen, 1882.

Everywhere the liberal professions are hardest hit, and agriculture the least. It is the same with the sexes. Woman has had less part than man in the movement of civilization. She participates less and derives less profit. She recalls, moreover, certain characteristics of primitive natures.[314] Thus, there is about one fourth the suicides among women as among men. But, it will be objected, if the ascending march of suicides indicates that unhappiness advances in certain respects, could it not be said at the same time that happiness increases in others? In that case, the increase of advantages would perhaps compensate for the losses suffered elsewhere. Thus, in certain societies, the number of poor increases without the public fortune diminishing. It is only concentrated in a smaller number of hands.

But this hypothesis itself is scarcely more favorable to our civilization. For, supposing that such compensations exist, one could conclude nothing except the fact that average happiness has remained almost stationary. Or, if it had increased, it could only have been in very small quantities which, being without relation to the great efforts progress has cost, would not be able to give an account of it. But the very hypothesis is without basis.

In fact, when a society is called more or less happy than another, average happiness is meant, that is, the happiness enjoyed by the average members of this society. As they are placed in conditions of similar existence, in so far as they are subject to the action of the same physical and social environment, there is necessarily a manner of living, and consequently a way of being happy which is common to them. If, from the happiness of individuals, there is taken away all that is due to individual or local causes in order to retain only the product of general and common causes, the residue thus obtained constitutes precisely what we term average happiness. It is, then, an abstracted magnitude, absolutely uniform, which cannot vary in two contrary senses at the same time. It can either grow or decrease, but it cannot do both. It has the same unity and the same reality as the average type of society, the average man of Quetelet, for it represents the happiness which this ideal being is supposed to enjoy. Consequently, in the same way that he cannot become at the same moment greater and smaller, more moral and immoral, he cannot at the same time become happier and unhappier.

But the causes upon which the progress of suicides among civilized peoples depends have a certain general character. Indeed, it does not occur in isolated points to the exclusion of others. One observes it everywhere. According to the region, the ascension is rapid or slow, but no region is exempt. Agriculture is less affected than industry, but the quota it furnishes to suicide is always increasing.

---

[314] Tarde, *Criminalité comparée*, p. 48.

Thus, we are before a phenomenon which is linked not to some local and particular circumstances, but to a general state of the social milieu. This state is diversely refracted by special milieux (provinces, occupations, religious confessions, etc.). That is why its action cannot be felt everywhere with the same intensity, but its nature does not change on that account.

The happiness whose regression is attested by the increase in suicides is the average happiness. What the mounting tide of voluntary deaths proves is not only that there is a greater number of individuals too unhappy to live—which would prove nothing in respect to the others who are in the majority—but that the general happiness of society is decreasing. Consequently, since this happiness cannot increase and decrease at the same time, it is impossible for it to increase, in whatever manner that may be, when suicides multiply. In other words, the growing deficiency they reveal has no compensation. The causes on which they depend exhaust only a part of their energy in suicides. The influence they exert is even more extensive. Where they do not lead man to kill himself, totally suppressing happiness, they reduce, at least, in variable proportions, the normal excess of pleasures over pains. Doubtless, it may happen by combinations of particular circumstances that, in certain cases, their action may be neutralized in a way to make possible even an increase of happiness, but these accidental, private variations are without effect upon *social happiness.* What statistician would hesitate to see in the progress of general mortality in the midst of a determined society a sure symptom of the weakening of public health?

Is that to say that it is necessary to impute these sad results to progress itself and to the division of labor which is its condition? This discouraging conclusion does not necessarily follow from the preceding facts. It is, on the contrary, very likely that these two orders of fact are simply concomitant. But this concomitance is sufficient to prove that progress does not greatly increase our happiness, since the latter decreases, and, in very grave proportions, at the very moment when the division of labor is developing with an energy and rapidity never known before. If there is no reason for believing that it has effectively diminished our capacity for enjoyment, it is still more impossible to believe it has perceptibly increased it.

Lastly, all we have just said is only a particular application of this general truth that pleasure is, as pain, a thing essentially relative. There is no absolute happiness, objectively determinable, which men approach as they progress. But in the same way as the happiness of man is not that of woman, according to Pascal, that of lower societies cannot be ours, and vice versa. One, however, is not greater than the other, for the relative intensity can be measured only by the force with which it attaches us to life in general, and to our kind of life in particular. Now, the most primitive peoples are as anxious to continue their existence as we ours. They renounce it even less willingly.[315] There is, then, no relation between the variations of happiness and the advances of the division of labor.

This proposition is of the utmost importance. From it results the fact that, to explain the transformations through which societies have passed, we must not look for the influence they exercise on the happiness of men, since it is not this influence which has determined them. Social science must resolutely renounce these utilitarian comparisons in which it has too often been involved. Besides, such considerations are necessarily subjective, for whenever pleasures or interests are compared, as all objective criterion is wanting, one cannot refrain from deciding on the basis of one's own ideals and preferences, and what is nothing more than personal sentiment is called scientific truth. It is a principle which Comte had already formulated very neatly. "The essentially relative spirit," he said, "in which any sort of idea of positive politics must necessarily be conceived, must first of all make us dismiss as vain and futile the vague metaphysical controversy concerning the increase of man's happiness in the various ages of civilization. . . . Since the happiness of each demands a sufficient harmony between the totality of the development of his different faculties and the total system of whatever circumstances dominate his life, and since, moreover, such an equilibrium always automatically remains within a certain range, there can be no place for positively comparing, either by any direct sentiment or by rational procedure, with respect to individual happiness, social situations which cannot be compared."[316]

But the desire to become happier is the only individual source which can take account of progress. If that is set aside, no other remains. Why should an individual cause changes which are painful, if he is no happier with the changes? It is, therefore, outside himself, in the surrounding environment, that the determinant causes of social evolution are to be found. If societies change, and if he changes, that is because this environment changes. On the other hand, as the physical environment is relatively constant, it cannot explain this uninterrupted succession of change. Consequently, it is in the social environment we must seek the original conditions. Variations are produced there provoking those through which societies and individuals pass. This is a rule of method we shall have occasion to apply and confirm in what follows.

---

[315] Except cases where the instinct of preservation is neutralized by religious or patriotic sentiments, etc. without its being weaker for that.

[316] *Cours de Philosophie positive*, 2nd ed., IV, p. 273.

III

It could still be asked, however, whether certain variations undergone by pleasure do not spontaneously cause man to change, and if, consequently, the progress of the division of labor cannot be explained in this way. Here is how this explanation could be conceived. If pleasure is not happiness, it is, however, one element. But it loses its intensity through repetition. If it becomes too continuous, it disappears completely. Time is sufficient to break the equilibrium tending to be established, and create new conditions of existence to which man can adapt himself only by changing. To the extent that we accustom ourselves to a certain type of happiness, it flees from us, and we are obliged to throw ourselves into new undertakings to recapture it. We must bring the extinguished pleasure to life again by means of more energetic stimuli, that is, multiply or render those which we have more intense. But that is possible only if work becomes more productive and, consequently, more divided. Thus, each realized advance in art, in science, in industry, would necessitate new advances, so as not to lose the fruits of the preceding advance. The development of the division of labor would then be explained by a net-work of individual causes, without the intervention of any social cause. To be sure, it would be said, if we specialize, it is not to acquire new pleasures, but to repair, as fast as it is produced, the corrosive influence that time exercises over acquired pleasures.

But no matter how real these variations of pleasure may be, they cannot play the role attributed to them. Indeed, they are produced wherever there is pleasure, that is, wherever there are men. There is no society where this psychological law does not apply, but there are some where the division of labor does not progress. We have seen, indeed, that a very great number of primitive people live in a stationary state from which they do not even think of emerging. They aspire to nothing new. Nevertheless, their happiness is submitted to the common law. It is the same in the country among civilized peoples. The division of labor only advances very slowly there, and the desire for changes is only weakly felt. Finally, in the midst of the same society, the division of labor is developed more or less quickly through the ages, but the influence of time on pleasures is always the same. It is not it which determines the development.

Indeed, one cannot see how it could have such a result. The equilibrium time destroys cannot be re-established, nor can happiness be maintained at a constant level without attempts which are the more disagreeable as they approach the higher limit of pleasure, for in the region adjoining the maximum point the increases are steadily lower than the corresponding stimuli. More trouble must be taken for the same reward. What is gained on one side is lost on the other, and loss is avoided only by new expenditure. Consequently, for the operation to be profitable, this loss would at least have to be important, and the need for reparation strongly felt.

But, in fact, it has only a very mediocre energy, because simple repetition brings nothing essential to pleasure. It is, indeed, necessary not to confuse the charm of variety with that of novelty. The first is the necessary condition of pleasure, since an uninterrupted enjoyment disappears or is changed into pain. But time alone does not suppress variety; continuity must be added to it. A state often repeated, but in discontinuous manner, can remain agreeable, for, if continuity destroys pleasure, it is either because it makes it unwitting, or because the play of each function demands an outlay which, prolonged without interruption, is exhausting and becomes painful. If, then, the act, in becoming habitual, returns only at separated intervals, it will continue to be felt, and the expenditures will be replaced in the intervals. That is why a healthy adult always feels the same pleasure in eating, drinking, sleeping, although he sleeps, eats, drinks every day. It is the same with needs of the spirit, which are, also, periodic as the psychical functions to which they correspond. The pleasures that music brings, or the arts, or science, are integrally maintained provided they alternate.

If continuity can do what repetition cannot, it does not inspire us with a need for new and unforeseen stimuli. For, if it totally abolishes the consciousness of the agreeable state, we cannot discover that the pleasure attached to it has vanished at the same time. It is replaced by that general feeling of well-being accompanying the regular exercises of functions normally continued which is not their least worth. We, then, regret nothing. Who of us has ever wanted to feel his heart beating, or his lungs functioning? If, on the contrary, there is pain, we simply aspire to a state different from the one annoying us. But to have this suffering cease, it is not necessary to tax our ingenuity. A known object which ordinarily leaves us cold can, even in this case, cause a piercing joy if it contrasts with the state annoying us. There is, then, nothing in the way in which time affects the fundamental element of pleasure that can provoke us to some sort of progress. It is true that it is otherwise with novelty, whose attraction is not durable. But if it gives greater freshness to pleasure, it does not constitute it. It is only one of its secondary and accessory qualities without which it can exist very well, although with the risk of being less savory. When obliterated, the resulting void is not very evident nor the need of filling it very intense.

What diminishes its intensity is that it is neutralized by a contrasting sentiment a great deal stronger and more firmly rooted in us: this is the need of stability in our enjoyments and regularity in our pleasures. At the same time that we like to change, we are attached to what we like and we cannot separate ourselves from it without difficulty. Besides, it is necessary that it be so in order that life be maintained, for if life is not possible without change, even if it is as flexible as it is complex, nevertheless it is above all a system of stable and regular functions. There are, to be sure, individuals whose need for the new attains exceptional intensity. Nothing existent satisfies them, they thirst for the impossible, they would like to put in the place of imposed reality another. But these incorrigible grumblers are unhealthy, and their pathological character only confirms what we have just said.

Finally, we must not forget that this need is intrinsically indeterminate. It attaches us to nothing precise, since it is a need of something which does not exist. It is then only half-constituted, for a complete need comprises two terms: a tension of the will and a certain object. As the object is not given without, it can have no other reality than that which imagination lends it. This process is half representative. It consists more in combinations of images, in a sort of intimate poetry, than in an effective movement of will. It does not take us out of ourselves; it is scarcely more than an internal agitation seeking a way out, not yet found. We dream of new sensations, but it is a bodiless desire floating about. Consequently, even where it is most energetic, it cannot have the force of firm and defined needs which, directing the will always in the same direction and by well-beaten paths, stimulates it so much more imperiously that they leave no place either for groping or deliberations.

In a word, one cannot admit that progress is only an effect of boredom.[317] This recasting, periodic and even, in certain respects, continuous in human nature, has been a laborious work which has been accompanied by suffering. It is impossible for humanity to have imposed upon itself so much trouble solely to be able to vary its pleasures a little and to keep their first freshness.

CHAPTER TWO. THE CAUSES

I

We must, then, look for the causes explaining the progress of the division of labor in certain variations of the social scene. The results of the preceding book enable us to infer at once what these variations are.

We saw how the organized structure, and, thus, the division of labor, develop as the segmental structure disappears. Hence, either this disappearance is the cause of the development, or the development is the cause of the disappearance. The latter hypothesis is inadmissible,

---

[317] This was the theory of Georges Leroy; we are acquainted with it only through Comte, *Cours de Philosophie positive*, IV, p. 449.

for we know that the segmental arrangement is an insurmountable obstacle to the division of labor, and must have disappeared at least partially for the division of labor to appear. The latter can appear only in proportion to the disappearance of the segmental structure. To be sure, once the division of labor appears, it can contribute towards the hastening of the other's regression, but it is in evidence only after the regression has begun. The effect reacts upon the cause, but never loses its quality of effect. The reaction it exercises is, consequently, secondary. The growth of the division of labor is thus brought about by the social segments losing their individuality, the divisions becoming more permeable. In short, a coalescence takes place which makes new combinations possible in the social substance.

But the disappearance of this type can have this consequence for only one reason. That is because it gives rise to a relationship between individuals who were separated, or, at least, a more intimate relationship than there was. Consequently, there is an exchange of movements between parts of the social mass which, until then, had no effect upon one another. The greater the development of the cellular system, the more are our relations enclosed within the limits of the cell to which we belong. There are, as it were, moral gaps between the various segments. On the contrary, these gaps are filled in as the system is leveled out. Social life, instead of being concentrated in a multitude of little centres, distinctive and alike, is generalized. Social relations,— more exactly, intra-social—consequently become more numerous, since they extend, on all sides, beyond their original limits. The division of labor develops, therefore, as there are more individuals sufficiently in contact to be able to act and react upon one another. If we agree to call this relation and the active commerce resulting from it dynamic or moral density, we can say that the progress of the division of labor is in direct ratio to the moral or dynamic density of society.

But this moral relationship can only produce its effect if the real distance between individuals has itself diminished in some way. Moral density cannot grow unless material density grows at the same time, and the latter can be used to measure the former. It is useless to try to find out which has determined the other; they are inseparable.

The progressive condensation of societies in historical development is produced in three principal ways:

1. Whereas lower societies are spread over immense areas according to population, with more advanced people population always tends to concentrate. As Spencer suggests, if we oppose the rate of population in regions inhabited by savage tribes to that of regions of the same extent in Europe; or again, if we oppose the density of the population in England under the Heptarchy to its present density, we shall recognize that the growth produced by the union of groups is also

accompanied by interstitial growth.[318] The changes brought about in the industrial life of nations prove the universality of this transformation. The industry of nomads, hunters, or shepherds implies the absence of all concentration, dispersion over the largest possible surface. Agriculture, since it necessitates a sedentary life, presupposes a certain tightening of the social fiber, but it is still incomplete, for there are stretches of land between families.[319] In the city, although the condensation was greater, the houses were not contiguous, for joint property was no part of the Roman law.[320] It grew up on our soil, and is proof that the social web has become tighter.[321] On the other hand, from their origins, European societies have witnessed a continuous growth in their density in spite of exceptions of short-lived regressions.[322]

2. The formation of cities and their development is an even more characteristic symptom of the same phenomenon. The increase in average density may be due to the material increase of the birth-rate, and, consequently, can be reconciled with a very feeble concentration, a marked maintenance of the segmental type. But cities always result from the need of individuals to put themselves in very intimate contact with others. They are so many points where the social mass is contracted more strongly than elsewhere. They can multiply and extend only if the moral density is raised. We shall see, moreover, that they receive recruits especially by immigration. This is only possible when the fusion of social segments is advanced.

As long as social organization is essentially segmental, the city does not exist. There are none in lower societies. They did not exist among the Iroquois, nor among the ancient Germans.[323] It was the same with the primitive populations of Italy. "The peoples of Italy," says Marquardt, "originally did not live in cities, but in familial communities or villages (*pagi*) over which farms (*vici, οἶκοι*) were spread."[324] But in a rather short time the city made its appearance. Athens and Rome are or become cities, and the same transformation is made in all Italy. In our Christian societies, the city is in evidence from the beginning, for those left by the Roman empire did not disappear with it. Since then, they have increased and multiplied. The tendency of

---

[318] *Principles of Sociology*, II, p. 31.

[319] "*Colunt diver si ac discreti*," said Tacitus of the Germans; "*suam quisque domum spatio circumdat.*" *Germania*, xvi.

[320] See in Accarias, *Précis*, I, p. 640, the list of urban servitudes. Cf. Fustel de Coulanges, *La cite antique*, p. 65.

[321] In reasoning thus, we do not mean to say that the development of density results from economic changes. The two facts mutually condition each other, and the presence of one proves the other's.

[322] See Levasseur, *La Population française*, passim.

[323] Tacitus, *Germania*, xvi.—Sohm, *Ueber die Entstehung der Städte*.

[324] *Römische Alterthümer*, IV, 3.

the country to stream into the city, so general in the civilized world,[325] is only a consequence of this movement. It is not of recent origin; from the seventeenth century, statesmen were preoccupied with it.[326]

Because societies generally begin with an agricultural period there has sometimes been the temptation to regard the development of urban centres as a sign of old age and decadence.[327] But we must not lose sight of the fact that this agricultural phase is as short as societies are elevated. Whereas in Germany, among the Indians of America, and with all primitive peoples, it lasts as long as the people themselves, in Rome and Athens, it ends rather soon, and, with us, we can say that it has never existed alone. On the other hand, urban life commences sooner, and consequently extends further. The regularly more rapid acceleration of this development proves that, far from constituting a sort of pathological phenomenon, it comes from the very nature of higher social species. The supposition that this movement has attained alarming proportions in our societies today, which perhaps no longer have sufficient suppleness to adapt themselves, will not prevent this movement from continuing either within our societies or after them, and the social types which will be formed after ours will likely be distinguished by a still more complete and rapid regression of agricultural civilization.

3. Finally, there are the number and rapidity of ways of communication and transportation. By suppressing or diminishing the gaps separating social segments, they increase the density of society. It is not necessary to prove that they are as numerous and perfected as societies are of a more elevated type.

Since this visible and measurable symbol reflects the variations of what we have called moral density,[328] we can substitute it for this latter in the formula we have proposed. Moreover, we must repeat here what we said before. If society, in concentrating, determines the development of the division of labor, the latter, in its turn, increases the concentration of society. But no matter, for the division of labor remains the derived fact, and, consequently, the advances which it has made are due to parallel advances of social density, whatever may be the causes of the latter. That is all we wish to prove.

But this factor is not the only one.

If condensation of society produces this result, it is because it multiplies intra-social relations. But these will be still more numerous,

---

[325] See Dumont, *Dépopulation et Civilisation*, Paris, 1890, ch. viii, on this point, and Oettingen, *Moralstatistik*, pp. 273 ff.

[326] Levasseur, *op. cit.*, p. 200.

[327] We believe this is the opinion of Tarde in his *Lois de l'imitation.*

[328] There are particular, exceptional cases, however, where material and moral density are perhaps not entirely in accord. See final note of this chapter.

if, in addition, the total number of members of society becomes more considerable. If it comprises more individuals at the same time as they are more intimately in contact, the effect will necessarily be re-enforced. Social volume, then, has the same influence as density upon the division of labor.

In fact, societies are generally as voluminous as they are more advanced, and consequently as labor is more divided. Societies, as living organisms, in Spencer's words, begin in the form of a bud, sprouting extremely tenuous bodies, compared to those they finally become. The greatest societies, as he says, have emerged from little wandering hordes, such as those of lower races. This is a conclusion which Spencer finds cannot be denied.[329] What we have said of the segmental constitution makes this an indisputable truth. We know, indeed, that societies are formed by a certain number of segments of unequal extent which mutually envelop one another. These moulds are not artificial creations, especially in origin, and even when they have become conventional, they imitate and reproduce, as far as possible, the forms of the natural arrangement which has preceded. There are a great many old societies maintained in this form. The most vast among these subdivisions, those comprising the others, correspond to the nearest inferior social type. Indeed, among the segments of which they are in turn composed, the most extensive are vestiges of the type which comes directly below the preceding, and so on. There are found traces of the most primitive social organization among the most advanced peoples.[330] Thus, the tribe is formed of an aggregate of hordes or clans. The nation (the Jewish nation, for example) and the city are formed of an aggregate of tribes; the city, in turn, with the villages subordinate to it, enters as an element of the most complex societies, etc. Thus, the social volume cannot fail to increase, since each species is constituted by a repetition of societies of the immediately anterior species.

There are exceptions, however. The Jewish nation, before the conquest, was probably more voluminous than the Roman city of the fourth century. Nevertheless, it was of an inferior species. China and Russia are a great deal more populous than the most civilized nations of Europe. With these people, consequently, the division of labor is not developed in proportion to the social volume. That is because the increase of volume is not necessarily a mark of superiority if the density does not increase at the same time and in the same relation, for a society can attain great dimensions because it comprises a very great number of segments, whatever may be the nature of the latter. If, then, even the most vast among them reproduce only societies of very inferior type, the segmental structure will remain very pronounced, and,

---

[329] *Principles of Sociology*, II, 23.
[330] The village, which is originally only a fixed clan.

consequently, social organization little elevated. Even an immense aggregate of clans is below the smallest organized society, since the latter has run through stages of evolution within which the other has remained. In the same way, if the number of social units has influence on the division of labor, it is not through itself and necessarily, but it is because the number of social relations generally increases with that of individuals. But, for this result to be attained, it is not enough that society take in a great many people, but they must be, in addition, intimately enough in contact to act and react on one another. If they are, on the contrary, separated by opaque milieux, they can only be bound by rare and weak relations, and it is as if they had small populations. The increase of social volume does not, then, always accelerate the advances of the division of labor, but only when the mass is contracted at the same time and to the same extent. Consequently, it is only an additional factor, but when it is joined to the first, it amplifies its effects by action peculiar to it, and therefore is to be distinguished from that.

We can then formulate the following proposition: *The division of labor varies in direct ratio with the volume and density of societies, and, if it progresses in a continuous manner in the course of social development, it is because societies become regularly denser and generally more voluminous.*

At all times, it is true, it has been well understood that there was a relation between these two orders of fact, for, in order that functions be more specialized, there must be more co-operators, and they must be related to co-operate. But, ordinarily, this state of societies is seen only as the means by which the division of labor develops, and not as the cause of its development. The latter is made to depend upon individual aspirations toward well-being and happiness, which can be satisfied so much better as societies are more extensive and more condensed. The law we have just established is quite otherwise. We say, not that the growth and condensation of societies *permit*, but that they *necessitate* a greater division of labor. It is not an instrument by which the latter is realized; it is its determining cause.[331]

---

[331] On this point, we can still rely on Comte as authority. "I must," he said, "now indicate the progressive condensation of our species as a last general concurrent element in regulating the effective speed of the social movement. We can first easily recognize that this influence contributes a great deal, especially in origin, in determining a more special division of human labor, necessarily incompatible with a small number of co-operators. *Besides, by a most intimate and little known property, although still most important, such a condensation stimulates directly, in a very powerful manner, the most rapid development of social-evolution*, either in driving individuals to new efforts to assure themselves by more refined means of an existence which otherwise would become more difficult, or by obliging society with more stubborn and better concentrated energy to fight more stiffly against the more powerful effort of particular divergences. With one and the other, we see that it is not a question here of the absolute increase of the number of individuals, but especially of their more intense concourse in a given space." *Cours,*

But how can the manner in which this double cause produces its effect be represented?

II

According to Spencer, the increase of social volume has an influence which does not determine the advances of the division of labor, but only accelerates these advances. It is only an adjunct condition of the phenomenon. Unstable by nature, all homogeneous masses become strongly heterogeneous, whatever their dimensions. They become more completely and more rapidly differentiated, however, the greater their extension. In effect, as this heterogeneity springs up because the different parts of the mass are exposed to the action of different forces, it is so much greater as there are more diversely situated parts. As Spencer says in this instance, when a community, becoming populous, is spread over a great area, and is so firmly established that its members live and die in their respective districts, it maintains its diverse sections in different physical circumstances, and thus these sections can no longer remain alike with respect to their occupations. Those who live dispersed continue to hunt and cultivate the soil; those on the sea-shore devote themselves to maritime occupations, the inhabitants of some site, chosen perhaps for its central position, as a place of periodic reunions, become merchants, and a city is founded. A difference in the soil or climate causes specialized occupations in diverse regions of the country, and singles out the production of cattle, sheep, or wheat.[332] In short, the variety of environments in which individuals are placed produces in them different aptitudes determining their specialization in divergent senses, and if this specialization grows with the dimensions of societies, it is because these external differences increase at the same time.

There is no doubt that external conditions leave their mark upon individuals, and through their diversity cause differentiation. But the question is whether this diversity, doubtlessly related to the division of labor, is sufficient to constitute it. To be sure, explanation can be made by referring to the properties of the soil and climatic conditions, inhabitants producing wheat here, elsewhere sheep and cattle. But functional differences are not always reduced, as in these examples, to simple distinctions. They are sometimes so marked off that the individuals among whom work is divided form a great many distinct and even opposed species. One might say there was deliberate conspiracy for the utmost deviation. What resemblance is there between the brain thinking and the stomach digesting? Likewise, what

---

IV, p. 455.
    [332] *First Principles*, p. 381.

is there in common between the poet entirely wrapped up in his dream, the scholar entirely in his researches, the workman spending his life making pin-heads, the plowman wielding his plow, the shopkeeper behind his counter? However great the variety of external circumstances may be, it nowhere presents disparities relative to the contrasts thus strongly indicated, and which consequently might be able to render an account of it. Even if one compares, not widely separated functions, but only the diverse branches of the same function, it is often entirely impossible to see to what external differences their separation can be due. Scientific work steadily becomes more specialized. What are the climatic, geological, or even social conditions which can have given birth to the different talents of the mathematician, chemist, naturalist, psychologist, etc.?

But, even where external circumstances most strikingly cause individuals to specialize in a definite sense, they are not sufficient to determine the specialization. By constitution, woman is predisposed to lead a life different from man. Nevertheless, there are societies in which the occupations of the sexes are in fact the same. Because of age, because of the blood relations he has with his children, the father is the one who exercises the authority in the family, an authority constituting paternal power. Nevertheless, in the matriarchal family, it is not in him that this authority rests. It appears quite natural that the different members of the family should have duties, that is to say, different functions according to their degree of relationship; that father and uncle, brother and cousin, have neither the same rights nor the same duties. There are, however, familial types where all the adults play the same role and are on the same plane of equality, whatever their relations of consanguinity. The inferior situation the prisoner of war occupies in the midst of a victorious tribe seems to condemn him—if his life is spared—to the lowest social functions. We have seen, however, that he is often assimilated into the conquering tribe and becomes an equal.

If these differences make possible the division of labor, they do not necessitate it. Because they are given, it does not rigorously follow that they are utilized. They count for little along side of the resemblances men continue to present among them. It is only an indistinct beginning. For specialization of activity to result, they must be developed and organized, and this development evidently depends on other causes than the variety of external conditions. But, says Spencer, it will come about of itself, because it follows the line of least resistance and all the forces of nature will invincibly bear in that direction. Assuredly, *if men specialize*, it will be in the sense marked by these natural differences, for it is in this way that they will have the least trouble and the most profit. But why do they specialize? What makes them lean towards distinguishing themselves from others? Spencer ably explains in what manner evolution will be produced, if it does take place, but he does not tell us the source producing it. As a matter of fact, the question is not even raised for him. He admits, in effect, that happiness increases with the productive power of work. Each time, then, that a new means of dividing work is made available, it seems to him impossible for us not to seize it. But we know things do not happen in this way. In truth, this means has value for us only if we find need of it, and as primitive man has no need of all the products civilized man has learned to desire and with which a more complex organization of work has provided him, we can understand the source of this increasing specialization of tasks only if we know how these new needs are constituted.

III

If work becomes divided more as societies become more voluminous and denser, it is not because external circumstances are more varied, but because struggle for existence is more acute.

Darwin justly observed that the struggle between two organisms is as active as they are analogous. Having the same needs and pursuing the same objects, they are in rivalry everywhere. As long as they have more resources than they need, they can still live side by side, but if their number increases to such proportions that all appetites can no longer be sufficiently satisfied, war breaks out, and it is as violent as this insufficiency is more marked; that is to say, as the number in the struggle increase. It is quite otherwise if the co-existing individuals are of different species or varieties. As they do not feed in the same manner, and do not lead the same kind of fife, they do not disturb each other. What is advantageous to one is without value to the others. The chances of conflict thus diminish with chances of meeting, and the more so as the species or varieties are more distant from one another. Thus, Darwin says that in a small area, opened to immigration, and where, consequently, the conflict of individuals must be acute, there is always to be seen a very great diversity in the species inhabiting it. He found turf three feet by four which had been exposed for long years to the same conditions of life nourishing twenty species of plants belonging to eighteen genera and eight classes. This clearly proves how differentiated they are.[333] Everybody, besides, has observed that in the same field with grain a great number of weeds can grow. Animals, themselves, prosper more when they differ more. On an oak-tree there were found two hundred species of insects having no other relationship than neighborhood. Some feed upon the fruits of the tree, others on the leaves, others on the bark and roots. "It would be," says Haeckel, "absolutely impossible for such a number of individuals to live on this

---

[333] *Origin of Species.*

tree if all belonged to the same species, if all, for example, lived upon the bark, or only the leaves."[334] Likewise, in the interior of the organism, what softens the conflict between different tissues is that they feed upon different substances.

Men submit to the same law. In the same city, different occupations can co-exist without being obliged mutually to destroy one another, for they pursue different objects. The soldier seeks military glory, the priest moral authority, the statesman power, the business man riches, the scholar scientific renown. Each of them can attain his end without preventing the others from attaining theirs. It is the same even when the functions are less separated from one another. The oculist does not struggle with the psychiatrist, nor the shoemaker with the hatter, nor the mason with the cabinet maker, nor the physicist with the chemist, etc. Since they perform different services, they can perform them parallelly.

The closer functions come to one another, however, the more points of contact they have; the more, consequently, are they exposed to conflict. As in this case they satisfy similar needs by different means, they inevitably seek to curtail the other's development. The judge never is in competition with the business man, but the brewer and the wine-grower, the clothier and the manufacturer of silks, the poet and the musician, often try to supplant each other. As for those who have exactly the same function, they can forge ahead only to the detriment of others. If, then, these different functions are represented as a series of branches issuing from a common trunk, the struggle is at its minimum between the extreme points, whereas it increases steadily as we approach the centre. It is so, not only in the interior of each city, but in all society. Similar occupations situated on different points of land are as competitive as they are alike, provided the difficulty of communication and transport does not restrict the circle of action.

That settled, it is easy to understand that all condensation of the social mass, especially if it is accompanied by an increase in population, necessarily determines advances in the division of labor.

Indeed, let us suppose an industrial centre providing a certain region of the country with a special product. The development it may possibly attain is doubly limited; first, by the extent of needs that must be satisfied, or, as has been said, by the size of the market, then by the control of the means of production at its disposal. Normally, it does not produce more than is necessary, still less does it produce more than it can. But if it is impossible to surpass the boundary thus marked, it tries to attain it, for it is in the nature of a force to develop all its energy as long as nothing intervenes to stop it. Once arrived at this point, it is

---

[334] *History of Natural Creation.*

adapted to conditions of existence. It is found in a position of equilibrium which cannot change if nothing else changes.

But it happens that a region, heretofore independent of this centre, is bound to it through means of communication which partially overcome the distance. At the same time, one of the barriers which hemmed it in is lowered or, at least, recedes. The market is extended, there are now more needs to satisfy. To be sure, if all the particular enterprises it comprises had already realized the maximum of production they could attain, things would remain in *statu quo*, since they could extend themselves no further. Such a condition, however, is wholly ideal. In reality, there is always a considerable number of enterprises which have not reached their limit and which have, consequently, power to go further. Since there is a free field for them, they necessarily seek to spread and fill it. If they meet similar enterprises which offer resistance, the second hold back the first; they are mutually limited, and, consequently, their mutual relationships are not changed. There are, to be sure, more competitors, but, as they share a greater market, the part of each remains the same. But if some of them present some inferiority, they will necessarily have to yield ground heretofore occupied by them, but in which they cannot be maintained under the new conditions of conflict. They no longer have any alternative but to disappear or transform, and this transformation must necessarily end in a new specialization. For if, instead of immediately creating another specialty, the feeblest preferred to adopt another occupation, already existent, they would have to compete with those in practice. The struggle would not then be over, but only placed somewhere else, and it would produce consequences in another sector. Finally, somewhere there would have to be elimination or a new differentiation. One need not add that, if society effectively includes more members at the same time as they are more closely in relation to each other, the struggle is still more acute and the resulting specialization more rapid and complete.

In other words, in proportion to the segmental character of the social constitution, each segment has its own organs, protected and kept apart from like organs by divisions separating the different segments. But as these divisions are swept away, inevitably like organs are put into contact, battling and trying to supplant one another. But, no matter how this substitution is made, it cannot fail to produce advances in the course of specialization. For, on the one hand, the triumphant segmental organ, as it were, can take care of the vaster task devolving upon it only by a greater division of labor, and, on the other hand, the vanquished can maintain themselves only by concentrating their efforts upon a part of the total function they fulfilled up to then. The small employer becomes a foreman, the small merchant becomes an employee, etc. This can be more or less considerable, depending upon whether the inferiority is more or less marked. It even happens that the original function is simply divided into two equal parts. Instead of entering into or remaining in competition, two similar enterprises establish equilibrium by sharing their common task. Instead of one being subordinate to the other, they co-ordinate. But, in all cases, new specialties appear.

Although the preceding examples are borrowed particularly from economic life, this explanation applies to all social functions indiscriminately. Scientific and artistic work is divided in no other manner, and for no other reason. It is, again, through the same causes that, as we have seen, the central regulative system absorbs the local regulative organs and reduces them to the role of special auxiliaries.

With all these changes, is there an increase in average happiness? There is no reason for so believing. The greater intensity of the struggle implies new and difficult attempts which are not naturally made to contribute towards making men happier. Everything takes place mechanically. A break in the equilibrium of the social mass raises conflicts which can be resolved only by a more developed division of labor. Such is the moving power of progress. As for external circumstances, the varied combinations of heredity, just as slopes of the earth determine the direction of the current, but do not create it, so they mark the sense in which specialization takes place where it is necessary, but they do not necessitate it. The individual differences they produce would remain in a state of potentiality if, to meet new difficulties, we were not forced to project and develop them.

The division of labor is, then, a result of the struggle for existence, but it is a mellowed *dénouement.* Thanks to it, opponents are not obliged to fight to a finish, but can exist one beside the other. Also, in proportion to its development, it furnishes the means of maintenance and survival to a greater number of individuals who, in more homogeneous societies, would be condemned to extinction. Among a great many lower peoples, all malformed organisms must perish, for they fulfill no function. Sometimes, law, advancing and in some way consecrating the results of natural selection, condemned those born infirm or weak to death, and Aristotle himself[335] found this custom natural. It is quite otherwise in more advanced societies. A sickly individual can find in the complex forms of our social organization a place where it is possible for him to render services. If he is physically weak, but has a good brain, he will devote himself to sedentary work, to speculative functions. If his brain is weak, "he will no doubt have to renounce intellectual competition, but society has in its secondary compartments unimportant posts which will prevent his elimination."[336]

---

[335] *Politics*, IV (VII), 16, 1335b, 20 ff.

[336] Bordier, *Vie des Sociétés*, p. 45.

In the same way, among primitive tribes, the vanquished enemy is put to death; where industrial functions are separated from military functions he lives as a slave beside the conqueror.

There are a number of circumstances where different functions enter into competition. Thus, in the individual organism, during a long fast, the nervous system is nourished at the expense of the other organs, and the same phenomenon is produced if cerebral activity develops too considerably. It is the same in society. In time of famine or economic crisis, the vital functions are obliged, in order to maintain themselves, to support themselves at the expense of less essential functions. Industries of luxury are ruined, and the part of the public fortune which served to support them is absorbed by food-industries, or objects of prime necessity. Or again, it may be that an organism attains a degree of abnormal activity, disproportionate to needs, and that, to provide the expense caused by this exaggerated development, it must take a share of others. For example, there are societies where there are too many functionaries, or too many soldiers, or too many officers, or too many intermediaries, or too many priests, etc. The other occupations suffer from this hypertrophy. But all these cases are pathological. They are due to the fact that the nutrition of the organism is irregularly taken care of, or that functional equilibrium has been broken.

But an objection presents itself:

An industry can exist only if it answers some need. A function can become specialized only if this specialization corresponds to some need of society. But all new specialization results in increasing and improving production. If this advantage is not the division of labor's reason for existing, it is its necessary consequence. Therefore, advance can be established in permanent form only if individuals really feel the need of more abundant products, or products of better quality. As long as transportation was not organized, each one traveled by the means at his disposal, and was adapted to this environment. For it to become a specialty, however, men had to cease being satisfied with what had, till then, satisfied them and become more exacting. But whence could these new demands come?

They are an effect of the same cause which determines the progress of the division of labor. We have just seen that such progress is due to the greater acuteness of the struggle. But a more violent struggle does not proceed without great depletion of forces, and, consequently, without great fatigue. But for life to be maintained, reparation must be proportionate to the expenditure. That is why the dispensations, until then sufficient to restore organic equilibrium, are insufficient from then on. There must be a more abundant and choicer sustenance. It is thus that the peasant whose work is less exhausting than that of the workman in the cities can bear a poorer sustenance. The latter cannot be content with vegetable food, and even so, there is a great deal of difficulty in counterbalancing the deficit that intense and continuous work each day causes in the budget of the organism.[337] On the other hand, it is especially the nervous system that supports all these burdens,[338] for it must devise ingenious methods to keep up the struggle, to create new specialties, to acclimatize them, etc. In general, the more subject to change the environment is, the greater the part intelligence plays in life, for it alone can have new conditions of equilibrium continually broken, and yet restore it. Cerebral life develops, then, at the same time as competition becomes keener, and to the same degree. These advances are observed not only among the elite, but in all classes of society. On this point, it is only necessary to compare the worker with the farmer. It is a known fact that the first is a great deal more intelligent in spite of the mechanical nature of the tasks to which he is often subject. Besides, it is not without cause that mental diseases keep pace with civilization, nor that they rage in cities rather than in the country, and in large cities more than in small ones.[339] Now, a more voluminous and more delicate brain makes greater demands than a less refined one. Difficulties and privations the latter does not even feel painfully disturb the former. For the same reason, more complex stimulants are needed to affect this organ agreeably once it is refined, and there is greater necessity for them, because it has been developing at the same time. Finally, more than all others, needs properly intellectual increase;[340] rough explanations no longer satisfy more perspicuous minds. Fresh insights are needed and science holds these aspirations together at the same time that it satisfies them.

All these changes are, then, mechanically produced by necessary causes. If our intelligence and sensibility develop and become keener, it is because we exercise them more, and if we exercise them more, it is because we are forced to by the greater violence of the struggle we have to live through. That is how, without having desired it, humanity is found apt to receive a more intense and more varied culture.

If another factor did not intervene, however, this simple predisposition would not of itself rear the means for satisfaction, for it constitutes only an aptitude for enjoyment. As Bain has said, simple aptitudes for enjoyment do not necessarily provoke desire; we can be so constituted that we take pleasure in cultivating music, painting, science, and yet do not desire them if we are always kept from them.[341] Even when we are impelled towards an object by hereditary and strong

---

[337] See Bordier, *op. cit.*, pp. 166 ff.

[338] Féré, *Dégénérescence et Criminalité*, p. 88.

[339] See article *Alienation mentale* in the *Dictionnaire encyclopédique des sciences médicales.*

[340] This development of intellectual or scientific life has still another cause, as we shall see in the following chapter.

[341] *The Emotions and the With*

impulsion, we can desire it only after having entered into relations with it. The adolescent who has never heard speak of sexual relations nor of their pleasures can feel a vague and indefinable restlessness, and feel the lack of something, but he does not know what, and, consequently, he has no sexual desires properly speaking. Besides, these indeterminate aspirations can rather easily deviate from their natural ends and their normal direction. But, at the very moment when man is in a position to taste these new enjoyments and calls for them, even unconsciously, he finds them within his reach, because the division of labor has developed at the same time, and furnishes them to him. Without there having been the least pre-established harmony, these two orders of fact meet, simply because they are effects of the same cause.

Here is how the meeting can be conceived. The attraction of novelty would be sufficient to impel man to taste these pleasures. It naturally follows that the greater richness and complexity of these stimulants would cause him to find those with which he had been content more mediocre. He can, besides, adapt himself to them mentally before having tried them, and as, in reality, they correspond to changes in his constitution, he hastens to benefit from them. Experience thus comes to confirm these presentiments; needs which were sleeping awaken, are determined, become aware of themselves, and are organized. This is not to say that this adjustment may be in all cases perfect, that each new product due to new advances in the division of labor always corresponds to a real need of our nature. It is, on the contrary, likely that rather often needs are contracted only because one has become accustomed to the object to which they are related. This object was neither necessary nor useful, but it has been experienced several times, and it has been so well enjoyed that it cannot be denied. Harmonies resulting from quite mechanical causes can never be anything but imperfect and proximate, but they are sufficient to maintain order in general. That is what happens to the division of labor. The advances it makes are, not in all cases, but generally, in harmony with changes in man, and that is what permits them to last.

But, to repeat, we are not happier for that. To be sure, once these needs are excited, they cannot be suspended without pain. But our happiness is no greater because they are excited. The point at which we measure the relative intensity of our pleasures is displaced. A subversion of all gradation results. But this confusion of classes of pleasures does not imply an increase. Because the environment is no longer the same, we have to change, and these changes have determined others in our manner of being happy, but changes do not necessarily imply progress.

The division of labor appears to us otherwise than it does to economists. For them, it essentially consists in greater production. For us, this greater productivity is only a necessary consequence, a repercussion of the phenomenon. If we specialize, it is not to produce more, but it is to enable us to live in new conditions of existence that have been made for us.

IV

A corollary of all that has preceded is that the division of labor can be effectuated only among members of an already constituted society. In effect, when competition places isolated and estranged individuals in opposition, it can only separate them more. If there is a lot of space at their disposal, they will flee; if they cannot go beyond certain boundaries, they will differentiate themselves, so as to become still more independent. No case can be cited where relations of pure hostility are transformed, without the intervention of any other factor, into social relations. Thus, as among individuals of the same animal or vegetable species, there is generally no bond, the war they wage has no other result than to diversify them, to give birth to dissimilar varieties which grow farther apart. It is this progressive disjunction that Darwin called the law of the divergence of characters. But the division of labor unites at the same time that it opposes; it makes the activities it differentiates converge; it brings together those it separates. Since competition cannot have determined this conciliation, it must have existed before. The individuals among whom the struggle is waged must already be solidary and feel so. That is to say, they must belong to the same society. That is why, where this feeling of solidarity is too feeble to resist the dispersive influence of competition, the latter engenders altogether different effects from the division of labor. In countries where existence is too difficult because of the extreme density of the population, the inhabitants, instead of specializing, retire from society, either permanently or temporarily and leave for other countries.

To represent what the division of labor is suffices to make one understand that it cannot be otherwise. It consists in the sharing of functions up to that time common. But this sharing cannot be executed according to a preconceived plan. We cannot tell in advance where the line of demarcation between tasks will be found once they are separated, for it is not marked so evidently in the nature of things, but depends, on the contrary, upon a multitude of circumstances. The division of labor, then, must come about of itself and progressively. Consequently, under these conditions, for a function to be divided into two exactly complementary parts, as the nature of the division of labor demands, it is indispensable that the two specializing parts be in constant communication during all the time that this dissociation lasts. There is no other means for one to receive all the movement the other abandons, and which they adapt to each other. But in the same way that an animal colony whose members embody a continuity of tissue form one individual, every aggregate of individuals who are in continuous contact form a society. The division of labor can then be produced only in the midst of a pre-existing society. By that, we do not mean to say simply that individuals must adhere materially, but it is still necessary that there be moral links between them. First, material continuity by itself produces links of this kind, provided it is durable. But, moreover, they are directly necessary. If the relations becoming established in the period of groping were not subject to any rule, if no power moderated the conflict of individual interests, there would be chaos from which no new order could emerge. It is thought, it is true, that everything takes place through private conventions freely disputed. Thus, it seems that all social action is absent. But this is to forget that contracts are possible only where a juridical regulation, and, consequently, a society, already exists.

Hence, the claim sometimes advanced that in the division of labor lies the fundamental fact of all social life is wrong. Work is not divided among independent and already differentiated individuals who by uniting and associating bring together their different aptitudes. For it would be a miracle if differences thus born through chance circumstance could unite so perfectly as to form a coherent whole. Far from preceding collective life, they derive from it. They can be produced only in the midst of a society, and under the pressure of social sentiments and social needs. That is what makes them essentially harmonious. There is, then, a social life outside the whole division of labor, but which the latter presupposes. That is, indeed, what we have directly established in showing that there are societies whose cohesion is essentially due to a community of beliefs and sentiments, and it is from these societies that those whose unity is assured by the division of labor have emerged. The conclusions of the preceding book and those which we have just reached can then be used to control and mutually confirm each other. The division of physiological labor is itself submitted to this law; it never appears except in the midst of polycellular masses which are already endowed with a certain cohesion.

For a number of theorists, it is a self-evident truth that all society essentially consists of co-operation. Spencer has said that a society in the scientific sense of the word exists only when to the juxtaposition of individuals co-operation is added.[342] We have just seen that this so-called axiom is contrary to the truth. Rather it is evident, as Auguste Comte points out, "that co-operation, far from having produced society, necessarily supposes, as preamble, its spontaneous existence."[343] What

---

[342] *Principles of Sociology*, III, p. 331.
[343] *Cours de Philosophie positive*, IV, p. 421.

bring men together are mechanical causes and impulsive forces, such as affinity of blood, attachment to the same soil, ancestral worship, community of habits, etc. It is only when the group has been formed on these bases that co-operation is organized there.

Further, the only co-operation possible in the beginning is so intermittent and feeble that social life, if it had no other source, would be without force and without continuity. With stronger reason, the complex co-operation resulting from the division of labor is an ulterior and derived phenomenon. It results from internal movements which are developed in the midst of the mass, when the latter is constituted. It is true that once it appears it tightens the social bonds and makes a more perfect individuality of society. But this integration supposes another which it replaces. For social units to be able to be differentiated, they must first be attracted or grouped by virtue of the resemblances they present. This process of formation is observed, not only originally, but in each phase of evolution. We know, indeed, that higher societies result from the union of lower societies of the same type. It is necessary first that these latter be mingled in the midst of the same identical collective conscience for the process of differentiation to begin or recommence. It is thus that more complex organisms are formed by the repetition of more simple, similar organisms which are differentiated only if once associated. In short, association and co-operation are two distinct facts, and if the second, when developed, reacts on the first and transforms it, if human societies steadily become groups of co-operators, the duality of the two phenomena does not vanish for all that.

If this important truth has been disregarded by the utilitarians, it is an error rooted in the manner in which they conceive the genesis of society. They suppose originally isolated and independent individuals, who, consequently, enter into relationships only to co-operate, for they have no other reason to clear the space separating them and to associate. But this theory, so widely held, postulates a veritable *creatio ex nihilo.*

It consists, indeed, in deducing society from the individual. But nothing we know authorizes us to believe in the possibility of such spontaneous generation. According to Spencer, for societies to be formed within this hypothesis, it is necessary that primitive units pass from the state of perfect independence to that of mutual dependence.[344] But what can have determined such a complete transformation in them? Is it the prospect of the advantages presented by social life? But they are counterbalanced, perhaps more than counterbalanced, by the loss of independence, for, among individuals born for a free and solitary life, such a sacrifice is most intolerable. Add to this, that in the first social types social life is as absolute as possible, for nowhere is the individual

---

[344] *Principles of Sociology,* III, p. 332.

more completely absorbed in the group. How would man, if he were born an individualist, as is supposed, be able to resign himself to an existence clashing violently with his fundamental inclination? How pale the problematical utility of co-operation must appear to him beside such a fall! With autonomous individualities, as are imagined, nothing can emerge save what is individual, and, consequently, co-operation itself, which is a social fact, submissive to social rules, cannot arise. Thus, the psychologist who starts by restricting himself to the ego cannot emerge to find the non-ego.

Collective life is not born from individual life, but it is, on the contrary, the second which is born from the first. It is on this condition alone that one can explain how the personal individuality of social units has been able to be formed and enlarged without disintegrating society. Indeed, as, in this case, it becomes elaborate in the midst of a pre-existing social environment, it necessarily bears its mark. It is made in a manner so as not to ruin this collective order with which it is solidary. It remains adapted to it while detaching itself. It has nothing anti-social about it because it is a product of society. It is not the absolute personality of the monad, which is sufficient unto itself, and could do without the rest of the world, but that of an organ or part of an organ having its determined function, but which cannot, without risking dissolution, separate itself from the rest of the organism. Under these conditions, co-operation becomes not only possible but necessary. Utilitarians thus reverse the natural order of facts, and nothing is more deceiving than this inversion. It is a particular illustration of the general truth that what is first in knowledge is last in reality. Precisely because co-operation is the most recent fact, it strikes sight first. If, then, one clings to appearance, as does common sense, it is inevitable that one see in it the primary fact of moral and social life.

But if it is not all of ethics, it is not necessary to put it outside ethics, as do certain moralists. As the utilitarians, the idealists have it consist exclusively in a system of economic relations, of private arrangements in which egotism is the only active power. In truth, the moral fife traverses all the relations which constitute co-operation, since it would not be possible if social sentiments, and, consequently, moral sentiments, did not preside in its elaboration.

Attention will be called to the international division of labor. It seems evident, in this case at least, that individuals among whom labor is divided do not belong to the same society. But it must be recalled that a group can, while keeping its individuality, be enveloped by another, vaster and containing several of the same kind. It can be affirmed that an economic or any other function can be divided between two societies only if they participate from certain points of view in the same common life, and, consequently, belong to the same society. Suppose, indeed, that these two collective consciences have no common meeting-ground, it is not possible for the two aggregates to have the continuous contact which is necessary, nor, consequently, for one to abandon its functions to the other. For one people to be penetrated by another, it must cease to hold to an exclusive patriotism, and learn another which is more comprehensive.

Moreover, this relation of facts can be directly observed in most striking fashion in the international division of labor that history offers us. It can truly be said that it has never been produced except in Europe and in our time. But it was at the end of the eighteenth century and at the beginning of the nineteenth that a common conscience of European societies began to be formed. "There is," says Sorel, "a prejudice it is important to get rid of. That is to represent Europe of the old regime as a society of regularly constituted states, in which each formed its conduct according to principles recognized by all, in which respect for established law governed transactions and dictated treaties, in which good faith directed their execution, where sentiment of solidarity of monarchies assured, with the maintenance of public order, the duration of engagements contracted by princes. ... A Europe where the rights of each resulted from the duties of all was something so foreign to statesmen of the old regime that they needed war for a quarter of a century, the most formidable yet seen, to impose this idea upon them and prove its necessity. The attempt made at the Congress of Vienna and at the meetings following to give Europe an elementary organization was progress, and not a return to the past."[345] Inversely, every return to strict nationalism always results in a protectionist spirit, that is, in a tendency of peoples to isolate themselves from one another economically and morally.

If, however, in certain cases, peoples tied by no bond, even regarding themselves as enemies,[346] exchange products in a more or less regular manner, it is necessary to see in these facts only simple relations of *mutualism* having nothing in common with the division of labor.[347] For, merely because two different organisms are found to have properties usefully adjusted, it does not follow that there is a division of functions between them.[348]

---

[345] *L'Europe et la Révolution française*, I, pp. 9 and 10.

[346] See Kulischer, *Der Handel auf den primitiven Kulturstufen* (*Zeitschrift für Voelkerpsychologie*, X, 1877, p. 378) and Schrader, *Linguistisch-historische Forschungen zur Handelsgeschichte*, Jena, 1886.

[347] It is true that mutualism is generally produced among individuals of different species, but the phenomenon remains identical, even when it takes place among individuals of the same species. (See on mutualism, Espinas, *Sociétés animales*, and Giraud, *Les Sociétés chez les animaux.*)

[348] We wish to point out at the close that in this chapter we have only studied how it happens that generally the division of labor steadily continues to advance, and we have elucidated the determinant causes of this advance. But it may very well happen that in a

CHAPTER THREE. SECONDARY FACTORS

Progressive Indetermination of the Common Conscience and Its Causes

We saw in the first part of this work that the collective conscience became weaker and vaguer as the division of labor developed. It is, indeed, through this progressive indetermination that the division of labor becomes the principal source of solidarity. Since these two phenomena are linked at this point, it will be useful to seek the causes for this regression. Doubtless, having demonstrated with what regularity this regression is produced, we have directly proved its certain dependence upon some fundamental conditions of social evolution. But this conclusion of the preceding book would be still more indisputable if we could find what these conditions are.

This question is, moreover, solidary with the one we are now treating. We have just shown that the advances of the division of labor are due to the stronger pressure exercised by social units upon one another which obliges them to develop in increasingly divergent directions. But this pressure is at each moment neutralized by a contrary pressure that the common conscience exercises on each particular conscience. Whereas one impels us to become a distinct personality, the other, on the contrary, demands our resemblance to

particular society a certain division of labor, and notably the division of economic labor, may be greatly developed, although the segmental type may be strongly pronounced there. This seems to be the case with England. Great industry and commerce appear to be as developed there as on the continent, although the cellular system is still very marked, as both the autonomy of local life and the authority of tradition serve to prove. (The symptomatic value of this last fact will be determined in the following chapter.)

That is because the division of labor, being a derived and secondary phenomenon, as we have just seen, passes on the surface of social life, and this is especially true of the division of economic labor. But, in all organisms, the superficial phenomena, by their very situation, are much more accessible to the action of external causes, even when internal causes on which they generally depend are not modified. It is sufficient, then, that some sort of circumstance excite an urgent need of material well-being with a people for the division of economic labor to be developed without the social structure sensibly changing. The spirit of imitation, the contact of a more refined civilization can produce this result. It is thus that understanding, being the culminating part and, consequently, the most superficial part of conscience, can rather easily be modified by external influences, as education, without the seat of psychical life being changed. One thus creates intelligences sufficient to assure success, but which are not deep-rooted. Hence, this kind of talent is not transmitted by heredity.

This comparison shows that one must not judge the place of a society on the social ladder according to its state of civilization, especially of its economic civilization, for the latter can be only an imitation, a copy, and conceal a social structure of inferior species. The case, it is true, is exceptional. It appears, however.

It is only in these instances that the material density of societies does not exactly express the state of moral density. The principle we have posed is then true in a very general manner, and that is sufficient for our proof.

everybody else. Whereas the first has us following our personal bent, the second holds us back and prevents us from deviating from the collective type. In other words, for the division of labor to be born and grow, it is not sufficient that there be potentialities for special aptitudes in individuals, nor that they be aroused to specialize in the direction of these aptitudes, but it is very necessary that individual variations be possible. But they cannot be produced when they are opposed to some strong and defined state of the collective conscience, for the stronger the state, the greater the resistance to all that may weaken it; the more defined, the less place it leaves for changes. It can thus be seen that the progress of the division of labor will be as much more difficult and slow as the common conscience is vital and precise. Inversely, it will be as much more rapid as the individual is enabled to put himself in harmony with his personal environment. But, for that, the existence of the environment is not sufficient; each must be free to adapt himself to it, that is to say, be capable of independent movement even when the whole group does not move with him. But we know that the movements of individuals are proportionately as rare as mechanical solidarity is more developed.

Examples are numerous where this neutralizing influence of the common conscience on the division of labor can be directly observed. As long as law and custom make a strict obligation of the inalienability and communism of real estate, the necessary conditions for the division of labor do not exist. Each family forms a compact mass, and all devote themselves to the same occupation, to the exploitation of the hereditary patrimony. Among the Slavs, the *Zadruga* is often increased to such proportions that great misery becomes prevalent. Nevertheless, as domestic spirit is very strong, they generally continue to live together, instead of taking up special occupations such as mariner and merchant outside. In other societies, where the division of labor is more advanced, each class has determinate functions, always the same, sheltered from all innovation. Elsewhere, there are entire classes of occupations whose cultivation is more or less forbidden to citizens. In Greece,[349] in Rome,[350] industry and commerce were scorned careers. Among the Kabyles, certain trades like those of butcher, shoemaker, etc. are held in low esteem by public opinion.[351] Specialization, thus, cannot move in these various directions. Finally, even with those peoples where economic life has already attained some development, as with us during the days of the old corporations, functions were regulated in such a way that the division of labor could not progress.

---

[349] Büsschenshütz, *Besitz und Erwerb.*

[350] According to Dionysius of Halicarnassus (IX, 25), during the first years of the Republic, no Roman could become merchant or worker. Cicero even speaks of all mercenary work as a degrading calling. (*De Off.*, I, 42.)

[351] Hanoteau and Letourneux, *La Kabylie*, II, p. 23.

Where everyone was obliged to manufacture in the same manner, all individual variation was impossible.[352]

The same phenomenon shows itself in the representative life of societies. Religion, the eminent form of the common conscience, originally absorbs all representative functions with practical functions. The first are not dissociated from the second until philosophy appears. But this is possible only when religion has lost something of its hold. This new way of representing things clashes with collective opinion which resists it. It has sometimes been said that free thought makes religious beliefs regress, but that supposes, in its turn, a preliminary regression of these same beliefs. It can arise only if the common faith permits.

The same antagonism breaks out each time a new science is founded. Christianity itself, although it instantly gave individual reflection a larger place than any other religion, could not escape this law. To be sure, the opposition was less acute as long as scholars limited their researches to the material world since it was originally abandoned to the disputes of men. Yet, as this surrender was never complete, as the Christian God does not entirely ignore things of this world, it necessarily happened that, on more than one point, the natural sciences themselves found an obstacle in faith. But it is especially when man became an object of science that the resistance became fierce. The believer, indeed, cannot but find repugnant the idea that man is to be studied as a natural being, analogous to others, and moral facts as facts of nature. It is well known how these collective sentiments, under the different forms they have taken, have hindered the development of psychology and sociology.

There has been no complete explanation of the progress of the division of labor when one has shown that it is necessary because of changes in the social environment, but it still depends upon secondary factors, which can either expedite or hinder it, or completely thwart its course. It must not be forgotten that specialization is not the only possible solution to the struggle for existence. There are also emigration, colonization, resignation to a precarious, disputed existence, and, finally, the total elimination of the weakest by suicide or some other means. Since the result is in part contingent, and since the combatants are not necessarily impelled towards one of these issues to the exclusion of others, they tend toward the one closest to their grasp. Of course, if nothing prevents the division of labor from developing, they specialize. But if circumstances make this too difficult or impossible, another means will be necessary.

The first of these factors consists of a greater independence of individuals in relation to the group, permitting them to diversify in

---

freedom. The division of physiological labor is submitted to the same condition. "Even related to one another," says Perrier, "the anatomic elements respectively conserve all their individuality. Whatever may be their number, in the most elevated organisms as in the humblest, they eat, increase, and reproduce with no thought of their neighbors. Herein lies the *law of independence of anatomic elements* become so fertile in the hands of physiologists. This independence must be considered as the necessary condition for the free exercise of a very general faculty of plastids, the variability under the action of external circumstances or even of certain forces immanent in protoplasm. Thanks to their aptitude for varying and their reciprocal independence, the elements, born of one another, and originally all alike, have been able to modify in different directions, to assume diverse forms, to acquire new functions and properties."[353]

In contrast to what takes place in organisms, this independence is not a pristine fact in societies, since originally the individual is absorbed in the group. But we have seen that independence later appears and progresses regularly with the division of labor and the regression of the collective conscience. There remains to discover how this useful condition of the division of social labor is realized in proportion to its necessity. Doubtless it depends upon causes which have determined the advances in specialization. But how can this increase of societies in volume and in density have this result?

I

In a small society, since everyone is clearly placed in the same conditions of existence, the collective environment is essentially concrete. It is made up of beings of all sorts who fill the social horizon. The states of conscience representing it then have the same character. First, they are related to precise objects, as this animal, this tree, this plant, this natural force, etc. Then, as everybody is related to these things in the same way, they affect all consciences in the same way. The whole tribe, if it is not too widely extended, enjoys or suffers the same advantages or inconveniences from the sun, rain, heat, or cold, from this river, or that source, etc. The collective impressions resulting from the fusion of all these individual impressions are then determined in form as well as in object, and, consequently, the common conscience has a defined character. But it changes its nature as societies become more voluminous. Because these societies are spread over a vaster surface, the common conscience is itself obliged to rise above all local diversities, to dominate more space, and consequently to become more abstract. For not many general things can be common to all these

---

[353] *Colonies animales*, p. 702.

diverse environments. It is no longer such an animal, but such a species; not this source, but such sources; not this forest, but forest *in abstracto.*

Moreover, because conditions of life are no longer the same everywhere, these common objects, whatever they may be, can no longer determine perfectly identical sentiments everywhere. The collective resultants then no longer have the same sharpness, and the more so in this respect as their component elements are more unlike. The more differences among individual portraits serving to make a composite portrait, the more indecisive the latter is. True it is that local collective consciences can keep their individuality in the midst of the general collective conscience and that, as they comprise less space, they more easily remain concrete. But we know they slowly tend to vanish from the first, in so far as the social segments to which they correspond are effaced.

The fact which perhaps best manifests this increasing tendency of the common conscience is the parallel transcendence of the most essential of its elements, I mean the idea of divinity. In the beginning, the gods are not distinct from the universe, or rather there are no gods, but only sacred beings, without their sacred character being related to any external entity as their source. The animals or plants of the species which serves as a clan-totem are the objects of worship, but that is not because a principle *sui generis* comes to communicate their divine nature to them from without. This nature is intrinsic with them; they are divine in and of themselves. But little by little religious forces are detached from the things of which they were first only the attributes, and become hypostatized. Thus is formed the notion of spirits or gods who, while residing here or there as preferred, nevertheless exist outside of the particular objects to which they are more specifically attached.[354] By that very fact they are less concrete. Whether they multiply or have been led back to some certain unity, they are still immanent in the world. If they are in part separated from things, they are always in space. They remain, then, very near us, constantly fused into our life. The Graeco-Latin polytheism, which is a more elevated and better organized form of animism, marks new progress in the direction of transcendence. The residence of the gods becomes more sharply distinct from that of men. Set upon the mysterious heights of Olympus or dwelling in the recesses of the earth, they personally intervene in human affairs only in somewhat intermittent fashion. But it is only with Christianity that God takes leave of space; his kingdom is no longer of this world. The dissociation of nature and the divine is so complete that it degenerates into antagonism. At the same time, the concept of divinity becomes more general and more abstract, for it is

---

[354] See Réville, *Religions des peuples non civilisés*, I, pp. 67 ff.; II, pp. 230 ff.

formed, not of sensations, as originally, but of ideas. The God of humanity necessarily is less concrete than the gods of the city or the clan.

Besides, at the same time as religion, the rules of law become universal, as well as those of morality. Linked at first to local circumstances, to particularities, ethnic, climatic, etc., they free themselves little by little, and with the same stroke become more general. What makes this increase of generality obvious is the uninterrupted decline of formalism. In lower societies, the very external form of conduct is predetermined even to the details. The way in which man must eat, dress in every situation, the gestures he must make, the formulae he must pronounce, are precisely fixed. On the contrary, the further one strays from the point of departure, the more moral and juridical prescriptions lose their sharpness and precision. They rule only the most general forms of conduct, and rule them in a very general manner, saying what must be done, not how it must be done. Now, all that is defined is expressed in a definite form. If collective sentiments had the same determination as formerly, they would not be expressed in a less determined manner. If the concrete details of action and thought were as uniform, they would be as obligatory.

It has often been remarked that civilization has a tendency to become more rational and more logical. The cause is now evident. That alone is rational which is universal. What baffles understanding is the particular and the concrete. Only the general is thought well of. Consequently, the nearer the common conscience is to particular things, the more it bears their imprint, the more unintelligible it also is. That is why primitive civilizations affect us as they do. Being unable to subsume them under logical principles, we succeed in seeing only bizarre and fortuitous combinations of heterogeneous elements. In reality, there is nothing artificial about them. It is necessary only to seek their determining causes in sensations and movements of sensibility, not in concepts. And if this is so, it is because the social environment for which they are made is not sufficiently extended. On the contrary, when civilization is developed over a vaster field of action, when it is applied to more people and things, general ideas necessarily appear and become predominant there. The idea of man, for example, replaces in law, in morality, in religion, that of Roman, which, being more concrete, is more refractory to science. Thus, it is the increase of volume in societies and their greater condensation which explain this great transformation.

But the more general the common conscience becomes, the greater the place it leaves to individual variations. When God is far from things and men, his action is no longer omnipresent, nor ubiquitous. There is nothing fixed save abstract rules which can be freely applied in very different ways. Then they no longer have the same ascendancy nor the same force of resistance. Indeed, if practices and formulae, when they are precise, determine thought and movements with a necessity analogous to that of reflexes, these general principles, on the contrary, can pass into facts only with the aid of intelligence. But, once reflection is awakened, it is not easy to restrain it. When it has taken hold, it develops spontaneously beyond the limits assigned to it. One begins by putting articles of faith beyond discussion; then discussion extends to them. One wishes an explanation of them; one asks their reasons for existing, and, as they submit to this search, they lose a part of their force. For reflective ideas never have the same constraining force as instincts. It is thus that deliberated movements have not the spontaneity of involuntary movements. Because it becomes more rational, the collective conscience becomes less imperative, and for this very reason, it wields less restraint over the free development of individual varieties.

II

But this is not the greatest contributing cause in producing this result.

What gives force to collective states is not only that they are common to the present generation, but especially that they are, for the most part, a legacy of previous generations. The common conscience is constituted very slowly and is modified in the same way. Time is necessary for a form of conduct or a belief to arrive at that degree of generality and crystallization; time is also necessary for it to lose it. It is, then, almost entirely a product of the past. But what comes from the past is generally the object of a very special respect. A practice to which everybody conforms has, without doubt, a great prestige, but if it is, in addition, strong because of the assent of ancestors, it is still less liable to derogation. The authority of the collective conscience is, then, in large part composed of the authority of tradition. We shall see that the latter necessarily diminishes as the segmental type is effaced.

Indeed, when the type is very pronounced, the segments form very small societies more or less closed in. Where they have a familial base, it is as difficult to change from them as to change families, and if, when they have only a territorial base, the barriers separating them are not as insurmountable, they nevertheless persist. In the middle ages, it was still difficult for a workman to find work in a city other than his own.[355] The internal customs, moreover, formed an enclosure around each social division protecting it from the infiltration of foreign elements. Under these conditions, the individual is held to the soil where he was born by ties attaching him to it, and because he is repulsed elsewhere. The rarity of means of communication and transportation is a proof of

---

[355] Levasseur, *op. cit.*, I, p. 239.

this exclusion of each segment. By repercussion, the causes maintaining man in his native land fix him in his domestic life. In the beginning the two are confounded and if, later, they are distinguished, one cannot draw far away from the second when the first cannot be passed. The force of attraction resulting from consanguinity exercises its action with a maximum of intensity, since each remains throughout life very near the source of this force. It is, indeed, a law without exception that the more the social structure is by nature segmental, the more families form great, compact, undivided masses, gathered up in themselves.[356]

On the other hand, in so far as the lines of demarcation separating the different segments are obliterated, this equilibrium is inevitably broken. As individuals are no longer held together in the places of their origin, and as these free spaces, opening before them, attract them, they cannot fail to expand there. Children no longer remain immutably attached to the land of their parents, but leave to seek their fortune in all directions. Populations are mingled, and, because of this, their original differences are lost. Statistics, unfortunately, do not permit our following the march of these interior migrations in history, but a fact sufficient to establish their growing importance is the formation and development of cities. Cities, indeed, are not formed by a sort of spontaneous growth, but by immigration. Far from owing their existence and progress to the normal preponderance of births over deaths, they present, from this point of view, a general deficiency. It is, then, from without that they receive the elements to which they owe their daily increase. According to Dunant,[357] the annual increase in the total population of thirty-one large cities of Europe owes 784.6 out of every thousand to immigration. In France, the census of 1881 presented an increase of 766,000 over that of 1876; the *departement* of the Seine and the forty-five cities having more than 30,000 inhabitants "absorbed more than 661,000 inhabitants of the quinquennial increase, leaving only 105,000 to be distributed among the average towns, the small towns, and the country."[358] It is not only toward the great cities that these great migratory movements tend; they radiate into neighboring regions. Bertillon has calculated that during the year 1886, while on the average in France 11.25 out of 100 were born outside the *departement*, in the *departement* of the Seine there were 34.67. This proportion of strangers is so much greater as *departements* of cities are more populous. It is 31.47 in the *Rhone*, 26.29 in the *Bouches-du-Rhone*,

---

[356] The reader himself sees facts verifying this law whose express proof we cannot present here. It results from researches we have made on the family, and that we hope to publish soon.

[357] Cited by Layet, *Hygiène des paysans*, last chapter.

[358] Dumont, *Dépopulation et Civilisation*, p. 175.

26.41 in the *Seine-et-Oise,*[359] 19.46 in the *Nord,* 17.62 in the *Gironde.*[360] This phenomenon is not peculiar to great cities. It is equally produced, although with less intensity, in small towns and market-towns. "All these agglomerations increase constantly at the expense of the smaller townships, so that one sees with each census the number of cities of each category increased by some units."[361]

But the greater mobility of social units which these phenomena of migration suppose causes a weakening of all traditions.

In fact, what especially gives force to tradition is the character of the persons who transmit it and inculcate it, the old people. They are its living expression. They alone have been witnesses of the acts of their ancestors. They are the unique intermediary between the present and the past. Moreover, they enjoy a prestige with generations reared under their eyes and their direction which nothing can replace. The child, indeed, is aware of his inferiority before the older persons surrounding him, and he feels he depends upon them. The reverential respect he has for them is naturally communicated to all that comes from them, to all they say, and all they do. Thus, it is the authority of age which gives tradition its authority. Consequently, all that can contribute to prolonging this influence beyond infancy can only fortify traditional beliefs and practices. That is what happens when a man continues to live in the environment where he was reared, for he then remains in relation with people who have known him as a child, and he submits to their action. The feeling he has for them lasts, and, consequently, it produces the same effects, that is to say, restrains the desire for innovation. To produce novelties in social life, it is not sufficient for a new generation to appear. It is still necessary for them not to be strongly impelled towards following in the footsteps of their forefathers. The more profound the influence of these latter—and it is as much more profound as it lasts longer—the more obstacles there are to change. Auguste Comte was right in saying that if human life was increased tenfold, without the respective proportion of ages being changed, there would result "an inevitable slowing up of our social development, although it would be impossible to measure."[362]

But it is the reverse that is produced when man, while emerging from adolescence, is transplanted into a new environment. To be sure, he finds there men older than himself as well, but they are not the same as those he obeyed in his infancy. The respect he has for them is then less, and by nature more conventional, for it corresponds to no reality, present or past. He does not depend upon and never has depended upon

---

[359] This increased number is an effect of the neighborhood of Paris.
[360] *Dictionnaire encyclop. des Sciences medic.*, art. *Migration*
[361] Dumont, *op. cit.*, p. 178.
[362] *Cours de Philosophie positive*, IV, p. 451.

them; he can then respect them only by analogy. It is, moreover, a known fact that the worship of age is steadily weakening with civilization. Though formerly developed, it is today reduced to some few polite practices, inspired by a sort of pity. One pities old men more than one fears them. Ages are leveled off. All men who have reached maturity are treated almost as equals. As a consequence of this, the ancestral customs lose their predominance, for they no longer have authorized representatives among adults. One is freer in contact with them because one is freer with those who incarnate them. The solidarity of time is less perceptible because it no longer has its material expression in the continuous contact of successive generations. To be sure, effects of primary education continue to be felt, but with less force, because they are not held together.

The prime of youth, moreover, is the time when men are most impatient with all restraint and most eager for change. The life circulating in them has not yet had time to congeal, or definitely to take determined forms, and it is too intense to be disciplined without resistance. This need will, then, be satisfied so much more easily as it is less restrained from without, and it can be satisfied only at the expense of tradition. The latter is most battered at the very moment when it loses its strength. Once given, this germ of weakness can only be developed with each generation, for one transmits with less authority principles whose authority is felt less.

A characteristic example shows the influence of age on the force of tradition.

Precisely because the population of great cities is recruited especially through immigration, it is essentially composed of people who, on becoming adult, have left their homes and been freed from the action of the old. Moreover, the number of old men there is small, whereas that of men in the prime of life, on the contrary, is very high. Cheysson has shown that the curves of population at each age group, for Paris and for the province, meet only at the ages of 15 to 20 and from 50 to 55. Between 20 and 50, the Parisian curve is a great deal higher; beyond that it is lower.[363] In 1881, there were in Paris 1,118 individuals from 20 to 25 to 874 in the rest of the country.[364] For the entire *departement* of the Seine, there is found in 1,000 inhabitants 731 from 15 to 60 and only 76 beyond that age, whereas the province has 618 of the first and 106 of the second. In Norway, according to Jacques Bertillon, the relations are the following in 1,000 inhabitants:

---

[363] *La Question de la population,* in *Annales d' Hygiène,* 1884.
[364] *Annales de la ville de Paris.*

	Cities	Country
From 15 to 30	278	239
From 30 to 45	205	183
From 45 to 60	110	120
From 60 and above	59	87

Thus, it is in the great cities that the moderating influence of age is at its minimum. At the same time, one observes that nowhere have the traditions less sway over minds. Indeed, great cities are the uncontested homes of progress; it is in them that ideas, fashions, customs, new needs are elaborated and then spread over the rest of the country. When society changes, it is generally after them and in imitation. Temperaments are so mobile that everything that comes from the past is somewhat suspect. On the contrary, innovations, whatever they may be, enjoy a prestige there almost equal to the one the customs of ancestors formerly enjoyed. Minds naturally are there oriented to the future. Consequently, life is there transformed with extraordinary rapidity; beliefs, tastes, passions, are in perpetual evolution. No ground is more favorable to evolutions of all sorts. That is because the collective life cannot have continuity there, where different layers of social units, summoned to replace one another, are discontinuous.

Observing that during the youth of societies and especially at the moment of their maturity the respect for traditions is much greater than during old age, Tarde believed he could present the decline of traditionalism as simply a transitory phase, a passing crisis of all social evolution. "Man," he says, "escapes the chains of custom only to be captured again, that is to say, to fix and consolidate, again falling a prey after his temporary emancipation."[365] This error results, we believe, from the method of comparison followed by the author, the objections to which we have several times pointed out. Doubtless, if one compares the end of a society to the beginnings of a succeeding one, a return to traditionalism can be seen. But this phase in which every social type begins is always a great deal less violent than it had been with the immediately anterior type. With us, the customs of ancestors have never been the object of the superstitious worship which was accorded to them at Rome. Never was there at Rome an institution analogous to the γραφὴ παρανόμων of the Athenian law, opposing all innovation.[366] Even at the time of Aristotle in Greece, it was still a question of whether it was good to change established laws in order to improve them, and the philosopher answers in the affirmative only with the greatest circumspection.[367] Finally, with the Jews all deviation from

---

[365] *Lois de l'imitation*, p. 271.
[366] See concerning this γραφὴ Meier and Schoemann, *Der attische Process.*
[367] Aristotle, *Politics*, II, 8, 1268b, 26.

traditional rule was still more completely impossible, since it was an impiety. But, to judge the march of social events, one must not put, end to end, the societies which succeed each other, but one must compare them at the corresponding period of their life. If, then, it is quite true that all social life tends to be fixed and to become habitual, the form it takes always becomes less resistant, more accessible to changes. In other words, the authority of custom diminishes in a continuous manner. It is, moreover, impossible for it to be otherwise, since this weakening depends upon the very conditions which dominate historical development.

Moreover, since common beliefs and practices, in large part, extract their strength from the strength of tradition, it is evident that they are less and less able to prevent the free expansion of individual variations.

III

Finally, in so far as society is extended and concentrated, it envelops the individual less, and, consequently, cannot as well restrain the divergent tendencies coming up.

To assure ourselves of this it is sufficient to compare great cities with small. In the latter, whoever seeks to free himself from accepted customs meets with resistance which is sometimes very acute. Every attempt at independence is an object of public scandal, and the general reprobation attached is of such a nature as to discourage all imitators. On the contrary, in large cities, the individual is a great deal freer of collective bonds. This fact of experience cannot be denied. It is because we depend so much more closely on common opinion the more it watches over conduct. When the attention of all is constantly fixed on what each does, the least misstep is perceived and immediately condemned. Inversely, each has as many more facilities to follow his own path as he is better able to escape this control. And, as the proverb has it, one is nowhere better hidden than in a crowd. The greater the extension and the greater the density of a group, the greater the dispersion of collective attention over a wide area. Thus, it is incapable of following the movements of each individual, for it does not become stronger as they become more numerous. It has to consider too many points at once to be able to concentrate on any. The watch is less piercing because there are too many people and too many things to watch.

Moreover, the great source of attention, that of interest, is more or less completely wanting. We wish to know the facts about, and movements of a person only if his image awakens in us memories and emotions which are linked to him, and this desire is more acute as the states of conscience thus awakened are more numerous and strong.[368] If, on the contrary, we look upon someone from afar, having no interest in his concerns, we are not aroused either to learn what happens to him or to observe what he does. Collective curiosity is, then, keener as personal relations between individuals are more continuous and more frequent. Moreover, it is clear that they are proportionately rarer and shorter as each individual is in contact with a greater number of persons.

That is why the pressure of opinion is felt with less force in great centres. It is because the attention of each is distracted in too many directions, and because, moreover, one is known less. Even neighbors and members of the same family are less often and less regularly in contact, separated as they are by the mass of affairs and intercurrent persons. Doubtless, if population is more numerous than it is dense, it may be that life, spread over a larger area, is less at each point. The great city is resolved, then, into a certain number of little cities, and, consequently, the preceding observations do not exactly apply.[369] But wherever the density of the agglomeration is related to the volume, personal bonds are rare and weak. One more easily loses others from sight; in the same way one loses interest even in those close by. As this mutual indifference results in loosing collective surveillance, the sphere of free action of each individual is extended in fact, and, little by little, the fact becomes a right. We know, indeed, that the common conscience keeps its strength only on condition of not tolerating contradictions. But, by reason of this diminution of social control, acts are committed daily which confute it, without, however, any reaction. If, then, there are some repeated with frequency and uniformity, they end by enervating the collective sentiment they shock. A rule no longer appears respectable when it ceases to be respected, and that with impunity. One no longer finds the same conviction in an article of faith too often denied. Moreover, once we have availed ourselves of some liberty, we feel the need for it. It becomes as necessary and appears as sacred to us as others. We judge a control intolerable when we have lost the habit of complying. An acquired right to greater autonomy is founded. It is thus that the encroachments the individual personality makes, when it is less strongly restrained from without, end by receiving the consecration of custom.

But if this fact is more marked in great cities, it is not special to them; it is also produced in others according to their importance. Since,

---

[368] It is true that, in a small city, the stranger, the unknown, is no less the object of curiosity than the inhabitant, but it is because of contrast, because he is the exception. It is not the same in a great city, where it is the rule, as it were, for everybody to be unknown.

[369] This is a question to be studied. We believe we have noticed that in populous cities, which are not dense, collective opinion keeps its strength.

then, the obliteration of the segmental type entails a steadily increasing development of urban centres, there is a primary reason for this phenomenon having to continue to become general. But, moreover, in so far as the moral density of society is increased, it itself becomes similar to a great city which contains an entire people within its walls.

In effect, as material and moral distance between different regions tend to vanish, they are, with relation to one another, steadily more analogous to that of different quarters of the same city. The cause which in great cities determines a weakening of the common conscience must then produce its effect throughout society. So long as divers segments, keeping their individuality, remain closed to one another, each of them narrowly limits the social horizon of individuals. Separated from the rest of society by barriers more or less difficult to clear, nothing turns us from local life, and, therefore, all our action is concentrated there. But as the fusion of segments becomes more complete, the vistas enlarge, and the more so as society itself becomes more generally extended at the same time. From then on, even the inhabitant of a small city lives the life of the little group immediately surrounding him less exclusively. He joins in relations with distant localities which are more numerous as the movement of concentration is more advanced. His more frequent journeys, the more active correspondence he exchanges, the affairs occupying him outside, etc., turn his attention from what is passing around him. He no longer finds the centre of his life and preoccupations so completely in the place where he lives. He is then less interested in his neighbors, since they take a smaller place in his life. Besides, the small city has less hold upon him for the very reason that his life is bursting that small shell, and his interests and affections are extending beyond it. For all these reasons, local public opinion weighs less heavily on each of us, and as the general opinion of society cannot replace its predecessor, not being able to watch closely the conduct of all its citizens, the collective surveillance is irretrievably loosened, the common conscience loses its authority, individual variability grows. In short, for social control to be rigorous and for the common conscience to be maintained, society must be divided into rather small compartments completely enclosing the individual. Both weaken as these divisions are done away with.[370]

But, it will be said, the crimes and delicts to which organized punishments are attached never leave the organs charged with suppressing them indifferent. Whether the city be great or small, whether society be dense or not, magistrates do not leave the criminal or delinquent go unpunished. It would seem, then, that the special

---

[370] To this fundamental cause must be added the contagious influence of great cities upon small, and of small upon the country. But this influence is only secondary, and, besides, assumes importance only to the extent that social density grows.

weakening whose cause we have just indicated must be localized in that part of the collective conscience which determines only diffuse reactions, without being able to extend beyond. But, in reality, this localization is impossible, for these two regions are so strictly solidary that one cannot be attacked without the other feeling it. The acts which custom alone must repress are not different in nature from those the law punishes; they are only less serious. If, then, there are some among them which lose their weight, the corresponding graduation of the others is upset by the same stroke. They sink one or several degrees, and appear less revolting. When one is no longer at all sensible to small faults, one is less sensible to great ones. When one no longer attaches great importance to simple neglect of religious practices, one is no longer as indignant about blasphemies or sacrileges. When one is accustomed complacently to tolerate free love, adultery is less scandalous. When the weakest sentiments lose their energy, the strongest sentiments, even those which are of the same sort and have the same objects, cannot keep theirs intact. It is thus that, little by little, the movement is communicated to the whole common conscience.

IV

It is now manifest how it happens that mechanical solidarity is linked to the existence of the segmental type, as we have shown in the preceding book. It is because this special structure allows society to enclose the individual more tightly, holding him strongly attached to his domestic environment and, consequently, to traditions, and finally contributing to the limitation of his social horizon, it also contributes[371] to make it concrete and defined. Wholly mechanical causes, then, bring it about that the individual is absorbed into the collective personality, and they are causes of the same nature as those which bring about the individual's freedom. To be sure, this emancipation is found to be useful, or, at least, it is utilized. It makes the progress of the division of labor possible; more generally, it gives more suppleness and elasticity to the social organism. But it is not because it is useful that it is produced. It is because it cannot be otherwise. Experience with the service it renders can only consolidate it once it exists.

One can, nevertheless, ask oneself if, in organized societies, the organ does not play the same role as the segment; if it is not probable that the corporative and occupational mind replaces the mind of the native village, and exercises the same influence as it did. In this case they would not gain anything by the change. Doubt is permitted to a

---

[371] This third effect results only in part from the segmental nature. The principal cause of it lies in the growth of social volume. It would still be asked why, in general, density increases at the same time as volume. It is a question we pose.

great extent, as the caste-mind has certainly had this effect, and the caste is a social organ. We also know how the organization of bodies of trades has, for a long time, hindered the development of individual variations; we have cited examples of this above.

It is certain that organized societies are not possible without a developed system of rules which predetermine the functions of each organ. In so far as labor is divided, there arises a multitude of occupational moralities and laws.[372] But this regulation, none the less, does not contract the sphere of action of the individual.

In the first place, the occupational mind can only have influence on occupational life. Beyond this sphere, the individual enjoys a greater liberty whose origin we have just shown. True, the caste extends its action further, but it is not an organ, properly speaking. It is a segment transformed into an organ;[373] it has the nature of both. At the same time as it is charged with special functions, it constitutes a distinct society in the midst of the total aggregate. It is a society-organ, analogous to those individual-organs observed in certain organisms.[374] That is what makes it enclose the individual in a much more exclusive manner than ordinary corporations.

As these rules have their roots only in a small number of consciences, and leave society in its entirety indifferent, they have less authority by consequence of this lesser universality. They offer, then, less resistance to changes. It is for this reason that, in general, faults properly occupational have not the same degree of gravity as others.

Moreover, the same causes which, in a general manner, lift the collective yoke, produce their liberating effect in the interior of the corporation as well as externally. In so far as segmental organs fuse, each social organ becomes more voluminous, and in proportion as the total volume of society grows at the same time. Common practices of the occupational group thus become more general and more abstract, as those which are common to all society, and, accordingly, they leave more free space for individual divergences. Indeed, the greater independence enjoyed by new generations in comparison with the older cannot fail to weaken traditionalism in the occupation. This leaves the individual even more free to make innovations.

Thus, not only does occupational regulation, because of its very nature, hinder less than any other the play of individual variation, but it also tends to do so less and less.

---

[372] See above, Book I, ch. v, especially pp. 179 ff.
[373] See above, p. 156.
[374] See Perrier, *Colonies animales*, p. 764.

CHAPTER FOUR. SECONDARY FACTORS (*Continued*)

Heredity

In the preceding pages, we reasoned as if the division of labor depended only upon social causes. It is also linked with organico-psychical conditions, however. The individual, at birth, receives tastes and aptitudes predisposing him to certain functions more than to others, and these predispositions certainly have an influence on the way in which tasks are distributed. According to the most common opinion, one would have to see the first condition of the division of labor in this diversity of natures. Its principal reason for existing would be to classify individuals according to their capacities.[375] It is, then, interesting to ascertain what precisely is the part of this factor, the more so since it constitutes an additional obstacle to individual variability, and, consequently, to the progress of the division of labor.

As these native talents are transmitted to us by our ancestors, they have to do, not with conditions in which the individual actually finds himself, but those of his forefathers. They chain us, then, to our race, as the collective conscience chains us to our group and shackles the liberty of our movements. As this part of us is entirely turned to the past, and toward a past not personal to us, it removes us from our own sphere of interests and the changes produced there. The greater its development, the more it controls us. Race and individuality are two contradictory forces which vary inversely with each other. As long as we only continue to follow in the path of our ancestors, we tend to live as they have lived, and remain adamant to all innovation. A human being who would receive from heredity an important and heavy legacy would be almost incapable of any change. Such is the case with animals, who can progress only very slowly.

The obstacle that progress meets in this quarter is even more difficult to surmount than that coming from a community of beliefs and practices. For the latter are imposed upon the individual only from without and by moral action, whereas hereditary tendencies are congenital and have an anatomical base. Thus, the greater the part of heredity in the distribution of tasks, the more invariable the distribution, the more difficult, consequently, the advances of the division of labor are, even when they may be useful. That is what happens in the organism. The function of each cell is determined by its birth. In a living animal, as Spencer says, progress in organization implies not only that the units composing each of the differentiated parts keep their places, but also that their descendants succeed them in

---

[375] Mill, J. S., *Political Economy.*

these places. Spencer adds that the hepatic cells, while fulfilling their function, enlarge and bring forth new hepatic cells to take their place when they are dissolved and disappear; the cells coming from them do not surrender to the kidneys, to the muscles, to the nervous centres to unite in the accomplishment of their functions.[376] Moreover, the changes produced in the organization of physiological work are very rare, very restricted, and very slow.

But a great many facts tend to prove that, in the beginning, heredity had a very considerable influence over the division of social functions.

To be sure, among entirely primitive people, it has no importance from this point of view. The several functions which have begun to be specialized are elective, but that is because they are not yet organized. The chief or chiefs are scarcely distinguishable from the crowd they direct; their power is as restricted as it is ephemeral; all members of the group are on a plane of equality. But as soon as the division of labor appears in characteristic fashion, it is fixed into a form transmitted by heredity. Thus castes grow up. India offers the most perfect model of this organization of work, but it is found elsewhere. With the Jews, the only functions which were sharply separated from others, sacerdotal functions, were strictly hereditary. It was the same at Rome for all public functions, which implied religious functions, which were the privilege of the patricians alone. In Assyria, Persia, Egypt, society is divided in the same manner. When castes tend to disappear, they are replaced by classes, which, in order to keep their close exclusion and privileges, rely on the same principle.

Assuredly, this institution is not a simple consequence of the fact of hereditary transmissions. A great many causes have contributed to bring it into being. But it would never have been able either to generalize to such a point, or to persist for so long a time, if, *in general*, it had not had the effect of putting each in a place fitting to him. If the system of castes had been contrary to individual aspirations and social interest, no artifice could have maintained it. If, in the average case, individuals were not really born for the function assigned them by custom or law, this traditional classification of citizens would have been quickly overthrown. The proof is that this overthrow is effected as soon as discordance breaks out. The rigidity of social forms, then, only explains the immutable manner in which these talents are distributed, and this immutability itself can be due only to the laws of heredity. To be sure, education, since it was carried on entirely in the midst of the family and was prolonged late for reasons we have cited, strengthened the influence, but it could not have alone produced such results. For it acts usefully and efficaciously only if it is employed in the same way as

---

[376] Spencer, *Principles of Sociology*, III, p. 349.

heredity. In short, this latter could become a social institution only where it effectively played a social role. In fact, we know that the ancients had a very acute feeling for it. We do not find traces only in customs of which we were speaking, and such like, but it is directly expressed in more than one literary testimonial.[377] It is impossible, however, that so general an error be a simple illusion and correspond to nothing in reality. "All peoples," says Ribot, "have faith, perhaps only vague, in hereditary transmission. It would even be possible to argue that this faith was stronger in primitive times than in civilized epochs. It is from this natural faith that heredity as an institution is born. It is certain that reasons, social, politic, or even prejudices, have had to contribute to its development and its strength, but it would be absurd to believe that it was invented."[378]

Moreover, occupational heredity was very often the rule, even when the law did not impose it. Thus, medicine, with the Greeks, was first cultivated by a small number of families. "The asclepiads, or priests of Aesculapius, were said to be of the posterity of this god. . . . Hippocrates was the seventeenth doctor in his family. The art of divination, the gift of prophecy, that high favor of the gods, was considered by the Greeks as being most often transmitted from father to son."[379] "In Greece," says Hermann, "heredity of function was enjoined by law only in some states and for certain functions bound narrowly to the religious life, as in Sparta, the cooks and flute players, but the custom had also played a greater part in artisans' occupations than is ordinarily believed."[380] Even now, in a great many lower societies, functions are distributed according to race. In a great number of African tribes, the blacksmiths descend from another race than the rest of the population. It was the same with the Jews in the time of Saul. "In Abyssinia, almost all the workers are of alien race: the mason is Jewish, the tanner and weaver are Mohammedans, the armorer and goldsmith Greeks and Copts. In the Indies, a great many differences of caste which indicate differences in trade coincide, even today, with those in race. In all countries of mixed population, the descendants of the same family are accustomed to consecrate themselves to certain occupations. It is thus that, in eastern Germany, fishers for centuries were Slavs."[381] These facts give great weight to Lucas' opinion that "the heredity of occupations is the primitive type, the elementary form of all institutions founded on the principle of the heredity of moral nature."

---

[377] Ribot, *L'Hérédité*, 2nd ed., p. 360.

[378] *Ibid.*, p. 345.

[379] *Ibid., op. cit.*, p. 365. Cf. Hermann, *Griech. Antiq.*, IV, p. 353, note 3.

[380] *Ibid.*, p. 395, note 2, ch. i, 33.—For the facts, see especially, Plato, *Euthyphro*, 11C; *Alcibiades*, 121A; *Republic*, IV, 421D; particularly *Protagoras*, 328A; Plutarch, *Apophth. Lacon*, 208B.

[381] Schmoller, *La division du travail*, in *Rev. econ. polit.*, 1889, p. 590.

But it is well known how slow and difficult progress is in these societies. For centuries, work remains organized in the same manner without any thought of innovation. "Heredity is shown to us here with its habitual characteristics: conservation, stability."[382] Consequently, for the division of labor to be able to develop, men had to succeed in shaking off the yoke of heredity, progress had to break up castes and classes. The progressive disappearance of these latter tends to prove the reality of this emancipation, for we cannot see how, if heredity had lost none of its claims over the individual, it could have been weakened as an institution. If statistics went back into the past, and particularly if they were better informed on this point, they would very likely inform us that cases of hereditary occupation become less numerous. What is certain is that faith in heredity, formerly so intense, has today been replaced by an almost opposed faith. We tend to believe the individual is in large part the son of his work, and even to scorn the bonds which attach him to his race and make him depend upon it. This is, at least, a popular opinion of which the psychologists of heredity complain. It is, indeed, a rather curious fact that heredity entered into science only at the time when it had almost completely emerged from the belief in it. There is no contradiction here. For what the common conscience basically affirms is not that heredity does not exist, but that its weight is lighter, and science, we shall see, does not contradict this sentiment.

But it is important to establish the fact directly, and especially to show its causes.

I

In the first place, heredity loses its hold in the course of evolution because new modes of activity are simultaneously brought about which owe nothing to its influence.

A first proof of the halt in heredity is the stationary position of the great human races. From most distant times, no new races have been formed, unless, with de Quatrefages,[383] we give this name to the different types which have issued from the three or four great fundamental types. It must be added that the further they develop from their points of origin, the less do they present the constitutive traits of the race. Indeed, everyone agrees in recognizing that what characterizes a race is the existence of hereditary likenesses. Thus, anthropologists take as the basis of their classifications physical characteristics, because they are the most hereditary of all. But the more circumscribed anthropological types are, the more difficult it becomes to define them as functions of exclusively organic properties, because the latter are

---

[382] Ribot, *op. cit.*, p. 360.
[383] See *L'Espèce humaine.*

neither numerous enough nor distinctive enough. There are completely moral resemblances which are established with the aid of linguistics, archaeology, comparative law, which become preponderant, but there is no reason for admitting they are hereditary. They serve to distinguish civilizations rather than races. As we advance, the human varieties which are formed become, then, less hereditary. These varieties are less and less racial. The progressive impotency of our species to produce new races makes a most striking contrast with the fecundity of animal species. Can any other meaning be found save that human culture, as it develops, becomes steadily more resistant to this kind of transmission? What men have added and each day add to this primitive base which has for many centuries been fixed in the structure of initial races increasingly escapes the action of heredity. But if this is true of the general current of civilization, with stronger reason it is true of each of the particular tributaries forming it, that is to say, of each functional activity and its products.

The following facts confirm this induction:

It is an established truth that the degree of simplicity of psychic facts gives the measure of their transmissibility. In fact, the more complex states are, the more easily do they decompose, since their great complexity keeps them in a state of unstable equilibrium. They resemble those skilful constructions whose architecture is so delicate that a trifle is sufficient seriously to trouble their arrangement and, at the least pressure, the shaken edifice crashes, laying bare the ground it covered. It is thus that, in the case of general paralysis, the ego is slowly dissolved until it rests, as it were, only upon the organic base on which it was fixed. Ordinarily, it is under the burden of sickness that these facts of disorganization are produced. But it is obvious that seminal transmission must have analogous effects. Indeed, in the act of impregnation, the strictly individual characteristics tend to be neutralized, for, as those special to one of the parents can be transmitted only to the detriment of the other, a sort of struggle from which they cannot emerge intact grows up between them. But the more complex a state of conscience is, the more personal it is, the more does it carry the mark of the particular circumstances in which we have lived, of our sex, of our temperament. We resemble one another a great deal more in the lower and fundamental parts of our being than in these higher parts. It is by these latter, on the contrary, that we are distinguished from one another. If, then, they do not completely disappear in hereditary transmission, they can survive only in an effaced and weakened state.

But aptitudes are as much more complex as they are special. It is, indeed, an error to believe that our activity is simplified as our tasks are delimited. On the contrary, it is when it is dispersed over a multitude of objects that it is simple, for, as it then neglects what is personal and distinct to aspire to the common, it is reduced to very general movements fitting into a host of diverse circumstances. But when it is a question of adapting ourselves to particular and special objects so as to realize all their shadings, we can succeed only by combining a great number of states of conscience, differentiated as the image of the very things to which they are related. Once arranged and set up, these systems no doubt function with more ease and rapidity, but they remain very complex. What a prodigious assemblage of ideas, images, customs one observes as the linotyper sets up a page of printing; as the mathematician combines a multitude of scattered theorems and sets up a new theorem; as the doctor, by an imperceptible sign, at once recognizes and at the same time foresees the course of a disease! Compare the elementary technique of the ancient philosopher, of the sage, who, by the strength of his thought alone, undertakes to explain the world, and that of today's scholar who resolves a very special problem only by a very complicated combination of observations and experiments, thanks to the reading of books written in all languages, correspondences, discussion, etc. It is the dilettante who conserves his original simplicity intact. The complexity of his nature is only apparent. As he assigns himself the task of being interested in everything, it seems that he has a multitude of diverse tastes and aptitudes. A pure illusion! Look to the bottom of things, and you will see that it all reduces to a small number of general, simple faculties, but which, having lost nothing of their early indetermination, turn with ease from objects to which they are attached to intend themselves upon others. From without one perceives an uninterrupted succession of varied events, but it is the same actor playing all the roles in somewhat different costumes. This surface upon which so many skillfully shaded colors shine covers a base of deplorable monotony. He has trained and refined the powers of his being, but he has not learned how to transform and recast them so as to extract a new and defined work. He has reared nothing personal and durable on the ground which nature has bequeathed to him.

Consequently, the more special faculties are, the more difficult they are to transmit. Or, if they succeed in passing from one generation to the other, they cannot fail to lose their strength and precision. They are less irresistible and more malleable. By reason of their greater indetermination, they can more easily change under the influence of circumstances of family, fortune, education, etc. In short, the more specialized the forms of activity, the more they escape the action of heredity.

Cases have nevertheless been cited where occupational aptitudes appear to be hereditary. From tables arranged by Galton, there seem to have been veritable dynasties of scholars, poets, and musicians. De

Candolle, on his part, has observed that sons of scholars "often busy themselves with science."[384] But these observations have no demonstrative value for the case in point. We do not think of maintaining that the transmission of special aptitudes is radically impossible. We simply mean that generally it does not take place because it can be effectuated only by a miracle of equilibrium which cannot often recur. Hence, nothing is proved by citing this or that particular case in which it was produced or appears to have been produced, but we must see what part they represent in the totality of scientific vocations. It is only then that one can judge if they truly prove heredity to be a great influence in the way in which social functions are divided.

But, although this comparison cannot be made methodically, a fact, established by de Candolle, tends to prove how restricted the action of heredity is in these careers. Of 100 foreign associates in the *Academie de Paris* whose genealogies de Candolle has been able to trace, 14 descend from Protestant ministers, only 5 from doctors, surgeons, chemists. Of 48 foreign members of the Royal Society of London in 1829, 8 are sons of pastors, only 4 have professional men as fathers. The total number of the latter, however, "in countries outside of France must be much greater for Protestant ecclesiastics. Indeed, among Protestant populations, considered alone, doctors, surgeons, chemists, and veterinarians are almost as numerous as churchmen and, when one adds those of purely Catholic countries other than France, they constitute a much more considerable total than that of pastors and Protestant ministers. The studies that medical men have made and the works to which they must habitually devote themselves for their profession are much more in the realm of science than the studies and work of a pastor. If success in science were solely a matter of heredity, there would be a great many more sons of doctors, chemists, etc. on our lists than sons of pastors."[385]

Still, it is not at all certain that these scientific vocations of sons of scholars are really due to heredity. To be justified in attributing them to it, it is not sufficient to observe a similarity of tastes between parents and children. The latter would have to manifest their aptitudes after being reared from infancy outside their families and in a place foreign to all scientific culture. But, in fact, all the sons of scholars who have been observed have been reared in their families, where they have naturally found more intellectual aid and encouragement than their fathers had received. There are also words of advice, and examples, the desire to resemble one's father, to make use of his books, his collections, his researches, his laboratory, which are for a generous and

---

[384] *Histoire des sciences et des savants*, 2nd ed., p. 293.

[385] *Op. cit.*, p. 294.

circumspect mind energetic stimulants. Finally, in the institutions where they pursue their studies, the sons of scholars are found in contact with minds cultivated and receptive to lofty culture, and the action of this new environment only strengthens that of the first. To be sure, in societies where it is the rule that the child follows the profession of his father, such regularity cannot be explained by a simple concourse of external circumstances, for it would be a miracle if it was produced in each case with so perfect an identity. But the case is not the same today with these coincidences; they are rare and very exceptional.

It is true that several of the English scientists addressed by Galton[386] have insisted on a special and innate taste they have felt since infancy for the science they were to cultivate later. But, as de Candolle observes, it is quite difficult to know whether these tastes "come from birth or acute impressions of youth and influences provoking and directing them. Besides, tastes change, and the only ones important for the career are those which persist. In that case, the individual who distinguishes himself in a science or who continues to cultivate it with pleasure never fails to say that it is an innate taste with him. On the contrary, those who have had special tastes in infancy and have thought no more of them do not speak of them. Think of the multitude of children who chase butterflies or make collections of shells, of insects, etc. who do not become naturalists. I am also familiar with a goodly number of examples of scholars who had, in their youth, a passion for poetry or the drama and who, in time, have taken up quite different occupations."[387]

Another observation of the same author shows how great the action of social environment on the genesis of these attitudes is. If they were due to heredity, they would be equally hereditary in all countries. The scholars born of scholars would be in the same proportion with all peoples of the same type. "However, the facts give evidence of something entirely different. In Switzerland, for two centuries there have been more scholars grouped by family than isolated scholars. In France and Italy, the number of scholars who are unique in their families constitute, on the contrary, the immense majority. Physiological laws are, however, the same for all men. Accordingly, education in each family, the examples and counsel given, must have exercised a more marked influence than heredity upon the special career of the young scholars. It is, moreover, easy to understand why this influence has been stronger in Switzerland than in most countries. Studies are carried on until the age of eighteen or twenty in each city and in such conditions that the students live at their homes close to their

---

[386] *English men of science*, 1874, pp. 144 ff.
[387] *Op. cit.*, p. 320.

fathers. It was especially true in the eighteenth century and in the first half of the nineteenth, particularly in Geneva and Basle; that is to say, in the two cities which have furnished the greatest proportion of scholars united by family bonds. Elsewhere, notably in France and in Italy, it has always been ordinary for young people to be reared in schools where they live and, consequently, are removed from family influences."[388]

There is, then, no reason for admitting "the existence of innate and imperious vocations for special objects."[389] At least, if there are, they are not the rule. As Bain similarly remarks, the son of a great philologist does not inherit one word; the son of a great traveler can be surpassed in geography in school by the son of a miner.[390] That is not to say that heredity is without influence, but that it transmits very general faculties and not a particular aptitude for this or that science. What a child receives from his parents is some power of attention, a capacity for perseverance, a wholesome judgment, imagination, etc. But each of these faculties can be suitable to a multitude of different specialties, and assure success in each. Here is a child gifted with a lively imagination: at a young age, he is put among artists; he will become a painter or a poet. If he lives in an industrial environment, he may become an engineer with inventive genius. If chance places him in the business world, he will perhaps be a fearless financier. Of course, he will always have his own nature, his need of creating and imagining, his passion for novelty, but the careers in which he will be able to use these talents and satisfy his inclinations are many. This is what de Candolle has proved by direct observation. He has revealed the qualities useful in the sciences his father inherited from his grandfather. Here is the list: will, orderliness, sane judgment, a certain power of attention, aversion for metaphysical abstractions, independence of opinion. It was assuredly a good heritage, but one with which he could equally have become an administrator, a statesman, an historian, an economist, a great manufacturer, an excellent doctor, or, finally, a naturalist, like de Candolle. It is, then, evident that circumstances played a large part in the choice of his career, and that is, in fact, what his son tells us.[391] Only the mathematical mind and musical feelings can be fairly often hereditarily transmitted directly from parents. This apparent anomaly will not be surprising if one recalls that these two talents were developed very early in the history of humanity. Music is the first of the arts and mathematics the first of the sciences which man cultivated. These two faculties must, then, be more general and less

---

[388] *Op. cit.*, p. 296.
[389] *Op. cit.*, p. 299.
[390] *The Emotions and the Will.*
[391] *Op. cit.*, p. 318.

complex than is believed, and that is what would explain their transmissibility.

One can say as much of another vocation, that of crime. According to Tarde, the different varieties of crimes and delicts are professions, although harmful. They sometimes even require a complex technique. The swindler, the counterfeiter, the forger, are obliged to use more science and more art in their work than a great many ordinary workers. And it has been maintained that not only moral perversion in general, but even the specific forms of criminality, were a product of heredity. It has even been believed that more than 40% are "criminal-born."[392] If this proposition were proved, we would have to conclude that heredity sometimes has a great influence on the way in which occupations, even special, are distributed. . To prove it, two different methods have been tried. Often, they have been content to cite cases of families who are entirely given to evil and that for several generations. But in this manner one cannot determine the relative part of heredity in the totality of criminal vocations. Such observations, as numerous as they may be, do not constitute demonstrative experiments. Because the son of a thief becomes a thief himself, it does not follow that his immorality is a heritage his father left him. To interpret the fact that way, we would have to be able to isolate the action of heredity from that of environment, education, etc. If the child manifested his aptitude for theft after having been reared in a perfectly healthy family, one would then be able, with good right, to invoke the influence of heredity, but we possess very few observations of this kind that have been made methodically. One does not escape the objection by observing that families thus involved in evil sometimes are very numerous. The number has nothing to do with it, for the domestic environment, which is the same for all the family, whatever its size, is sufficient to explain this endemic criminality.

The method followed by Lombroso would be more conclusive if it gave the results its author promised. Instead of enumerating a certain number of particular cases, he sets up, anatomically and physiologically, the criminal type. As anatomical and physiological characters, and especially the first, are congenital, that is to say, determined by heredity, it will be sufficient to establish the proportion of delinquents who present the type thus defined, in order to measure exactly the influence of heredity on this special activity.

It has been seen that, according to Lombroso, it would be considerable. But the cited number expresses only the relative frequency of the criminal type in general. All that one can conclude, in consequence, is that the propensity toward evil in general is often hereditary,. but one can deduce nothing relative to the particular forms

---

[392] Lombroso, *L'Homme criminel*, p. 669.

of crime and delict. We know today, moreover, that this pretended criminal type has, in reality, nothing specific about it. A great many traits constituting it are found elsewhere. All one sees is that it resembles that of degenerates and neurasthenics.[393] But, if this fact is a proof that among criminals there are a great many neurasthenics, it does not follow that neurasthenia inevitably and always leads to crime. There are at least as many degenerates who are honest, if they are not men of talent and genius.

If aptitudes, then, are so much less transmissible as they are more specialized, the part of heredity in the organization of social work is so much greater as the latter is less divided. In lower societies, where functions are very general, they demand only aptitudes equally general which can most easily and most integrally pass from one generation to the other. Each receives at birth all that is essential to his character. What he himself must acquire is a trifle compared to what he gets from heredity. In the middle ages, the nobleman, to fulfill his duty, had no need of a great deal of knowledge, or of very complicated practices, but especially of courage, and he inherited that. The Levite and the Brahman, for their work, had no need of a voluminous science—we can measure its dimensions from the books containing it—but they had to have a native superiority in intelligence which made them susceptible to ideas and sentiments closed to the vulgar. To be a good doctor in the time of Aesculapius, it was not necessary to receive a wide culture; it was enough to have a natural taste for observation and concrete things, and as this taste is general enough to be easily transmissible, it inevitably was perpetuated in certain families, and, consequently, the medical profession was hereditary.

In these conditions, it is clear, heredity became a social institution. To be sure, these wholly psychological causes could not give rise to the organization of castes, but once the latter was born through other circumstances, it lasted because it was found to conform perfectly both to the tastes of individuals and the interests of society. Since professional aptitude was a quality of the race rather than the individual, it was very natural that it be the same with the function. Since functions were immutably distributed in the same manner, it could have advantages only in so far as the law consecrated the principle of this distribution. When the individual has only a very small part in the formation of his mind and character, he cannot have any greater choice in his career, and if greater liberty were permitted him, he generally would not know what to do with it. Yet, what if the same general capacity could serve in different occupations! But precisely because work is not specialized much, there exists only a small number of functions sharply separated from one another. Consequently, one

---

[393] See Féré, *Dégénérescence et Criminalité*.

could seldom succeed in more than one of them. The margin left to individual combinations is, then, still restricted on that side. Finally, the case of heredity of functions is like that of heredity of goods. In lower societies, the heritage transmitted by the forefathers, and which most often consists of real estate, represents the most important part of the patrimony of each particular family. The individual, because of the small importance economic functions then have, cannot add much to the hereditary base. Thus, it is not he who possesses, but the family, the collective being, composed not only of all the members of the present generation, but of all generations. That is why patrimonial goods are inalienable. None of the ephemeral representatives of domestic life can dispose of them, for they do not belong to him. They are to the family what their function is to the house. Even when law tempers its first restrictions, an alienation of patrimony is still considered a forfeiture; it is for all classes of population what a misalliance is to the aristocracy. It is a betrayal of the race, a defection. Thus, while tolerating it, the law, for a long time, puts all sorts of obstacles in its path. That is where the law of reversion comes from.

It is not the same in more voluminous societies where work is more specialized. As functions are more diversified, the same faculty can serve in different professions. Courage is as necessary to the miner, the aviator, the doctor, the engineer, as to the soldier. Taste for observation can make a man either a novelist, a dramatist, a chemist, a naturalist, a sociologist. In short, the orientation of the individual is less necessarily predetermined by heredity.

But what especially decreases the relative. importance of heredity is the fact that individual acquirements become more considerable. To make the hereditary legacy valuable, a great deal more must be added than formerly. In effect, in so far as functions are more specialized, simply general aptitudes are no longer enough. They must be submitted to active elaboration, they must acquire a whole world of ideas, movements, habits, they must co-ordinate them, systematize them, recast their nature, give a new form and new face to it. Let us compare—and we take rather related points of comparison—the reasonable man of the seventeenth century with his open and little-informed mind, and the modern scholar armed with all the technique, all the necessary knowledge of the science he cultivates; the nobleman of former times with his natural courage and pride, and the officer today with his laborious and complicated technique, and we can judge the importance and variety of the combinations which have been slowly superimposed upon the primitive foundation.

But because they are very complex, these scholarly combinations are fragile. They are in a state of unstable equilibrium which cannot resist a strong shake-up. If they were identical with both parents, they could perhaps survive the crisis of the generation. But such identity is wholly exceptional. First of all, they are special to each sex; then, as societies extend and condense, cross-breedings are made over a larger area, bringing together individuals of very different temperaments. All this superb growth of states of conscience, then, dies with us and we transmit to our descendants only an indeterminate germ. It is then their duty to reproduce it anew, and, consequently, they can more easily, if necessary, modify its development. They are no longer so narrowly restricted to repeat what their fathers did before them. To be sure, it would be an error to believe that each generation begins the work of centuries afresh and as a whole. That would make all progress impossible. Because the past is not transmitted with blood, it does not follow that it is reduced to nothing. It remains fixed in monuments, in traditions of all sorts, in habits inculcated by education. But tradition is a considerably less rigid bond than heredity. It predetermines thought and conduct in a much less rigorous and precise manner. We have seen, moreover, how it became more flexible as societies became denser. A larger field is thus found open to individual variations, and it steadily enlarges as work is divided more.

In short, civilization can be fixed in the organism only through the most general foundations on which it rests. The more elevated it is, the more, consequently, is it free of the body. It becomes less and less an organic thing, more and more a social thing. But, then, it is no longer through the intermediary of the body that it can perpetuate itself; that is to say, that heredity is more and more incapable of assuring its continuity. Thus, it loses its hold, not because it has ceased to be a law of our nature, but because, to five, we must have means that it cannot provide us with. To be sure, we cannot extract something from nothing, and the raw materials that it alone gives us have prime importance, but those which are added are no less important. The hereditary patrimony preserves a great value, but it no longer represents any more than a steadily restricted part of individual fortune. Under these conditions, we have already explained why heredity has disappeared from social institutions, and why people, no longer seeing the hereditary foundation under the additions covering it over, no longer feel its importance as much.

II

But, furthermore, there is room for believing that the hereditary contribution diminishes, not only in relative value, but in absolute value. Heredity becomes a lesser factor of human development, not only because there is an ever greater multitude of new acquisitions it cannot transmit, but also because those it transmits disturb individual variations less. This is a conjecture which the following facts render very likely.

One can measure the importance of the hereditary legacy for a given species according to the number and strength of the instincts. But it is, indeed, very remarkable that instinctive life is weakened as one mounts in the animal scale. Instinct, indeed, is a manner of defined action adjusted to a strictly determined end. It impels the individual to acts which are invariably the same when the necessary conditions are given. It is congealed in its form. No doubt, one can make it deviate, but such deviations, in order to be stable, require long development, and have no other effect than the substitution of one instinct for another, of one special mechanism for another of the same nature. On the contrary, the more elevated the species to which an animal belongs, the more discretionary instinct becomes. "It is no longer," says Perrier, "the unconscious aptitude of combining indetermined acts; it is the aptitude to act differently according to the circumstances."[394] To say that the influence of heredity is more general, more vague, less imperious, is to say that it is smaller. It no longer imprisons the activity of the animal in a rigid form, but leaves him with freer activity. As Perrier says, "with the animal, at the same time that intelligence grows, the conditions of heredity are profoundly modified."

When from animals one passes to man, this regression is still more marked. "Man does all that animals do and more; only he does it knowing what he does and why he does it. The consciousness of his acts alone seems to free him from all the instincts which would necessarily impel him to accomplish these same acts."[395] It would take too long to enumerate all the movements which, instinctive with animals, have ceased to be hereditary with man. Even where instinct survives, it has less force, and the will can more easily subdue it.

But, then, there is no reason for supposing that this movement of recoil, followed in an uninterrupted manner from the inferior animal species to the most developed, and from those to man, abruptly ceases at the advent of humanity. Was man, from the day he came into history, totally freed from instinct? But we still feel its yoke today. Have the causes determining this progressive enfranchisement whose continuity we have just seen, suddenly lost their energy? But evidently they are merged with the same causes determining the general progress of species, and as it does not stop, they cannot themselves be stopped. Such an hypothesis is contrary to all analogies. It is even contrary to well-established facts. It is indeed proved that intelligence and instinct always vary in inverse ratio to each other. We do not have to seek for the source of this relation at this time; we are content to affirm its existence. But, from the beginning, the intelligence of man has not

---

[394] *Anatomie et Physiologie animales*, p. 201. Cf. the preface of *Intelligence des animaux*, of Romanes, p. xxiii.

[395] Guyau, *Morale anglaise*, 1st ed., p. 330.

stopped developing. Instinct has, then, had to follow a backward course. Consequently, although one cannot establish this proposition by a positive observation of the facts, one must believe that heredity has lost ground in the course of human evolution.

Another fact corroborates the preceding. Not only has evolution not caused new races to spring up since the beginning of history, but, in addition, ancient races are always regressing. In effect, a race is formed by a certain number of individuals who present, in relation to the same hereditary type, a conformity sufficiently great for individual variations to be negligible. But the importance of the latter is steadily increasing. Individual types always assume more importance to the detriment of the generic type whose constitutive traits, dispersed on all sides, confused with a multitude of others, indefinitely diversified, can no longer be easily reassembled in a whole which has any unity. This dispersion and effacement have begun, moreover, even with people little advanced. Because of their isolation, the Eskimos seem placed in very favorable conditions for the maintenance of the purity of their race. Nevertheless, "the variations of height surpass the permitted individual limits there. ... In the passage of Hotham, an Eskimo exactly resembled a negro; in the inlet of Spafarret, he resembled a Jew (Seeman). The oval face, associated with a Roman nose, is not rare (King). Their complexion is sometimes very dark and sometimes very light."[396] If this is so in such restricted societies, the same phenomenon must be much more in evidence in our great contemporary societies. In central Europe, one finds, side by side, all the possible varieties of skulls, all possible forms of faces. It is the same with complexion. According to observations made by Virchow, out of ten million children taken in different classes of Germany, the blond type, characteristic of the Germanic race, was found only from 43 to 33 times out of a 100 in the North; from 32 to 25 times in the Centre, and from 24 to 18 times in the South.[397] This explains why in these conditions, which are always becoming worse, the anthropologist can hardly set up strictly defined types.

The recent researches of Galton affirm, at the same time that they enable us to explain, this weakening of hereditary influence.[398]

According to this author, whose observations and calculations appear irrefutable, the only characters transmitted regularly and integrally by heredity in a given social group are those whose reuniting sets up the average type. Thus, a son born of exceptionally tall parents will not be of their height, but will come close to a medium height.

---

[396] Topinard, *Anthropologie*, p. 458.
[397] Wagner, *Die Kulturzüchtung des Menschen*, in *Kosmos*, 1886, Vol. I, p. 27.
[398] *Natural Inheritance*, London, 1889.

Inversely, if they are very small, he will be taller than they. Galton has even been able to measure, at least in proximate fashion, this relation of deviation. If one agrees to call the average parent a composite being who represents the average of the two real parents (the characters of the woman are transposed in such a way as to be able to be compared with those of the father, added and divided together), the deviation of the son, in relation to the fixed standard, will be two-thirds of that of the father.[399]

Galton has not only established this law for height, but also for the color of eyes and artistic faculties. It is true he has made these observations only as to quantitative deviations, and not as to qualitative deviations which individuals present in relation to the average type. But one cannot see why the law applies to one and not the other. If the rule is that heredity transmits constitutive attributes of this type only to the degree of development in which they are there found, it must also transmit only attributes which are found there. What is true of the abnormal extent of normal characters must be true, with stronger reason, of abnormal characters themselves. They must, in general, pass from one generation to another in a weakened condition and on the verge of disappearance.

This law, moreover, is easily explained. Indeed, a child does not inherit from his parents alone, but from all his ancestors. Doubtless, the action of the first is particularly strong because it is immediate, but that of anterior generations is susceptible of accumulation when it is exercised in the same direction, and thanks to this accumulation which makes up for the effects of remoteness, it can attain a degree of force sufficient to neutralize or attenuate the precedent. But the average type *of a natural group* is the one which corresponds to the conditions of average life, consequently, to the most ordinary. It expresses the manner in which individuals have adapted themselves to what one may call the average environment, physical as well as social; that is to say, to the environment where the greatest number live. These average conditions were most frequent in the past for the same reason that they are most general at present. They are, then, those in which the major part of our powers are found situated. It is true that with time they have been able to change, but they are generally modified slowly. The average type remains, then, perceptibly the same for a long time. Consequently, it is it which is repeated most often and in most uniform manner in the series of anterior generations, at least in those near enough to make us feel their action efficaciously. Thanks to this constancy, it acquires a fixity which makes it the centre of gravity of the hereditary influence. Characteristics constituting it are those which have the most resistance, which tend to be transmitted with most force

---

[399] *Op. cit.*, p. 104.

and precision. Those, on the contrary, which are dispersed survive only in a state of indetermination so much greater as the dispersion is more considerable. That is why the deviations produced are never more than short-lived, and succeed in being maintained for a time only in very imperfect fashion.

Still, this explanation itself, in some respects a little different from that proposed by Galton himself, allows one to conjecture that his law, to be perfectly exact, would need some slight rectifying. Indeed, the average type of our powers is merged with that of our generation only to the extent that average life has not changed. But, in fact, variations are produced from one generation to the other which entail changes in the average type. If the facts collected by Galton nevertheless seem to confirm the law as he has formulated it, that is because he has scarcely verified it save by physical characteristics relatively immutable, as height or color of eyes. But if observation is made, following the same method, of other properties, whether organic, or psychical, it is certain one would see the effects of evolution. Consequently, to speak rigorously, characteristics whose degree of transmissibility is of the highest are not those whose entirety constitutes the average type of a given generation, but those obtained in taking the average between average types of successive generations. Without this correction, furthermore, one cannot explain how the average of the group can advance, for if one takes Galton's proposition literally, societies would always be invincibly led back to the same level, since the average type of two generations, even distant from each other, would be identical. But, far from this identity being the law, on the contrary, even with physical characteristics as simple as average height or the average color of eyes, there is seen a gradual change, albeit slow.[400] The truth is that, if enduring changes are produced in the environment, the resulting organic and psychical modifications end by being fixed and integrated in the average evolving type. The variations produced on the way cannot, then, have the same degree of transmissibility as the elements repeated constantly.

The average type results from the superposition of individual types, and expresses what they have most in common. Consequently, the traits of which it is formed are as much more defined as they are more identically repeated in the different members of the group, for, when this identity is complete, they are found again intact, with all their characteristics and in all their details. On the other hand, when they vary from one individual to the other, since the points on which they coincide are rarer, what subsists in the average type is reduced to features as general as the differences are greater. But we know that individual differences steadily multiply, that is to say, the constitutive

---

[400] Arréat, *Récents travaux sur l'hérédité*, in *Rev. phil.*, April 1890, p. 414.

elements of the average type are more diversified. This type itself must, then, comprise fewer determined traits and still less as society is more differentiated. The average man assumes a physiognomy less and less precise and recognizable, and more and more schematic. He is an abstraction more and more difficult to fix and delimit. Further, the more elevated the species to which societies belong, the more rapidly they evolve, since tradition becomes more supple, as we have proved. The average type changes, then, from one generation to the other. Consequently, the doubly composed type which results from the superposition of all these average types is still more abstract than each of them, and becomes steadily more so. Since, then, it is heredity of this type which constitutes normal heredity, we see that, as Perrier says, the conditions of normal heredity have been profoundly modified. To be sure, that does not mean that it transmits fewer things in an absolute manner, for if individuals present more unlike characteristics, they also present more characteristics. But what it transmits consists more and more of indeterminate predispositions, general ways of feeling and thinking which can be specialized in a thousand different ways. It is no longer, as it was formerly, a set of complete mechanisms exactly set up for special ends, but of very-vague tendencies which do not definitely prejudge the future. Heritage has not become less rich, but it no longer resides entirely in transmittable goods. Most of the values of which it is composed are not yet realized, and everything depends upon the use to which they are put.

This greater flexibility of hereditary characteristics is not due only to their state of indetermination, but to the shaking up they have received because of the changes through which they have passed. We know, indeed, that a type is so much more unstable as it has been subject to more deviations. "Sometimes," says de Quatrefages, "the smallest causes rapidly transform these organisms which have become unstable. The Swiss bull, transported to Lombardy, becomes a Lombard bull in two generations. Two generations are also sufficient for our bees of Burgundy, small and brown, to become large and yellow in Bresse."[401] For all these reasons, heredity always leaves more room for new combinations. Not only is there a growing number of things over which it has no power, but the properties whose continuity it assures become more plastic. The individual is, thus, less strongly chained to his past; it is easier for him to adapt himself to new circumstances which are produced, and the progress of the division of labor thus becomes easier and more rapid.[402]

---

[401] Article *Races* in *Dictionnaire encyclopédique des sciences medicates*, lxxx, p. 372.

[402] What appears to be most solid in the theories of Weismann would serve to confirm what precedes. Doubtless, it is not proved, as this scholar maintains, that individual variations are radically intransmissible by heredity. But it seems to have been

CHAPTER FIVE. CONSEQUENCES OF THE PRECEDING

I

The preceding enables us to have a better understanding of the manner in which the division of labor functions in society. From this point of view, the division of social labor is distinguished from the division of physiological labor by an essential characteristic. In the organism, each cell has its defined role, and cannot change it. In societies, tasks have never been so immutably distributed. Even where the forms of organization are most rigid, the individual can move about in the interior of the form in which he is fixed with a certain liberty. In primitive Rome, the plebeian could freely undertake all the functions not exclusively reserved to the patricians. Even in India, the careers which were allowed to each caste had sufficient generality[403] to permit some choice. In every land, if the enemy has seized the capital, that is to say, the very brain of the nation, social life is not suspended because of that, but, at the end of a relatively short time, another city is found to fulfill this complex function, although it had in no way been prepared for it.

As work is divided more, this suppleness and liberty become greater. The same individual is seen to raise himself from the most humble to the most important occupations. The principle according to which all employments are equally accessible to all citizens would not be generalized to this point if it did not receive constant applications. What is still more frequent is that a worker leaves his career for a neighboring one. When scientific activity was not specialized, the scholar, encompassing all science, could scarcely change his function,

---

well established that the normally transmissible type is not the individual type, but the generic type which has, in some way, for organic substratum the reproductive elements, and that this type is not as easily affected by individual variations as has sometimes been supposed. (See Weismann, *Essais sur l'hérédité* (tr. Fr.), Paris, 1892, especially the third essay; and Ball, *Hérédité et Exercice* (tr. Fr.), Paris, 1891.) The result of this is that the more undetermined and plastic this type is, the more the individual factor gains ground.

From another point of view, these theories interest us. One of the conclusions of our work to which we attach the most importance is this idea that social phenomena derive from social causes, and not from psychological causes; that the collective type is not a simple generalization of an individual type, but, on the contrary, that the latter is born from the former. In another order of facts, Weismann proves in the same way that the race is not a simple prolongation of the individual; that the specific type, from the physiological and anatomical point of view, is not an individual type perpetuated in time, but that it has its own evolution, that the second is detached from the first, far from being its source. His doctrine is, like ours, it seems to us, a protest against the artless theories which reduce the complex to the simple, the whole to the part, society or the race to the individual.

[403] *Laws of Manou*, I, 87-91.

for it would have been necessary to renounce science itself. Today, it often happens that he devotes himself to different sciences, passing from chemistry to biology, from physiology to psychology, from psychology to sociology. This aptitude for successively taking very diverse forms is nowhere so discernible as in the economic world. As nothing is more variable than the tastes and needs these functions answer to, commerce and industry must be held in a perpetual state of unstable equilibrium to be able to yield to all the changes produced in the demand. Whereas formerly immobility was the almost natural state of capital, even the law forbidding too easy mobilization, today it can scarcely be followed in all its transformations, so great is the rapidity with which it is engaged in enterprise, withdrawing from one to rest elsewhere where it remains only for some moments. Thus, workers must be ready to follow it, and, consequently, to serve in different employments.

The nature of the causes upon which the division of labor in society depends explains this character. If the role of each cell is fixed in an immutable manner, it is because this is imposed by birth. It is imprisoned in a system of hereditary customs which mark its path, and which cannot be overcome. It cannot even sensibly modify them, because these customs have too profoundly affected the substance from which it is formed. Its structure predetermines its life. We have just seen that it is not the same in society. Origins do not determine the special career of an individual; his congenital constitution does not predestine him necessarily to one role alone, making him incapable for any other, but he receives from heredity only very general dispositions, consequently very supple, and able to take different forms.

It is true that he determines them himself by the use which he makes of them. As he must employ his faculties in particular functions and specialize them, he is forced to make those immediately required for his use undergo very intensive cultivation, and let the others partially atrophy. Thus, he cannot develop his brain beyond a certain point without losing a part of his muscular force, or his reproductive power; he cannot rouse his powers of analysis and reflection to a high pitch without enfeebling the energy of his will and the vivacity of his sentiments, nor make a habit of observation without losing his ability at dialectic. Moreover, by the very force of things, that faculty which he makes keen to the detriment of others is forced to assume definite forms in which it becomes imprisoned little by little. This faculty gets into the habit of certain practices, of functioning in a set way which becomes more difficult to change as it continues to endure. But, as this specialization results from purely individual efforts, it has neither the fixity nor the rigidity which a long heredity alone can produce. These practices are very supple, because they are very young. As it is the individual who engaged himself in them, he can disengage himself, and betake himself to new ones. He can call forth faculties dulled through dormancy, infuse new fife into them, replace them in their original state, although, truly, this kind of resurrection is by that time very difficult.

One is tempted, at first glance, to see in these facts of the phenomena of regression either proof of a certain inferiority, or at least a transitory state of an incomplete being in process of formation. In effect, it is especially among lower animals that the different parts of the aggregate can quite easily change their functions and substitute them for others. But in so far as organization becomes perfected, it becomes more and more impossible for them to leave the role which is assigned to them. One is thus led to ask whether society may not someday arrive at a point where it will assume an arrested form, where each organ, each individual, will have a definite function and will no longer change. This was, it seems, Comte's idea;[404] it is certainly Spencer's.[405] This induction, however, is precipitate, for the phenomenon of substitution is not special to very simple beings, but is equally observable in the highest ranks of the hierarchy, and especially in the higher organs of the higher organisms. Thus, "the consecutive disturbances in the ablation of certain domains of the cerebral surface very often disappear after a lapse of time. This phenomenon can only be explained by the following supposition: other elements come in to take over the function of the suppressed elements. This implies that the substituted elements are employed at new functions. ... An element which, during the normal relations of conduction, causes a visual sensation, becomes, thanks to a change of conditions, the cause of a tactile sensation, of a muscular sensation, or of a motor innervation. Indeed, one is almost obliged to suppose that, if the central network of nervous cords has the power to transmit phenomena of diverse natures to one and the same element, this element will be able to unite in itself a plurality of different functions."[406] Thus, the motor-nerves can become centripetal, and the sensible nerves centrifugal.[407] Finally, if a new partition of all these functions can occur when the conditions of transmission are modified, there is reason for presuming, according to Wundt, that "even in its normal state, it presents oscillations or variations which depend upon the variable development of individuals."[408]

Thus it is that a rigid specialization is not necessarily a mark of superiority. It is far from being a good thing in every circumstance; often what the organ does *not* congeal in its role is of advantage. Of

[404] *Cours de Philosophie positive*, VI, p. 505.
[405] *Principles of Sociology*, II, p. 57.
[406] Wundt, *Physiological Psychology* (tr. Fr.), I, p. 234.
[407] Notice the experiment of Kühne and Paul Bert reported by Wundt, *ibid.*, p. 233.
[408] *Ibid.*, I, p. 239.

course, where the environment itself is fixed, even a very great fixity is useful. This is the case, for example, with the nutritive functions of the individual organism. They are not subject to great changes in the same organic type. Consequently, there is an advantage rather than inconvenience from their assuming a definitely stationary form. That is why the polyp, whose internal and external tissue so easily replace each other, is less well armed for the struggle than more elevated animals with whom this substitution is always incomplete and almost impossible. But it is quite otherwise when the circumstances upon which the organ depends change often. Then it must itself change or perish. That is what happens with complex functions which adapt us to complex milieux. The latter, because of their very complexity, are essentially unstable. Some break in equilibrium, or some innovation, is always being produced. To remain adapted, the function must always be ready to change, to accommodate itself to new situations. But, of all existing environments, there is none more complex than the social. Thus, it is very natural that the specialization of social functions is not as definitive as that of biological functions, and, since this complexity increases with a greater division of labor, this elasticity becomes ever greater. No doubt, it is always enclosed in certain limits, but they steadily recede.

What definitely attests to this relative and ever growing flexibility is that the function is becoming more and more independent of the organ. In effect, nothing realizes a function as much as being tied to a structure that is highly defined, for, of all arrangements, there is none more stable nor more opposed to changes. Structure is not only a way of acting; it is a way of existing that necessitates a certain way of acting. It implies not only a certain manner of vibrating, special to molecules, but an arrangement of the latter which makes any other kind of vibrations almost impossible. If, then, function gains greater suppleness, it is because it is less strictly related to the form of the organ, because the tie between the two becomes looser.

We observe, in effect, that this loosening comes about in proportion to the greater complexity of societies and their functions. In lower societies, where tasks are general and simple, the different classes charged with their execution are distinguished from one another by morphological characters. In other words, each organ is anatomically distinguished from the others. As each caste, each stratum of the population, has its way of eating, dressing, etc., so these differences are accompanied by physical differences. As Spencer tells us, Fijian chiefs are very tall, strongly built, and very muscular; the people of lower class are emaciated from excessive work and poor food. In the Sandwich Islands, Spencer continues, the chiefs are large and vigorous, and their external appearance is so different from the people of lower station that one might think the latter were of a different race. We learn from Spencer that Ellis, confirming Cook, says that the Tahitian chiefs are almost without exception as far above the peasants in physical force as they are in station and wealth, and that Erskine notices an analogous difference among the natives of the Tonga Islands.[409] In higher societies, on the contrary, these differences disappear. Many facts tend to prove that men executing different social functions are distinguished less than heretofore by the form of their bodies, by their features, and their appearance. Some are even offended because they do not have the traits of their calling. If, according to Tarde, statistics and anthropometry were used to determine the constitutive characters of various occupational types with greater precision, we would probably find that they differ less than in the past, particularly if we consider the greater differentiation of functions.

A fact which confirms this assumption is that the custom of occupational dress more and more falls into desuetude. In effect, although modes of dress have assuredly served to make functional differences clear, we cannot see in this role their only reason for existing, since they disappear as social functions become more differentiated. They must, then, correspond to differences of another nature. If, moreover, before the institution of this practice, the men of different classes had not already presented apparent somatic differences, we do not see why they should have thought of distinguishing themselves in this fashion. These external signs of conventional origin must have been invented only in imitation of external signs of natural origin. Dress, to us, does not signify anything other than the occupational type which, in order to manifest itself in clothes, marks them with its imprint, and differentiates them in its own image. They are, as it were, a prolongation of it. This is particularly evident with the distinctions which play the same role as dress and certainly derive from the same causes, such as the custom of cutting the beard in a certain way, or of not having a beard at all, or of having the hair cut short or left long, etc. They are the very traits of the occupational type which, after being produced and spontaneously constituted, reproduces itself imitatively and artificially. The diversity of dress symbolizes, then, above all, morphological differences. Consequently, if differences in dress disappear, it is because morphological differences are obliterated. If the members of different occupations no longer see the need of distinguishing themselves from others by visible signs, it is because this distinction no longer corresponds to anything in reality. Functional differences, however, tend to become more numerous and more pronounced; this is because morphological types are leveling off. That certainly does not mean that

---

[409] *Principles of Sociology*, III, p. 406.

all brains are indifferently apt at every function, but that their functional indifference, while remaining limited, becomes greater.

But this enfranchisement of function, far from being a mark of inferiority, only proves that it is becoming more complex. For if it is more difficult for the constitutive elements of tissues to arrange themselves in a certain way and incarnate it, and, consequently, to keep it together and imprison it, that is because it is made up of dispositions that are too subtle and delicate. It may even be asked if, beginning with a certain degree of complexity, it does not definitely escape them, if it does not end by breaking away from the organ in such a way that it is impossible for the latter to reabsorb it completely. That, in fact, it is independent of the form of the substratum is a truth long ago established by naturalists. When it is general and simple, however, it cannot long remain in this state of liberty because the organ easily assimilates it, and, at the same time, shackles it. But there is no reason for supposing that this power of assimilation is indefinite. Everything points, on the contrary, to the fact that, from a certain moment, the disproportion between the simplicity of the molecular arrangements and the complexity of functional arrangements becomes ever greater. The link between the second and the first loosens. Of course, it does not follow that function can exist without any organ, nor even that it can ever lack all relation with it. But the relation does become less immediate.

Progress would then result in more and more detaching, without ever separating, however, function from the organ, life from matter; consequently, in spiritualizing it, in making it more supple, more unrestrained, more complex. It is because spiritualism believes that the character of higher forms of existence is such that it always refuses to consider the psychic life a simple consequence of the molecular constitution of the brain. In fact, we know that the functional indifference of different regions of the encephalos, if not absolute, is nevertheless great. Hence, cerebral functions are the last to assume an immutable form. They remain plastic longer than the others, and defend their plasticity the more complex they are. Thus, their evolution is prolonged much later with the learned man than with the uncultivated. If, then, social functions present this same character in still more telling fashion, it is not in accordance with an exception without precedent, but because they correspond to a still more elevated stage in the development of nature.

II

In determining the principal cause of the progress of the division of labor, we have at the same time determined the essential factor of what is called civilization.

Civilization is itself the necessary consequence of the changes which are produced in the volume and in the density of societies. If science, art, and economic activity develop, it is in accordance with a necessity which is imposed upon men. It is because there is, for them, no other way of living in the new conditions in which they have been placed. From the time that the number of individuals among whom social relations are established begins to increase, they can maintain themselves only by greater specialization, harder work, and intensification of their faculties. From this general stimulation, there inevitably results a much higher degree of culture. From this point of view, civilization appears, not as an end which moves people by its attraction for them, not as a good foreseen and desired in advance, of which they seek to assure themselves the largest possible part, but as the effect of a cause, as the necessary resultant of a given state. It is not the pole towards which historic development is moving and to which men seek to get nearer in order to be happier or better, for neither happiness nor morality necessarily increases with the intensity of life. They move because they must move, and what determines the speed of this march is the more or less strong pressure which they exercise upon one another, according to their number.

This does not mean that civilization has no use, but that it is not the services that it renders that make it progress. It develops because it cannot fail to develop. Once effectuated, this development is found to be generally useful, or, at least, it is utilized. It responds to needs formed at the same time because they depend upon the same causes. But this is an adjustment after the fact. Yet, we must notice that the good it renders in this direction is not a positive enrichment, a growth in our stock of happiness, but only repairs the losses that it has itself caused. It is because this super activity of general life fatigues and weakens our nervous system that it needs reparations proportionate to its expenditures, that is to say, more varied and complex satisfactions. In that, we see even better how false it is to make civilization the function of the division of labor; it is only a consequence of it. It can explain neither the existence nor the progress of the division of labor, since it has, of itself, no intrinsic or absolute value, but, on the contrary, has a reason for existing only in so far as the division of labor is itself found necessary.

We shall not be astonished by the importance attached to the numerical factor if we notice the very capital role it plays in the history of organisms. In effect, what defines a living being is the double property it has of nourishing itself and reproducing itself, and reproduction is itself only a consequence of nourishment. Therefore, the intensity of organic life is proportional, all things being equal, to the activity of nourishment, that is, to the number of elements that the organism is capable of incorporating. Hence, what has not only made possible, but even necessitated the appearance of complex organisms is that, under certain conditions, the more simple organisms remain grouped together in a way to form more voluminous aggregates. As the constitutive parts of the animal are more numerous, their relations are no longer the same, the conditions of social life are changed, and it is these changes which, in turn, determine both the division of labor, polymorphism, and the concentration of vital forces and their greater energy. The growth of organic substance is, then, the fact which dominates all zoological development. It is not surprising that social development is submitted to the same law.

Moreover, without recourse to arguments by analogy, it is easy to explain the fundamental role of this factor. All social life is made up of a system of facts which come from positive and durable relations established between a plurality of individuals. It is, thus, as much more intense as the reactions exchanged between the component units are themselves more frequent and more energetic. But, upon what does this frequency and this energy depend? Upon the nature of the elements present, upon their more or less great vitality? But we shall see in this very chapter that individuals are much more a product of common life than they are determinants of it. If from each of them we take away everything due to social action, the residue that we obtain, besides being picayune, is not capable of presenting much variety. Without the diversity of social conditions upon which they depend, the differences which separate them would be inexplicable. It is not, then, in the unequal aptitudes of men that we must seek the cause for the unequal development of societies. Will it be in the unequal duration of these relations? But time, by itself, produces nothing. It is only necessary in bringing latent energies to light. There remains no other variable factor than the number of individuals in relation and their material and moral proximity, that is to say, the volume and density of society. The more numerous they are and the more they act upon one another, the more they react with force and rapidity; consequently, the more intense social life becomes. But it is this intensification which constitutes civilization.[410]

---

[410] We do not here have to look to see if the fact which determines the progress of the division of labor and civilization, growth in social mass and density, explains itself automatically; if it is a necessary product of efficient causes, or else an imagined means in view of a desired end or of a very great foreseen good. We content ourselves with stating this law of gravitation in the social world without going any farther. It does not seem, however, that there is a greater demand here than elsewhere for a teleological explanation. The walls which separate different parts of society are torn down by the force of things, through a sort of natural usury, whose effect can be further enforced by the action of violent causes. The movements of population thus become more numerous and rapid and the passage-lines through which these movements are effected—the means of communication—deepen. They are more particularly active at points where several of these lines cross; these are cities. Thus social density grows. As for the growth in volume,

But, while being an effect of necessary causes, civilization can become an end, an object of desire, in short, an ideal. Indeed, at each moment of a society's history, there is a certain intensity of the collective life which is normal, given the number and distribution of the social units. Assuredly, if everything happens normally, this state will be realized of itself, but we cannot bring it to pass that things will happen normally. If health is in nature, so is sickness. Health is, indeed, in societies as in individual organisms, only an ideal type which is nowhere entirely realized. Each healthy individual has more or less numerous traits of it, but there is none that unites them all. Thus, it is an end worthy of pursuit to seek to bring society to this degree of perfection.

Moreover, the direction to follow in order to attain this end can be laid out. If, instead of letting causes engender their effects by chance and according to the energy in them, thought intervenes to direct the course, it can spare men many painful efforts. The development of the individual reproduces that of the species in abridged fashion; he does not pass through all the stages that it passed through; there are some he omits and others he passes through more quickly because the experiences of the race help him to accelerate them. But thought can produce analogous results, for it is equally a utilization of anterior experience, with a view to facilitating future experience. By thought, moreover, one must not understand exclusively scientific knowledge of means and ends. Sociology, in its present state, is hardly in a position to lead us efficaciously to the solution of these practical problems. But beyond these clear representations in the milieu in which the scholar moves, there are obscure ones to which tendencies are linked. For need to stimulate the will, it is not necessary that it be clarified by science. Obscure gropings are enough to teach men that there is something lacking, to awaken their aspirations and at the same time make them feel in what direction they ought to bend their efforts.

Hence, a mechanistic conception of society does not preclude ideals, and it is wrong to reproach it with reducing man to the status of an inactive witness of his own history. What is an ideal, really, if not an anticipated representation of a desired result whose realization is possible only thanks to this very anticipation? Because things happen in accordance with laws, it does not follow that we have nothing to do. We shall perhaps find such an objective mean, because, in sum, it is only a question of living in a state of health. But this is to forget that, for the cultivated man, health consists in regularly satisfying his most

---

it is due to causes of the same kind. The barriers which separate peoples are analogous to those which separate the different cells of the same society and they disappear in the same way.

elevated needs as well as others, for the first are no less firmly rooted in his nature than the second. It is true that such an ideal is near, that the horizons it opens before us have nothing unlimited about them. In any event, it cannot consist in exalting the forces of society beyond measure, but only in developing them to the limit marked by the definite state of the social milieu. All excess is bad as well as all insufficiency. But what other ideal can we propose? To seek to realize a civilization superior to that demanded by the nature of surrounding conditions is to desire to turn illness loose in the very society of which we are part, for it is not possible to increase collective activity beyond the degree determined by the state of the social organism without compromising health. In fact, in every epoch there is a certain refinement of civilization whose sickly character is attested by the uneasiness and restlessness which accompanies it. But there is never anything desirable about sickness.

But if the ideal is always definite, it is never definitive. Since progress is a consequence of changes in the social milieu, there is no reason for supposing that it must ever end. For it to have a limit, it would be necessary for the milieu to become stationary at some given moment. But such an hypothesis is contrary to the most legitimate inductions. As long as there are distinct societies, the number of social units will necessarily be variable in each of them. Even supposing that the number of births ever becomes constant, there will always be movements of population from one country to another, through violent conquests or slow and unobtrusive infiltrations. Indeed, it is impossible for the strongest peoples not to tend to incorporate the feeblest, as the most dense overflow into the least dense. That is a mechanical law of social equilibrium not less necessary than that which governs the equilibrium of liquids. For it to be otherwise, it would be necessary for all human societies to have the same vital energy and the same density. What is irrepresentable would only be so because of the diversity of habitats.

It is true that this source of variations would be exhausted if all humanity formed one and the same society. But, besides our not knowing whether such an ideal is realizable, in order for progress to cease it would still be necessary for the relations between social units in the interior of this gigantic society to be themselves recalcitrant to all change. It would be necessary for them always to remain distributed in the same way, for not only the total aggregate but also each of the elementary aggregates of which it would be formed, to keep the same dimensions. But such a uniformity is impossible, solely because these partial groups do not all have the same extent nor the same vitality. Population cannot be concentrated in the same way at all points; it is inevitable that the greatest centres, those where life is most intense, exercise an attraction for the others proportionate to their importance.

The migrations which are thus produced result in further concentrating social units in certain regions, and, consequently, in determining new advances there which irradiate little by little from the homes in which they were born into the rest of the country. Moreover, these changes call forth others, without it being possible to say where the repercussions stop. In fact, far from societies approaching a stationary position in proportion to their development, they become, on the contrary, more mobile and more plastic.

If, nevertheless, Spencer could claim that social evolution has a limit which cannot be passed,[411] that is because, according to him, progress has no other reason for existing than to adapt the individual to the cosmic environment which surrounds him. For this thinker, perfection consists in the growth of individual life, that is, in a more complete correspondence between the organism and its physical conditions. As for society, it is one of the means by which this correspondence is established rather than the object of a special correspondence. Because the individual is not alone in the world, but is surrounded by rivals who dispute over the means of existence, he has every interest in establishing between himself and those like him relations such that they will be of use to him rather than harm him. Thus society was born, and all social progress consists in ameliorating these relations in such a way as to make them more completely produce the effect in view of which they were established. Thus, in spite of the biological analogies upon which he lays stress Spencer does not see a reality *sui generis* in society, which exists by itself and by virtue of specific and necessary causes, and which, consequently, confound themselves with man's own nature, and to which he is held to adapt himself in order to live, just as to his physical environment—but he sees it as an arrangement instituted by individuals to extend individual life in length and breadth.[412] It consists entirely in co-operation, whether positive or negative, and both have no other object than the adapting of the individual to his physical environment. Of course, society is in this sense a secondary condition of this adaptation; it can, in accordance with the way in which it is organized, lead man to, or keep him from, a state of perfect equilibrium, but it is not itself a contributory factor in the determination of the nature of this equilibrium. Moreover, as the cosmic environment is relatively constant, as changes in it are infinitely few and far between, the development whose object is to put us in harmony with it is necessarily limited. It is inevitable that a moment will arrive when there will no longer be any external relations to which some internal relations do not correspond. Then, social progress cannot fail to halt, since it will have

---

[411] *First Principles*, pp. 454 ff.
[412] See his work on ethics.

arrived at the goal for which it was headed and which was its reason for existing. It will have been achieved.

But, under these conditions, the very progress of the individual becomes inexplicable.

In short, why should he aim for this more perfect correspondence with the physical environment? In order to be happier? We have already disposed of this point. We cannot say of a correspondence that it is more complete than another simply because it is more complex. Indeed, we speak of an organism being in equilibrium when it responds in an appropriate manner, not to all external forces, but only to those which make an impression upon it. If there are some which do not affect it, it is as if they did not exist, and, accordingly, it does not have to adapt itself to them. Whatever may be their material proximity, they are outside its circle of adaptation because it is outside the sphere of their action. If, then, the subject is of a simple, homogeneous constitution, there will be only a small number of external circumstances which will naturally arouse it, and consequently it will respond to these stimuli, that is, realize a state of irreproachable equilibrium with very little effort. If, on the contrary, it is very complex, the conditions of adaptation will be more numerous and more complicated, but the adaptation itself will not be more complete on that account. Because many stimuli which received no response from the nervous system of men who came before us act upon us, we are forced, in order to adjust ourselves, to a more considerable development. But the product of this development, that is, the adjustment which results from it, is not more perfect in one case than in the other. It is only different because the organisms which are adjusted are themselves different. The savage whose epidermis does not feel the variations in temperature very much is as well adapted as the civilized man who protects himself with clothes.

If, then, man does not depend upon a variable milieu, we do not see what reason he would have had for varying. Hence, society is itself, not the secondary condition, but the determining factor in progress. It is a reality which is no more our work than the external world, and to which, consequently, we must submit in order to exist. It is because it changes that we must change. For progress to halt, it would be necessary at some moment for the social milieu to come to a stationary position, and we have just shown that such an hypothesis is contrary to all the precepts of science.

Thus, not only does a mechanistic theory of progress not deprive us of an ideal, but it permits us to believe that we shall never lack for one. Precisely because the ideal depends upon the essentially mobile social milieu, it ceaselessly changes. There is no reason for fearing that the world will ever fail us, that our activity will come to an end and that our horizon will be closed. But, although we never pursue any but definite, limited ends, there is, and there will always be, between the extreme points at which we arrive and the end towards which we are tending, a free field open to our efforts.

III

With societies, individuals are transformed in accordance with the changes produced in the number of social units and their relations.

First, they are made more and more free of the yoke of the organism. An animal is almost completely under the influence of his physical environment; its biological constitution predetermines its existence. Man, on the contrary, is dependent upon social causes. Of course, animals also form societies, but, as they are very restricted, collective life is very simple. They are also stationary because the equilibrium of such small societies is necessarily stable. For these two reasons, it easily fixes itself in the organism. It not only has its roots in the organism, but it is entirely enveloped in it to such a point that it loses its own characteristics. It functions through a system of instincts, of reflexes which are not essentially distinct from those which assure the functioning of organic life. They present, it is true, the particular characteristic of adapting the individual to the social environment, not to the physical environment, and are caused by occurrences of the common life. They are not of different nature, however, from those which, in certain cases, determine without any previous education the necessary movements in locomotion. It is quite otherwise with man, because the societies he forms are much vaster. Even the smallest we know of are more extensive than the majority of animal societies. Being more complex, they also change more, and these two causes together see to it that social life with man is not congealed in a biological form. Even where it is most simple, it clings to its specificity. There are always beliefs and practices common to men which are not inscribed in their tissues. But this character is more manifest as the social mass and density grow. The more people there are in association, and the more they react upon one another, the more also does the product of these reactions pass beyond the bounds of the organism. Man thus finds himself placed under the sway of causes *sui generis* whose relative part in the constitution of human nature becomes ever more considerable.

Moreover, the influence of this factor increases not only in relative value, but also in absolute value. The same cause which increases the importance of the collective environment weakens the organic environment in such a manner as to make it accessible to the action of social causes and to subordinate it to them. Because there are more individuals living together, common life is richer and more varied, but for this variety to be possible, the organic type must be less definite to be able to diversify itself. We have seen, in effect, that the tendencies and aptitudes transmitted by heredity became ever more general and more indeterminate, more refractory consequently, to assuming the form of instincts. Thus, a phenomenon is produced which is exactly the inverse of that which we observe at the beginning of evolution. With animals, the organism assimilates social facts to it, and, stripping them of their special nature, transforms them into biological facts. Social life is materialized. In man, on the contrary, and particularly in higher societies, social causes substitute themselves for organic causes. The organism is spiritualized.

The individual is transformed in accordance with this change in dependence. Since this activity which calls forth the special action of social causes cannot be fixed in the organism, a new life, also *sui generis*, is superimposed upon that of the body. Freer, more complex, more independent of the organs which support it, its distinguishing characteristics become ever more apparent as it progresses and becomes solid. From this description we can recognize the essential traits of psychic life. To be sure, it would be exaggerating to say that psychic life begins only with societies, but certainly it becomes extensive only as societies develop. That is why, as has often been remarked, the progress of conscience is in inverse ratio to that of instinct. Whatever may be said of them, it is not the first which breaks up the second. Instinct, the product of the accumulated experience of generations, has a much greater resistive force to dissolution simply because it becomes conscious. Truly, conscience only invades the ground which instinct has ceased to occupy, or where instinct cannot be established. Conscience does not make instinct recede; it only fills the space instinct leaves free. Moreover, if instinct regresses rather than extends as general life extends, the greater importance of the social factor is the cause of this. Hence, the great difference which separates man from animals, that is, the greater development of his psychic life, comes from his greater sociability. To understand why psychic functions have been carried, from the very beginnings of the human species, to a degree of perfection unknown among animal species, one would first have to know why it is that men, instead of living in solitude or in small bands, were led to form more extensive societies. To put it in terms of the classical definition, if man is a reasonable animal, that is because he is a sociable animal, or at least infinitely more sociable than other animals.[413]

This is not all. In so far as societies do not reach certain dimensions nor a certain degree of concentration, the only psychic life

---

[413] The definition of de Quatrefages which makes man a religious animal is a particular instance of the preceding, for man's religiosity is a consequence of his eminent sociability. See *supra*, pp. 168 ff.

which may be truly developed is that which is common to all the members of the group, which is found identical in each. But, as societies become more vast and, particularly, more condensed, a psychic life of a new sort appears. Individual diversities, at first lost and confused amidst the mass of social likenesses, become disengaged, become conspicuous, and multiply. A multitude of things which use to remain outside consciences because they did not affect the collective being become objects of representations. Whereas individuals use to act only by involving one another, except in cases where their conduct was determined by physical needs, each of them becomes a source of spontaneous activity. Particular personalities become constituted, take conscience of themselves. Moreover, this growth of psychic life in the individual does not obliterate the psychic life of society, but only transforms it. It becomes freer, more extensive, and as it has, after all, no other bases than individual consciences, these extend, become complex, and thus become flexible.

Hence, the cause which called forth the differences separating man from animals is also that which has forced him to elevate himself above himself. The ever growing distance between the savage and the civilized man has no other source. If the faculty of ideation is slowly disengaged from the confused feeling of its origin, if man has learned to formulate concepts and laws, if his spirit has embraced more and more extensive portions of space and time, if, not content with clinging to the past, he has trespassed upon the future, if his emotions and his tendencies, at first simple and not very numerous, have multiplied and diversified, that is because the social milieu has changed without interruption. In effect, unless these transformations were born from nothing, they can have had for causes only the corresponding transformations of surrounding milieux. But, man depends only upon three sorts of milieux: the organism, the external world, society. If one leaves aside the accidental variations due to combinations of heredity,—and their role in human progress is certainly not very considerable,—the organism is not automatically modified; it is necessary that it be impelled by some external cause. As for the physical world, since the beginning of history it has remained sensibly the same, at least if one does not take account of novelties which are of social origin.[414] Consequently, there is only society which has changed enough to be able to explain the parallel changes in individual nature.

It is not, then, audacious to affirm that, from now on, whatever progress is made in psycho-physiology will never represent more than a fraction of psychology, since the major part of psychic phenomena does not come from organic causes. This is what spiritualist philosophers

---

[414] Transformations of the soil, of streams, through the art of husbandry, engineers, etc.

have learned, and the great service that they have rendered science has been to combat the doctrines which reduce psychic life merely to an efflorescence of physical life. They have very justly felt that the first, in its highest manifestations, is much too free and complex to be merely a prolongation of the second. Because it is partly independent of the organism, however, it does not follow that it depends upon no natural cause, and that it must be put outside nature. But all these facts whose explanation we cannot find in the constitution of tissues derive from properties of the social milieu. This hypothesis assumes, at least, very great probability from what has preceded. But the social realm is not less natural than the organic realm. Consequently, because there is a vast region of conscience whose genesis is unintelligible through psycho-physiology alone, we must not conclude that it has been formed of itself and that it is, accordingly, refractory to scientific investigation, but only that it derives from some other positive science which can be called socio-psychology. The phenomena which would constitute its matter are, in effect, of a mixed nature. They have the same essential characters as other psychic facts, but they arise from social causes.

It is not necessary, then, with Spencer, to present social life as a simple resultant of individual natures, since, on the contrary, it is rather the latter which come from the former. Social facts are not the simple development of psychic facts, but the second are in large part only the prolongation of the first in the interior of consciences. This proposition is very important, for the contrary point of view exposes the sociologist, at every moment, to mistaking the cause for the effect, and conversely. For example, if, as often happens, we see in the organization of the family the logically necessary expression of human sentiments inherent in every conscience, we are reversing the true order of facts. On the contrary, it is the social organization of the relations of kinship which has determined the respective sentiments of parents and children. They would have been completely different if the social structure had been different, and the proof of this is, in effect, that paternal love is unknown in a great many societies.[415] One could cite many other examples of the same error.[416] Of course, it is a self-evident truth that there is nothing in social life which is not in individual consciences. Everything that is found in the latter, however, comes from society. The major part of our states of conscience would not have been produced among isolated beings and would have been produced quite otherwise among beings grouped in some other manner. They

---

[415] This is the case in societies where the matriarchal family rules.

[416] To cite only one example of this,—religion has been explained by the movements of individual feeling, whereas these movements are only the prolongation in the individual of social states which give birth to religion. We have developed this point further in an article in the *Révue Philosophique, Etudes de science sociale*, June, 1886. Cf. *Année Sociologique*, Vol. II, pp. 1-28.

come, then, not from the psychological nature of man in general, but from the manner in which men once associated mutually affect one another, according as they are more or less numerous, more or less close. Products of group life, it is the nature of the group which alone can explain them. Of course, they would not be possible if individual constitutions did not lend themselves to such action, but individual constitutions are only remote conditions, not determinate causes. Spencer in one place[417] compares the work of the sociologist to the calculation of a mathematician who, from the form of a certain number of balls, deduces the manner in which they must be combined in order to keep them in equilibrium. The comparison is inexact and does not apply to social facts. Here, instead, it is rather the form of all which determines that of the parts. Society does not find the bases on which it rests fully laid out in consciences; it puts them there itself.[418]

Book Three. Abnormal Forms

CHAPTER ONE. THE ANOMIC DIVISION OF LABOR

Up to now, we have studied the division of labor only as a normal phenomenon, but, like all social facts, and, more generally, all biological facts, it presents pathological forms which must be analyzed. Though normally the division of labor produces social solidarity, it sometimes happens that it has different, and even contrary results. Now, it is important to find out what makes it deviate from its natural course, for if we do not prove that these cases are exceptional, the division of labor might be accused of logically implying them. Moreover, the study of these devious forms will permit us to determine the conditions of existence of the normal state better. When we know the circumstances in which the division of labor ceases to bring forth solidarity, we shall better understand what is necessary for it to have that effect. Pathology, here as elsewhere, is a valuable aid of physiology.

One might be tempted to reckon as irregular forms of the division of labor criminal occupations and other harmful activities. They are the very negation of solidarity, and yet they take the form of special activities. But to speak with exactitude, there is no division of labor here, but differentiation pure and simple. The two terms must not be

---

[417] *Study of Sociology*, ch. i.

[418] This is a sufficient reply, we believe, to those who think they prove that everything in social life is individual because society is made up only of individuals. Of course, society has no other substratum, but because individuals form society, new phenomena which are formed by association are produced, and react upon individual consciences and in large part form them. That is why, although society may be nothing without individuals, each of them is much more a product of society than he is its maker.

confused. Thus, cancer and tuberculosis increase the diversity of organic tissues without bringing forth a new specialization of biologic functions.[419] In all these cases, there is no partition of a common function, but, in the midst of the organism, whether individual or social, another is formed which seeks to live at the expense of the first. In reality, there is not even a function, for a way of acting merits this name only if it joins with others in maintaining general life. This question, then, does not enter into the body of our investigation.

We shall reduce to three types the exceptional forms of the phenomenon that we are studying. This is not because there can be no others, but rather because those of which we are going to speak are the most general and the most serious.

I

The first case of this kind is furnished us by industrial or commercial crises, by failures, which are so many partial breaks in organic solidarity. They evince, in effect, that at certain points in the organism certain social functions are not adjusted to one another. But, in so far as labor is divided more, these phenomena seem to become more frequent, at least in certain cases. From 1845 to 1869, failures increased 70 %.[420] We cannot, however, attribute this fact to the growth in economic life, since enterprises have become a great deal more concentrated than numerous.

The conflict between capital and labor is another example, more striking, of the same phenomenon. In so far as industrial functions become more specialized, the conflict becomes more lively, instead of solidarity increasing. In the middle ages, the worker everywhere lived at the side of his master, pursuing his tasks "in the same shop, in the same establishment."[421] Both were part of the same corporation and led the same existence. "They were on an almost equal footing; whoever had served his apprenticeship could, at least in many of the occupations, set himself up independently if he had the means."[422] Hence, conflicts were wholly unusual. Beginning with the fifteenth century things began to change. "The occupational circle is no longer a common organization; it is an exclusive possession of the masters, who alone decided all matters. . . . From that time, a sharp line is drawn between masters and workers. The latter formed, so to speak, an order

---

[419] This is a distinction that Spencer does not make. It seems that, for him, the two terms are synonymous. The differentiation, however, which disintegrates (cancerous, microbic, criminal) is very different from that which brings vital forces together (division of labor).

[420] Block, *Statistique de la France.*

[421] Levasseur, *Les classes ouvrières en France jusqu'à la Révolution,* II, p. 315.

[422] *Ibid.,* i, p. 496.

apart; they had their customs, their rules, their independent associations."[423] Once this separation was effected, quarrels became numerous. "When the workers thought they had a just complaint, they struck or boycotted a village, an employer, and all of them were compelled to obey the letter of the order. . . . The power of association gave the workers the means of combating their employers with equal force."[424] But things were then far from reaching "the point at which we now see them. Workers rebelled in order to secure higher wages or some other change in the condition of labor, but they did not consider the employer as a permanent enemy whom one obeyed because of his force. They wished to make him concede a point, and they worked energetically towards that end, but the conflict was not everlasting. The workshops did not contain two opposing classes. Our socialist doctrines were unknown."[425] Finally, in the seventeenth century, the third phase of this history of the working classes begins: the birth of large-scale industry. The worker is more completely separated from the employer. "He becomes somewhat regimented. Each has his function, and the system of the division of labor makes some progress. In the factory of Van-Robais, which employed 1692 workers, there were particular shops for wheel-wrighting, for cutlery, for washing, for dyeing, for warping, and the shops for weaving themselves contained several types of workers whose labor was entirely distinct."[426] At the same time that specialization becomes greater, revolts become more frequent. "The smallest cause for discontent was enough to upset an establishment, and cause a worker unhappiness who did not respect the decision of the community."[427] We well know that, since then, the warfare has become ever more violent.

To be sure, we shall see in the following chapter that this tension in social relations is due, in part, to the fact that the working classes are not really satisfied with the conditions under which they five, but very often accept them only as constrained and forced, since they have not the means to change them. This constraint alone, however, would not account for the phenomenon. In effect, it does not weigh less heavily upon all those generally bereft of fortune, and yet this state of permanent hostility is wholly special to the industrial world. Then, in the interior of this world, it is the same for all workers indiscriminately. But, small-scale industry, where work is less divided, displays a relative harmony between worker and employer.[428] It is only in large-

---

[423] Levasseur, I, p. 496.
[424] *Ibid.*, I, p. 504.
[425] Hubert Valleroux, *Les Corporations d'arts et de métiers*, p. 49.
[426] Levasseur, II, p. 315.
[427] *Ibid.*, p. 319.
[428] See Cauwes, *Précis d'économie politique*, II, p. 39.

scale industry that these relations are in a sickly state. That is because they depend in part upon a different cause.

Another illustration of the same phenomenon has often been observed in the history of sciences. Until very recent times, science, not being very divided, could be cultivated almost entirely by one and the same person. Thus was had a very lively sense of its unity. The particular truths which composed it were neither so numerous nor so heterogeneous that one could not easily see the tie which bound them in one and the same system. Methods, being themselves very general, were little different from one another, and one could perceive the common trunk from which they imperceptibly diverged. But, as specialization is introduced into scientific work, each scholar becomes more and more enclosed, not only in a particular science, but in a special order of problems. Auguste Comte had already complained that, in his time, there were in the scientific world "very few minds embracing in their conception the total scope of even a single science, which is, however, in turn, only a part of a greater whole. The greater part were already occupied with some isolated consideration of a more or less extensive section of one certain science, without being very much concerned with the relation of the particular labors to the general system of positive knowledge."[429] But then, science, parceled out into a multitude of detailed studies which are not joined together, no longer forms a solidary whole. What best manifests, perhaps, this absence of concert and unity is the theory, so prevalent, that each particular science has an absolute value, and that the scholar ought to devote himself to his special researches without bothering to inquire whether they serve some purpose and lead anywhere. "This division of intellectual labor," says Schaeffle, "offers good reason for fearing that this return to a new Alexandrianism will lead once again to the ruin of all science."[430]

II

What makes these facts serious is that they have sometimes been considered a necessary effect of the division of labor after it has passed beyond a certain stage of development. In this case, it is said, the individual, hemmed in by his task, becomes isolated in a special activity. He no longer feels the idea of a common work being done by those who work side by side with him. Thus, the division of labor could not be pushed farther without becoming a source of disintegration. "Since all such decomposition," says Auguste Comte, "necessarily has the tendency to determine a corresponding dispersion, the fundamental

---

[429] *Cours de philosophie positive*, I, p. 27.
[430] *Bau und Leben des sozialen Körpers*, IV, p. 113.

partition of human labors cannot avoid evoking, in a proportionate degree, individual divergences, both intellectual and moral, whose combined influence must, in the same measure, demand a permanent discipline able to prevent or unceasingly contain their discordant flight. If, on the one hand, indeed, the separation of social functions permits a felicitous development of the spirit of detail otherwise impossible, it spontaneously tends, on the other hand, to snuff out the spirit of togetherness or, at least, to undermine it profoundly. Likewise, from the moral point of view, at the same time that each is thus placed in strict dependence upon the mass, he is naturally deterred by the peculiar scope of his special activity which constantly links him to his own private interest whose true relation with the public interest he perceives but very vaguely. . . . Thus it is that the same principle which has alone permitted the development and the extension of general society threatens, in a different aspect, to decompose it into a multitude of incoherent corporations which almost seem not to be of the same species."[431] Espinas has expressed himself almost in the same terms: "Division," he says, "is dispersion."[432]

The division of labor would thus exercise, because of its very nature, a dissolving influence which would be particularly obvious where functions are very specialized. Comte, however, does not conclude from his principle that societies must be led to what he himself calls the age of generality, that is, to that state of indistinctness and homogeneity which was their point of departure. The diversity of functions is useful and necessary, but as unity, which is no less indispensable, does not spontaneously spring up, the care of realizing it and of maintaining it would constitute a special function in the social organism, represented by an independent organ. This organ is the State or government. "The social destiny of government," says Comte, "appears to me to consist particularly in sufficiently containing, and preventing, as far as possible, this fatal disposition towards a fundamental dispersion of ideas, sentiments, and interests, the inevitable result of the very principle of human development, and which, if it could follow its natural course without interruption, would inevitably end by arresting social progress in all important respects. This conception, in my eyes, constitutes the first positive and rational basis of an elementary and abstract theory of government properly so called, seen in its noblest and greatest scientific extension, as characterized in general by a universal and necessary reaction, at first spontaneous and then regulated, of the totality of the parts that go to make it up. It is clear, in effect, that the only real means of preventing such a dispersion consists in this indispensable reaction in a new and

---

[431] *Cours*, IV, p. 429.
[432] *Sociétés animales*, conclusion, IV.

special function, susceptible of fittingly intervening in the habitual accomplishment of all the diverse functions of social economy, so as to recall to them unceasingly the feeling of unity and the sentiment of common solidarity."[433]

What government is to society in its totality philosophy ought to be to the sciences. Since the diversity of science tends to disrupt the unity of science, a new science must be set up to re-establish it. Since detailed studies make us lose sight of the whole vista of human knowledge, we must institute a particular system of researches to retrieve it and set it off. In other words, "we must make an even greater specialty of the study of scientific generalities. A new class of scholars, prepared by suitable education, without devoting themselves to a special culture of any particular branch of natural philosophy, will busy themselves with considering the various positive sciences in their present state, with exactly determining the spirit of each of them, with discovering their relations and their continuity, with summing up, if possible, all their principles in a very small number of principles common to all, and the division of labor in the sciences will be pushed, without any danger, as far as the development of the various orders of knowledge demand."[434]

Of course, we have ourselves shown[435] that the governmental organ develops with the division of labor, not as a repercussion of it, but because of mechanical necessity. As organs are rigorously solidary where functions are very divided, what affects one affects the others, and social events take on a more general interest. At the same time, with the effacement of the segmental type, they penetrate more easily throughout the extent of the same tissue or the same system. For these two reasons, there are more of them which are retained in the directive organ whose functional activity, more often exercised, grows with the volume. But its sphere of action does not extend further.

But beneath this general, superficial life there is an intestine, a world of organs which, without being completely independent of the first, nevertheless function without its intervention, without its even being conscious of them, at least normally. They are freed from its action because it is too remote for them. The government cannot, at every instant, regulate the conditions of the different economic markets, fixing the prices of their commodities and services, or keeping production within the bounds of consumptionary needs, etc. All these practical problems arise from a multitude of detail, coming from thousands of particular circumstances which only those very close to

---

[433] *Cours de Philosophie positive*, IV, pp. 430-431.

[434] This bringing together of government and philosophy ought not to surprise us, for, in Comte's eyes, the two institutions are inseparable. Government, as he conceives it, is possible only upon the institution of the positive philosophy.

[435] See above, Book I, ch. vii, § 3.

the problems know about. Thus, we cannot adjust these functions to one another and make them concur harmoniously if they do not concur of themselves. If, then, the division of labor has the dispersive effects that are attributed to it, they ought to develop without resistance in this region of society, since there is nothing to hold them together. What gives unity to organized societies, however, as to all organisms, is the spontaneous consensus of parts. Such is the internal solidarity which not only is as indispensable as the regulative action of higher centres, but which also is their necessary condition, for they do no more than translate it into another language and, so to speak, consecrate it. Thus, the brain does not make the unity of the organism, but expresses and completes it. Some speak of the necessity of a reaction of the totality of parts, but it still is necessary for this totality to exist; that is to say, the parts must be already solidary with one another for the whole to take conscience of itself and react in this way. Else, as work is divided, one would see a sort of progressive decomposition produced, not only at certain points, but throughout society, instead of the ever stronger concentration that we really observe.

But, it is said, there is no need for going into detail. It is sufficient to call to mind whenever necessary "the spirit of the whole and the sentiment of common solidarity," and this action the government alone can execute. This is true, but it is much too general to assure the concourse of social functions, if that has not been realized by itself. In effect, what is the point at issue? Is it to make each individual feel that he is not self-sufficient, but is a part of a whole on which he depends? But such an abstract, vague, and, withal, intermittent representation, just as all complex representations, can avail nothing against lively, concrete impressions which occupational activity at every instant evokes in each one of us. If, then, occupational activity has the effects that are adduced, if the occupations which fill our daily life tend to detach us from the social group to which we belong, such a conception, which is quite dormant and never occupies more than a small part of the field of conscience, will not be sufficient to hold us to it. In order that the sentiment of our state of dependence be effective, it would be necessary for it also to be continuous, and it can be that only if it is linked to the very practice of each special function. But then specialization would no longer have the consequences which it is said to produce. Or else governmental action would have as its object the maintenance of a certain moral uniformity among occupations, the preventing of "social affections gradually concentrated in individuals of the same occupation from becoming more and more foreign to other classes, for want of sufficient likeness in customs and thoughts."[436] But this uniformity cannot be maintained by force and against the nature of

---

[436] *Cours de Philosophie positive*, IV, p. 42.

things. Functional diversity induces a moral diversity that nothing can prevent, and it is inevitable that one should grow as the other does. We know, moreover, why these two phenomena develop in parallel fashion. Collective sentiments become more and more impotent in holding together the centrifugal tendencies that the division of labor is said to engender, for these tendencies increase as labor is more divided, and, at the same time, collective sentiments are weakened.

For the same reason, philosophy becomes more and more incapable of assuring the unity of science. As long as the same mind could, at once, cultivate different sciences, it was possible to acquire the competency necessary for their unification. But, as they become specialized, these grand syntheses can no longer be anything more than premature generalizations, for it becomes more and more impossible for one human intelligence to gain a sufficiently exact knowledge of this great multitude of phenomena, of laws, of hypotheses which must be summed up. "It would be interesting to speculate," Ribot justly says, "what philosophy, as the general conception of the universe, will be when particular sciences, because of their growing complexity, become overwhelming in their detail and philosophers are reduced to knowledge of the most general results, which are necessarily superficial."[437]

To be sure, there is some reason for judging as excessive this pride of the scholar, who, hemmed in by his special researches, refuses to recognize any other control. It is certain, however, that to gain an exact idea of a science one must practice it, and, so to speak, live with it. That is because it does not entirely consist of some propositions which have been definitively proved. Along side of this actual, realized science, there is another, concrete and living, which is in part ignorant of itself, and yet seeks itself; besides acquired results, there are hopes, habits, instincts, needs, presentiments so obscure that they cannot be expressed in words, yet so powerful that they sometimes dominate the whole life of the scholar. All this is still science; it is even its best and largest part, for the discovered truths are a little thing in comparison with those which remain to be discovered. Moreover, in order to possess a good idea of the first and understand what is found condensed therein, one must have been close to scientific life while it was still in a free state; that is to say, before it became fixed in the form of definite propositions. Otherwise, one will have the letter, but not the spirit. Each science has, so to speak, a soul which lives in the conscience of scholars. Only a part of this soul assumes sensible bodily form. The formulas which express it, being general, are easily transmitted. But such is not the case with this other part of science which no symbol translates without. Here, all is personal and must be acquired through

---

[437] *Psychologie allemande*, Introduction, p. xxvii.

personal experience. To take part in it, one must put oneself to work and place oneself before the facts. According to Comte, to assure the unity of science, it would be enough to have methods reduced to unity;[438] but it is just the methods which are most difficult to unify, for, as they are immanent in the very sciences, as it is impossible to disengage them completely from the body of established truths in order to codify them separately, we can know them only if we have ourselves practiced them. But it is now impossible for the same man to practice a large number of sciences. These grand generalizations can rest only on a very summary view of things. If, moreover, we remember how slowly and with what patient precautions scholars ordinarily proceed in the discovery of even their most particular truths, we see that improvised disciplines no longer have anything more than a very feeble authority over them.

But, whatever may be the value of these philosophic generalities, science would not find therein the unity it needs. They well express what there is in common among the sciences,—laws, specific method,—but, besides these resemblances, there are differences which have to be integrated. We often say that the general holds in its power particulars that it sums up, but the expression is not exact. It contains only what is common to them. Now, there are no two phenomena in the world which resemble each other, simple as they may be. That is why every general proposition lets a part of the material it tries to master escape. It is impossible to establish the concrete characters and distinctive properties of things in the same impersonal and homogeneous formula. But, as long as resemblances exceed differences, they are sufficient to integrate the representations thus brought together. The dissonances of detail disappear in the total harmony! On the contrary, as the differences become more numerous, cohesion becomes more unstable and must be consolidated by other means. If we picture the growing multiplicity of special sciences, with their theorems, their laws, their axioms, their conjectures, their methods of procedure, we shall see that a short and simple formula, as the principle of evolution, for example, is not enough to integrate such a prodigious complexity of phenomena. Even when these total views exactly correspond to reality, the part they explain is too small a thing beside what they leave unexplained. It is not, then, by this means that we shall ever be able to take the positive sciences out of their isolation. There is too great a chasm between detailed researches which are their backbone and such syntheses. The tie which binds these two orders of knowledge together is too slight and too loose, and, consequently, if particular sciences can take cognizance of their mutual dependence

---

[438] *Op. cit.*, I, p. 45.

only through a philosophy which embraces all of them, the sentiment of unity they will have will always be too vague to be efficacious.

Philosophy is the collective conscience of science, and, here as elsewhere, the role of the collective conscience becomes smaller as labor is divided.

III

Although Comte recognized that the division of labor is a source of solidarity, it seems that he did not perceive that this solidarity is *sui generis* and is little by little substituted for that which social likenesses give rise to. That is why, in remarking that the latter were very much obliterated where functions are very specialized, he considered this obliteration a morbid phenomenon, a menace to social cohesion due to the excess of specialization, and by that he explained the facts of lack of co-ordination which sometimes accompany the development of the division of labor. But since we have shown that the enfeeblement of the collective conscience is a normal phenomenon, we cannot consider it as the cause of the abnormal phenomena that we are studying. If, in certain cases, organic solidarity is not all it should be, it is certainly not because mechanical solidarity has lost ground, but because all the conditions for the existence of organic solidarity have not been realized.

We know, in effect, that, wherever organic solidarity is found, we come upon an adequately developed regulation determining the mutual relations of functions.[439] For organic solidarity to exist, it is not enough that there be a system of organs necessary to one another, which in a general way feel solidary, but it is also necessary that the way in which they should come together, if not in every kind of meeting, at least in circumstances which most frequently occur, be predetermined. Otherwise, at every moment new conflicts would have to be equilibrated, for the conditions of equilibrium can be discovered only through gropings in the course of which one part treats the other as an adversary as much as an auxiliary. These conflicts would incessantly crop out anew, and, consequently, solidarity would be scarcely more than potential, if mutual obligations had to be fought over entirely anew in each particular instance. It will be said that there are contracts. But, first of all, all social relations are not capable of assuming this juridical form. We know, moreover, that a contract is not self-sufficient, but supposes a regulation which is as extensive and complicated as contractual life itself. Besides, the links which have this origin are always of short duration. A contract is only a truce, and very precarious; it suspends hostilities only for a time. Of course, as precise

---

[439] See Book I, ch. vii.

as this regulation may be, it will always leave a place for many disturbances. But it is neither necessary nor even possible for social life to be without conflicts. The role of solidarity is not to suppress competition, but to moderate it.

Moreover, in the normal state, these rules disengage themselves from the division of labor. They are a prolongation of it. Assuredly, if it only brought together individuals who united for some few moments to exchange personal services, it could not give rise to any regulative action. But what it brings face to face are functions, that is to say, ways of definite action, which are identically repeated in given circumstances, since they cling to general, constant conditions of social life. The relations which are formed among these functions cannot fail to partake of the same degree of fixity and regularity. There are certain ways of mutual reaction which, finding themselves very conformable to the nature of things, are repeated very often and become habits. Then these habits, becoming forceful, are transformed into rules of conduct. The past determines the future. In other words, there is a certain sorting of rights and duties which is established by usage and becomes obligatory. The rule does not, then, create the state of mutual dependence in which solidary organs find themselves, but only expresses in clear-cut fashion the result of a given situation. In the same way, the nervous system, far from dominating the evolution of the organism, as we have already said, results from it.[440] The nerve-cords are probably only the lines of passage which the streams of movements and excitations exchanged between different organs have followed. They are the canals which fife has hewed for itself while steadily flowing in the same direction, and the ganglia would only be the place of intersection of several of these lines.[441] Because they misunderstood this aspect of the phenomena, certain moralists have claimed that the division of labor does not produce true solidarity. They have seen in it only particular exchanges, ephemeral combinations, without past or future, in which the individual is thrown on his own resources. They have not perceived the slow work of consolidation, the network of links which little by little have been woven and which makes something permanent of organic solidarity.

But, in all the cases that we have described above, this regulation either does not exist, or is not in accord with the degree of development of the division of labor. Today, there are no longer any rules which fix the number of economic enterprises, and, in each branch of industry, production is not exactly regulated on a level with consumption. We do not wish to draw any practical conclusion from this fact; we are not contending that restrictive legislation is necessary; we do not here have

---

[440] Perrier, *Colonies animales,* p. 746.
[441] See Spencer, *Principles of Biology,* II, pp. 438 ff.

to weigh its advantages and disadvantages. What is certain is that this lack of regulation does not permit a regular harmony of functions. The economists claim, it is true, that this harmony is self-established when necessary, thanks to rises or declines in prices which, according to needs, stimulate or slacken production. But, in every case, this is established only after ruptures of equilibrium and more or less prolonged disturbances. Moreover, these disturbances are naturally as much more frequent as functions are more specialized, for the more complex an organization is, the more is the need of extensive regulation felt.

The relations of capital and labor have, up to the present, remained in the same state of juridical indetermination. A contract for the hire of services occupies a very small place in our Codes, particularly when one thinks of the diversity and complexity of the relations which it is called upon to regulate. But it is not necessary to insist upon a gap whose presence is keenly felt by all, and which everybody seeks to fill.[442]

Methodological rules are for science what rules of law and custom are for conduct; they direct the thought of the scholar just as the others govern the actions of men. But if each science has its method, the order that it realizes is wholly internal. It co-ordinates the findings of scholars who cultivate the same science, not their relations with the outside world. There are hardly any disciplines which bring together the work of the different sciences in the light of a common end. This is particularly true of the moral and social sciences, for the sciences of mathematics, physics, chemistry, and even biology, do not seem to be strangers to one another in this respect. But the jurist, the psychologist, the anthropologist, the economist, the statistician, the linguist, the historian, proceed with their investigations as if the different orders of fact they study constituted so many independent worlds. In reality, however, they penetrate one another from all sides; consequently, the case must be the same with their corresponding sciences. This is where the anarchical state of science in general comes from, a state that has been noted not without exaggeration, but which is particularly true of these specific sciences. They offer the spectacle of an aggregate of disjointed parts which do not concur. If they form a whole without unity, this is not because they do not have a sentiment of their likenesses; it is because they are not organized.

These different examples are, then, varieties of the same species. If the division of labor does not produce solidarity in all these cases, it is

---

[442] This was written in 1893. Since then, industrial legislation has taken a more important place in our law. This is proof of how serious the gap was, and that there was need of its being filled.

because the relations of the organs are not regulated, because they are in a state of *anomy*.

But whence comes this state?

Since a body of rules is the definite form which spontaneously established relations between social functions take in the course of time, we can say, *a priori*, that the state of *anomy* is impossible wherever solidary organs are sufficiently in contact or sufficiently prolonged. In effect, being contiguous, they are quickly warned, in each circumstance, of the need which they have of one another, and, consequently, they have a lively and continuous sentiment of their mutual dependence. For the same reason that exchanges take place among them easily, they take place frequently; being regular, they regularize themselves accordingly, and in time the work of consolidation is achieved. Finally, because the smallest reaction can be felt from one part to another, the rules which are thus formulated carry this imprint; that is to say, they foresee and fix, in detail, the conditions of equilibrium. But, on the contrary, if some opaque environment is interposed, then only stimuli of a certain intensity can be communicated from one organ to another. Relations, being rare, are not repeated enough to be determined; each time there ensues new groping. The lines of passage taken by the streams of movement cannot deepen because the streams themselves are too intermittent. If some rules do come to constitute them, they are, however, general and vague, for under these conditions it is only the most general contours of phenomena that can be fixed. The case will be the same if the contiguity, though sufficient, is too recent or has not endured long enough.[443]

Generally, this condition is found to be realized in the nature of things. A function can be apportioned between two or several parts of an organism only if these parts are more or less contiguous. Moreover, once labor is divided, since they need one another, they naturally tend to lessen the distance separating them. That is why as one goes up in the animal scale, one sees organs coming together, and, as Spencer says, being introduced in the interstices of one another. But a set of exceptional circumstances can bring this about differently.

This is what happens in the cases we are discussing. In so far as the segmental type is strongly marked, there are nearly as many economic markets as there are different segments. Consequently, each of them is very limited. Producers, being near consumers, can easily reckon the

---

[443] There is, however, a case where *anomy* can be produced although the contiguity is sufficient. This occurs when the necessary regulation can be established only by submitting to transformations of which the social structure is incapable. The plasticity of societies is not indefinite. When it reaches its limit, even necessary changes are impossible.

extent of the needs to be satisfied. Equilibrium is established without any trouble and production regulates itself. On the contrary, as the organized type develops, the fusion of different segments draws the markets together into one which embraces almost all society. This even extends beyond, and tends to become universal, for the frontiers which separate peoples break down at the same time as those which separate the segments of each of them. The result is that each industry produces for consumers spread over the whole surface of the country or even of the entire world. Contact is then no longer sufficient. The producer can no longer embrace the market in a glance, nor even in thought. He can no longer see its limits, since it is, so to speak, limitless. Accordingly, production becomes unbridled and unregulated. It can only trust to chance, and in the course of these gropings, it is inevitable that proportions will be abused, as much in one direction as in another. From this come the crises which periodically disturb economic functions. The growth of local, restricted crises which result in failures is in all likelihood an effect of the same cause.

As the market extends, great industry appears. But it results in changing the relations of employers and employees. The great strain upon the nervous system and the contagious influence of great agglomerations increase the needs of the latter. Machines replace men; manufacturing replaces hand-work. The worker is regimented, separated from his family throughout the day. He always lives apart from his employer, etc. These new conditions of industrial life naturally demand a new organization, but as these changes have been accomplished with extreme rapidity, the interests in conflict have not yet had the time to be equilibrated.[444]

Finally, the explanation of the fact that the moral and social sciences are in the state we have suggested is that they were the last to come into the circle of positive sciences. It is hardly a century since this new field of phenomena has been opened to scientific investigation. Scholars have installed themselves in them, some here, some there, according to their tastes. Scattered over this wide surface, they have remained until the present too remote from one another to feel all the ties which unite them. But, solely because they will push their researches farther from their points of departure, they will necessarily end by reaching and, consequently, taking conscience of their solidarity. The unity of science will thus form of itself, not through the abstract unity of a formula, far too scanty for the multitude of things that it must embrace, but through the living unity of an organic whole.

---

[444] Let us remember, however, that, as we shall see in the following chapter, this antagonism is not entirely due to the rapidity of these changes, but, in good part, to the still very great inequality of the external conditions of the struggle. On this factor, time has no influence.

For science to be unitary, it is not necessary for it to be contained within the field of one and the same conscience—an impossible feat anyhow—but it is sufficient that all those who cultivate it feel that they are collaborating in the same work.

The preceding has removed one of the most serious charges brought against the division of labor.

It has often been accused of degrading the individual by making him a machine. And truly, if he does not know whither the operations he performs are tending, if he relates them to no end, he can only continue to work through routine. Every day he repeats the same movements with monotonous regularity, but without being interested in them, and without understanding them. He is no longer a living cell of a living organism which unceasingly vibrates with neighboring cells, which acts upon them, and to whose action it responds and with whose needs and circumstances it changes. He is no longer anything but an inert piece of machinery, only an external force set going which always moves in the same direction and in the same way. Surely, no matter how one may represent the moral ideal, one cannot remain indifferent to such debasement of human nature. If morality has individual perfection as its goal, it cannot thus permit the ruin of the individual, and if it has society as its goal, it cannot let the very source of social life be drained, for the peril does not threaten only economic functions, but all social functions, as elevated as they may be. "If," says Comte, "we have often justly deplored, in the material world, the workman being exclusively occupied during his whole life with the manufacture of knife-handles or pin-heads, healthy philosophy ought not less bemoan, in the intellectual order, the exclusive and continuous employment of the human brain in the resolution of some equations or in the classification of some insects. The moral effect, in one case, as in the other, is unfortunately very much the same."[445]

As a remedy, it has sometimes been proposed that, in addition to their technical and special instruction, workers be given a general education. But, suppose that we can thus relieve some of the bad effects attributed to the division of labor; that is not a means of preventing them. The division does not change its nature because it has been preceded by general culture. No doubt, it is good for the worker to be interested in art, literature, etc., but it is none the less bad that he should be treated as a machine all day long. Who cannot see, moreover, that two such existences are too opposed to be reconciled, and cannot be led by the same man! If a person has grown accustomed to vast horizons, total views, broad generalities, he cannot be confined, without impatience, within the strict limits of a special task. Such a remedy

---

[445] *Cours*, IV, p. 430.

would make specialization inoffensive by making it intolerable, and, consequently, more or less impossible.

What solves the contradiction is that, contrary to what has been said, the division of labor does not produce these consequences because of a necessity of its own nature, but only in exceptional and abnormal circumstances. In order for it to develop without having such a disastrous influence on the human conscience, it is not necessary to temper it with its opposite. It is necessary and it is sufficient for it to be itself, for nothing to come from without to denature it. For, normally, the role of each special function does not require that the individual close himself in, but that he keep himself in constant relations with neighboring functions, take conscience of their needs, of the changes which they undergo, etc. The division of labor presumes that the worker, far from being hemmed in by his task, does not lose sight of his collaborators, that he acts upon them, and reacts to them. He is, then, not a machine who repeats his movements without knowing their meaning, but he knows that they tend, in some way, towards an end that he conceives more or less distinctly. He feels that he is serving something. For that, he need not embrace vast portions of the social horizon; it is sufficient that he perceive enough of it to understand that his actions have an aim beyond themselves. From that time, as special and uniform as his activity may be, it is that of an intelligent being, for it has direction, and he knows it. The economists would not have left this essential character of the division of labor in the shade and, accordingly, would not have exposed it to this unmerited reproach, if they had not reduced it to being merely a means of increasing the produce of social forces, if they had seen that it is above all a source of solidarity.

CHAPTER TWO. THE FORCED DIVISION OF LABOR

I

It is not sufficient that there be rules, however, for sometimes the rules themselves are the cause of evil. This is what occurs in class-wars. The institution of classes and of castes constitutes an organization of the division of labor, and it is a strictly regulated organization, although it often is a source of dissension. The lower classes not being, or no longer being, satisfied with the role which has devolved upon them from custom or by law aspire to functions which are closed to them and seek to dispossess those who are exercising these functions. Thus civil wars arise which are due to the manner in which labor is distributed.

There is nothing similar to this in the organism. No doubt, during periods of crises, the different tissues war against one another and nourish themselves at the expense of others. But never does one cell or organ seek to usurp a role different from the one which it is filling. The reason for this is that each anatomic element automatically executes its purpose. Its constitution, its place in the organism, determines its vocation; its task is a consequence of its nature. It can badly acquit itself, but it cannot assume another's task unless the latter abandons it, as happens in the rare cases of substitution that we have spoken of. It is not so in societies. Here the possibility is greater. There is a greater distance between the hereditary dispositions of the individual and the social function he will fill. The first do not imply the second with such immediate necessity. This space, open to striving and deliberation, is also at the mercy of a multitude of causes which can make individual nature deviate from its normal direction and create a pathological state. Because this organization is more supple, it is also more delicate and more accessible to change. Doubtless, we are not, from birth/predestined to some special position; but we do have tastes and aptitudes which limit our choice. If no care is taken of them, if they are ceaselessly disturbed by our daily occupations, we shall suffer and seek a way of putting an end to our suffering. But there is no other way out than to change the established order and to set up a new one. For the division of labor to produce solidarity, it is not sufficient, then, that each have his task; it is still necessary that this task be fitting to him.

Now, it is this condition which is not realized in the case we are examining. In effect, if the institution of classes or castes sometimes gives rise to anxiety and pain instead of producing solidarity, this is because the distribution of social functions on which it rests does not respond, or rather no longer responds, to the distribution of natural talents. For, despite the claim,[446] it is not solely because of the spirit of imitation that lower classes are ambitious to elevate themselves to higher classes. Indeed, imitation can by itself explain nothing, since it supposes something other than itself. It is possible only between beings who already resemble each other and only in proportion to their resemblance. It is not produced between different species or different varieties. It is the same with moral contagion as with physical contagion; it manifests itself only on predisposed ground. For needs to flow from one class to another, differences which originally separated these classes must have disappeared or grown less. Through changes produced in society, some must have become apt at functions which were at first beyond them, while the others lost their original superiority. When the plebeians aimed to dispute the right to religious and administrative functions with the patricians, it was not only in imitation of the latter, but it was also because they had become more intelligent, richer, more numerous, and their tastes and ambitions had in

---

[446] Tarde, *Lois de l'imitation.*

consequence been modified. In accordance with these transformations, the agreement between the aptitudes of individuals and the kind of activity assigned to them is found to be broken in every region of society; constraint alone, more or less violent and more or less direct, links them to their functions. Consequently, only an imperfect and troubled solidarity is possible.

Thus, this result is not a necessary consequence of the division of labor. It comes about only under particular circumstances, that is, when it is an effect of an external force. The case is quite otherwise when it is established in virtue of purely internal spontaneity, without anything coming to disturb the initiative of individuals. In this condition, harmony between individual natures and social functions cannot fail to be realized, at least in the average case. For, if nothing impedes or unduly favors those disputing over tasks, it is inevitable that only those who are most apt at each kind of activity will indulge in it. The only cause determining the manner in which work is divided, then, is the diversity of capacities. In the nature of things, the apportioning is made through aptitudes, since there is no reason for doing otherwise. Thus, the harmony between the constitution of each individual and his condition is realized of itself. It will be said that it is not always sufficient to make men content, that there are some men whose desires go beyond their faculties. This is true, but these are exceptional and, one may say, morbid cases. Normally, man finds happiness in realizing his nature; his needs are in relation to his means. Thus, in the organism, each organ demands only as much food as it requires.

The forced division of labor is, then, the second abnormal type that we meet. But the sense of the word "forced" must not be misunderstood. Constraint is not every kind of regulation, since, as we have just seen, the division of labor cannot do without regulation. Even when functions are divided in accordance with pre-established rules, this apportioning is not necessarily the result of constraint. This is what takes place even under the rule of castes, in so far as that is founded in the nature of the society. This institution is never arbitrary throughout, but when it functions in a society in regular fashion without resistance, it expresses, at least in the large, the immutable manner in which occupational aptitudes distribute themselves. That is why, although tasks are, in certain measure, divided by law, each organ executes its own automatically. Constraint only begins when regulation, no longer corresponding to the true nature of things, and, accordingly, no longer having any basis in customs, can only be validated through force.

Inversely, we may say that the division of labor produces solidarity only if it is spontaneous and in proportion as it is spontaneous. But by spontaneity we must understand not simply the absence of all express violence, but also of everything that can even indirectly shackle the free unfolding of the social force that each carries in himself. It supposes, not only that individuals are not relegated to determinate functions by force, but also that no obstacle, of whatever nature, prevents them from occupying the place in the social framework which is compatible with their faculties. In short, labor is divided spontaneously only if society is constituted in such a way that social inequalities exactly express natural inequalities. But, for that, it is necessary and sufficient that the latter be neither enhanced nor lowered by some external cause. Perfect spontaneity is, then, only a consequence and another form of this other fact,—absolute equality in the external conditions of the conflict. It consists, not in a state of anarchy which would permit men freely to satisfy all their good or bad tendencies, but in a subtle organization in which each social value, being neither overestimated nor underestimated by anything foreign to it, would be judged at its true worth. It will be objected that, even under these conditions, there will still be conflict between the conquerors and the conquered, and that the latter will never accept defeat except when forced to do so. But this constraint does not resemble the other; they have only their name in common. What really constitutes constraint is the making of conflict itself impossible and refusing to admit the right of combat.

It is true that this perfect spontaneity is never met with anywhere as a realized fact. There is no society where it is unadulterated. If the institution of castes corresponds to the natural apportionment of capacities, it is, however, only in a very proximate and rough and ready manner. Heredity never acts with such precision that, even where it meets with most favorable conditions for its purpose, children can be identical with their parents. There are always exceptions to this rule, and, consequently, cases where the individual is not in harmony with the functions which are attributed to him. These discrepancies become more numerous as society develops, until, one day, the framework becomes too narrow and breaks down. When the regime of castes has lost juridical force, it survives by itself in customs, and, thanks to the persistence of certain prejudices, a certain distinction is attached to some individuals, a certain lack of distinction attached to others, independent of their merits. Finally, even where there remains no vestige of the past, hereditary transmission of wealth is enough to make the external conditions under which the conflict takes place very unequal, for it gives advantages to some which are not necessarily in keeping with their personal worth. Even today among the most cultivated peoples, there are careers which are either totally closed to or very difficult to be entered into by those who are bereft of fortune. It would thus seem that we have not the right to consider as normal a character which the division of labor never purely presents if it is noted that the more we advance on the social scale the more the segmental type disappears into the organized type, and the more these inequalities tend to become completely level.

The progressive decline of castes, beginning from the moment the division of labor is established, is an historical law, for, as they are linked to the politico-familial organization, they necessarily regress along with this organization. The prejudices to which they have given rise and which they leave behind do not survive them indefinitely, but slowly become obliterated. Public office is more and more freely open to everybody with no question as to wealth. Finally, even this last inequality, which comes about through birth, though not completely disappearing, is at least somewhat attenuated. Society is forced to reduce this disparity as far as possible by assisting in various ways those who find themselves in a disadvantageous position and by aiding them to overcome it. It thus shows that it feels obliged to leave free space for all merits and that it regards as unjust any inferiority which is not personally merited. But what manifests this tendency even more is the belief, so widespread today, that equality among citizens becomes ever greater and that it is just that this be so. A sentiment so general cannot be a pure illusion, but must express, in confused fashion, some aspect of reality. But as the progress of the division of labor implies, on the contrary, an ever growing inequality, the equality which public conscience thus affirms can only be the one of which we are speaking, that is, equality in the external conditions of conflict.

It is, moreover, easy to understand what makes this leveling process necessary. We have just seen that all external inequality compromises organic solidarity. There is nothing vexatious in this for lower societies where solidarity is assured pre-eminently by the community of beliefs and sentiments. However strained the ties which come from the division of labor, nevertheless, since they are not the ones which most strongly attach the individual to society, social cohesion is not menaced. The uneasiness which results from contrary aspirations is not enough to turn those who harbor them against the social order which is their cause, for they cling to this social order, not because they find in it the necessary field for the development of their occupational activity, but because it contains a multitude of beliefs and practices by which they live. They cling to it because their whole internal life is linked with it, because all their convictions presuppose it, because, serving as a basis for the moral and religious order, it appears to them as sacred. Private disturbances of a temporal nature are evidently too slight to upset states of conscience which derive such an exceptional force from such an origin. Moreover, as occupational life is but little developed, these disturbances are only intermittent. For all these reasons, they are weakly felt. They occur without trouble ensuing. Men even find inequalities not only tolerable but natural.

It is quite the contrary which is produced when organic solidarity becomes predominant, for, then, whatever undermines it attacks the social tie in its vital part. First of all, since under these conditions special activities are pursued in a somewhat continuous manner, they cannot be opposed without resulting in continuous suffering. Then, as the collective conscience becomes weak, the anxieties which are thus produced can no longer be as completely neutralized. Common sentiments no longer have the same force to keep the individual attached to the group under any circumstances. Subversive tendencies, no longer having the same consequences, occur more frequently. More and more losing the transcendent character which placed it in a sphere higher than human interests, social organization no longer has the same force of resistance while it is breaking down. A work wholly human, it can no longer so well oppose human demands. When the flood becomes very violent, the dam which holds it in is broken down. It thus becomes more dangerous. That is why, in organized societies, it is indispensable that the division of labor be more and more in harmony with this ideal of spontaneity that we have just defined. If they bend all their efforts, and must so bend them, to doing away with external inequalities as far as possible, that is not only because enterprise is good, but because their very existence is involved in the problem. For they can maintain themselves only if all the parts of which they are formed are solidary, and solidarity is possible only under this condition. Hence, it can be seen that this work of justice will become ever more complete, as the organized type develops. No matter how important the progress already realized in this direction, it gives, in all likelihood, only a small idea of what will be realized in the future.

II

Equality in the external conditions of conflict is not only necessary to attach each individual to his function, but also to link functions to one another.

Contractual relations necessarily develop with the division of labor, since the latter is not possible without exchange, and the contract is the juridical form of exchange. In other words, one of the important varieties of organic solidarity is what one might call contractual solidarity. Of course, to believe that all social relations come under the heading of contracts is false, because a contract supposes something other than itself. They are, however, special links which have their origin in the will of individuals. There is a consensus of a certain kind which is expressed in contracts and which, in higher species, represents an important factor in general consensus. It is thus necessary that, in these same societies, contractual solidarity be, as far as possible, protected from all that can disturb it. For if, in less advanced societies, it can be unstable without great inconvenience (for the reasons we have given), where it is one of the eminent forms of social solidarity it cannot be threatened without threatening the unity of the social body at the same time. Conflicts arising from contracts become more serious as contract itself assumes greater importance in general life. Thus, whereas primitive societies do not even intervene in their resolution,[447] the contractual law of civilized peoples becomes ever more voluminous. But it has no other object than to assure the regular concourse of functions which enter into relations in this manner.

For this result to be attained, however, it is not enough for public authority to desire that engagements contracted for be kept; it is still necessary, at least in the great majority of cases, that they be spontaneously kept. If contracts were observed only by force or through fear of force, contractual solidarity would be very precarious. A wholly external order would badly cover disturbances too general to be indefinitely controlled. But, it is said, to alleviate this fear it is sufficient that contracts be freely consented to. That is true, but the difficulty is not resolved by that; for what constitutes free consent? Verbal or written acquiescence is not sufficient proof; one may acquiesce only through force. It is then necessary that all constraint be absent. But where does constraint begin? It does not consist solely in the direct use of violence, for indirect violence suppresses liberty quite as well. If the engagement which I have extorted by threatening someone with death is morally and legally void, why should it be valid if, to obtain it, I profited from some situation which I did not cause but which put someone else under the necessity of yielding to me or dying?

In a given society each object of exchange has, at each moment, a determined value which we might call its social value. It represents the quantity of useful labor which it contains. By that must be understood, not the integral labor which it might have cost, but that part of the energy capable of producing useful social effects, that is, effects which reply to normal needs. Although this magnitude cannot be mathematically calculated, it is none the less real. It is very easy to perceive the principal conditions in relation to which it varies. They are, above all, the sum of efforts necessary to produce the object, the intensity of the needs which it satisfies, and finally the extent of the satisfaction it brings. In fact, it is around this point that average value oscillates. It deviates from it only under the influence of abnormal factors, and, in that case, public conscience generally has a somewhat lively sentiment of this deviation. It finds unjust every exchange where the price of the object bears no relation to the trouble it cost and the services it renders.

This definition set forth, we shall say that a contract is fully consented to only if the services exchanged have an equivalent social value. Under these conditions each receives in effect the thing he desires and delivers what he gives in return so that each has a value for

---

[447] See Strabo, p. 702. Even in the *Pentateuch* no regulation of contracts is found.

the other. This equilibrium of wills which a contract establishes and consecrates is, thus, produced and maintained of itself, since it is only a consequence and another form of the very equilibrium of things. It is truly spontaneous. To be sure, we sometimes desire more for our product than it is worth; our ambitions are limitless and, consequently, are moderated only because they are restrained by those of others. But this constraint which prevents us from satisfying our unchecked desires without measure must not be confused with that which deprives us of the means of obtaining the just remuneration for our work. For the reasonable man the first kind of constraint does not exist. The second alone deserves to be called by this name; by itself, it alters the conditions of consent. But it does not exist in the case we have just spoken of. If, on the contrary, the values exchanged are not balanced, they can be put into equilibrium only if some external force has been thrown into the balance. Suppose there had been injury done from one side to the other; the wills could not be put in accord without one of them being submitted to direct or indirect pressure, and this pressure constitutes violence. In short, for the obligatory force of a contract to be complete, it is not sufficient that it be the object of an expressed assent. It is still necessary for it to be just, and it is not just by virtue of mere verbal consent. A simple state of the subject cannot bestow upon the contract this power of linking which is inherent in conventions. At least, for consent to have this virtue it must rest upon an objective foundation.

In order that this equivalence be the rule for contracts it is necessary that the contracting parties be placed in conditions externally equal. Since the appreciation of things cannot be determined *a priori*, but comes out of exchanges themselves, the individuals who are exchanging must have no other force than that which comes from their social worth if their labor is to be properly evaluated. In this way, the values of things exactly correspond to the services that they render and the trouble that they cost, for every other factor capable of making them vary is, by hypothesis, eliminated. To be sure, the unequal merit of men will always bring them into unequal situations in society, but these inequalities are external only in appearance, for they are only the external manifestations of internal inequalities. They have no other influence over the determination of values except to establish a gradation among the latter parallel to the hierarchy of social functions. The situation is no longer the same if some receive supplementary energy from some other source, for that necessarily results in displacing the point of equilibrium, and it is clear that this displacement is independent of the social value of things. All superiority has its effect on the manner in which contracts are made. If, then, it does not derive from the persons of the individuals, from their social services, it falsifies the moral conditions of exchange. If one class of society is obliged, in order to live, to take any price for its services, while another can abstain from such action thanks to resources at its disposal which, however, are not necessarily due to any social superiority, the second has an unjust advantage over the first at law. In other words, there cannot be rich and poor at birth without there being unjust contracts. This was still more the case when social status itself was hereditary and law sanctioned all sorts of inequalities.

These injustices are not strongly felt, however, as long as contractual relations are but little developed and the collective conscience is strong. Because of the rarity of contracts, there are fewer occasions for them, and, then, common beliefs neutralize their effects. Society does not suffer from this situation since it is not endangered by it. But, as labor becomes more divided and social faith grows weak, these same injustices become more insupportable, since the circumstances which give rise to them reappear very often and also because the sentiments which they evoke can no longer be as completely tempered by contrary sentiments. This is shown in the history of contract-law, which tends more and more to detract all value from conventions where the contracting parties are found in situations that are too unequal.

Originally, every contract, drawn up as formally prescribed, had obligatory force, no matter how it was obtained. Assent was not even the chief factor. The accord of wills was not sufficient to link them, and the links formed did not directly result from this accord. For a contract to exist, it was necessary, and it was sufficient, for certain ceremonies to be accomplished, such as the pronouncing of certain words, and the nature of the engagement was determined, not by the intent of the parties, but by the formulas employed.[448] The contract of consent appears only in a relatively recent epoch.[449] It is the first progress made in the system of justice. But, for a long time, the consent which sufficed to validate compacts was very imperfect, that is, extorted by force or by fraud. It was at a much later date that the Roman praetor accorded to victims of fraud and violence the action *de dolo* and the action *quod metus causa*;[450] still violence had legal existence only if there had been the threat of death or corporal punishment. Our law has become more exacting on this point. At the same time, injury, duly established, was put among the causes which could, in certain cases, annul contracts.[451]

---

[448] See the contract *verbis, litteris, et re* in Roman law. Cf. Esmein, *Études sur les contrats dans le très ancien droit français*, Paris, 1883.

[449] Ulpian looks at contracts of consent as being *juris gentium*. But the whole *jus gentium* is certainly of later origin than civil law. See Voigt, *Jus gentium*.

[450] The action *quod metus causa* which is slightly earlier than the action *de dolo* is later than the dictatorship of Sulla. The date is put at 674.

[451] Diocletian decided that a contract could be rescinded if the price was lower than one half of the real value. Our law permits rescindment because of injury only in the case

Is this not the reason why civilized peoples refuse to recognize an usurious contract? It is because the usurious contract presupposes that one of the contracting parties is too much at the mercy of the other. Finally, common morality very severely condemns every kind of leonine contract wherein one of the parties is exploited by the other because he is too weak to receive the just reward for his services. Public conscience demands, in an ever more pressing manner, an exact reciprocity in the services exchanged, but it recognizes only one obligatory form highly curtailed through conventions which do not fulfill this fundamental condition of all justice. It shows itself much more indulgent than law towards those who violate them.

Credit is due the economists for first having seen the spontaneous character of social life, and having shown that constraint could only make it deviate from its natural direction and that, normally, it results, not in arrangements which are external and imposed, but in a free internal elaboration. In this regard, they have rendered an important service to the science of morality. They have, however, been mistaken as to the nature of this liberty. Since they see it as a constitutive attribute of man, since they logically deduce it from the concept of the individual in itself, it seems to them to be entirely a state of nature, leaving aside all of society. Social action, according to them, has nothing to add to it; all that it can and must do is to regulate the external functioning in such a way that the competing liberties do not harm one another. And, if it is not strictly confined within these limits, it encroaches on the legitimate domain of the individual and diminishes it.

But, besides the fact that it is false to believe that all regulation is the product of constraint, it happens that liberty itself is the product of regulation. Far from being antagonistic to social action, it results from social action. It is far from being an inherent property of the state of nature. On the contrary, it is a conquest of society over nature. Naturally, men are unequal in physical force; naturally, they are placed under external conditions unequally advantageous; domestic life itself, with the heredity of goods that it implies and the inequalities which come from that, is, of all the forms of social life, that which depends most strictly on natural causes, and we have just seen that these inequalities are the very negation of liberty. In short, liberty is the subordination of external forces to social forces, for it is only in this condition that the latter can freely develop themselves. But this subordination is rather the reverse of the natural order.[452] It can, then,

---

of real property.
    [452] We do not mean that society is outside of nature, if one understands by that the totality of phenomena which obey the law of causality. By natural order, we mean only

realize itself progressively only in so far as man raises himself above things and makes law for them, thus depriving them of their fortuitous, absurd, amoral character; that is, in so far as he becomes a social being. For he can escape nature only by creating another world where he dominates nature. That world is society.[453]

The task of the most advanced societies is, then, a work of justice. That they, in fact, feel the necessity of orienting themselves in this direction is what we have already shown and what every-day experience proves to us. Just as the ideal of lower societies was to create or maintain as intense a common life as possible, in which the individual was absorbed, so our ideal is to make social relations always more equitable, so as to assure the free development of all our socially useful forces. When one remembers, however, that for centuries men have been content with a much less perfect justice, one may ask if these aspirations might not perhaps be due to unreasonable impatience; if they do not represent a deviation from the normal state rather than an anticipation of the coming normal state; if, in short, the means for curing the evil whose existence these aspirations reveal is through their satisfaction or elimination. The propositions established in the preceding books permit us to reply to this question with precision. There are no needs more firmly entrenched than these tendencies, for they are a necessary consequence of changes which have occurred in the structure of societies. Because the segmental type is effaced and the organized type develops, because organic solidarity is slowly substituted for that which comes from resemblances, it is indispensable that external conditions become level. The harmony of functions and, accordingly, of existence, is at stake. Just as ancient peoples needed, above all, a common faith to live by, so we need justice, and we can be sure that this need will become ever more exacting if, as every fact presages, the conditions dominating social evolution remain the same.

CHAPTER THREE. ANOTHER ABNORMAL FORM

We must now describe one last abnormal form.

It often happens in a commercial, industrial, or other enterprise that functions are distributed in such a way that they do not offer sufficient material for individual activity. There is evidently a deplorable loss of effort in that, but we need not trouble ourselves with the economic aspects of the situation. What should be of interest to us is another fact which always accompanies this waste,—a more or less great lack of co-

---

that which is produced in what is called the state of nature, that is, under the exclusive influence of physical and organic-psychic forces.

[453] See Book II, ch. v.—Once more it is seen that free contract is not in itself sufficient, since it is possible only through a very complex social organization.

ordination of these functions. It is well known that in a business where each employee is not sufficiently occupied movements are badly adjusted to one another, operations are carried on without any unity; in short, solidarity breaks down, incoherence and disorder make their appearance. At the court of the lower Empire, functions were infinitely specialized, and yet veritable anarchy resulted. Thus, there are cases where the division of labor, pushed very far, produces a very imperfect integration. How does this happen? We might be tempted to reply that what is lacking is a regulative organ, a direction. This explanation is not very satisfying, since, very often, this unhealthy state is the work of the directive power itself. For the evil to disappear, it is not enough that there be regulative action, but this must be employed in a certain way. We are well aware of the way in which it should be used. The first care of an intelligent, scientific chief will be to suppress useless tasks, to distribute work in such a way that each one will be sufficiently occupied, and, consequently, to increase the functional activity of each worker. Thus, order will be achieved at the same time that work is more economically managed. How is this to be done? We have already seen it badly done. For, ultimately, if each functionary has a well determined task, if he performs it well, he will necessarily need help from neighboring functionaries, and will not feel solidary without it. Is it important whether this task is small or large, so long as it is specialized? Is it important whether or not it absorbs his time and energies?

It is very important. In general fashion, solidarity depends very greatly upon the functional activity of specialized parts. The two terms vary with each other. Where functions languish, they are not well specialized, they are badly co-ordinated, and incompletely feel their mutual dependence. A few examples clearly make this fact evident. In man, as Spencer says, suffocation stops the flow of blood through the capillaries, and this obstacle is followed by a congestion and arresting of the heart; in a few seconds, great distress is produced in the organism, and in a minute or two functions cease.[454] All life depends very greatly upon respiration. But, in a frog, respiration can be stopped for a long time without causing any disorder, the aeration of the blood which takes place through the skin being enough, or, being wholly deprived of respirable air, it finds the oxygen coming from its tissues sufficient. Thus, there is great independence of, and consequently an imperfect solidarity between the respiratory function of the frog and the other functions of the organism, as the latter can subsist without the aid of the former. This results from the fact that the tissues of the frog, not having as great a functional activity as man's, have less need for renewing their oxygen, and throwing off carbon dioxide produced by

---

[454] *Principles of Biology*, II, p. 131.

their combustion. To take another instance: a mammifer has to take nourishment very regularly; the rhythm of its respiration, in its normal state, obviously remains the same; its rest-periods are never very long. In other words, its respiratory functions, its nutritive functions, its relational functions, are ceaselessly necessary to one another, and to the whole organism, to such a degree that none of them can long remain suspended without danger to the others and to general life. A snake, on the other hand, takes nourishment only at long intervals; its periods of activity and rest are remote from each other; its respiration, sometimes very apparent, is occasionally almost nil. That is to say, its functions are not strongly linked, and can without inconvenience be isolated from one another. The reason for this is that its functional activity is less than that of mammifers. The loss to tissues being smaller, they need less oxygen; their wear being smaller, and movements designated to pursue and seize booty less frequent, reparation is less often necessary. Spencer has further noticed that we find in unorganized nature examples of the same phenomenon. He tells us to look at a very complicated machine whose parts are not well adjusted or have become very loose through wear, and then to examine it when it is stopping. You then observe, he says, certain irregularities of movement about the time it reaches a state of rest; some parts stop first, recover movement by the effect of the continuance of movement in others, and then they become in turn causes of renewal of movement in other parts which had ceased to move. In other words, he continues, when the rhythmical changes of the machine are rapid, the actions and reactions that they exercise on one another are regular, and all the movements are well integrated, but, as speed slackens, irregularities are produced, movements disintegrate.[455]

What makes this growth of functional activity determine a growth of solidarity is that the functions of an organism can become more active only on condition of also becoming more continuous. Consider one of them in particular. As it can do nothing without the help of the others, so it can produce more only if the others produce more. But the tasks of these can be elevated, in their turn, only if that one can elevate itself by a new effort. All growth of activity in a function, implying a corresponding growth in solidary functions, implies a new growth in the former. This is possible only if it becomes more continuous. Carefully considered, moreover, these counterblows are not indefinitely produced, but a time comes when equilibrium is established anew. If the muscles and the nerves work more, richer nourishment will be necessary for them, which the stomach will furnish on condition of functioning more actively; but to accomplish this, it will be necessary for it to receive more materials to work with, and these materials will

---

[455] Spencer, *Principles of Biology*, II, p. 131.

be obtained only through a new dispensation of nervous and muscular energy. A very great industrial production necessitates the investment of a very great quantity of capital in the form of machines, but this capital, in its turn, in order to hold itself together, to repair its losses, that is to say, to pay the price of its hire, demands a very great industrial production. When the movement which animates all the parts of a machine is very rapid, it is uninterrupted because it passes without disturbance from one to the other. They mutually come together. If, moreover, not only an isolated function, but all of them at the same time become more active, the continuity of each will be still more increased.

Accordingly, they will be more solidary. Being more continuous, they are in a much closer relation and more continually have need of one another. They feel their dependence more. Under large-scale industry, the entrepreneur is more dependent upon the workers, provided that they act together, for strikes, by stopping production, hinder capital from holding together. But the worker himself can less easily stop work since his needs grow with his work. When, on the contrary, activity is smaller, needs are more intermittent, and so are the relations which unite functions. Only occasionally do they feel their solidarity, which is much looser.

If, then, the work furnished is not only not considerable but even insufficient, it is natural that solidarity itself is not only less perfect, but becomes more and more completely faulty. This is what happens in enterprises where tasks are apportioned in such a way that the activity of each worker is lower than it would normally be. The different functions are, then, too discontinuous to be able to adjust themselves exactly to one another and move in concert. This is how the incoherence spoken about comes into being.

But exceptional circumstances must arise for the division of labor to be placed in such a situation. Normally, it does not develop without functional activity growing at the same time and in the same proportion. In effect, the same causes that oblige us to specialize more also oblige us to work more. When the number of competitors becomes greater in society, it also becomes greater in each particular profession. The struggle becomes more lively, and, consequently, more efforts are necessary to sustain it. Moreover, the division of labor tends of itself to make these functions more active and more continuous. Economists have, for a long time, assigned reasons for this phenomenon. These are the principal ones: 1. When work is not divided, it must ceaselessly upset us, we must pass from one occupation to another. The division of labor economizes on all this lost time. In Karl Marx's words, it contracts the pores of the working-day. 2. Functional activity grows with the competency, the talent of the workman as the division of labor develops; there is less time lost in hesitation and vacillation.

The American sociologist, Carey, has strongly stated this characteristic of the division of labor. "In the movements of the isolated settler, however, there can be no continuity. Dependent for supplies upon his powers of *appropriation*, and compelled to wander over extensive surfaces, he finds himself not infrequently in danger of perishing for want of food. Even when successful, he is compelled to intermit his search, and provide for effecting the *change of place* required for bringing his food, his miserable habitation, and himself together. There arrived, he is forced to be, in turn, cook and tailor, mason and carpenter. Deprived of artificial light", his nights are wholly useless, while his power productively to apply his days is dependent altogether upon the chances of the weather. . . . Discovering, however, at length, that he has a neighbor,[456] exchanges arise between them; but, occupying different parts of the island, they find themselves compelled to approach each other precisely as do the stones with which they pound their grain. . . . Further, when they meet, difficulties exist in settling the terms of trade, by reason of the irregularity of the supply of the various commodities with which they desire to part. The fisherman has had good luck, and has taken many fish; but chance has enabled the hunter to obtain a supply of fish, and now he wants only fruit, which the fisherman has not.—Difference being, as we already know, indispensable to association, the want of difference would here oppose a bar to association difficult to be surmounted. ... In time, however, wealth and population grow, and with that growth there is an increase of motion in the community—the husband now exchanging services with the wife, the parents with the children, and the children with each other—one providing fish, a second meat, and, a third grain; while a fourth converts the wool into cloth, and a fifth the skins into shoes. ... At every step we witness an increased rapidity of motion, with increase of force on the part of man."[457]

In fact, besides this, we may observe that labor becomes more continuous as it is more divided. Animals and savages work in a very capricious manner when they are forced by necessity to satisfy some immediate need. In societies which are exclusively agricultural and pastoral, labor is almost entirely suspended during the season of bad weather. In Rome, it was interrupted by a multitude of holidays and days of rest.[458] In the middle ages, cessation from work occurred even more often.[459] As we go forward, however, work becomes a permanent occupation, a habit, and indeed, if this habit is sufficiently

---

[456] This is really only a metaphorical way of putting things. They did not occur thus historically. Man did not discover one fine day that he had a neighbor.

[457] Carey, *Principles of Social Science*, pp. 202-204.

[458] Marquardt, *Römische Staatsverwaltung*, III, pp. 545 ff.

[459] See Levasseur, *Les classes ouvrières en France jusqu'à la Révolution*, I, p. 474 and p. 475.

strengthened, a need. But it would not have been set up and the corresponding need would not have arisen, if work had remained irregular and intermittent as heretofore.

We are thus led to the recognition of a new reason why the division of labor is a source of social cohesion. It makes individuals solidary, as we have said before, not only because it limits the activity of each, but also because it increases it. It adds to the unity of the organism, solely through adding to its life. At least, in its normal state, it does not produce one of these effects without the other.

CONCLUSION

I

We are now in a position to solve the practical problem that we posed for ourselves at the beginning of this work.

If there is one rule of conduct which is incontestable, it is that which orders us to realize in ourselves the essential traits of the collective type. Among lower peoples, this reaches its greatest rigor. There, one's first duty is to resemble everybody else, not to have anything personal about one's beliefs or actions. In more advanced societies, required likenesses are less numerous; the absences of some likenesses, however, is still a sign of moral failure. Of course, crime falls into fewer different categories; but today, as heretofore, if a criminal is the object of reprobation, it is because he is unlike us. Likewise, in lesser degree, acts simply immoral and prohibited as such are those which evince dissemblances less profound but nevertheless considered serious. Is this not the case with the rule which common morality expresses when it orders a man to be a man in every sense of the word, which is to say, to have all the ideas and sentiments which go to make up a human conscience? No doubt, if this formula is taken literally, the man prescribed would be man in general and not one of some particular social species. But, in reality, this human conscience that we must integrally realize is nothing else than the collective conscience of the group of which we are a part. For what can it be composed of, if not the ideas and sentiments to which we are most attached? Where can we find the traits of our model, if not within us and around us? If we believe that this collective ideal is that of all humanity, that is because it has become so abstract and general that it appears fitting for all men indiscriminately. But, really, every people makes for itself some particular conception of this type which pertains to its personal temperament. Each represents it in its own image. Even the moralist who thinks he can, through thought, overcome the influence of transient ideas, cannot do so, for he is impregnated with them, and no matter what he does, he finds these precepts in the body of his deductions. That is why each nation has its own school of moral philosophy conforming to its character.

On the other hand, we have shown that this rule had as its function the prevention of all agitation of the common conscience, and, consequently, of social solidarity, and that it could accomplish this role only by having a moral character. It is impossible for offenses against the most fundamental collective sentiments to be tolerated without the disintegration of society, and it is necessary to combat them with the aid of the particularly energetic reaction which attaches to moral rules.

But the contrary rule, which orders us to specialize, has exactly the same function. It also is necessary for the cohesion of societies, at least at a certain period in their evolution. Of course, its solidarity is different from the preceding, but though it is different, it is no less indispensable. Higher societies can maintain themselves in equilibrium only if labor is divided; the attraction of like for like less and less suffices to produce this result. If, then, the moral character of the first of these rules is necessary to the playing of its role, it is no less necessary to the second. They both correspond to the same social need, but satisfy the need differently, because the conditions of existence in the societies themselves differ. Consequently, without speculating concerning the first principle of ethics, we can induce the moral value of one from the moral value of the other. If, from certain points of view, there is a real antagonism between them, that is not because they serve different ends. On the contrary, it is because they lead to the same end, but through opposed means. Accordingly, there is no necessity for choosing between them once for all nor of condemning one in the name of the other. What is necessary is to give each, at each moment in history, the place that is fitting to it.

Perhaps we can even generalize further in this matter.

The requirements of our subject have obliged us to classify moral rules and to review the principal types. We are thus in a better position than we were in the beginning to see, or at least to conjecture, not only upon the external sign, but also upon the internal character which is common to all of them and which can serve to define them. We have put them into two groups: rules with repressive sanctions, which may be diffuse or organized, and rules with restitutive sanctions. We have seen that the first of these express the conditions of the solidarity, *sui generis*, which comes from resemblances, and to which we have given the name mechanical; the second, the conditions of negative solidarity[460] and organic solidarity. We can thus say that, in general, the characteristic of moral rules is that they enunciate the fundamental conditions of social solidarity. Law and morality are the totality of ties

---

[460] See Book I, ch. iii, § 2.

which bind each of us to society, which make a unitary, coherent aggregate of the mass of individuals. Everything which is a source of solidarity is moral, everything which forces man to take account of other men is moral, everything which forces him to regulate his conduct through something other than the striving of his ego is moral, and morality is as solid as these ties are numerous and strong. We can see how inexact it is to define it, as is often done, through liberty. It rather consists in a state of dependence. Far from serving to emancipate the individual, or disengaging him from the environment which surrounds him, it has, on the contrary, the function of making him an integral part of a whole, and, consequently, of depriving him of some liberty of movement. We sometimes, it is true, come across people not without nobility who find the idea of such dependence intolerable. But that is because they do not perceive the source from which their own morality flows, since these sources are very deep. Conscience is a bad judge of what goes on in the depths of a person, because it does not penetrate to them.

Society is not, then, as has often been thought, a stranger to the moral world, or something which has only secondary repercussions upon it. It is, on the contrary, the necessary condition of its existence. It is not a simple juxtaposition of individuals who bring an intrinsic morality with them, but rather man is a moral being only because he lives in society, since morality consists in being solidary with a group and varying with this solidarity. Let all social life disappear, and moral life will disappear with it, since it would no longer have any objective. The state of nature of the philosophers of the eighteenth century, if not immoral, is, at least, *amoral.* Rousseau himself recognized this. Through this, however, we do not come upon the formula which expresses morality as a function of social interest. To be sure, society cannot exist if its parts are not solidary, but solidarity is only one of its conditions of existence. There are many others which are no less necessary and which are not moral. Moreover, it can happen that, in the system of ties which make up morality, there are some which are not useful in themselves or which have power without any relation to their degree of utility. The idea of utility does not enter as an essential element in our definition.

As for what is called individual morality, if we understand by that a totality of duties of which the individual would, at the same time, be subject and object, and which would link him only to himself, and which would, consequently, exist even if he were solitary,—that is an abstract conception which has no relation to reality. Morality, in all its forms, is never met with except in society. It never varies except in relation to social conditions. To ask what it would be if societies did not exist is thus to depart from facts and enter the domain of gratuitous hypotheses and unverifiable flights of the imagination. The duties of the individual towards himself are, in reality, duties towards society. They correspond to certain collective sentiments which he cannot offend, whether the offended and the offender are one and the same person, or whether they are distinct. Today, for example, there is in all healthy consciences a very lively sense of respect for human dignity, to which we are supposed to conform as much in our relations with ourselves as in our relations with others, and this constitutes the essential quality of what is called individual morality. Every act which contravenes this is censured, even when the agent and the sufferer are the same person. That is why, according to the Kantian formula, we ought to respect human personality wherever we find it, which is to say, in ourselves as in those like us. The sentiment of which it is the object is not less offended in one case than in the other.

But not only does the division of labor present the character by which we have defined morality; it more and more tends to become the essential condition of social solidarity. As we advance in the evolutionary scale, the ties which bind the individual to his family, to his native soil, to traditions which the past has given to him, to collective group usages, become loose. More mobile, he changes his environment more easily, leaves his people to go elsewhere to live a more autonomous existence, to a greater extent forms his own ideas and sentiments. Of course, the whole common conscience does not, on this account, pass out of existence. At least there will always remain this cult of personality, of individual dignity of which we have just been speaking, and which, today, is the rallying-point of so many people. But how little a thing it is when one contemplates the ever increasing extent of social life, and, consequently, of individual consciences! For, as they become more voluminous, as intelligence becomes richer, activity more varied, in order for morality to remain constant, that is to say, in order for the individual to remain attached to the group with a force equal to that of yesterday, the ties which bind him to it must become stronger and more numerous. If, then, he formed no others than those which come from resemblances, the effacement of the segmental type would be accompanied by a systematic debasement of morality. Man would no longer be sufficiently obligated; he would no longer feel about and above him this salutary pressure of society which moderates his egoism and makes him a moral being. This is what gives moral value to the division of labor. Through it, the individual becomes cognizant of his dependence upon society; from it come the forces which keep him in check and restrain him. In short, since the division of labor becomes the chief source of social solidarity, it becomes, at the same time, the foundation of the moral order.

We can then say that, in higher societies, our duty is not to spread our activity over a large surface, but to concentrate and specialize it. We must contract our horizon, choose a definite task and immerse ourselves in it completely, instead of trying to make ourselves a sort of creative masterpiece, quite complete, which contains its worth in itself and not in the services that it renders. Finally, this specialization ought to be pushed as far as the elevation of the social type, without assigning any other limit to it.[461] No doubt, we ought so to work as to realize in ourselves the collective type as it exists. There are common sentiments, common ideas, without which, as has been said, one is not a man. The rule which orders us to specialize remains limited by the contrary rule. Our conclusion is not that it is good to press specialization as far as possible, but as far as necessary. As for the part that is to be played by these two opposing necessities, that is determined by experience and cannot be calculated *a priori*. It is enough for us to have shown that the second is not of a different nature from the first, but that it also is moral, and that, moreover, this duty becomes ever more important and pressing, because the general qualities which are in question suffice less and less to socialize the individual.

It is not without reason that public sentiment reproves an ever more pronounced tendency on the part of dilettantes and even others to be taken up with an exclusively general culture and refuse to take any part in occupational organization. That is because they are not sufficiently attached to society, or, if one wishes, society is not sufficiently attached to them, and they escape it. Precisely because they feel its effect neither with vivacity nor with the continuity that is necessary, they have no cognizance of all the obligations their positions as social beings demand of them. The general ideal to which they are attached being, for the reasons we have spoken of, formal and shifting, it cannot take them out of themselves. We do not cling to very much when we have no very determined objective, and, consequently, we cannot very well elevate ourselves beyond a more or less refined egotism. On the contrary, he who gives himself over to a definite task is, at every moment, struck by the sentiment of common solidarity in the thousand duties of occupational morality.[462]

---

[461] There is, however, probably' another limit which we do not have to speak of since it concerns individual hygiene. It may be held that, in the light of our organico-psychic constitution, the division of labor cannot go beyond a certain limit without disorders resulting. Without entering upon the question, let us straightaway say that the extreme specialization at which biological functions have arrived does not seem favorable to this hypothesis. Moreover, in the very order of psychic and social functions, has not the division of labor, in its historical development, been carried to the last stage in the relations of men and women? Have not there been faculties completely lost by both? Why cannot the same phenomenon occur between individuals of the same sex? Of course, it takes time for the organism to adapt itself to these changes, but we do not see why a day should come when this adaptation would become impossible.

[462] Among the practical consequences that might be deduced from the proposition that we have just established there is one of interest to education. We always reason, in educational affairs, as if the moral basis of man was made up of generalities. We have just seen that such is not the case at all. Man is destined to fill a special function in the

II

But does not the division of labor by making each of us an incomplete being bring on a diminution of individual personality? That is a reproach which has often been levelled at it.

Let us first of all remark that it is difficult to see why it would be more in keeping with the logic of human nature to develop superficially rather than profoundly. Why would a more extensive activity, but more dispersed, be superior to a more concentrated, but circumscribed, activity? Why would there be more dignity in being complete and mediocre, rather than in living a more specialized, but more intense life, particularly if it is thus possible for us to find what we have lost in this specialization, through our association with other beings who have what we lack and who complete us? We take off from the principle that man ought to realize his nature as man, to accomplish his ὁικεῖον ἔργον, as Aristotle said. But this nature does not remain constant throughout history; it is modified with societies. Among lower peoples, the proper duty of man is to resemble his companions, to realize in himself all the traits of the collective type which are then confounded, much more than today, with the human type. But, in more advanced societies, his nature is, in large part, to be an organ of society, and his proper duty, consequently, is to play his role as an organ.

Moreover, far from being trammeled by the progress of specialization, individual personality develops with the division of labor.

To be a person is to be an autonomous source of action. Man acquires this quality only in so far as there is something in him which is his alone and which individualizes him, as he is something more than a simple incarnation of the generic type of his race and his group. It will be said that he is endowed with free will and that is enough to establish his personality. But although there may be some of this liberty in him, an object of so many discussions, it is not this metaphysical, impersonal, invariable attribute which can serve as the unique basis for concrete personality, which is empirical and variable with individuals. That could not be constituted by the wholly abstract power of choice between two opposites, but it is still necessary for this faculty to be exercised towards ends and aims which are proper to the agent. In other words, the very materials of conscience must have a personal character.

---

social organism, and, consequently, he must learn, in advance, how to play this role. For that an education is necessary, quite as much as that he should learn his role as a man. We do not, however, wish to imply, that it is necessary to rear a child prematurely for some certain profession, but that it is necessary to get him to like the idea of circumscribed tasks and limited horizons. But this taste is quite different from that for general things, and cannot be aroused by the same means.

But we have seen in the second book of this work that this result is progressively produced as the division of labor progresses. The effacement of the segmental type, at the same time that it necessitates a very, great specialization, partially lifts the individual conscience from the organic environment which supports it, as from the social environment which envelops it, and, accordingly, because of this double emancipation, the individual becomes more of an independent factor in his own conduct. The division of labor itself contributes to this enfranchisement, for individual natures, while specializing, become more complex, and by that are in part freed from collective action and hereditary influences which can only enforce themselves upon simple, general things.

It is, accordingly, a real illusion which makes us believe that personality was so much more complete when the division of labor had penetrated less. No doubt, in looking from without at the diversity of occupations which the individual then embraces, it may seem that he is developing in a very free and complete manner. But, in reality, this activity which he manifests is not really his. It is society, it is the race acting in and through him; he is only the intermediary through which they realize themselves. His liberty is only apparent and his personality borrowed. Because the life of these societies is, in certain respects, less regular, we imagine that original talents have more opportunity for free play, that it is easier for each one to pursue his own tastes, that a very large place is left to free fantasy. But this is to forget that personal sentiments are then very rare. If the motives which govern conduct do not appear as periodically as they do today, they do not leave off being collective, and, consequently, impersonal, and it is the same with the actions that they inspire. Moreover, we have shown above how activity becomes richer and more intense as it becomes more specialized.[463]

Thus, the progress of individual personality and that of the division of labor depend upon one and the same cause. It is thus impossible to desire one without desiring the other. But no one today contests the obligatory character of the rule which orders us to be more and more of a person.

One last consideration will make us see to what extent the division of labor is linked with our whole moral life.

Men have long dreamt of finally realizing in fact the ideal of human fraternity. People pray for a state where war will no longer be the law of international relations, where relations between societies will be pacifically regulated, as those between individuals already are, where all men will collaborate in the same work and live the same life. Although these aspirations are in part neutralized by those which have

---

[463] See above, pp. 218 ff. and p. 246.

as their object the particular society of which we are a part, they have not left off being active and are even gaining in force. But they can be satisfied only if all men form one society, subject to the same laws. For, just as private conflicts can be regulated only by the action of the society in which the individuals live, so intersocial conflicts can be regulated only by a society which comprises in its scope all others. The only power which can serve to moderate individual egotism is the power of the group; the only power which can serve to moderate the egotism of groups is that of some other group which embraces them.

Truly, when the problem has been posed in these terms, we must recognize that this ideal is not on the verge of being integrally realized, for there are too many intellectual and moral diversities between different social types existing together on the earth to admit of fraternalization in the same society. But what is possible is that societies of the same type may come together, and it is, indeed, in this direction that evolution appears to move. We have already seen that among European peoples there is a tendency to form, by spontaneous movement, a European society which has, at present, some idea of itself and the beginning of organization.[464] If the formation of a single human society is forever impossible, a fact which has not been proved,[465] at least the formation of continually larger societies brings us vaguely near the goal. These facts, moreover, in no wise contradict the definition of morality that we have given, for if we cling to humanity and if we ought to cling to it, it is because it is a society which is in process of realizing itself in this way, and with which we are solidary.[466]

But we know that greater societies cannot be formed except through the development of the division of labor, for not only could they not maintain themselves in equilibrium without a greater specialization of functions, but even the increase in the number of those competing would suffice to produce this result mechanically; and that, so much the more, since the growth of volume is generally accompanied by a growth in density. We can then formulate the following proposition: the ideal of human fraternity can be realized only in proportion to the progress of the division of labor. We must choose: either to renounce our dream, if we refuse further to

---

[464] See pp. 224-225.

[465] There is nothing that forces the intellectual and moral diversity of societies to be maintained. The ever greater expansion of higher societies, from which there results the absorption or elimination of less advanced societies, tends, in any case, to diminish such diversity.

[466] Thus, the duties that we have toward it do not oppress those which link us to our country. For the latter is the only actually realized society of which we are members; the other is only a desideratum whose realization is not even assured.

circumscribe our activity, or else to push forward its accomplishment under the condition we have just set forth.

III

But if the division of labor produces solidarity, it is not only because it makes each individual an *exchangist*, as the economists say;[467] it is because it creates among men an entire system of rights and duties which link them together in a durable way. Just as social similitudes give rise to a law and a morality which protect them, so the division of labor gives rise to rules which assure pacific and regular concourse of divided functions. If economists have believed that it would bring forth an abiding solidarity, in some manner of its own making, and if, accordingly, they have held that human societies could and would resolve themselves into purely economic associations, that is because they believed that it affected only individual, temporary interests. Consequently, to estimate the interests in conflict and the way in which they ought to equilibrate, that is to say, to determine the conditions under which exchange ought to take place, is solely a matter of individual competence; and, since these interests are in a perpetual state of becoming, there is no place for any permanent regulation. But such a conception is, in all ways, inadequate for the facts. The division of labor does not present individuals to one another, but social functions. And society is interested in the play of the latter; in so far as they regularly concur, or do not concur, it will be healthy or ill. Its existence thus depends upon them, and the more they are divided the greater its dependence. That is why it cannot leave them in a state of indetermination. In addition to this, they are determined by themselves. Thus are formed those rules whose number grows as labor is divided, and whose absence makes organic solidarity either impossible or imperfect.

But it is not enough that there be rules; they must be just, and for that it is necessary for the external conditions of competition to be equal. If, moreover, we remember that the collective conscience is becoming more and more a cult of the individual, we shall see that what characterizes the morality of organized societies, compared to that of segmental societies, is that there is something more human, therefore more rational, about them. It does not direct our activities to ends which do not immediately concern us; it does not make us servants of ideal powers of a nature other than our own, which follow their directions without occupying themselves with the interests of men. It only asks that we be thoughtful of our fellows and that we be just, that we fulfill our duty, that we work at the function we can best execute,

---

[467] The word is de Molinari's, *La morale économique*, p. 248.

and receive the just reward for our services. The rules which constitute it do not have a constraining force which snuffs out free thought; but, because they are rather made for us and, in a certain sense, by us, we are free. We wish to understand them; we do not fear to change them. We must, however, guard against finding such an ideal inadequate on the pretext that it is too earthly and too much to our liking. An ideal is not more elevated because more transcendent, but because it leads us to vaster perspectives. What is important is not that it tower high above us, until it becomes a stranger to our lives, but that it open to our activity a large enough field. This is far from being on the verge of realization. We know only too well what a laborious work it is to erect this society where each individual will have the place he merits, will be rewarded as he deserves, where everybody, accordingly, will spontaneously work for the good of all and of each. Indeed, a moral code is not above another because it commands in a drier and more authoritarian manner, or because it is more sheltered from reflection. Of course, it must attach us to something besides ourselves but it is not necessary for it to chain us to it with impregnable bonds.

It has been said[468] with justice that morality—and by that must be understood, not only moral doctrines, but customs—is going through a real crisis. What precedes can help us to understand the nature and causes of this sick condition. Profound changes have been produced in the structure of our societies in a very short time; they have been freed from the segmental type with a rapidity and in proportions such as have never before been seen in history. Accordingly, the morality which corresponds to this social type has regressed, but without another developing quickly enough to fill the ground that the first left vacant in our consciences. Our faith has been troubled; tradition has lost its sway; individual judgment has been freed from collective judgment. But, on the other hand, the functions which have been disrupted in the course of the upheaval have not had the time to adjust themselves to one another; the new life which has emerged so suddenly has not been able to be completely organized, and above all, it has not been organized in a way to satisfy the need for justice which has grown more ardent in our hearts. If this be so, the remedy for the evil is not to seek to resuscitate traditions and practices which, no longer responding to present conditions of society, can only live an artificial, false existence. What we must do to relieve this anomy is to discover the means for making the organs which are still wasting themselves in discordant movements harmoniously concur by introducing into their relations more justice by more and more extenuating the external inequalities which are the source of the evil. Our illness is not, then, as has often been believed, of an intellectual sort; it has more profound causes. We shall not suffer

---

[468] Beaussire, *Les principes de la morale*, Introduction.

because we no longer know on what theoretical notion to base the morality we have been practicing, but because, in certain of its parts, this morality is irremediably shattered, and that which is necessary to us is only in process of formation. Our anxiety does not arise because the criticism of scholars has broken down the traditional explanation we use to give to our duties; consequently, it is not a new philosophical system which will relieve the situation. Because certain of our duties are no longer founded in the reality of things, a breakdown has resulted which will be repaired only in so far as a new discipline is established and consolidated. In short, our first duty is to make a moral code for ourselves. Such a work cannot be improvised in the silence of the study; it can arise only through itself, little by little, under the pressure of internal causes which make it necessary. But the service that thought can and must render is in fixing the goal that we must attain. That is what we have tried to do.

Appendix

I

Ordinarily, to ascertain whether a rule of conduct is moral, it is confronted with a pre-established general formula of morality. To the extent that the rule can be deduced from the formula, or contradicts it, one assigns, or refuses to assign, a moral value to it.

We cannot follow this method, for in order to give it any efficacy, it would be necessary for the formula serving as criterion to be an incontestable scientific truth. But each moralist has his own particular doctrine, and the diversity of doctrines proves the flimsiness of the so-called objective value. Furthermore, we shall show that the doctrines which have been successively proposed are faulty, and that, to find one more exact, a whole science that cannot be improvised is necessary.

Indeed, in spite of the implicit or express avowals of all moralists, such a formula cannot be accepted unless it fits the reality it expresses, which means that it must realize all the facts whose moral nature is undisputed. Even those who do without, or believe that they do without, observation and experience, are obliged, in fact, to submit their conclusions to this control, for they have no other means to prove their correctness, and thus confute their opponents. "If close examination is made," Janet justly says, "it will be seen that in the theory of duties, more reliance is placed upon the conscience of men and on their innate or acquired idea of their duties than upon this or that abstract principle. . . . The proof of this is that in discussions against false systems of ethics examples can always be brought up, and from them, arguments that are granted by all sides. ... In short, all science must rest on facts. Now, the facts which are used as a foundation for ethics are those duties generally admitted or at least admitted by those with whom one is arguing."[469]

Now, of all the formulas that have been given of the general law of morality, we do not know of one which can undergo this proof.

Vainly Kant has tried to deduce from his categorical imperative that group of duties, surely badly defined, but universally recognized, called the duties of charity. His method of argument is reduced to a game of concepts;[470] and can be summarized as follows: We act morally only when the maxim of our action can be universalized. Consequently, to be moral in refusing aid to our fellow-men when they are in need, we would have to be able to make of the egotistical maxim a law applying to all cases without exception. We cannot generalize to this point without contradicting ourselves; for, in fact, every time we are in distress we want to be aided. Charity is then a general duty of humanity, since egotism is irrational. But, we shall reply, all that constitutes this so-called irrationality is the fact that it is in conflict with the need we sometimes feel to be helped ourselves. These two tendencies contradict each other. Why should the second supersede the first? Doubtless, to remain consistent with oneself, one must choose, once for all, between the two systems of conduct; but why choose one rather than the other? The antinomy can be otherwise solved; that is, be a consistent and systematic egotist, apply a rule that one might well apply to others, a law which will require nothing from others. The egotistical maxim is no more stubborn than the other in assuming a universal form; it can be practiced with all its implied consequences. This logical rigor will be especially easy for men who feel themselves capable of being sufficient unto themselves in any circumstance, and are quite ready to do without others provided others will always do without them. Shall one say that under these conditions human society becomes impossible? That would bring up considerations extraneous to the Kantian imperative.

It is true that in another passage,[471] Kant has tried to demonstrate the duties of charity in another manner, deducing them from the concept of the human person. But the proof is no more probing. To treat the human being as an end in itself, he says, is not only to respect it negatively, but also to develop it as much as possible in relation to others, as well as in itself. But such an explanation can, at most, give an account of the inferior charity dispensed by our wealth and superfluity. On the other hand, true charity, which consists in self-giving, necessarily implies that I subordinate myself to an end transcending

---

[469] *Manuel de Philosophie*, p. 569.

[470] *Metaphysik der Sitten*, Part II, § 30; and *Grundlegung der Metaphysik der Sitten*, Hartenstein edition, vol. IV, p. 271.

[471] *Grundlegung*, ed. Hartenstein, vol. IV, p. 278.

me. I wish this end to be the human persons of other people; but I can exalt the humanity of others only by virtue of humiliating myself, lowering myself to the role of means. Such acts would then be denuded of all positive moral value, since, if, on the one hand, they conform to the law, they violate it on the other. They are not exceptional and rare; life is filled with them; otherwise it would be impossible. For example, does conjugal society deny that man and wife give themselves mutually and wholly to one another? Nothing is more pathetic than to see the manner in which Kant deduces the constitutive rules of marriage. According to him, that act of sacrifice by which one mate consents to be an instrument of pleasure for the other is in itself immoral,[472] and cannot lose that quality unless it is compensated for by a similar and reciprocal sacrifice on the part of the other. It is this barter of personalities which puts things in their places and which establishes the moral equilibrium again!

The difficulties are as great for the moral law of perfection. It enables us to understand why the individual seeks his development to the extreme; but why is he to think of others? The perfection of others does not concern his perfection. If he remain consistent with himself, he will have to practice the most ungovernable moral egotism. Vainly shall we call attention to sympathy, familial instincts, patriotic sentiments, considered our natural, even our most noble, propensities, and ask that they be cultivated. The duties one will be able to deduce, strictly speaking, from such considerations, in no way resemble those really binding us to our fellow men; for these rest in the obligations to serve others, and not from service to our personal perfection.[473]

To escape this inference, the principle of perfection has been reconciled with another complimenting it, called the principle of the community of essence. "Whether one sees in humanity," says Janet, "a body whose individuals are its members, or, on the other hand, an association of individuals, similar and ideally the same, one must recognize in this common community something more than a simple collection or juxtaposition of parts, a meeting of atoms, a mechanical and purely exterior aggregate. There is between men an internal bond, *vinculum sociale*, which manifests itself in affections, sympathy, language, civil society, and is yet something more profound than all that, hidden in the recesses of the human essence. . . . Men, bound by a community of essence, cannot say: 'I am indifferent to what concerns others.'"[474] But whatever this solidarity may be, whatever its nature and

---

[472] In diesem Akt macht sich ein Mensch selbst zur Sache; welches dem Rechte der Menscheit an seiner eigenen Person widerstreitet. (*Metaphysik der Sitten*, Part I, § 25.)
[473] We are using Janet's argument, *Morale*, p. 123.
[474] *Ibid.*, pp. 124-125.

its origins, it can only be presented as a *fact*, with no basis for presenting it as a *duty*. The observation that man is not, in practice, entirely master of himself does not warrant the conclusion that he must not be master of himself. No doubt, we are bound to our neighbors, to our ancestors, to our past; many of our beliefs and feelings do not originate with us, but come from outside sources. But where is the proof that this dependence is a good thing? What invests it with moral value? Why should it not be, on the contrary, a burden from which we seek to free ourselves, so that duty would then He in a complete deliverance? That was the Stoic doctrine. The answer is given that the attempt cannot be realized; but why not attempt to carry it as far as possible? If the success cannot be truly complete, we would have to submit to this solidarity only in so far as we cannot oppose it. Perhaps it is inevitable; it does not therefore follow that it is moral. This conclusion is imposed when the principle of duty is extracted from the concept of personal perfection. Do I participate in all that I do for the sake of others, because, for some reason, others are part of me? But I am most completely myself in that part of my make-up which is not confused with others; that subjective realm alone is characteristic of me; I shall then perfect myself only by concentrating all my efforts on it. The utilitarians have been criticized because no inference could be made of the identity of interests from the solidarity of interests; but it is the same with the solidarity of perfection. The choice must be made; if my first duty is to be a person, I must reduce to the minimum all that is impersonal in me.

The insufficiency of these doctrines would be still more apparent if we were to ask them to explain not the very general duties, like those we have just considered, but more particular rules, like those prohibiting either the marriage between near relatives, or "companionate marriages," or those determining the right of succession, or even those imposing the duties of guardianship upon the relative of an orphan, etc. The more explicit and concrete moral maxims are, the more sharply defined the relationships, the more difficult it becomes to perceive the bond attaching them to such abstract concepts. Thus, certain thinkers, pushing logic to the extreme, give up trying to incorporate into the simplicity of their formula the details of the moral life as it is manifested in experience. For them, experiential ethics is not an application, but a degradation of abstract ethics. The moral law must be altered in order to be adjusted to the facts; the ideal is corrected, and more or less adulterated in order to reconcile it with the exigencies of practice. In other words, there are two ethics in the one law of ethics: one, which alone is true, but which is impossible by definition; the other, which is practicable, consisting only in semi-conventional arrangements in which concessions, inevitably but regretfully, are made to the necessities of experience. It is a sort of inferior and perverted law of ethics with which we content ourselves by reason of our imperfection, but to which more elevated spirits cannot resign themselves without sadness. Thus, there is at least the advantage of not presenting an insoluble problem, for the facts which confute the narrow formula form no part of it. But if the theory, thus corrected, is consistent with itself, it is not consistent with experience, for it relegates to this inferior sphere of ethics institutions of unquestioned morality, as, for example, marriage, the family, the right of property, etc. Furthermore, the principal cause of this corruption which the moral ideal would undergo by descending into reality would be what has been called the solidarity of men and of time.[475] Now, really, solidarity is not only a duty not less obligatory than others, but is perhaps the very source of morality.

Unfaithful to the claims they have made, the so-called empirical doctrines are no more adequate than the former theories in the light of the moral reality.

We shall say nothing of the law of ethics based upon individual interest, for that may well be regarded as abandoned. Nothing comes from nothing; it would be a miracle of logic if altruism could be deduced from egotism, the love of society from the love of oneself, the whole from the part.[476] The best proof of this lies in the form Spencer has recently given the doctrine. He has been able to remain consistent with his principle only by criticizing the most generally accepted ethics, only by treating as superstitious practices duties implying a genuine disinterestedness, a more or less complete forgetfulness of self. Thus, he has been able to say of his own conclusions that they will probably gain little adherence since they agree neither with current ideas nor the most widely scattered sentiments.[477] What would be said of a biologist who, instead of explaining biological phenomena, would contest their right to existence?

A formula more widely known today defines morality as a function, not of individual utility, but of social interest.[478] But although this expression of morality is certainly more comprehensive than is the preceding theory, it still cannot be regarded as a good definition.

First of all, a number of things are useful or even necessary to society without being moral. Nowadays a nation cannot do without a large and well-equipped army, or great industry; and yet people possessing the most cannons or steam-engines are not considered the

---

[475] Renouvier, *Science de la Morale*, vol. i, p. 349.

[476] See Guyau, *Morale Anglaise*; Wundt, *Ethik*, pp. 356 ff.

[477] In his work on ethics.

[478] Wiart, *Des Principes de la Morale considérée comme science.*—The theory-has often been sustained in Germany, and with considerable gusto in recent times. (See herring, *Der Zweck im Recht*; Post, *Die Grundlage des Rechts*; Schaeffle, *Bau und Leben des sozialen Koerpers.*)

most moral. There are even completely immoral acts which are nevertheless sometimes profitable to society.

On the other hand, there are a number of moral practices no less obligatory than others, but which render no particular service to the community. What is the social utility of honoring the dead? Yet its violation is particularly odious to us. Or of the refined modesty that cultivated classes observe as if it were an imperative duty? Spencer has clearly shown that the great philanthropy so completely a part of our customs is not only useless, but harmful to society. It conserves the lives of, and puts upon public charge, a crowd of incompetents, who are not only good for nothing, but by their presence disturb the free development of others. In our hospitals, we support a population of imbeciles, idiots, lunatics, incurables of all sorts, of no use at all, yet whose existence is prolonged, thanks to the privations imposed upon the normal, healthy workers. Dialectic subtleties cannot argue away the facts.[479] It may be objected that these incurable infirmities are the exception;[480] but sickly constitutions are cared for, thanks to this same philanthropy, and that to the detriment of the average health and collective well-being! Without speaking of the scrofulous, of the consumptive, of those suffering from rickets who can never be more than mediocre workers and are scarcely able to return to society what they have cost it, there are among present nations an ever increasing crowd of degenerates, perpetual candidates for suicide and crime, creators of disorder and disorganization upon whom we lavish maternal cares, whom we constantly favor, although they steadily become a more formidable menace to the future. Without granting, as does Spencer, that this generosity does more harm than good, we must, however, recognize that it is gratuitous, and presents only problematical advantages. Nevertheless, the more we advance, the greater the development of this uneconomical virtue. Spencer and the last disciples of Bastiat try in vain to stop the movement; it grows steadily stronger.

To all these examples, many others could be added, such as the rule commanding respect for age, that which forbids our making animals suffer, and the innumerable religious practices imposed upon the conscience of the believer with an authority properly moral, which, however, do not present the least social utility. For the Jew, formerly, to eat pork was a moral abomination; however, it could never be sustained on the ground that the practice was indispensable to Jewish society. These exceptions have been numerous, as examination proves. Whether or not moral practices are useful to society, surely it is not usually in the light of such a purpose that they are established, for in order for collective utility to be the spring of moral evolution, it would

---

[479] Spencer, *Study of Sociology.*
[480] See Fouillée, *Propriété sociale*, p. 83.

have to be, in most cases, the object of a rather distinct idea in order to determine moral conduct. Now, these utilitarian calculations, though they be exact, are too intelligently contrived to have had any great effect upon the will; the elements are too many, and the relations uniting them too confused. To hold them all united by conscience and in the wished-for order, all our available energy is necessary, and there would be none left for action. That is why, as long as interest is not immediate and apparent, it is too feebly felt to set activity in motion. Moreover, there is nothing as obscure as these questions of utility. No matter how simple the situation appears to be, the individual cannot see clearly where his interest lies. So many diverse conditions and circumstances must be taken into account, so adequate a notion must be had, that in such matters certainty is impossible. Whichever side one takes, there is the feeling that it is all still conjectural, that a large place remains open to risks. But evidence is still more difficult to obtain when it is the interest, not of an individual, but of a society that is at stake; for then it is no longer sufficient to observe the relatively proximate consequences an action in our restricted personal milieu can produce, but we must measure the repercussions which can result from it in all directions in the social organism. For that, faculties of foresight and ingenuity are necessary that the average man is far from possessing. Even if those rules whose social utility has been best demonstrated are examined, it is seen that the services they render could not be known in advance. Thus, statistics have recently shown that domestic life is a powerful preservative against the tendency to suicide and crime; can it be said that the constitution of the family has been determined by the anticipated knowledge of these beneficent results?

It is, then, quite certain that the rules of ethics, even the simplest, have not originally had, as end, the interest of society. Their origins might just as well have been rooted in aesthetic or religious aspirations, passions of all kinds, but without utilitarian objective. No doubt, once they exist, selection has its influence upon them. Those which disturb the collective life are eliminated; for, otherwise, the society in which they are produced could not last, and, at any rate, they would disappear with it. But a great many must, in the nature of things, persist, although they may not be directly useful, and be maintained as they are by the causes which have created them. For natural selection is, in the last analysis, a rather coarse method of perfection. It can rid itself of the most imperfect beings, and thus insure the victory of those comparatively the most gifted. But it is reduced to a simple process of sorting; by itself it creates nothing, adds nothing. It can obliterate from ethics the most harmful practices which invest societies with marked inferiority; but it cannot make those which survive useful if, originally, they were not so.

II

We admit that this examination is hardly complete. Moral doctrines are so numerous that it is impossible to consider them all. But the method by which they are constructed leaves us certain that they are manufactured from subjective points of view, which are more or less similar. But since a general law of ethics can only be of scientific value by taking into account the diversity of moral facts, these must first be studied if we wish to arrive at a law. Before discovering a summarizing formula, the facts must be analyzed, their qualities described, their functions determined, their causes sought out; and only by comparing the results of all these special studies shall we be able to extract the common characteristics of all moral rules, the constitutive properties of the law of ethics. When we are not even definite about the nature of particular duties and particular rights, how can we understand the nature of their principle? This method is used even when the source of morality is made to rest in some *a priori* datum, as is so often presumed. For, if this initial basis really does exist, the difficulty of defining it, the very different ways of expressing it, prove that, in any case, it is confused and hidden. Evidently, to extract and formulate the law, it is not sufficient to examine it introspectively; but wherever it exists, whether it be within or outside us, to reach it we must start from the facts in which the law is incarnated and which alone manifest it.

The necessity for this process will be better understood if the moral law is seen in all its complexity. It does not consist of two or three very general rules used as the connecting threads of life and needing variation according to circumstances, but in a great number of special precepts. There is not one duty, but many duties. Here, as elsewhere, what exists is the individual and the particular; the general is only a schematic expression. Suppose we are faced with a question of domestic ethics? The case is far from complete when it has been said that children must obey their parents, who must in turn protect their children; that husband and wife must be faithful to each other and co-operate. The *real* relations uniting different members of the family are more numerous and more defined. The relations between parents and child are not abstractly based upon protection on the one side and respect on the other; what really exists is a great crowd of particular rights, of particular duties, some being real, others personal; rights and duties mingled with a multitude of others, solidary and inseparable. There are, specifically, the right of punishment, which law and custom limit; the right of the father over the lives of his minor children; rights and duties to wardship, others concerning heredity; they take different forms, depending upon whether the child is illegitimate, legitimate, or adopted; according to whether the powers are exercised by father or mother, etc. If we submit marriage to analysis, we find the same great diversity of relations. Suppose it is a question of property. The idea cannot be simplified and defined in one word. The *ius utendi* and *abutendi* and all the other definitions which have been propounded are only very imperfect expressions. What is called the right of property is after all a *complexus* of rights determined through a great number of rules which complement or delimit each other: rules on the right of accession, on legal servitudes, on expropriation because of public utility, on the limitation of the law of reversionary interest, on the right of the lawful heirs to reclaim investment lost through waste, on questions of limitation, etc. Far from being corollaries of more general precepts, far from deriving their authority from higher maxims, these particular rules are, on the contrary, directly and without intermediary laid upon the will. In all important situations, when we wish to know what our action should be, we do not need to examine the higher principles with the object of learning how they apply to the particular case. There are specific and definite ways of acting imposed upon us. When we obey the law of modesty, do we feel the relation it has with the fundamental axioms of ethics and how it has been derived from them? When we feel an instinctive repulsion for incest, do we discover the same reason that the savants have discovered? What if I am a father? In order to know what must be done in a given situation I do not need to deduce from the general idea of paternity the particular duties it implies, but I find, among facts, a certain number of rules tracing my conduct in the ordinary circumstances of life. A rather just idea of the knowledge and the role of these practices can be had by comparing them to the reflexes of organic life; they are, indeed, so many moulds in which activities must run. Only, they are reflexes inscribed, not in the interior of the organism, but in law and customs; these are social phenomena and not biological phenomena; they do not determine the activity from within, but stimulate it from without by means proper to them.

It is evidently impossible ever to find the law dominating so vast and varied a world, if one begins by observing it in its entirety. Have the moralists proceeded in this way? Quite on the contrary. They believe they can attain this superior law with one bound and without intermediary. They begin by reasoning as if the moral law was to be entirely invented, as if they were before a clear table on which they could erect their system to suit their taste; as if it were a question of finding, not a law summarizing and explaining a system of facts actually realized, but the principle of a moral law which would settle everything. From this point of view the schools cannot be distinguished. The argument of the empiricists is no less premature nor summary than that of the rationalists. The maxim of utility has not been obtained with the help of a truly inductive method any more than the others. The procedure of one, as well as the other, is the following: they start from the concept of man, deducing the ideal from what seems to them suitable to a being who is thus defined; and having set up this ideal, they derive from it the supreme rule of conduct, the moral law. The differences distinguishing the doctrines rest uniquely in the fact that man is not everywhere conceived in the same manner. With some, he is made a creature of pure will; elsewhere place is given to the sensibilities; some see an autonomous creature made for solitude; others, an essentially social being. For some, he is made so that he cannot live without a law surpassing and dominating him, imposing upon him an imperative authority. Others, on the contrary, are struck by the fact that there is spontaneity and freedom in all he does; they conclude the ideal must have an attraction which stimulates the desire. But if the inspiration varies, the method is everywhere the same. All talk abstractly of the existing reality; and if some tardily attempt to find it, the tardy control is always made in an expeditious manner. The most general duties are quickly passed in review, but the generalities are not put aside; indeed, it is a question, not of proceeding to verify the rule, but of illustrating with some examples the abstract proposition that was set up at the very first.[481]

With such a method, it is impossible to reach a truly objective conclusion. First of all, this concept of man, serving as the basis of these deductions, cannot be the product of a scientific elaboration, methodically conducted; for science is not able to give us that information precisely. We begin by knowing some of the elements of man, but there are a great many of which we are ignorant, and we have only a very confused notion of the totality that they form. There is, then, the probability that the moralist has determined his concept in the light of his beliefs and personal aspirations. Moreover, even were it perfectly exact, the conclusions extracted through the process of deduction would be, in any case, conjectural. When an engineer deduces from theoretical principles, even though uncontested, practical consequences, he can be certain of the results of his logic only when experience has verified the theories. Deduction, by itself, does not constitute sufficient proof. Why should it be otherwise with the moralist? The rules he establishes in the manner we have described are

---

[481] So far as we know, Janet is the only French moralist who has assigned more importance to the improperly called "practical" ethics than to the so-called "theoretical." We believe this innovation important. But to be efficacious, this examination of duties must not be reduced to a purely descriptive and very general analysis. Each would have to be established in all its complexity, its comprising elements determined, the conditions upon which its development depends, studied, either in relation to the individual or society, etc. Only by these particular researches can we little by little extricate notions of the whole and a philosophical generalization.

only hypotheses as long as they have not been submitted to verification by the facts. Experience alone can decide if they are suitable to man.

But what is still more serious is that all these logical operations are based upon a simple postulate. They suppose, in fact, that the only reason for the existence of the law of ethics is to assure the development of man. Now, there is no proof that such is indeed the case. On what grounds is it asserted that it does not serve exclusively social aims to which the individual is held subordinate?—Then, it will be said, the formula is deduced from the concept of society!—But even ignoring that the proposition itself has not been proved, we would still have to know what these aims are. It is useless to say that its object is to safeguard great social interests; we have seen that this expression of morality was at once both too loose and too narrow. In short, even supposing that the deductive method was applicable to this problem, in order to be able to extract the general law of morality from some notion, what would have to be known, at least, is the function of ethics; and the only means to that is through the observation of moral facts; which is to say, that multitude of particular rules effectively governing conduct. It would have to be begun by establishing a science, which, after having classed the moral phenomena, would look for the conditions upon which each of these types depends, and would determine its role. This means a positive science of ethics that would be an application neither of sociology nor of psychology, but a science purely speculative and autonomous, although, as we shall see later, it belongs to the cycle of social sciences.[482]

If, as has often been claimed, moral rules are eternal verities receiving their value from themselves or from a transcendental source, such researches could be considerably shortened. On this hypothesis, indeed, the circumstances of time and place have a completely secondary influence on the development of ethics. These circumstances bring it about that these truths are revealed to man sooner or later, but it is not because of them that rules of conduct have or have not a moral nature. It may, then, be of interest to follow the development of the moral ideas, in order to be able to find in these facts the idea incarnated in them and progressively realized; but, for that, it is sufficient to see the general direction in which the current moves. It is not necessary to study in detail the ground it covers, since it affects it only superficially and can, at the most, facilitate or hinder the march. Thus, in order that this study of facts render all the services of which it is capable, it would be sufficient to make a rapid and summary review of the principal stages through which the historical development of ethics has passed.[483]

---

[482] We take the liberty of calling attention to our articles on *Science Positive de la Morale* in the *Révue Philosophique*, July, August, September, 1887.

[483] This is approximately the method of Wundt, in his *Ethik*, eine Untersuchung der

But this text appears actually unsustainable to us, for history has shown that what was moral for one people was immoral for another, and not only in fact, but in law. It is, indeed, impossible to regard some practices as moral which would be subversive of the societies observing them, for it is a fundamental duty everywhere to assure the existence of the fatherland. Now, there is no doubt that if the peoples who have preceded us had had the respect for personal dignity we profess today, they could not have lived. To maintain themselves, given their conditions, it was absolutely necessary for the individual to be less covetous of his independence. If, then, the ethics of the city-state or of the tribe are so different from our own in certain respects, it is not because these societies were deceived about the destiny of man, but simply that their destiny, as it was determined by the conditions in which they found themselves, would not allow any other ethic. Thus, moral rules are moral only in relation to certain experimental conditions; and, consequently, the nature of moral phenomena cannot be understood if the conditions on which they are dependent are not determined. Possibly, there is an eternal law of morality, written by some transcendental power, or perhaps immanent in the nature of things, and perhaps historical morality is only a series of successive approximations; but this is a metaphysical hypothesis that we do not have to discuss. But, in any case, this morality is relative to a certain state of humanity, and as long as this state is not realized, not only will it not be obligatory for healthy consciences, but it will even be our duty to fight against it.

This science of moral facts is, then, very laborious and very complex. It can now be understood why the attempts of the moralists necessarily had to fail. Such a question cannot be tackled at the beginning of the scientific investigation; it can be solved only in proportion to the advance of the science.

III

But how then shall we recognize the facts which are the object of this science, that is, the moral facts? By some external and visible sign, and not according to a formula trying to express their essence. Thus a biologist recognizes a biological fact by certain apparent characteristics, without any necessity for setting up a philosophic idea of the phenomenon.

First of all, they clearly consist of rules of conduct; but even so there are a number of facts of this kind which have no moral character about them. For example, there are rules of conduct a doctor must follow in the treatment of this or that illness; others informing the

---

manufacturer, the merchant, the artist, the way to proceed to success. They must not be confused with moral rules, distinguished by the two following characteristics:

1. When an act, which, by its very nature, is obliged to conform to a moral rule, deviates from it, society, if it knows of it, intervenes to oppose the deviation. It actively sets up forces against its author. He who has committed a murder or a theft, for example, is specifically punished; he who acts contrary to the laws of honor incurs public scorn; he who fails in obligations voluntarily contracted is obliged to repair the harm he has caused, etc. The same phenomenon is not produced when other precepts of conduct are violated. If I do not conduct my affairs with art, I run the risk of not succeeding, but society does not oppose my acting in that way. It leaves me free to my actions. They may not result in the intended aims, but because of that they are not repressed.

2. This social reaction pursues the infringement with true necessity; sometimes it is predetermined even in its modalities. Everyone knows in advance what will happen if the act is recognized as contrary to the rule either of competent courts of justice or of public opinion. A material or moral constraint, according to the case, will be exercised over the agent, either to punish, or to oblige him to compensate for the damage, or to do both. On the contrary, the consequences which arise from ignoring principles of traditional technique are the most contingent. All that can be said is that this reaction is more or less likely; but it may also happen that this deflection from the rules, even if made with the knowledge and in the presence of the world, may be greeted with favor. One can be certain of nothing until the event has occurred. It is this dependence upon chance which makes changes a great deal easier and quicker in the field of social activity; these individual variations can be produced not only with complete liberty, but even with success. On the other hand, when the infraction is one formally opposed by society, the individual can make no innovations, since all innovation is fought against as if it were error. The only possible steps of progress are those which society makes collectively.

This predetermined reaction, exercised by society on the agent who has violated the rule, constitutes what is called a *sanction*. We are limiting the meaning of this word that has so often been used in a more general sense. We now have the criterion for which we have been looking: we can say that all moral facts consist in a rule of sanctioned conduct.

This definition, moreover, does not differ from the one generally admitted; it is simply a more precise and scientific definition. What is meant, in short, when we speak of what distinguishes moral rules, is that they are obligatory. But how can we recognize the presence of this quality? Is it by questioning our conscience and observing by direct intuition that this obligation is felt? We know, however, that all consciences are not the same, even in the midst of one society. There are some delicate, others more vulgar, others which are the antithesis of the moral sense. To which shall we address ourselves? To that of the cultivated man, to the workingman, to the delinquent? Evidently, only the normal conscience, the most general in society, is meant. But as it is impossible to see directly what happens there, to know in what manner the rules of conduct are there represented we must refer to some external fact reflecting this internal state. Nothing can better play this role than the sanction. It is impossible, indeed, for the members of a society to recognize a rule of conduct as obligatory without reacting against all those acts violating it; this reaction is so necessary that every normal conscience reproves even the very thought of such an act. If, then, we define the moral rule by the sanction which is attached to it, it is not as if we were considering the sentiment of obligation as a product of the sanction. On the contrary, it is because the latter derives from the former that it can symbolize it; and as this symbol has the great advantage of being objective, accessible to observation and even to measurement, it is a good method to prefer it to the thing it represents. For, to become scientific the study of moral facts must follow the example of the other sciences. These try, by all possible means, to eliminate the personal feelings of the observer to reach the facts in themselves. In the same way, the moralist must proceed to take as obligatory only what *is* obligatory, and not what *appears* so to him; he must take for the material of his researches realities and not subjective appearances. Now, the reality of an obligation is certain only if it is manifested by some sanction.

But, then, if this definition is held, does all law enter the domain of ethics? We believe these two domains too intimately united to be radically separated. Continual exchanges take place between them; now there are moral rules which become juridical, and now juridical rules which become moral. Very often the law cannot be detached from the customs which are its substratum, nor the customs from the law which realizes and determines them. Moreover, the moralists have never pushed logic to the extent of making all law distinct from ethics. Most of them recognize a moral character in the most general and most essential juridical prescriptions. But it is difficult for such a selection not to be arbitrary, for there is no criterion which allows it to be made methodically. How shall we distinguish the rules of law according to their importance and relative generality, and how shall we be able to predict when all morality disappears?

The distinction, moreover, cannot be made without falling into inextricable difficulties, for these general principles can pass into facts only by becoming solidary with juridical rules under which particular cases are subsumed. If, then, this special regulation is foreign to morality, this solidarity inevitably compromises the morality of the principles, and these can no longer descend into reality without decaying, without ceasing to be themselves. To be just, says the moralist, respect the property of others. But this property can only have been acquired by conforming to the particular rules of law, for example, springing up from a heritage or usucaption or accession. If, then, these different sources from which the law of property is derived are not moral, or are simply amoral, how is it possible for property to have a moral value? Legal authority must be respected; that is still a rule whose morality is not contested. But this authority has been instituted according to the prescriptions of constitutional law; if that is not moral, how could the powers it creates have a claim on our respect? The examples could be multiplied. If morality is allowed to penetrate into law, it invades it; and if it does not penetrate, it remains as a sort of dead letter, as a pure abstraction, instead of being an effective discipline of wills.

These two orders of phenomena are thus inseparable and spring from one and the same science. Nevertheless, the sanction attached to the rules called more specifically moral present some particular characteristics that can be determined. This name is generally reserved for those which cannot be violated without the offender incurring blame from public opinion which can range from utter disgrace to simple disapproval, passing through all the shades of reproach. This reproach constitutes a repression, for it is a misfortune imposed upon the agent whose prospect can sometimes turn the agent from the reproved act. It has often been distinguished from the one the courts apply as being distinctly moral. But the distinction is not exact, for all moral punishment necessarily assumes a material form. For the reproach to be efficacious, it must be expressed outwardly by movements in space; for example, the offender will be excluded from the society in which he has been accustomed to live. He will be exiled. This exile is not different from the one imposed by the regular courts of law. Besides, there are, and there have always been, legal punishments which are purely moral; such are those which consist in the deprivation of certain rights, as infamy among the Romans, dishonor among the Greeks, civic degradation, etc. The difference separating these two sorts of punishment is not based upon their intrinsic characters, but upon the manner in which they are administered. The one is applied by one and all, the other by defined and constituted bodies; the one is diffuse, the other organized. The first can also be coupled with the other; the reproach of public opinion can be accompanied by a legal punishment properly called. But every rule of conduct to which a repressive diffuse sanction is attached, whether it stand alone or not, is moral, in the ordinary sense of the word.

This definition alone proves that the positive science of morality is a branch of sociology, for every sanction is principally a social thing. The duties comprising that part of ethics called individual morality are sanctioned in the same manner as the others. That is to say, they are individual only in appearance, for they, too, depend upon social conditions. Furthermore, they have been conceived in different ways, according to the epochs in which they existed. Now, of all the milieux in which man has lived, only the social milieu has passed through changes profound enough to get a clear idea of the transformations.

But are all the moral facts included in this definition? Do they consist of imperative rules; or will they rather belong to a more elevated sphere in ethics transcending duty? Experience seems to show that there are acts which are praiseworthy without being obligatory; that there is a free ideal that one is not bound to attain. "For example, a wealthy man will be praised for using his fortune to favor the development of the arts and sciences. That is evidently praiseworthy and fine, and yet it cannot be said to be a duty for every rich man to make similar use of his fortune. A fairly well-to-do man will be praised, will be admired, if he assumes charge of aiding and raising a family not his own; however, he who does not act in that way is not guilty, and how could he not be guilty if this kind of action were indispensably obligatory?"[484]

There are, as a matter of fact, moralists who do not admit this distinction. According to Janet, if certain acts we admire do not appear obligatory to us, it is because they are not effectively obligatory for the average man who cannot raise himself to so high a standard of perfection. But if it is not a duty for everybody, it does not follow that it is not a duty for anyone. Quite on the contrary, those enabled to achieve that degree of heroism or holiness are strictly bound, unless, of course, it is possible for them to do as well in another way; inversely, if they are not bound to such acts, it is because those are not the best they can accomplish, and, consequently, are not moral. "It would be absurd to maintain that when a certain degree of perfection is possible to me, I have the right to content myself with a lesser; and at the same time it would be absurd to demand from me a degree of perfection alien to my nature."[485]

But the distinction holds good in its entirety. It is true that certain acts are imposed by public opinion, others abandoned to private initiative. These last are then gratuitous and free. But the agent obliges himself to accomplish them. If he does not realize his ideal, he will blame himself; but he will not be blamed. Still, one must not confuse

---

[484] Janet, *La Morale*, p. 223.
[485] *Loc. cit.*, p. 234.

the reproach inflicted upon oneself for having neglected to do a good turn with the remorse a genuine fault determines. These two sentiments have neither the same characters nor the same intensity. Both are punishments, but the second is a violent pain due to the wound we have made with our hands to the living parts of our moral conscience; the other is reduced to regret for having let a delicious joy escape. One arises because an irreparable loss has been suffered; the other because we have missed an opportunity to enrich ourselves. The internal reaction which follows the act does not differ perceptibly from the external reaction, and the moral conscience of the agent makes the same distinctions as the public conscience. Shall we go further and say that it is wrong to make these distinctions? Under these circumstances, discussion becomes impossible, for we seek only to observe the moral reality as it exists, not knowing for the moment the criterion which allows us to correct it. Furthermore, Janet ends by recognizing implicitly these differences and admitting there exists, at the very least, two quite distinct forms of virtue. "Virtue," he says, "is ... in its most sublime form, a free and individual act, which leads to unexpected forms of grandeur and generosity. The inferior form of virtue is the legal form which, with no spontaneity, faithfully follows a given rule. . . . But true virtue, as genius, escapes the rule, or rather creates the rule."[486]

Then it seems that our definition does not include all that is specific. But that does not matter, since if it is true that there are acts which are the object of admiration, and which, moreover, are not obligatory, they need not be moral. To put them thus outside of ethics, we need not refer to an abstract idea of morality and show that they cannot be deduced from it. We maintain only that it would be contrary to all method to unite under one rubric acts which are compelled to conform to a pre-established rule and others which are free from all regulation. If, then, to remain faithful to usage, we reserve for the first the qualification of moral, we cannot equally give it to the second. But what proof is there that they do not play the same role? It is an hypothesis which, for the moment, we do not have to discuss, for we have not the means. We are only searching now to classify phenomena according to their most important external characteristics, and it seems impossible to us to confuse facts which present properties so greatly opposed.

The contrast between them will appear still more striking if one observes that the properly called moral fact does not consist of the act conforming to the rule, but of the rule itself. Now, there is no rule where there is no obligation. Independent creations of private initiative keep their characters only by virtue of having been brought forth in no

---

[486] *Loc. cit.*, p. 239.

other way. Sometimes, indeed, they catch the moral conscience so unexpectedly that the latter, not having ready-made judgments to apply to them, remains hesitant and confused. To be sure, there is a very general precept which promises encomia or public gratitude to whoever does more than his duty; but besides the fact that this maxim has nothing imperative about it, the reward attached to it sanctions no determined action. It leaves an immense area open to the individual wherein he can move with complete freedom. The different ways of doing more than one's duty cannot be more specific than the different ways of doing less.

Besides, it is easy to see that these external differences correspond to internal and profound differences. For what this contingency indicates, this area made for the imagination, is that these acts are not necessary, are adjusted to no vital end, and in short, are a superfluity; that is to say, they belong to the domain of art. After we have directed a part of our energy towards doing its daily task, we like to play freely, indulging ourselves to exert energy for its own sake, without any use, without any definite goal in sight. This is the pleasure of playing a game, and aesthetic pleasure is only a superior form of it. At the same time that our energies are freed from their daily obligations, from their regular duties, they feel the need of tearing loose, of playing in new circumstances where rules are neither determined nor imposed, for the pleasure of doing and the joy of being free. It is this need which inspires all gratuitous acts we accomplish, from the refinements of worldly urbanity, the ingenuities of politeness, the loosing of sympathy in the midst of the family, the kind attentions, the gifts, affectionate words or caresses between friends or relatives, up to the heroic sacrifices that no duty demands. For it is wrong to believe that these noble inventions, as they are very justly called by Janet, are met with only in extraordinary circumstances. They are invested with the greatest importance; life is full of them; they invest it with charm.[487] The sentiment they inspire in us is of the same nature and depends upon the same cause. If we admire them, it is not because of their consequences, the utility of which is often doubtful. The father of a family risks his life for a stranger; who would dare say that was useful? What we love is the free use of moral strength, whatever be its effective consequences.

But, if such manifestations are in the domain of art they belong to a very special sphere. Of course, they have something moral about them, for they are derived from customs and tendencies which have been acquired in the practice of the properly called moral life, such as the

---

[487] It is, therefore, not the difficulty of these actions which separates them from the others. Some of them are easily accomplished. Consequently this distinction cannot arise, since we willingly regard as discretionary everything that is somewhat difficult.

need for giving oneself, of going outside oneself, of interesting oneself in others, etc. But these dispositions, moral in origin, are no longer used morally because, with the disappearance of the obligation, morality disappears.[488] Just as sport is the aesthetic of the physical life, art the aesthetic of the intellectual life, so this activity *sui generis* is the aesthetic of the moral life.[489]

IV

Our definition is still faulty, however. Indeed, the moral conscience of societies is a subject where error is quite possible. It can attach the external sign of morality to rules of conduct which are not themselves moral; and, contrariwise, leave without sanctions rules which should be sanctioned. We must complete our criterion, so that we shall not be exposed to accepting as moral, facts which are not so; or, on the other hand, excluding from ethics facts which in their very nature are moral.

The question does not differ essentially from the one the biologist asks when he seeks to separate the sphere of normal physiology from that of pathological physiology, for it is a fact of moral pathology that a rule may unduly present the character of an obligation or may be unduly deprived of it. We have, then, only to follow the method employed by the naturalists in similar circumstances. They call a biological phenomenon normal in a determined species when it is found in the average specimen of that species, when it is a part of the average type; and, contrariwise, it is pathological when it is not within the average, whether it be above or below it. But the average type need not signify an individual being whose characteristics are denned, quantitatively and qualitatively, with mathematical precision. There is, on the contrary, nothing absolute or fixed about it; it varies within certain limits; and it is only above and below these limits that the domain of pathology begins. If, for example, in a given society, the heights of all individuals are taken and if one puts in columns the figures thus obtained, beginning with the highest, one observes that the most numerous and most closely related statistics are massed in the centre. Beyond that, whether above or below, they are not only more

---

[488] This is not to be confused with the doctrine of those who admit the existence of discretionary duties; the last two words contradict each other.

[489] We do not wish to inject practical considerations into this scientific examination. However, it seems to us that the distinction between these two domains is very necessary even from the practical point of view. For they cannot be confused without putting them on the same plane. There is very often attributed to the aesthetic-moral activity a certain superiority. Now, the sentiment of obligation, that is, the existence of duty, is in danger of being weakened in admitting there is a morality, and perhaps a higher, which rests in the independent creations of the individual, which no rule determines, which is essentially *anomie*. We believe, on the contrary, that *anomy* is the contradiction of all morality.

rare but more widely interspaced. It is this central dense mass which constitutes the average, and if this is often expressed by a single figure, it is because all those in the average region may be represented by the one around which they gravitate.

The same method must be followed in ethics. A moral fact is normal for a determined social type when it is observed in the average of that species; it is pathological in antithetical circumstances. That is what makes the moral character of particular rules vary; they depend upon the nature of social types. For example, in all societies, with totems, clans, and aggregations of clans, there is a law forbidding the killing and eating of the animal used as emblem for the group; we shall say that this rule is normal for that social type. In all our European societies, infanticide, which formerly went unpunished, is severely forbidden; we shall say that this rule is normal for the social type to which our societies belong. One can even measure, in this way, the degree of coercive force which each normal rule must normally have; we need only determine the normal intensity of the social reaction which follows the violation of the rule. In Italy custom sometimes indulgently judges acts of brigandage that public conscience strongly reproves in other countries of Europe; such a fact is then abnormal. At the same time, it must not be forgotten that the normal type is not some stable thing whose traits can be fixed at an indivisible instant. On the contrary, it evolves, as do societies themselves and all organisms. We are, it is true, disposed to believe that it blends with the average type of the species during maturity, for it is only at that time that the organism is truly itself, for it is then all it can be. But if the normal or pathological state of an animal were determined in infancy or old age, from its adult normalcy, one would commit the same fault as judging the state of health of an insect by the standard of a mammifer. We would then see genuine maladies in infancy and decline. However, the presence of characteristics proper to the adult in either the infant or declining stage is an indication of a pathological state. A too precocious awakening in infancy, an over-prolonged persistence of genetic instincts in decline, are really morbid phenomena.[490] Thus, there is a normal type in infancy, another in the prime of life, another in old age, with societies as with individual organisms.

Consequently, to know if a moral fact is normal for a society, we must take into account the age of the society and determine the normal type which serves as landmark. Thus, during the infancy of our European societies, certain restrictive rules of liberty of thought which have disappeared in a more advanced age were normal. To be sure, one cannot be specific about what moment of evolution either a society or

---

[490] That does not mean that sickness is part of the normal type of old age. On the contrary, the illnesses of old age are abnormal facts just as those of the adult.

an organism has reached. To number the years would not be enough; one may be older or younger than one's age. Only according to certain characteristics of the structure and functions is it possible scientifically to distinguish old age from infancy, or maturity,[491] and these have not yet been determined with sufficient precision. However, besides being the only method of procedure, we shall find nothing insoluble about the problem. Certain of these objective signs are already known;[492] on the other hand, if the number of years is not always a satisfactory criterion, it may, however, be usefully employed, provided it be used with reserve and precaution. Ultimately, the progress of science will make this determination more exact. However, there are cases where, to distinguish the healthy state from the sick, it is not enough to refer to the normal type. This is so when all of its traits have not been formed; when, disturbed in certain particulars by a passing crisis, it is itself in process of becoming. That is what happens when the moral conscience of nations is not yet adapted to the changes which have been produced in the milieu, changes which, partaking of the past which holds it from behind and the necessities of the present, keep it from becoming fixed. Then there appear rules of conduct whose moral character is indecisive, because they are in the midst of acquiring or losing it without having definitely either acquired or lost it. These are badly determined passing fancies which are, however, general, and present themselves in social life in proportion to its process of transformation. However, the method remains the same. One must begin by fixing the normal type; and towards that the only means is to compare it with itself. We can determine the new conditions of the state of health only in the functions of the old, for we have no other point of comparison. To know if such and such a precept has moral value, we must compare it with others whose intrinsic morality is established. If it plays the same role, which is to say, if it is used for the same ends; if, moreover, it follows from causes which have brought forth the other moral facts as well; if, in sum, these last demand it on penalty of not existing if the other does not at the same time exist, it can rightfully be concluded from this functional identity and this solidarity that it must be accepted with the same claims and in the same manner as the other obligatory rules of conduct. Consequently, it is moral.

To be sure, it is not certain, even with this correction, that the normal type realizes the last degree of perfection. To have maintained itself in so general a manner, it must, in its essential characteristics, be

---

[491] Thus, the fact that an aged man presents the complete type of adult has nothing morbid about it; what is pathological is that, in presenting the anatomic and physiological type of old age in its essential lines, he may, at the same time, have certain characteristics of the adult.

[492] For example, for a society, regular lowering of the birth-rate may be used as proof that the limits of maturity have been reached or passed.

sufficiently well adapted to these conditions of existence; but that does not prove that anything will derive from it. Health is one thing, perfection another. Now, for the moment, we are looking especially for the characteristic signs of moral health, and if the division of labor presents them, that is enough for us. Let us add, besides, that this highest perfection can be determined only in the function of the normal state, for that is the only model from which corrections can be made. One can have only one intelligible reason for finding certain elements faulty; that is because they differ from the average of the others and constitute anomalies in the average type. One is then always led back to this last factor; it is only in relation to itself that it can be judged inadequate. To perfect it is to make it more like itself. To proceed otherwise would be to admit an ideal, coming from some unknown source, imposing itself from outside, a perfection whose value has not been brought forth from the nature of things and under the conditions they depend upon, but which brings forth the desire from I know not what transcendental and mystical virtue; a sentimental theory which has no part in scientific discussion. The only ideal that the human mind can propose is to improve what is. It is in reality alone that one can learn the improvements it demands.

We arrive, then, at the following definition:

One considers as a normal moral fact for a given social type, at a determinate phase of its development, every rule of conduct to which a repressive diffuse sanction is attached in the average society of this type, considered at the same period of evolution; secondly, the same qualification applies to every rule, which, without precisely presenting this criterion, is, however, analogous to certain of the preceding rules; that is to say, serves the same ends, and depends upon the same causes.

It may be said that this criterion is too empirical. But, in fact, the moralists of all schools use it more or less explicitly. We know, indeed, that they are obliged to take as their point of departure for their speculations a recognized and uncontested ethic, which can only be the one generally followed during their time and in their environment. It is from a summary observation of this ethic that they extract a law which is supposed to explain it. It is that which furnishes the material for their inferences; it is that also which they find in the phraseology of their deductions. To be otherwise, it would be necessary for the moralist, in the silence of his study, to construct solely by the strength of his thought the complete system of social relations, since the moral law penetrates all. This is obviously an impossible undertaking. Even when he appears to be original, he is only translating reformatory tendencies in motion about him. He adds something to them because he makes them clear, because he is weaving a theory about them; but this theory is reduced to showing that they are arriving at the same end as some moral practice whose authority is indisputable. Since this method is imposed, is it not wisest to practice it openly, resolutely meeting the great difficulties, and surrounding ourselves with all possible guarantees against error?

THE END